Rare and Resilient

ONE in 5000 Anthology

"Out of suffering have emerged the strongest souls;
the most massive characters are seared with scars."

- Khalil Gibran

Compiled by

Greg Ryan

All profits support the work of
ONE in 5000 Foundation Incorporated
ABN: 18393396753

A registered charity with Australian Charities and Not-for-profits Commission

DISCLAIMER:

ISBN: 978-0-646-83152-7

Editors: Greg Ryan; Anne Holland; Susan Setford; Meghan Douglass

Published by ONE in 5000 Foundation Incorporated
ABN: 18393396753
A registered charity with Australian Charities and Not-for-profits Commission

Contents

Foreword

It is with great pleasure that I write this foreword for Greg Ryan's new book, "Rare and Resilient – ONE in 5000 Anthology." Today, many people are referred to as heroes. However, for many, this title is overused and not deserved. Greg is a true hero, for the thousands of families and patients across the world affected by anorectal malformations. His tireless advocacy is not limited to newborns in his home town of Melbourne, nor to the many ARM adults in Australia. Instead, Greg provides support, understanding, hope and assistance for children, adolescents, adults and families across the globe.

Yet another example of Greg's dedication to those affected by anorectal malformations is this new anthology of inspiring stories from families and patients from 26 countries. For the very first time, we have a collection of ARM voices from whom we may all learn. The universal themes that come through so clearly in this anthology are of joy, pain, distress, acceptance and, ultimately, resilience. It is the resilience of the new parents confronting the sight of their child in the neonatal unit following surgery, the resilience of the school-aged child tackling toileting, and the resilience of the adult establishing intimate relationships for the first time. This resilience is shown across all parts of the world and reconfirms the universality of the human experience. I know that readers will not fail to be inspired and humbled by the words so passionately put down by this incredible collection of families and patients.

Associate Professor Sebastian King
Director, Colorectal and Pelvic Reconstruction Service
The Royal Children's Hospital, Melbourne, Australia

Introduction

Over these last three years I have been moved by the impact that my memoir "A Secret Life – Surviving a Congenital Condition" has reportedly had on people's understanding of living with Imperforate Anus (IA)/Anorectal Malformation (ARM), as well as the impact the ONE in 5000 Foundation has had on the global IA/ARM community.

I am continually amazed and inspired by the resilience shown by those born with IA/ARM and their families. Their stories, ideas and experiences never fail to enlighten and inspire me, as well as enabling others within our community to feel less isolated and able to live more comfortable lives.

I believed it was now time to collect some of those stories and for the world to hear them. So, on 15 September 2020, I launched the "ONE in 5000 Anthology Project" and asked people through our ONE in 5000 Foundation social media platforms if they would care to share their stories for a book.

The response was overwhelming and I received contributions from people in many countries from across the world. I am honoured to be able to share these stories from children, adolescents and adults who were born with IA/ARM, as well as parents and family members who play such an important role in supporting and sharing their experience.

The aim of the book is to promote awareness, education and acceptance of a condition which is unknown by 99.99% of the general population, and to lessen the stigma, embarrassment and taboo nature which still relates to an open discussion of bowel and bladder issues associated with IA/ARM.

Also, my hope is that the book gives the medical community as a whole an understanding that IA/ARM is not just a "paediatric issue". It is so important that the adult colorectal medical professionals open themselves to being educated by paediatric colorectal surgeons who specialise and play such a pivotal role in the treatment and care of young IA/ARM patients. The issues faced by patients as children usually have long-term implications throughout their adulthood. However, many adults struggle to find and maintain effective ongoing, and continuity of, care and treatment that specifically addresses the unique problems presented by IA/ARM as they battle through life.

I am also very passionate about our lifelong condition being recognised and accepted in the same manner as other colorectal issues i.e., Irritable Bowel Syndrome (IBS), Colitis, Crohn's Disease, Hirschsprung Disease etc.

And equally importantly, it has become increasingly evident that we must highlight and identify the mental health ramifications of the condition and the effect it has on childhood, adolescent and adult years. This can be just as problematic as the physical challenges. Also, there needs to be greater support provided to parents who have to carry the burden of caring for their child in the early years, for this too comes at a significant emotional and mental cost.

As you read these raw and honest stories you will be taken on many emotional journeys. You will learn the challenges that a child born with IA/ARM and their families endure on a daily basis. Most start with distressed and stunned parents sitting at the side of their fragile babies in the NICU ward. But in some instances, the diagnosis is not identified until much later which can cause even more distress.

Then, as they struggle along the difficult and winding road ahead, we hear of the challenges faced by the parent and child with potty training, day-care and school.

Next, we take a journey through their lives as they navigate adolescence and come to the realisation that they are "different" but look the same as everyone else.

As adulthood arrives, new challenges are faced with relationships, working and trying to survive an adult healthcare system into which they do not fit.

The book will take you through a range of emotions, even within just a single story. You may feel heartbroken, love, sorrow, joy, anger, relief, sadness, laughter, shock and frustration. But you will also have an overriding feeling of inspiration, admiration and respect.

You may find a repetitiveness in many of the stories, but I know you will be continually amazed at what the human spirit can achieve. The absolute love and commitment of families to adjust their lives to care for their child under so many varied circumstances will continue to inspire you as you read each individual story.

My hope is that by the end of this book, you the reader will have a greater understanding and insight into this rare congenital anomaly that affects ONE in 5000 births globally - as well as understand why I chose the title RARE AND RESILIENT!

Rare and Resilient

To be born Rare and Resilient
You face a battle every day

When your born with a condition
Which will never go away

It tests you to your limits
Both in body and mind

As you always question
Why you're one of a kind

We rely on our resilience
When the real bad days come

They can challenge us in a way
That can bring us undone

As living with our condition
At times can be a cross to bear

But we never surrender to it
Because we all are Resilient and Rare

Greg Ryan

On 25ᵗʰ October 2020 I visited two-year-old Bailey and his Mum at the Royal Children's Hospital, Melbourne.
That week he was having the same surgery I had at the same hospital, but 54 years apart

What is Imperforate Anus (IA)/Anorectal Malformation (ARM)?

Imperforate Anus (IA) also known as Anorectal Malformation (ARM), is a rare congenital condition that affects one in 5000 births and is slightly more common in males than in females. The majority of cases are diagnosed soon after birth. It is rare for children to be diagnosed during the prenatal period, and the cause is still unknown.

At birth, doctors should always check to make sure that a newborn baby's anus is open and in the correct position. If an issue is found, the doctor will do many tests to better understand the problems and to develop a long-term plan for the best outcome.

In a baby born with the condition, any of the following can happen:
- The anal opening may be too small or in the incorrect location – which can cause difficult and painful bowel movements, or severe constipation.
- The anal opening may be absent, and the rectum enters other organs in the pelvic area (including the urethra, bladder or vagina). This can lead to chronic infections or bowel obstruction (a dangerous condition where stool becomes trapped inside the body).
- The anal opening may be absent, and the rectum, reproductive system, and urologic system form a single channel called a cloaca, where both urine and stool are passed. This can also lead to chronic infections.

In addition, almost 50 percent of children are born with other associated anomalies. This is known as the VACTERL association. Each letter in VACTERL represents an area where an anomaly may be present:

V – Vertebrae

A – Anorectal Malformation

C – Cardiac

TE – Tracheo-Esophageal fistula and Esophageal disorders

R – Renal

L – Limb

The most commonly associated syndrome with IA/ARM is Down Syndrome (Trisomy 21), with a higher incidence rate seen than the general population.

Other syndromes that may be commonly associated with an ARM include Currarino syndrome, Townes-Brock syndrome, and Pallister-Hall syndrome.

There has been an evolution in the surgical repair of ARM patients over the last century, with the rectum connected to the anal opening in what is known as a 'pull-through'.

In 1952, Prof F. Douglas Stephens from The Royal Children's Hospital, Melbourne, Australia introduced a new technique which came to be known as the 'Stephens procedure'. This was the standard surgical practice performed on ARM patients until 1980, when Dr Alberto Pena first performed what is known as a PSARP (Posterior Sagittal Anorectoplasty) or "Pena pull-through procedure" at the Institute of Paediatrics in Mexico City, Mexico.1

The PSARP became the standard surgical technique used by paediatric surgeons globally for ARM patients. In 2000, a new technique was introduced by Dr Keith Georgeson from Children's Hospital of Alabama, Birmingham, Alabama, USA. Dr Georgeson demonstrated that laparoscopy (keyhole surgery) could be used for some children with ARM. This procedure is called a LAARP (Laparoscopic assisted anorectoplasty).

As well as evolving surgical techniques, the name of this congenital anomaly has changed. Traditionally the condition was called an Imperforate Anus and classified as:

- High
- Intermediate
- Low

At an international meeting to celebrate the centenary of The Royal Children's Hospital Melbourne, Australia in 1970, leading paediatric colorectal surgeons from across the world attended, and a consensus was reached to standardise an international classification system for Imperforate Anus.

The Melbourne meeting classification of Imperforate Anus (1970)

TYPE	MALE			FEMALE	
High (Supra-levator)	Anorectal Agenesis	Without fistula		Without Fistula	
		With fistula	Rectovesical Rectourethral	With Fistula	Rectovesical Rectocloacal Rectovaginal
	Rectal atresia				
Intermediate	Anal agenesis	Without fistula		Without fistula	Rectovaginal - low
		With fistula	Rectobulbar		Rectovestibular
Low (Trans-levator)	At normal site	Covered anus – complete / Anal stenosis			
	At perineal site	Anterior perineal anus / Anocutaneous fistula – covered anus (incomplete)			
	At vulvar site			Vulvar anus / Anovulvar fistula / Anovestibular fistula	

Following the conference at Wingspread, Wisconsin, USA in 1984, the following re-classification of Imperforate Anus was adopted:

The Wingspread Classification of Imperforate Anus (1994)

LEVEL OF ANOMALY	MALE	FEMALE

High	Anorectal agenesis
	   a. Rectoprostatic-urethral fistula
	   b. Without fistula
	Rectal atresia
		Anorectal agenesis
		   a. Rectovaginal fistula
		   b. Without fistula
		Rectal atresia

Intermediate	Rectobulbar-urethral fistula Anal agenesis without fistula	Rectovestibular fistula Rectovaginal fistula Anal agenesis without fistula
Low	Anocutaneous (perineal) fistula Anal stenosis (perineal) fistula	Anovestibular (perineal) fistula Anocutaneous Anal stenosis
Miscellaneous	Rare malformations	Persistent cloacal anomaly Rare malformations

With the advancement in medical research and modern technology, several other colorectal anomalies were introduced which were not documented in the 'Wingspread's classification'. In 1995, Dr Alberto Pena introduced a new classification system which replaced the traditional high, intermediate and low Imperforate Anus classifications. The various anomalies were now identified as a collective, under the name of Anorectal Malformations.

The Pena classification for Anorectal malformations (1995)

MALE	FEMALE
Perineal fistula	Perineal fistula

Rectourethral fistula
   Bulbar
   Prostatic
	Vestibular fistula

Rectovesical fistula	Persistent cloaca
	   3 cm common channel
	   3 cm common channel

Imperforate anus without fistula	Imperforate anus without fistula
Rectal atresia	Rectal atresia

An international conference was held at Krickenback Castle, Germany in 2005, which bought together 26 international authorities on congenital malformations. At this meeting, a new international classification system was developed for management of ARM patients. The 'Pena classification of ARM (2005)' was modified and the 'Krickenbeck classification' was established and to this day is used to diagnose the correct type of ARM.

The Krickenback classification for Anorectal malformations (2005)

Major clinical groups	Rare/regional variants
Perineal (Cutaneous) fistula	Pouch colon

Rectourethral fistula
    Bulbar
    Prostatic
	Rectal atresia/stenosis

Rectovesical fistula	Rectovaginal fistula
Vestibular fistula	H fistula
Cloaca	Others
No fistula	
Anal stenosis	

There is still much confusion and inconsistency worldwide as to the correct way to identify the condition. The overwhelming majority of the IA/ARM community, from a patient or family perspective, use the Imperforate Anus description. However, the paediatric colorectal medical community typically uses the Anorectal Malformation description.

For more information on the current type of care and treatments available to patients, please refer to Chapter 13 - Patient Care.

Also, many medical terms used in the stories which you may not be familiar with are listed in the Glossary at the end of the book.

References:
1. Holschneider AM, Hutson JM (2006) Anorectal Malformations in Children. Springer, Berlin Heidelberg New York
2. Pena A, (2011) Monologues of a Pediatric Surgeon. USA
3. Georgeson KE, Inge TH, Albanese CT. Laparoscopically Assisted Anorectal Pull-Through for High Imperforate Anus – A New Technique. Journal of Paediatric Surgery, Vol 35, No 6 (June), 2000: pp 927-931 35
4. Lane VA, Wood, RJ, Reck-Burneo CA, Levitt MA (2017) Pediatric Colorectal and Pelvic Surgery – Case Studies. CRC Press, Boca Rotan London New York
5. Vilanova-Sanchez A, Levitt MA (2020) Pediatric Colorectal and Pelvic Reconstructive Surgery. CRC Press, Boca Rotan London New York

Chapter 1 - Children/Adolescents Living with IA/ARM

1. My Story – Kruna - 6 Years Old (Serbia)

This is a small story about a big fighter. My name is Kruna. In my native Serbian language, it means crown. I am exactly what my name stands for - fighter, winner, queen.

I was born six years ago in a small town. It was a Wednesday, and it was raining. I got the highest grade at birth. My mom went to bed to rest, but the doctors woke her up very quickly and said they had to take me away from her. They told her I was born as an ARM baby and there was no doctor in my town who could address my problem.

When we arrived in Belgrade, they put me in a room with other babies without their mothers. I was alone for five days, but I knew my mom was thinking of me and she would come to me as soon as they would allow her, and of course, she came. She found me alone in a large room prepared just for the two of us. Everything was new to my mom. I was her first baby and she had never heard of such an anomaly before. But she learned with a little help from me and the doctors who showed her how. I always helped her, at first by not complaining and not crying and now that I have grown, I can do much more.

My mom never let my problem affect me growing up. In our country, we have the very best doctor, Marija L. who is our greatest friend and guardian angel.

My mom called, wrote and asked for other opinions and solutions for my problem. That is how I met the doctors from USA and Russia who had only one thing to tell us. There is no cure, but time is working for us and all we can do is apply the 'trial and error' principle.

My problem is completely invisible to others. I can do everything other children can. I know how to swim, ride rollerblades, ride a bike, practise gymnastics. I love all sports. It is just that I have to go home early. For me getting ready for bedtime takes a little longer. And when I go to bed, I dream of everything other children do.

The only difference is my birthday wish was to have a day without an enema.

Portrait by Michelle Collins

Footnote: *Kruna's mother, Alexsandra established a "ONE in 5000 Balkan's "Facebook page for families in her region under the name: "Udruženje za podršku deci sa anorektalnim anomalijama JEDAN u 5000 Balkan"*

2. Blake's Words and Art - 7 Years Old (USA)

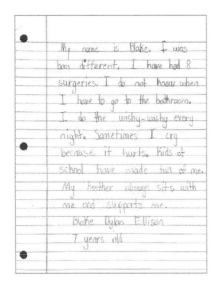

"My name is Blake. I was born different.

I have had 8 surgeries.

I do not know when I have to go to the bathroom. I do wishy-washy every night.

Sometimes I cry because it hurts. Kids at school have made fun of me.

My brother always sits with me and supports me."

Blake Dylan Ellison
7 years old

Footnote: Blake's mother Amanda and twin brother Austin share their stories (No's 76 & 77)

3. Xavier's Story in His Own Words - 7 Years Old (Canada)

My name is Xavier and I was born with an Imperforate anus. Life has been not so good because I have to get washed out every week. That means I have to take medication such as laxatives to clear out my stomach because I cannot control my poo.

I feel like I don't blend in with the other kids and that makes me feel left out. I wish I born with a good bum so that I could be like normal kids. I have been getting through my challenges pretty good because I have a good support system and I try to stay positive.

But sometimes it is hard because I keep having accidents or having too many bathroom breaks. I just want to have fun with my friends. I also have to wear training pants so that I don't mess myself. I wish I could wear normal underwear and not have to worry about those things.

I get frustrated when I use the washroom because sometimes it is hard for me to poo. I have to sit on the toilet for a long time only for nothing or a little of my poo to come out. I hope that one day I will be able to control my poo and use the washroom like everyone else.

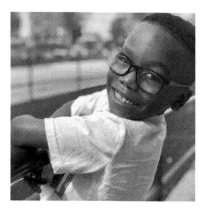

My mom says I am a brave boy because I have been through so much. She also tells me that I have a lot of courage. I have had six surgeries, which were not fun but I think my scar is cool. We call it my warrior scar.

I am an IA Warrior because I battle challenges every day. I started my Instagram page @xcie_xbox_dix so that I could tell people my story so that they could know more about me and my IA condition.

I am just a regular kid with a few challenges but my condition does not define me.

I define who I am and I am a warrior!

Footnote: Xavier's mother share's her story (No. 78)

4. X's Drawing and Her Own Words - 8 Years Old (England)

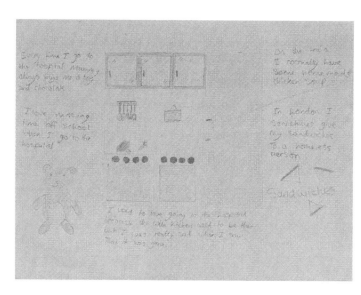

"Every time I go to the hospital Mummy always buys me a toy and chocolate"

"I love missing time off school when I go to the hospital"

"I used to love going to the hospital because the little kitchen used to be their but I was really sad that it was gone.

"On the train I normally have some homemade chicken soup"

"In London sometimes I give my sandwiches to a homeless person"

Footnote: X's mother Natalie share's her story (No. 79)

5. Incredibly Awesome – Jack - 10 Years Old (Canada)

May 28, 2010 - A normal day, except I was being born. The first two or three hours of my life was perfect - I was a healthy baby - nothing wrong. Then a nurse noticed that my stomach was getting big. And I mean BIG.

At first, they were not sure what was going on, but then they knew - I could not poop.

I was put in a helicopter and rushed to the IWK. There, when I was less than a day old, I had emergency surgery, where they put an opening for me to poop. But not pooping like normal people, nope.

For the next nine months I was pooping into a bag by my belly button. Poop would go into a bag, called a colostomy bag and it would need to be changed every couple of hours. I have one big scar.

And that is not the end of the story. They built me an anus, that was not perfect, but the best they could do. I have had to grow up with this and it has made life difficult for me. I have to take many medicines. We finally found a good one. I also have to go to the hospital two times a year.

For the first nine years of my life, I kept bits and pieces secret. People knew I had VACteRL. People knew I was born without an anus. People knew I was different. But I did not want them to know about the diaper. From kindergarten to grade two I kept it completely a secret from anyone and everyone. Then only one or two people knew in school. A couple of times people started to get suspicious and a couple of people asked me, and I would be 'No, No, I don't wear a diaper.'

Then in grade two, I started coming out and telling my friends and people who I trusted, about it. And things started to get better. At the moment it is going really well. For the first nine years of my life, I was wearing a diaper, but this year that has all changed - and I am now in underwear!! Everything is getting better and I am finally starting to live a semi-normal life, now that I am in grade five. I am pretty sure everyone knows that I used to wear a diaper, but now that I have stopped, I have not been teased and I have started to feel normal.

People look at me, people walk by me outside, and they notice me but do not pay any attention to me, because to them, I am just a normal kid. I look normal. I seem normal. But they do not know - they do not know that actually, I have VACteRL.

It is tough because, with all of this, I still have to put up with the normal stressors of life - school, friends, all of it - plus so much more. And VACteRL has affected all of this. Like at school I sometimes have trouble working because I am in pain, cramping from the medicine. And I have even been picked on due to it. It makes my life difficult in ways no one can see.

My future is unpredictable - we do not know what is going to happen in the future. But what we are hoping, what we are guessing, is that I am going to have a bright future and I am going to overcome all of this. And my life will finally be normal.

My dream is to someday become a big actor and be in movies like Star Wars, Marvel, whatever is big when I am an adult. I have travelled a lot, I have travelled from my home on PEI to NFLD, Toronto, Florida, California, Vegas, and more. I have walked the Hollywood walk of fame, went to Hell's Kitchen, been on stage with Penn and Teller, been on TV, done some small acting parts, and so much more.

I have done lots in my life, gone to lots of places, had lots of fun times and during it all I still put up with this. It has not changed it. VACteRL or not, I have still done all this, and I am pushing through. I have accomplished so much in my ten years of life with VACteRL and I will accomplish so much more, in my who knows how many more years of life, with VACteRL.

I do not care about people knowing. I want people to know it, because then people will know, 'Hey that kid has a tough life, but he still lives a normal life.' Then they will know that I am tough, I am different and I am not normal. And it is absolutely okay to not be normal. I am living an amazing life and I would not trade it for anything.

My advice to others with IA - It gets better - for the first while it is going to be hard, very hard to find the right medicine, to find the right people to tell about it and getting bullied about it. But just keep pushing through, it gets better I promise you.

IA stands for Imperforate Anus, but it also stands for Incredibly Awesome!!!!

And this is Jack Pickering signing off.

6. Heidi's Story in Her Own Words - 10 Years Old (Scotland)

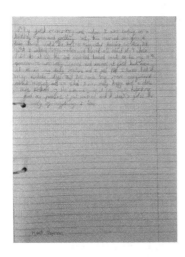

"My first memory was when I was curling in a ball of pain and yelling sick. This carried on for a long time until the doctors suggested having an ACE. At first I watched some videos and learnt all about it. I chose to do it in the end which turned out to be my 9th operation.

I was really scared and nervous at first but now it is my daily routine and I feel like I have had it my whole life. This has made me more confident about myself and in school.

I am really happy that I done this instead of the enemas as it has really helped me and my problems. I feel normal and it doesn't get in the way of anything I love."

Footnote: Heidi's mother Nicola share's her story (No. 86)

7. A Conversation with Noah – 13 Years Old (USA)

Newly thirteen-year-old Noah sat down with his mom, Amy, to talk about life with an anorectal malformation. Noah was born with imperforate anus, including a bladderneck/rectourethral fistula which caused kidney issues. He has undergone multiple surgeries and currently follows a daily bowel management program as described below.

AMY: Talk to me about what it's like to have imperforate anus.
NOAH: It's kind of like the same as having—like, once I understood I have it and it's for life, it just became part of our family's life, something that's just there.

AMY: What do you mean when you say it's just part of our life?
NOAH: I don't feel like we're different than other families in the way they run, except for the process I have to do every morning and feeling like I have to hide it.

AMY: Feeling like you have to hide it?
NOAH: I guess because, well, it doesn't bother me anymore because I'm getting older, but our life feels extremely different than other people's, other families'. I feel like we run as smoothly as other families, but because of my disability, it feels different. It comes down to wishing I didn't have to do a daily medical routine all the time—or at all.

But there are privileges that come along with it too.

AMY: Like?

NOAH: Like when I do my 45 minutes on the toilet, I usually get to watch a video and it's a great time to have some privacy. Because of how creative my family is, I have a table and it's like sitting at a dining room table on a chair, only I'm buck naked.

[We both laugh]

NOAH: I do schoolwork on the toilet, except on the weekends. Because it's so much quieter in there, it's easier to do my work. Usually this could take a couple hours, but sometimes I get everything done in that 45 minutes because it's so quiet.

And I only have to go to the restroom once a day.

AMY: Once a day?

NOAH: I only have to poop once a day.

[Pause while Noah looks thoughtful]

NOAH: But there are "downs" as well, like how I can't have too many foods with a lot of fibre. I can't have too much soda pop; it's a once-in-a-while treat. Not too much rice, not too much bread.

AMY: Weird things can cause issues.

NOAH: Oh, chewing gum actually can cause a problem for me!

AMY: What happens when you have certain foods and drinks?

NOAH: I sometimes get lots of gas, acid reflux, constipation, diarrhea, very bad stomach cramps, or start to literally poop during the day when I'm not supposed to.

I get a pretty good connection with my family through it, though. It's like our family's thing. It's not for everyone to know, so it feels like our secret.

It's fun to keep the secret sometimes because other people are like, why do you carry a bag around all the time?

And I can tell the truth and say, "I have to carry pull-ups [disposable undergarments]." And they'll say, "No, you don't." And I'll say, "Do you want to see?" And they say no usually.

AMY: What are the most important things your family and friends can do for you?

NOAH: Stay supportive. If they do a really good job, they make me feel like it's not getting in the way of things they want to do. Getting up at 6 a.m. to make it to soccer is already hard, as an example.

AMY: What do you have to do before you go to soccer?

NOAH: My whole morning routine, including breakfast, takes about 2.5-3 hours.

AMY: And that's before you can leave the house. [Noah nods] So what's your morning routine?

NOAH: I have imperforate anus and it's caused by not having muscles near my anus--not having an opening. This causes the poop to have trouble coming out, to pile up on itself and to get hard.

The process I talked about consists of getting the hard stool softened by using a liquid mixture of saline, glycerin and Carole soup [autocorrect turned "castile soap" into "Carole soup" and Noah laughed so hard and begged me to leave that for all of you to read] to moisturize the poop and irritate the colon. It makes contractions in my belly that stimulate my intestine to push. It kind of washes me out.

AMY: What else would you like people to know? Any final thoughts?
NOAH: If people have questions, ask my mom. Or google it.

AMY: Do you think there will ever come a time when you want to answer questions yourself?
NOAH: Nah. I don't really want to answer questions. I get pretty stressed out trying to tell people all about it. But it's a good thing for people to know. It's a really bad thing to keep secrets from friends, even for a good reason. It makes breaks in my relationships, and I always feel like I'm trying to hide something from someone, and it's really, really hard to do that.

Drawing by Noah

"Mike and I are endlessly proud of our boy, who handles all of the above (plus kidney issues which require cathing a couple times a day) with grace, strength and a tremendous sense of humour." Amy

8. My Story – Aiden - 13 Years Old (USA)

It all started on April 18, 2007, 13 years ago.

I was born with IA. I didn't know it yet, but my life was about to get a whole lot crazier. On April 20th, I had my first surgery. It was a Colostomy, a treatment that a lot of the people with my condition have (among other things). I don't remember most of the early days, however I do remember attending a PTN convention.

That's where I learned that I wasn't the only one and that I wasn't different. I was confused, but I got the premise pretty quickly. After all, I was at a convention for people with my condition. The first surgery I remember vaguely was in 1st grade. I was six and it was to get my Malone. The only things I remember from it was having a button for painkillers and a fear of going into a swimming pool.

The Youth Rally is what made the biggest impression on me. It's the one place where everyone gets what we're going through. Youth Rally is a camp that moves on a rotating schedule (Boulder, Seattle, San Diego). The camp takes place at a college campus and we stay in the dorms usually with a roommate. When you're there, you meet up with your group for the week. The groups are organized by age, so most of the time you have a wide range of conditions in one group.

During the week, they have fun events every night as well as support groups for self-esteem, condition, treatment, etc. At the end of the week, there's a big party and graduation for the senior campers which is always an emotional experience.

The next morning, everyone either gets on a bus or is picked up by their parents or family. This year, we had our Youth Rally at Zoom, ZM. It was a new, but fun adventure for everyone involved. It had its own set of new challenges that we all overcame and managed to have a fantastic week. I hope that next time we can all see each other in person.

In recent years, I've had a couple of surgeries and would like to thank Dr. Pena, Dr. Bischoff, Dr. Levitt, Dr. Wood, Dr. Ching & Dr. Anderson for all of their help.

For anyone going through the surgeries for IA, hang in there, it gets better.

Footnote: Aiden's parents, Michelle and Dave share their stories (Nos. 93 & 94)

9. My Story – Laura - 15 Years Old (Austria)

My name is Laura, and I am 15 years old. I live in Lower Austria.

I am currently in the 9th Grade at school with my main study focus being on music. I have two older siblings, Raffael and Viktoria, and they are both very important to me. And then there is my mum, who is one of the strongest people I know. She is always there for me and she is very selfless. My Dad does not want to be a part of my life, so he is not important to me. Now that you know some things about me, I will tell you my story.

It all began on 7th January 2005, the day I was born. At first everyone thought I was healthy, until they took my temperature and discovered something was wrong. Just two hours later I was sent to a hospital in Vienna where paediatric surgeons, who had experience in dealing with anorectal malformations (ARM), could better care for me.

The next day I had my first surgery to create a colon stoma. My mum has told me that throughout her pregnancy she had always felt something was wrong, but none of her doctors believed her. So, I got my stoma and had all my corrective surgeries performed over the next ten months.

When my surgeries were finished, everybody in my family thought that I would now have a normal life. But that wasn't to be the case and I needed diapers until the age of three and a half years.

In the 2nd Grade I began to deal with autoimmunity and because of this I started therapy. When I turned seven, we found out that my bladder did not function properly. We were told that it wasn't such a big deal at the time but would cause problems in the future. Until the age of eight I sometimes needed diapers as, on many days, I would have accidents.

When I went to Kindergarten, children started to bully me, and I never had many friends because of it. The bullying got less in middle school and stopped completely after a few years. Then for a long time, nothing serious or tragic happened to my body other than only a few hospital stays.

In 2017 I started to have suffer cramps daily and nobody could understand why. Over six months I had several hospital stays and many examinations until we found out what the problem was. It was my bladder, which had become too big and had be treated accordingly. After that treatment I thought it was all over and I could now live a normal life, but then the very worst time of my life began.

On March 21st, 2019, I had to have emergency surgery because of an ileus (an obstruction caused by the lack of bowel movement). The surgery took eleven hours and they had to open up my whole belly. Against my expectations, I felt better after a short time and everything went well until 1st of April when I had to have a second emergency surgery because of a new ileus. This surgery took six hours, and I spent a week feeling absolutely dreadful in the ICU. On 3rd of May I was discharged from hospital.

At the end of May I came very close to needing a third surgery for the same reason, but fortunately my body recovered without the need for it. Then on 27th July I did have a third emergency surgery because of another ileus. This surgery took six hours and I had to stay in the ICU again, and it was a month before I could go home. Five days later I had a sub-ileus (partial bowel obstruction) and so I went back to hospital for five more weeks.

Now in 2020, I have already had a few more hospital admissions because of recurring sub-ileus plus some other problems, but it has always gotten better and hasn't been as frequent as last year. Since I changed hospital in December 2019, everything has been better for me and my new surgeons Dr Carlos Reck and Dr Wilfried Krois are extremely nice and kind.

Now you know my medical history, let me tell you a few things about my daily life and the problems I have to deal with. I play four instruments and I love to sing and dance. Music is one of my greatest passions. When I sing, dance or play an instrument everything else becomes silent and my world seems better for a short time. Many people think it's not healthy for me to play the double bass, because it is so heavy, or even the flute. They do not understand that ARM does not affect your ability to play any instrument you want.

The biggest problem I have with school is that I cannot attend very often because of my ileus problems, and many teachers have wanted me to change school or drop out completely, neither of which I want to do. I want to become a surgeon and I like school, so it hurts me a great deal to hear things like that. Many teachers give me unsolicited advice, like you have to go for walks, try to get healthy again, eat healthier, eat more vegetables and so on. They all have no clue as to what ARM or my ileus issues are all about. Instead, they read about it on the Internet and give unhelpful advice based on how they think it relates to me. Some of my teachers don't even understand why I can't do any schoolwork when I am in hospital.

Just a few weeks ago, one of my teachers recommended that I try to get healthy again because I am in hospital so often and, at the age of 15, that shouldn't be happening to me. So, it's not easy with my teachers as they just do not understand. My classmates, on the other hand, are totally cool with it and when there is something, they want to know they simply ask.

When we have sports, school is even harder for me as I am always scared of having an "accident". Because of the attitude of my teachers with regard to my problems, I fear being at school and hearing things like "You can't do it", "It would be better if you changed school", "Maybe it's better to drop out" or even "I don't think you can become a surgeon".

I try my best to ignore such things but it's not easy. The sad truth is, I have many problems to deal with as part of my everyday life. Often people tell me things like "My neighbour had an ileus too" and I know they all want to be nice, but it just doesn't help. Things I hear about ten times a day include "Yeah it's not that bad, it could be worse", or the opposite "Wow! That must be so hard. I couldn't live like that". Both things are very unhelpful.

I've had many health issues in my life which are hard to deal with and sometimes I've wanted to run from them, but of course I cannot. People even tell me I look healthy and I can't possibly be that sick and they just can't see that something is wrong. My absolute favourite is "You've gained weight! Everything must be fine now!".

It really hurts when someone tells me these things. Nobody understands I also have problems with my mental health, not just as a result of my physical health, but also because of other people's reactions to it. I know it's hard for others to understand everything, but it would be nice if people just asked questions instead of giving uneducated advice.

Everybody has their own medical story and, when speaking to someone with chronic illness or disability, I believe it is best to simply ask questions and not offer advice or stories about someone else you know who you think has the same problems. Everyone is different, so please always keep that in mind when speaking to someone with medical issues and offer you're your attention by just asking questions.

I would like to tell you more about myself, my life with ARM and many other things, but it cannot be done in this short story. If you see my book in a few years I would be very grateful if you could read it. I started it a few months ago, writing about myself and my journey and I hope that people will gain some better understanding when they read it.

I want to say thank you to a few people because, without them, I may never have been able to talk about my condition. I am so thankful for my mum and my siblings and how strong and supportive they have been. I want to say thank you to the best physiotherapists in the whole universe, Patrick and Stefan, who have made my ileus journey so much funnier and easier to bear.

Thank you to my best friend Stefanie who is a VACTERL survivor - I love her dearly. And thank you to Greg for believing in us and for the way he is helping us to find our voice and tell the world who we are.

10. Nick's Story - 17 Years Old (USA)

Just like my mom says, **YOU ARE NOT ALONE.** The ONE in 5000 foundation has opened my eyes and showed me the beautiful community of people who are born with IA just like me. I have always believed it has been God's plan for me to help people struggling with IA, whether it is the children or the parents of those children.

If there is any advice I could give to parents, it would be to always be considerate of what your child is going through. Put yourselves in their shoes when it feels like there is no solution to accidents and other struggles that come with IA. As much as you try to help, you will never truly know what your child is going through. In my experience, doctors were basically telling my parents I should magically be having no accidents, based on a teaspoon of MiraLAX. This just did not work for me. It is not because I was lazy or did not mind having accidents. I just could not feel the urge to use the bathroom, so I would have leakage. It was awfully hard for the doctors and my family to understand that. No kid wants to have accidents, but sometimes, because of IA, we just cannot help it. To all the parents out there, make sure you put yourselves in your child's shoes and NEVER GIVE UP. My parents never gave up on me and it allowed me to keep my IA a secret, find a solution that works for me and live a happy life.

In my experience my mental health deteriorated because I did not think I would ever find a solution. I was in a constant negative state of mind and if there is one thing I want kids to learn from this message, it is to stay positive and never let your birth defect define you. Trust me, I know how hard it gets; I know how easy it is to slip into a depressed state. However, as I have gotten older, I have learned to stay positive and see the good in every situation. You have to take what God has given you and make the absolute best out of it. You are never going to get a second shot at life. You do not want to waste your one chance on this beautiful Earth by being sad all of the time because of a birth defect.

For example, when I had an accident at school when I was younger, I would go home and cry because my negative mindset was telling me that I was disappointing my family and they had to fix my problems. Nowadays if I have an accident, it is still hard on me, but instead of being sad and letting it ruin my day, I always think about how blessed I am that nobody knew it happened.

Keeping a positive mindset is not easy at all, but I promise you it will be a benefit to your life, just as it has been to mine. Another point I want to stress to you is to not let a birth defect define you. What I mean is, do not let anything hold you back from your dreams, playing sports you want to play, or doing activities you want to do. Parents this is for you as well. I know it is scary to allow your kids to do certain things, considering the problems they face with IA, however, you cannot hold them back. If they want to go play basketball let them play basketball, if they want to be a WWE wrestler let them pursue that.

You can do anything you want to in life kids, take what life gives you and make the best out of it, because you only live once. **YOU ARE NOT ALONE** and never, ever, forget it.

Footnote: Nick's mom April shares her story (No. 97)

Chapter 2 - Parents/Family with Infant (0-23 Months)

11. Ethan's Story – Mandi (USA)

The 27th May 2020 at 11:51 am was when our son Ethan was born via c-section and our journey through the one in 5000 began.

Everything went well throughout the pregnancy; however, they did notice he only had one vein and one artery within his umbilical cord. So, they wanted to watch his development closely. Once he was born, they informed me that it seems that your son was born without an anus. I was so confused with what I had just heard, I looked at my husband trying to see if he had heard what I did.

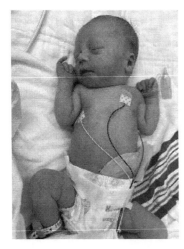

They took Ethan to the NICU immediately and they put a suction tube down into his stomach to help keep air and liquid from going down. I did not get to see him for about six hours or more. The next morning, he had his first surgery for the colostomy and fistula. They had to keep him on the ventilator just a bit longer, so his little lungs did not have to work so hard.

He then spent the next eight days in the NICU before we were finally able to go home. The staff helped us to learn about how to change the colostomy bags. It was a new experience for us, as we were first time parents. It was hard in the beginning, as we had to change his bag four times a day because it would leak. It just broke my heart to change them because each time it caused him pain and discomfort. I would cry along with him, trying to understand why he had to be born this way.

I have learned so much each day and eventually I worked out how to remove the bags without him screaming. I also figured out how to make a bag last three days, versus the three times a day, so as Ethan was growing, so was I.

On 3rd August, Ethan went in for his PSARP. He woke up in pain but with cuddles from mommy and daddy he recovered quickly. He was not yet three months old. Once we had his follow up surgery, we then had to start to do the dilations, which I have to say were super hard to do. Seeing my boy cry during these was still just as hard, however, I can say it does get easier. We started at a size five and before he could have his reconnect surgery, he had to be at a ten. It took the full eight weeks to get to the ten and he no longer cried during his dilation.

We had his stoma closure surgery on the 8th October, and he is doing very well with the healing. It is so amazing how fast he has recovered from the surgery.

He is now four months old and he is such a happy little boy, he is almost always smiling. He loves to go outside and look around at everything. I feel like Ethan has taken his journey through IA better than his daddy and myself.

It is so amazing how someone so small can do so well when everything is different. All Ethan knows is how he was born. He acts just like any other baby.

Every day he is learning something new and every day I am learning as well. Learning to be more aware and learning to speak up for my son when something is not right. My son is not any different from any other child, he just happens to have custom parts. I believe that educating others is the key. I had never heard of IA until my son was born, and I have learned that it is far more common than you would think.

I love my son more than anything in the world and I will help him throughout his journey. I want him to know he is not alone.

Our journey has barely started, but we are all in it together and he is going to be five months old in a few days. He amazes us every day.

12. Raven's Story - Our Little Warrior's Big Battle - Chloe (Australia)

Becoming a new parent is in itself challenging, however I never imagined being faced with this many difficulties so soon after becoming one. I look back now and often wonder how we even got through it.

During pregnancy, it was discovered I had a single umbilical artery, which is a malformation of the umbilical cord. I was told the only major concern would be that bub might be growth restricted, therefore we were carefully monitored for that. Otherwise, all the antenatal scans were normal.

Raven Belle was born not growth restricted, but simply SGA (Small for Gestational Age). The midwives placed her on my chest and for that brief ten seconds my heart was completely full. Before I could comprehend what was happening, they immediately took Raven from me. She was apnoeic for the first three minutes of her life and required resuscitation. Little did we know this was the beginning of our overwhelming and traumatic journey.

For the first two days of Raven's life, we actually got to experience that newborn bliss. She seemed perfect in every way. She was examined and passed her paediatric discharge check, so we were able to go home.

However, it was only a matter of hours before we had to return. We had decided to give Raven her first bath. When my husband was wiping her, he suddenly became very anxious and told me he couldn't see a little bum hole. Initially I dismissed it, thinking he must have missed it somehow. After I examined her very closely, confusion, fear and anxiety coursed through my body.

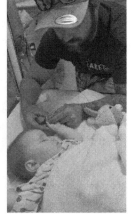

My midwife was also dismissive of the idea that Raven didn't have one, however she returned to double check to essentially reassure us. I still recall the colour vanish from her face when she opened Raven's nappy and inspected her. After a series of events and a flood of different emotions, a whirlwind of information thrown at us and Raven was scheduled for emergency surgery to create her colostomy.

We spent a week in NICU, where we were told Raven was born with an Imperforate Anus, and also with a rectovaginal fistula through which she was passing stool. As you can imagine, we had so many questions, the first being "How on earth was this missed?". Unfortunately, this wasn't the first time the hospital let us down and it was one of many questions that seemed to go unanswered.

Being a first time Mum, who had never even changed a nappy before, I felt extremely overwhelmed as I was now faced with having to look after a baby with a stoma! The NICU nurses informed us that the Stomal therapist was on leave, so they gave us one demonstration and sent us on our way.

For the first five weeks of Raven's life, we had to do it on our own - the trial and error, the tears, the failures and learning how to order the stoma bags, all without any support whatsoever.

Despite being located in regional Australia, we still had access to a large hospital. It was disappointing that they were unable to provide a skilled health professional or even access to another located elsewhere. Not only did this affect the day to day management of Raven's stoma at first, but such a simple thing like 'can my child go swimming?' was so daunting for us. We were made to feel like we had to hide Raven's condition, as we were so unsure of people's reaction and fearful of their judgement.

However, we wanted Raven to experience activities that all babies should have the opportunity to do. After contacting our local swim school, Raven was welcomed with open arms. To our surprise, her swim teacher had suffered her own silent battle with a bowel disease and was willing to share her story with us. This has created a very special bond between her and Raven, which assures us it's OK to share her journey.

At two months old, Raven underwent her Anterior Sagittal Rectoplasty and recovered tremendously well. However, it was the post-operative management she had to endure and that I had to subject her to which will haunt me for a very long time. I simply cannot explain the gut-wrenching emotion I felt hearing my daughter's painful screams during her dilatations. I know it NEEDED to be done for her, but I really struggled with the fact that I was the one causing this trauma.

Once again, I felt so alone. My husband and I had nobody to turn to for help, advice, guidance or support. We had no choice but to be strong on our own for our little girl.

At 7 months old, Raven has just undergone her stoma reversal. That was two weeks ago at the time of writing this. While we are managing the nappy rash at this stage, which appears to be one of the most common associated problems, there is a small part of me that remains anxious.

Yes, a parent will always worry about their child, but what about the parents of children whose future is so unknown, whose quality of life is dependent on so many different factors and who have already faced so much adversity? How much more can they handle?

These are worries unique to parents with children who have a rare condition such as IA. What feeds anxiety is the unknown. Unfortunately, there is simply not enough education and knowledge surrounding this. Compounding the issue is the lack of support we, as parents, receive during a very demanding and trying time in our life.

Raven is incredibly resilient and this is what drives me and gives me the strength to be the Mummy she needs. All anxieties aside, I know she will achieve great things in her life.

"With Brave Wings, She Flies".

13. Jovi's Story – Stella (New Zealand)

Our little Trooper was born on 6th April 2020, eight weeks premature due to pregnancy complications. This did not stop Jovi Quinn from making his presence known in the world, from the minute he arrived. Back at our twelve week scan we learnt there was a large fluid filled sac in the abdomen of our baby and we were unable to find out what it really was until much later in the pregnancy. Then we learnt little one had a Duplex right kidney and ureter seal which had caused severe dilation to his bladder, ureter and kidney.

After having our second child diagnosed with Turner Syndrome at six months old, we were optimistic that this little one would also beat all the odds. We put our faith and our little one's life in God's hands. After hearing it was a wee boy, after two girls, we were too excited to worry. We knew everything would be okay and could not wait to meet him.

At thirty-two weeks it was time to deliver via Caesarean Section, which was under general anaesthetic, due to the complications with the placenta.

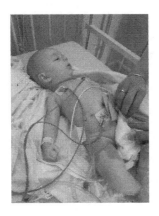

Jovi was born at 4lbs 8oz, with a distended abdomen, but other than that, the initial response was that he was a beautiful, perfect little boy. He was taken to the NICU where they completed their assessment and we found out that he was actually, a beautiful, perfectly imperfect little boy.

He was found to have no anus, so off he went to have a colostomy. The weeks went by and Jovi continued to thrive. However, at four weeks he developed a hernia and underwent surgery to repair that and he had a circumcision to prevent kidney infections due to his renal reflux. At five weeks we brought him home with us and two days later he was off the NG feeding and taking every meal via bottle. He did not stop growing.

Jovi went on to have a pull through procedure, where they also repaired an anorectal fistula. This surgery took three hours longer than expected because the bowel was so severely attached to the ureter. Also, there was not enough length of bowel to attach to the new anus. After five and a half hours, we finally got the call, to say, as always, our wee trooper had come through and was doing well. He continued to thrive once more.

We are now six and a half months in on our amazing journey with Jovi. He has had four surgeries, twenty trips to the hospital, uncountable tests and dozens of small procedures and he just loves life.

On our journey we have met so many amazing people, all of whom are part of our family now. Each and every one of them have special hearts, but it is our little trooper Jovi Quinn that has taught us all how to keep smiling through the toughest times of your life.

If you smile you have already won.

14. How Giovanni's Defect Began Helping Others – Amber (USA)

It was anything but a normal birthday for me. Just hours before I had to face my ex-husband and his fiancé at a father-daughter dance, the digital test I had taken in my boyfriend's bathroom read "pregnant." Terrified, I said nothing. We had plans for a later reveal, something fun for the kids and our families.

Richie and I had begun a whirlwind romance, discovering our Little Mouse in my pouch just a month into the relationship, but we embraced it and each other. He was by my side planning a fun little treasure hunt for the kids on St. Patrick's Day. We had an egg roulette gender reveal party, and I decided to take my first float trip (a leisurely raft ride) before my older kids would spend their first summer away from me.

I had a difficult pregnancy, with ex-husband issues giving me high blood pressure and doctors ordering me to have three months of bed rest so as to avoid pre-term labour.

On a gorgeous fall morning, Giovanni was born at 9.00am. Due to his size he had got stuck, but it was still a relatively quick delivery. The nurses weighed him twice because they were certain he was 10 pounds! However, he was actually 8 pounds and 10 ounces – still quite big!

He was perfect except the doctor thought his genitals were a little off and she said she would check again tomorrow. Richie and I thought nothing more of it as we were enveloped in new baby bliss, with family and friends coming in and out to visit and with lots of love and laughter.

Giovanni breast fed like a champion then and has never had a problem with it since. The doctor arrived cheerfully the next morning, asking "Hey guys, how was the first 24?" I told her "They were perfect! He nursed every few hours. He's a such little piggy and has a great latch. But do we need to see urology, is his penis okay? He hasn't pooped yet."

As a parent of three, you NEVER think to check your kid's butthole, right? Every human has a butthole, sphincter, rectum, intestines and so on. Basic anatomy. She checked him out, lifting his chubby cheeks and said, "OH!"

"What? Doc, wait, what's OH?" She turned his little bottom to me, and I said "OH! So, what now?"

His sweet little cheeks were sealed completely shut with no opening for poop to come out. My whole world stopped, knowing the next answer was NICU. I had just spent three months of my pregnancy on complete bed rest to avoid preterm labour, so we could avoid NICU. The doctor said to me "Honey, I'm going to make some calls and you're going to NICU. Call your family."

Giovanni is one of the one in 5,000 kids born with an anorectal malformation, commonly known as imperforate anus. Like autism and PTSD, there are spectrums; a 1 to 10 scale of how bad things can be and Giovanni was a 9. His lower intestine was attached to his bladder, and it was to be determined whether he had a rectum in a fold or even an anal canal, which meant he may or may not have the muscle function to understand bowel movements.

At four days old we were told that Giovanni needed surgery for a diverting colostomy with a fistula. Essentially, they attached a small piece of his colon to an opening in his outer belly called a stoma, and created a fistula from his lower intestine which was attached to the outside of below his belly button (the doctors would use the fistula to later diagnose that his lower intestine was leading down to his bladder)

After the surgery, they brought my tiny baby back to me wrapped in globs of Aquaphor ointment and mounds of pads and diapers. I quickly learned "skin care" or double diapering. Slathering that sweet belly in cream and covering it in mounds of gauze and pads, then wrapping a diaper sideways around his belly to hold it all in.

When his belly healed from the first wave of rashes, I began to learn the routine of using a colostomy bag. Cutting a hole to match his stoma and applying barrier cream, adhesives and tapes, and using cotton ball after cotton ball. We had a friend give us 4,000 cotton balls for Christmas which only lasted six months.

We learned after three months that all brands of disposable diapers caused an allergic reaction on his skin, so we switched to cloth diapers. His bottom healed but his belly didn't.

I remember at 3.00am one morning, when Giovanni was almost four months old, both Richie and I lay on the living room floor crying. We couldn't get bags to stick to his belly, and his belly was as red as fire covered in little blisters. We were going through diaper cream after diaper cream, gauze after gauze, disposable brand after disposable brand. Nothing was making his belly better, so I switched to using cloth flats; a large thin layer of cotton fabric folded and wrapped around his belly with a disposable wrapped on top. It slowly seemed to make his belly better, but then the diaper wouldn't fit around his ribs without cutting into them.

At around six months, my mom and I created "Tummy Huggers" - abdominal cloth diapers for bellies, to create what is commonly known as "double-diapering". It replaces the use of any adhesive bag for collecting output and is environmentally friendly, leak-proof, discreet, and machine washable (note my catchy sales pitch!).

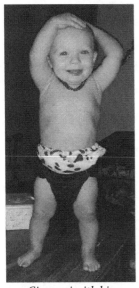

Giovanni with his Tummy Hugger

Not only can a Tummy Hugger be used as a replacement for a bag, it can also be used even if there is a bag. Say you are out and the bag leaks, which can be very stressful as a parent (not to mention as an adult suffering from the same issues), you can grab a Tummy Hugger to hold everything in (including the bag) until you can clean up properly and safely.

Tummy Huggers can be used for bathing and swimming and can also double as a simple support wrap. They are low cost and extremely effective, there are different styles for different types of ostomy patients and snaps are used for secure closure. We ask for measurements of the client for adequate sizing.

We went live on Facebook for marketing, to turn this into a small business. Posting in other groups we realised what a great need there is for something like this and how greatly they can impact lives. I returned to working overtime within a week of taking our idea live, suddenly my hours spent writing donation requests and hunting for angel investors all seemed futile.

Around eight months of age, we had yet another Giovanni storm. Our little guy swallowed a penny! Constipation is detrimental to anyone with a colostomy and after a few days we realised something wasn't right. We went to the local hospital ER for the first time and left after three days.

From that visit we stablished that Giovanni should be seen by a colorectal surgeon. His defect requires more than just a general paediatric surgeon. Upon medical advice, we decided that we should travel to Ohio for our next surgery. His posterior sagittal anorectoplasty (PSARP) surgery is scheduled for 20 November 2020, and will disconnect his intestine from his bladder, pulling it down to form and create a rectum and anus. On a 1 to 10 scale, this procedure is a 9, and it requires seven to nine hours of surgery.

After the penny debacle, I decided I was working too much and I shifted my focus to school, enrolling in the Cannabis Training University. Cutting my hours at work, I was taking more time for school, Tummy Huggers and Giovanni. I was blessed even further by receiving a single parent scholarship to MacCormac College a week into the school semester. I am now enrolled at two colleges and I dove in headfirst, pushing aside everything except Giovanni.

We had his first "vacation", an eight-hour road trip to Ohio from 18 to 23 November and Giovanni is now sporting a fancy new bum hole. You can only understand the excitement if you've gone through this. Our first day was a buzz, exploring a hospital in a town twice the size of home, covered with tall buildings and Christmas lights.

Giovanni's first appointment was pretty rough, taking quite a few doctors to hold him and get the images they needed. The urology team worked alongside the radiology team to determine the muscle function in his pelvic region and the size and function of his bladder and kidneys, watching his bladder empty after filling it with dye.

The urologist thought there was an area that looked a little funny and wanted to do a scope before surgery using a tiny camera to go in and look. Other than using the scope to have a better look, we received an all clear on his check-up. His kidneys looked beautiful, his bladder functioned well and surgery would be minimal.

Our next day began early, full of a whirlwind of events - A COVID-19 test at 8.30am and then back to radiology for x-rays. It was the day we would discover exactly where his connection was at. We would know whether it could be done with a few small spots on his belly or if the doctor would have to turn him on his belly and open him at the tail bone area. We also would know how long this surgery would take.

The x-rays showed that the lower intestine connected to the bladder, with a weird little fistula that urology wanted to look at with the camera. It also showed there was enough intestine to stretch down to his bum. But the doctor wouldn't know the exact location of his new bum until he got into surgery, as it depended on where the muscles lay.

We were scheduled for 12.00pm surgery. We checked in, we played and then we waited. Finally, it was time for him to go, the surgery then taking seven hours to complete. I spent the time working on school assignments that I had missed during appointments. I paced the floor. I grabbed lunch. I waited for my phone to ring - for the doctor to be done and out of surgery.

Finally, my phone rang. They were closing up in surgery and the doctor would be out soon. I rushed back across the street and up to the surgery floor. The surgeon explained to me that the little fistula urology saw on the camera was a part of the intestine. It was attached to his bladder, but also snaked around behind the bladder.

Most cases are usually cut and dry and each kid has a diagnosis category they fit in, like a box for each different one. But Giovanni was outside all the boxes. He was his own special case. The first time I saw him after surgery, he was laid over on his belly with his sweet little face swollen from the ordeal. We spent the next three days cuddling him in a rocking chair. Now we are back home and he is healing well.

We will return to Ohio in February of 2021 for his colostomy take down.

During our journey we learned about the ONE in 5000 Foundation, which was created by Greg Ryan to raise awareness for IA/ARM children and adults. I contacted him for a logo, to have a special cloth diaper made to help raise awareness with Giovanni and Tummy Huggers. The ultimate goal of "Tummy Huggers" is to donate to NICU's for children born needing ostomies and to families overseas who may not have the means to provide supplies.

While talking to Greg, I learned of the anthology project which allows us to share our stories and ideas with the world. IA/ARM is a One in 5000 condition. It is common enough that it can be fixed, but undetectable until birth. We always compare it to winning the lottery - you just don't know until it happens.

Giovanni is now one year old, weighs 21 pounds and is 29 inches long. Walking, sporting six teeth, speaking seven words and using ten different signs in sign language, he is such a happy, calm child. We have a hash tag saying #noshameinourostomygame because there is no shame in our ostomy game!

We are IA strong, and we will continue to persevere!

15. Rory's Story – Lucy and Rob (England)

Rory was born at 37 weeks gestation on the eleventh of November 2019. Everything seemed great and he latched on straight away. He only had two feeds when he became disinterested and did not want feeding.

Over the next couple of days, I expressed, and bottle fed him my milk (as advised by the midwives), although he became more and more lethargic and sleepy and certainly did not want any milk! We were then sent home three days later after having been seen by a paediatrician who said all was well and that we had to wake him every three hours to feed him. By this point he had only had a smear of poo!

The next day, a midwife came to see us and immediately sent us back to hospital where the situation became serious very quickly. Rory's tummy had become so distended that he was struggling to breathe; he was intubated, and blood tests were taken. It was then that the doctor discovered Rory had no anus, just a very tiny hole to the right where it should have been (he did have an indent where the anus should have been) and so he was blocked up with poo all the way up his colon.

We needed to be transferred ASAP to another hospital who could operate on Rory (because it is so specialised). We were blue lighted to the Norfolk and Norwich University Hospital (two hours from home) who were incredible!

Rory was diagnosed with an Imperforate Anus (he also had sepsis and was very close to dying); he needed to have surgery to remove the back up of poo and have a colostomy and a stoma bag (on the fifteenth of November 2020).

This was a huge shock for us, and Rory was in NICU for two weeks; the surgeon and nurses at NNUH were so supportive and incredible. They taught us how to change the stoma bag and care for him so well that we needed no further support back home.

On the ninth of March 2020, we then went back to NNUH for Rory to have anoplasty (creating an anus); following this we needed to do dilatations with a metal rod every day. This was fairly distressing because Rory got upset and it was painful; we needed to increase the size of the rod every week to ten days from a size seven to a size thirteen. We had to judge when to increase the size as we could not have appointments at the hospital due to COVID19 and the lockdown.

The surgeon called us on a weekly basis though to check. Rory made a speedy recovery after this surgery and we then just needed to wait for his anus to fully heal before we could have his colostomy reversed. However, again, due to COVID19, this surgery was delayed to August 2020 (three months after it was expected); it was so tough managing the stoma with Rory moving and it was leaking a lot and needed changing up to six times a day.

The surgery day finally arrived (twenty-sixth of August 2020) and Rory was the only patient in surgery that morning (due to COVID19). He was in surgery for six hours, but all went smoothly, and he was now without a stoma bag.

The wait was then on to see when Rory would do his first poo!! He pooed that night which was amazing and even the nurses and doctors were surprised!

Rory was not allowed any milk until forty-eight hours after surgery and even then, it was only thirty ml. every three hours to start with.

He continued to make excellent progress and day by day he appeared brighter. He started eating three days after surgery and this passed through absolutely fine. We were discharged five days after surgery which was super speedy!

Since being home, Rory has come on leaps and bounds and is now just like any other little boy his age.... he is also pooing like a trooper!

I know we may come across some difficult times in the future when we start potty training but for now, we are enjoying our happy little boy.

16. Amila's Story – Maria (Philippines)

My husband and I were in a relationship for seventeen years. Right after our wedding, we wished for a baby girl. Then a month later I became pregnant with a baby boy. Seven months after his birth I then became pregnant with our second baby, another boy.

After seven years of being married, we finally decided to try again to have a baby girl. It was a planned pregnancy, and after four months I finally conceived.

At our appointment with the OB-GYN, the ultrasound report revealed a six-week-old embryo. I had suddenly experienced a subchorionic haemorrhage which threatened a spontaneous abortion, so I was given medication and needed bed rest to overcome this trial.

At seven months of pregnancy, our relatives threw us a gender reveal party. The moment is still fresh to me. When the final reveal of the gender through the colour of smoke happened, I was jumping for joy when I saw that it was pink. Finally, our long-time wish was being granted. My husband and I were both so happy that we could not believe we would be having a baby girl after years of waiting.

Our strength was tested again on my twenty-seventh week of pregnancy, as I was experiencing feelings of being in labour. We went to the hospital immediately and were told that I was two centimetres dilated and contracting. After monitoring me for two hours, the hospital sent us home with one week worth of medication to stop the contractions.

On my thirty-fifth week of pregnancy, my waters broke. As my husband brought me to the hospital, we chatted about how excited we were to see our baby girl. At the hospital I was immediately checked and injected with dexamethasone to aid on my baby's lungs in case she was to be delivered early. The healthcare staff did the best they could to try and delay the labour, so that there would be more time for my baby's lungs to develop properly.

After eleven hours, I was experiencing very close contractions and then another hour later I delivered my baby via NSD (natural spontaneous delivery). The feeling was surreal. I heard my baby cry and then the OB-GYN said "Good job mommy! Congrats, it's a baby girl". I was crying tears of joy.

I still couldn't believe that I finally had a baby girl. The healthcare staff brought me to our room, with my baby left in the recovery room. The paediatrician told me that my baby needed to have dextrose and be supported with oxygen through a canula, because she had respiratory distress with her lungs not being fully developed.

After five hours of waiting, my baby girl was finally brought to me. She was so cute and tiny. My husband and I were so excited to meet her and so glad to finally hold her in our arms. She is a gift to us.

The first thing I did I was check her diaper, but there was no poop. I asked about this and her paediatrician said to wait until the next day because it might be that the baby still hasn't drunk milk. After twenty-four hours the paediatrician came to check her again and I asked again why she still hadn't pooped. We were told wait a bit longer, but after thirty-two hours the paediatrician returned, anxious and asking us for a thermometer.

The paediatrician showed my husband and I that two of the openings of my baby were present but the anus was not. We were so shocked as she told us to find a paediatric surgeon.

In my 34 years of existence, this was the first time I had heard that such a condition existed. My parents-in-law immediately went to the hospital and were very angry that the staff had taken so long to tell us about it. We were very scared we might lose my baby girl. We were then transferred to another hospital for the operation.

The travel time to the hospital was thirty to sixty minutes and the feelings I had then are still fresh to me now. I travelled in an ambulance with our baby and two nurses, while my husband drove in another car behind. It was a very sad ride and the streets were silent because of a strict curfew implemented at the peak of the COVID-19 pandemic.

When we reached the hospital, we were not attended to immediately because of the pandemic health protocols. I was crying because it was an emergency and I saw my baby vomiting as her tummy was already getting big. It was the scariest moment of my life.

After two hours, we were finally given a room and doctors were constantly coming in and out of it. What was happening still hadn't really sunk in for us. The excitement had turned into fear as we feared losing our much-awaited gift.

We thought that it would be a simple surgery, that the skin on my baby's anus might overlap the opening and could be fixed right away. We totally had no idea what the condition of our baby really was. All I knew that night was that my baby needed an urgent operation because her tummy was growing big. She kept on vomiting and I feared that she might aspirate it.

We were told that an X-ray of our baby showed neonatal pneumonia which had to be cured. There were a series of tests, ECG, a physical exam and lots of pricking and injections. All I remember was the cry of my baby. I felt so helpless because I couldn't rescue her from the pain she was experiencing. I wanted to stop her cries that seemed to be begging me to ease her suffering. There were many times I would go to the bathroom and cry so hard myself, but it didn't help my pain.

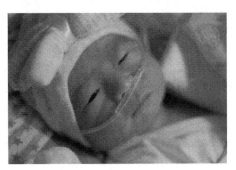

We were finally called for the ultrasound and x-ray of my baby. Because only one parent was allowed to accompany her, I went. The x-ray needed the baby to lie flat, and there I saw her purple feet and legs, eighty pricks from the foot and eighty pricks from the hand.

Tears from my eyes just kept on falling because I could not bear seeing the pain my baby was in. I just wanted to make her feel a princess like when I delivered her.

There was no family allowed to accompany us during that time, because it was the height of health precautionary measures due to COVID-19. On that day it was just me, my husband and our baby in that battle.

I can still remember how the nurse took my daughter to the operating room, but we were told we needed to wait in our room. We were very nervous every time the hospital phone rang, but hopeful of good news. My husband and I prayed to God, that whatever His plans were for us we would obey Him.

The phone rang and we were told that her operation was successful. We both cried. After nine hours of waiting, my baby was brought by the nurse to our room. She was still sedated and we saw her stoma. We were not afraid of the stoma; we were relieved that finally our daughter had survived her operation to finally be with us again.

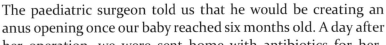

The paediatric surgeon told us that he would be creating an anus opening once our baby reached six months old. A day after her operation, we were sent home with antibiotics for her. That's how strong my baby is. She recovered easily from the operation.

As our baby grew, we thought that imperforate anus was her only problem, but then I noticed there was poop coming out of her vagina. We discovered that urine was also coming out of her vagina and she is prone to urinary tract infections because of a fistula. A deep sacral dimple on her back was also noticed that needed to be checked by a neurologist and neurosurgeon.

At five months of age, we went back to the hospital where she underwent series of tests. The 2D echocardiogram revealed she also has Patent Ductus Arteriosus and needs to undergo a cardiac catheterisation procedure. The diagnosis is that my baby girl has VACTERL association.

We are now just waiting for our baby girl to gain weight so she will be able to undergo the next operation.

I am very thankful for the parents on the Facebook support group who have the same diagnosis as my baby. I have experienced depression and finally overcome it by talking to other IA parents. It is a very helpful network that helps us gain the courage to move on with our lives and face this struggle, and also with the help of God.

It gives us hope that even as we deal with this condition with our beloved daughter, there are stories of adult IA that inspire us. We will do everything we can to meet our daughter's needs.

We have put up a fundraising page "Be a blessing to baby Amila", where I sell baby products like bolsters, bibs and dresses that are created and designed by myself. This is to raise funds for my baby's operation, medical needs and ongoing care.

They say it is a long journey, but we are very willing to join this journey with our daughter, with the help and mercy of God.

Portrait by Michelle Collins

17. My Warrior Baby – Laura Mancini (England)

Nine months he was growing as my belly grew fat and proud,
A voice inside me woke, so strong and loud

The doctors just ignored me said the voice was from trauma long before,
So, I kept my worries silent, I put them away and locked the door

The big day arrived, he was born, all was well
That voice was growing quieter now as we cuddled and in love I fell

But it never fully left me as the nurses took the lead,
Nurses came and went as we got him to feed

Six hours he had been in the world and home we were sent,
To bed I had to go exhausted, happy and spent

But in the night during a nappy change,
I noticed that something looked terribly strange

The voice was right of course, one nappy change and I could see,
His bum looked odd no hole where it should be

I begged them to come see him, be quick, make haste,
My boy had no anus, no exit for his waste

They told me it was crazy depression they would say,
These things were all checked before we were sent away

But when finally, the midwife came she confirmed our fears,
The voice I had ignored came rushing back and so did tears

To hospital we went but the wrong one at first,
as my child grew yellow and floppy with thirst

A transfer happened but not before,
Six students would come knocking at the door

Eager to see the boy with no bum,
the child so poorly and the overwhelmed mum

So rare it was to see a child with this disease,
They examined and discussed as if he were a leaf on the breeze

And all the while as the hospital apologized,
I felt sick to the stomach that I had not sooner realized

And out came the guilt, how could I have failed him so much?
I had failed to make him healthy, safe, happy and such

A transfer was done a new hospital we were delivered
With flashing lights in an ambulance, I shivered

More doctors and nurses and words I didn't understand,
I needed someone to tell me it's ok and to hold my hand

Three surgeries he would need. 1 down 2 more to go,
Beeping machines and faces but none that you know

Mum becomes nurse and son into patient,
You read up on anything you can find or get sent

Two operations down, one more to go,
He has a hole now but not quite normal, you know

Dilations are the enemy of a mother's spirit,
Nothing to do but suck it up and get on with it

Three operations under the knife, the last one will be soon,
I dread the moment he goes to sleep in that room

I dread the hours of waiting and not knowing
The pacing of the hospital halls, the toing and froing

Realising your strength comes from the smallest part of you,
The part that is not inside anymore. It's the part that you once grew

So much pain he has to suffer for a chance at a normal life,
Or as normal as can be after this trouble and strife

But normal he won't ever be despite their promises to me,
He will always be extraordinary, my warrior IA baby

18. Noelle's Story – Jill and Joe Peters (USA)

Noelle was born on the twenty-second of August 2019, she was born with IA/ARM, which unfortunately, the hospital and paediatrician overlooked. She was also born with a rectal vestibular fistula and because she was having poopy diapers, we did not notice it either.

Once she got to about six or seven months old and started cereal I noticed she had lots of straining. It seemed like she was pooping just a tiny bit all day long. Sometimes she would strain so hard her face would turn red and her hands would shake. I took her to her paediatrician and he wanted me to switch over to soy formula.

When that did not work, I took her to a GI specialist. Prior to the appointment with the specialist, I had started doing research myself. I thought she had an anterior anus, but I did not realize it was a fistula. We met with the GI specialist on a Friday and I told him what I thought it was.

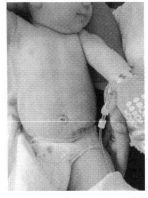

He confirmed she had an Anorectal Malformation/Imperforate Anus within about thirty seconds. He sent us to the children's hospital to meet with a surgeon that same day. Noelle underwent her first surgery, a bowel cleanout and colostomy three days later.

After doing lots of research I decided to switch her care to Nationwide Children's Hospital with Dr Richard Wood. He performed the second surgery which was the reconstruction and anal opening. He found that she had several large stool balls. To help with those we had to insert a catheter into her mucus fistula next to her stoma.

We would give her fifty cc's of mucomist every other day. Eight weeks later Dr. Wood was able to remove the stool balls and do the colostomy takedown. We are now almost a month out from that surgery and she is thriving and doing amazingly well.

Thankfully, she did not get the terrible diaper rash. This past six months have been a whirlwind!

There were so many unknowns and there was so much to learn. Finding the ONE in 5000 Group and family support groups helped me so much and I truly appreciate all the information I was given.

It really helps to speak to other parents who have gone through or are going through the same thing Being able to speak to IA adults can also shed a light on many things.

19. Willow's Story – Hattie (England)

Willow is our fifth child, but our first girl. She was born at thirty-seven weeks by a planned c-section weighing a healthy 7lb10oz and was perfect in every way. She passed all her newborn checks and we left the hospital just over twenty-four hours after she was born and we settled in at home, to life with a new baby.

She seemed a little unsettled, but nothing we had not dealt with before although she struggled a bit taking her formula and we thought maybe she had a tummy ache. At three days old I noticed blood in her stools. No need to panic I thought, unless it happens again. With the next nappy there was more bleeding and I instantly called the maternity hotline at our local hospital, where a disgruntled doctor told me it was normal for little girls. I insisted this was not normal and she dismissively told me if I were really worried to head to A&E.

I checked in at the A&E desk twenty minutes later, but they had not been told we were coming. Before my husband had even managed to park the car, we had been whisked into children's assessment. There we met the loveliest doctor, who admitted us instantly and started to run tests, he was so determined to find her the right help.

She had blood taken, an X-ray, they told us to stop feeding her and they put her on a drip instead. By the morning they had decided we needed to be seen by a specialist and so we were transferred by ambulance to another hospital.

The doctors at the new hospital instantly picked up that her anal opening was too small and we were given a fact sheet about Anal Stenosis. We were told we would need to dilate her anus to gradually stretch it to the right size. A surgical nurse came and taught us how to do it. The first time was a little scary, but we were determined to get it right to help her.

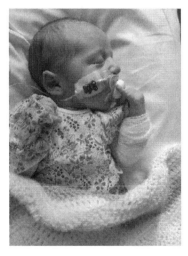

The doctors were concerned about the bleeding, which had continued despite being nil by mouth. She had an ultrasound, an MRI and at five days old she was taken for investigation under general anaesthetic, as they were concerned about Hirschsprung's Disease. Handing over my tiny baby was the hardest thing I had ever had to do as a parent. I was still too sore from the c-section to walk to theatre, so my husband went with her.

It was also our youngest boy's first birthday and I was full of guilt about missing his birthday, as well as being worried for Willow. My mum brought him up to visit us and the lovely play nurses opened the playroom on the ward for him and even gave him a birthday present. The gesture was lovely, we were overwhelmed with their kindness and it was a welcome distraction.

I made the walk to recovery where the surgeon explained she had found a section of inflamed bowel and had managed to dilate the anus a little further, whilst she was relaxed. We spent three more days in hospital during which her bleeding stopped and the gastroenterology team gave her the ok to start on neocate milk, a hypoallergenic amino acid formula. She did well and as no more bleeding occurred we were allowed to go home.

We had to continue with the dilations twice daily, the hospital 3D printed the dilator rods on site, so they were plastic and a bit nicer than the ones I had seen online. We started at a size seven and over the next few weeks worked up to a size nine.

At fifteen weeks old, Willow had her second investigative surgery, a recto sigmoidoscopy where they took a sample of tissue from her bowel. This time they found the inflammation had gone and we soon had the results back that they had not found any other problems. It was decided the inflammation must have been the result of a severe cow's milk allergy.

We were so relieved to find nothing serious and her doctor told us that without the bleeding, we may not have known about the stenosis, until she was much older. By six months old we had managed to get up to our target dilator size of twelve and we slowly reduced the dilations until we no longer needed to do them anymore.

On one occasion just after we had stopped dilating, Willow became very constipated and had to have a bowel washout, after which she was put on Movicol which she still takes. Other than that, we have had no more complications.

Anal Stenosis is mild compared to what most in the ARM family have to go through. We had just a glimpse of the struggle this condition brings and yet it still had a huge impact on our entire family. It took us away from our newborn bubble. I found the weeks leading up to and beyond her first birthday difficult, reliving what we had been through and feeling those emotions all over again.

Willow is now 19 months old and will remain under the care of her doctor until she potty trains. However, she is doing really well and they are exceptionally pleased with her progress.

Chapter 3 - Parents/Family - Down Syndrome

20. A Little Boy with a Little Extra and No Anus – Cassandra (USA)

As a young military couple that had no idea if conception was possible due to my health challenges, the idea of starting a family seemed daunting. In August of 2017, our prayers were answered, and we became pregnant with our first child. Lillian was born on May 8, 2018. Life was very easy early on, as we enjoyed life with Lilly and we wanted to give her a sibling as soon as possible.

In June of 2019, we found out we were yet again, pregnant! Another answered prayer. Our family moved back to Florida from Virginia in August of 2019. Our pregnancy was relatively easy, although high risk. There were many ultrasounds and growth checks but the only thing discovered was IUGR (Intrauterine growth restriction). The decision was made to deliver our team green baby at thirty-seven weeks.

On January 16, 2020, our team green baby turned team blue and Malachi Ryan was born weighing 4.15oz and 19in. long. The first thing noticed during his newborn exam was the absence of an anus. The nurse brought over my tiny baby, showed me his bottom where a gathering of skin was and stated, 'Your son has no anus but it's OK. It's an easy fix.'

I had never heard of a baby being born without an anus, but all I wanted was to hold my sweet boy. He was not allowed to nurse right away, as we had planned, and I held him for only a few minutes before he was taken away.

He was then transported via incubator to the local children's hospital to stay in the NICU and have his colostomy surgery. At one day old a colostomy was placed on Malachi's stomach for use until he grew, and an anus could be created. Genetic testing was done to see if Malachi had any other related genetic conditions.

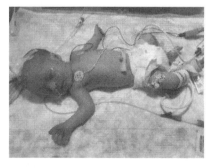 He spent time in the NICU recovering from surgery, growing stronger, learning to eat from a bottle and overcoming bradycardia. I did a lot of research during these long NICU days about imperforate anus and learned as much as I could. It seemed like a complex condition that the nurse boiled down to being 'no big deal' and 'an easy fix'. But I was learning that this condition, although 'fixable' was lifelong and bowel management, once surgeries were over, was forever.

At ten days old, in the NICU he finally received his genetic testing. This testing confirmed our little boy was EXTRAordinary and has Trisomy 21 (Down Syndrome). This diagnosis came as a huge surprise, because we saw no 'soft-markers' in utero. So, at this point it was determined that his IA (Imperforate Anus) was either the rare three percent of kids with DS who have IA, or in fact VACTERL. At fourteen days we were released from the NICU and our reality with two children under two years old, one with special needs began!

I am able to stay at home right now and I am so thankful for that. Bag changes were plentiful, every couple of hours to be exact! It was so hard to get something to stick to Malachi's skin in between his fistula and stoma, which was a very small area. Trial and error with bags, pastes, wafers, powder and spray began. We finally found a system at about four months old that lasted for threeish days!

Big sister Lillian enjoyed 'helping' with Malachi's 'Boo-Boo'. She also likes to help with his poopy and do all things to assist him and me. As Malachi grew and as a family, we learned more about IA and Down Syndrome, we began to really think where we wanted to have his future surgeries done. Locally we did not have a colorectal center, only a general surgeon who was going to do everything. But from my personal research we made the decision to find a specialised Colorectal Center to treat Malachi's IA and follow him long term.

This to us would give him the best outcome and a chance to have long term continence. We began PT, feeding therapy and seeing all the specialists that come with Down Syndrome. Malachi has two congenital heart defects that do not need surgery right now. In May, the decision to travel to Ohio to a Colorectal Center was made. I began contacting all the necessary people and determining when we needed to travel for his PSARP.

The COVID-19 pandemic complicated things a little and caused surgery to be pushed back a bit, but, overall, things worked out and the Colorectal Center at Cincinnati Children's Hospital in Ohio was very easy to work with even though it was long distance. Dr. Aaron Garrison was assigned to Malachi's case and I could not have asked for a better doctor and surgeon!

In early July Grandma Tina (my mother), Malachi and I travelled to Cincinnati for procedures and PSARP. A fistulogram was done first to determine the level of his IA and whether he had a fistula or not. It was determined his colon was 3.3cm from the placement of the rectal opening and that he has no fistula! The absence of a fistula is rare, but more common in kids with Down Syndrome.

We met with the Dr. Garrison and discussed the surgery. Malachi then had his PSARP and it went very well. He recovered very quickly with minimal pain. We travelled back home to Florida with no issues. October arrived very quickly, and we found ourselves on the long drive back to Cincinnati from Florida again. This time it was for a colostomy closure and reconnection surgery! No bag! What will that look like? Poopy diapers will take some getting used to and be celebrated!

We arrived in Cincinnati and were grateful for the cooler temperatures. Malachi had a few procedures the day before surgery including urodynamics and an MRI of his spine. The urodynamics showed no bladder problems and the MRI showed no tethered cord. We were so thankful and sang praises for this amazing news! Malachi was admitted to the hospital for clean out and the surgery anxiety set in. I was so excited to get him 'hooked up correctly', but nervous because any surgery is risky.

On October 14, 2020 Malachi had his big surgery, it went well but his recovery was a little rougher than last time. He was in a lot of pain and very out of it due to the pain medications. The day after surgery was hard for the both of us. He began to poop on October 15th! It was a joyful sight and a day we will celebrate forever!

By October 16th Malachi was back to his smiley, happy, loving little self. All the nurses were in awe of him and wanted to snuggle him. Grandma also got Malachi to start saying 'Mama' while we were in the hospital, which was amazing to hear!

We stayed for a few days in the hospital as a precaution and to wait to see the surgeon the following Monday. Dr. Garrison gave us the OK to head out and then head home at the end of the week.

Malachi had a pretty severe diaper rash, which we were warned about, but we were able to keep him comfortable with a variety of creams. The trip back to Florida was easy and uneventful. As I write this it has been two weeks since surgery and he is doing amazingly! If you did not know Malachi was born without an anus and had a colostomy bag for nine months you would never be able to guess! Malachi poops about five times a day and seems to be in no pain.

We are so grateful for the advances in medical procedures and treatments and the PSARP surgery that saved his life. Now we can focus on intense therapies to get him sitting up, crawling and then walking!

We are also anxiously awaiting a BAHA hearing device and cannot wait to see how Malachi responds to the new sounds he will be able to hear!

We know our IA journey does not end here. He will need lifelong follow up and most likely bowel management, but we will continue to take everything day by day. We will keep smiling, leaning on each other, having fun and enjoying all the little things in life!

Our family is so excited about our journey together. We will continue to raise awareness for IA/ARM and advocate for the Down Syndrome community! We will also continue to celebrate poop and toots!!

Thank you for reading our story and I hope Malachi's strength, happiness, smiles and story help you, inspire you and give you hope!

21. Johnny's Story – Michele & John (USA)

My husband and I have always wanted children, however the doctors said it was impossible. We still tried because we believed that if it were God's plan then it would happen. After ten years, we finally got our positive test. As you can imagine, we were over-joyed and in our excitement told everyone. Unfortunately, at our five-week ultrasound there was no heartbeat. We knew that if we were able to get pregnant once we could do it again, and it gave us hope.

When we got another positive test two years later, we were scared. At the first ultrasound, we held our breaths waiting for the sound of the heartbeat and were able to hear it clearly as soon as it started, with our baby wiggling all over. I have never been so happy in my life! We opted to have the NIPT test to check for genetic abnormalities. Our baby was a boy and tested 98% positive for Down's Syndrome. It was crushing and took some time to finally accept our boy's diagnosis.

The anatomy scans informed us that our boy had a clubbed foot, and also that he may have a small hole in his heart as well as an aortic arch. At the foetal ECHO appointment, we were told the hole was quite large (7mm). Holes like this can close on their own, but our boy's hole would not. He would need open heart surgery at about 4-6 months old and, while all very devastating, it could be fixed.

At 37 weeks I had to be induced due to preeclampsia. Baby Johnny was born through a c-section and whisked away to the NICU. When we went to see Johnny, we were told that he took his bottles great and drank more than most babies normally do.

However, the doctor needed to speak with us. The doctor explained that Johnny was born with an imperforate anus, explaining that he had no anal opening. We were in shock. Due to Johnny's foot, and heart and anal deformities, he was diagnosed with VACTERL.

We needed to meet with a paediatric surgeon who was going to do Johnny's surgery for a colostomy. He also brought us a book to read, so that we could better understand his diagnosed condition, called 'A Secret Life by Greg Ryan'. Thankfully, everything with the surgery went great. Being given a crash course in stoma care and how to change an ostomy bag was awkward, and the three weeks he was in the NICU was an adjustment time for us all.

We had been home for two weeks and were leaving Johnny's orthopaedic casting appointment when Johnny started crying and stopped breathing. I snatched him out of his car seat and ran back inside. One of the nurse practitioners took him and performed CPR on Johnny and got him breathing again. Apparently when Johnny would cry, he would bear down, causing his oxygen levels to drop due to his heart issues.

It took a week in the hospital before he was stable enough to be released. We spent the next few months terrified and praying that we would not have to go through that again. God was merciful and we did not.

Johnny's pull through surgery was scheduled for the end of August. The day finally arrived and we went to the hospital at 5.00am to get checked in and speak with the surgeon. We settled into the waiting room surrounded by our family to wait for Johnny to come out. After several hours, the surgeon came out and all had gone well. The anaesthesiologist came out a short time later and told us he was off the ventilator and we would be able to go see him soon.

A nurse came to show us to his recovery room and informed us that he'd had a setback and had to be re-intubated. We were unprepared for what we saw when we entered the room. Doctors and nurses all around the bed giving meds and bagging him. We followed a team of nurses to the PICU where he was put back on a ventilator. His oxygen levels were dropping as we sat there, and they had to bag him again and several more times throughout the night.

We just tried to stick to a corner of the room, rooting for Johnny to breathe again and unable to do much else besides pray our boy could last the night. The next morning Johnny showed what an incredible fighter he was with a marked improvement. When he was taken off the ventilator a second time, he stopped breathing after several hours. The medical team rushed in and resuscitated him again and Johnny remained stable after that. With his recovery going well, we were able to go home days later.

After a week, at his follow-up appointment, the doctor said we needed to start doing dilations. The doctor marked an 8mm dilator and then showed us how to insert it. Johnny cried, peed and then vomited due to being so upset. The only thought in my mind was how could I do this twice a day to my child! It was jarring and we left the visit a bit numb. The doctor had said that if we did not do the dilations, that scar tissue could form and cause a need for more surgeries to fix it. We made a schedule with heavy hearts and the two of us performed the dilations, following the doctor's recommendations for when to go up in size. It was difficult, but life continued with this new normal for a few months.

We were able to get Johnny's heart surgery scheduled for October but, as usual, Johnny had other plans. We noticed that he was not acting like himself and took him to his paediatrician. She said to take him to the hospital to get checked out. He tested positive for para influenza so he was admitted and we spent weeks at the hospital with supportive care. One morning his heart rate kept climbing and the hospital we were in said they could no longer continue to treat him as they did not have a paediatric cardiac unit. After being transferred he spent two more weeks in cardiac PICU.

Johnny had cleared the infection really well and we were able to go home after a month in the hospital. My husband took all our stuff to the car and then called to ask if I needed help to bring Johnny down. But I had to let him know that Johnny had decided that we needed to stay a while longer. The nurse and I had placed him in his car seat, and because it was cold outside I'd put a hat on him to keep his head warm. He didn't appreciate the motherly concern and started to cry, then his oxygen dropped and he turned blue. Fortunately, he bounced back without intervention but now we had to stay in hospital until after he was able to have his heart surgery.

So we lived at the hospital and his condition kept deteriorating, needing more medicine to keep his lungs clear of fluids. The cardiologist decided that it was time and his surgery was scheduled for later that week. It was now December. Johnny seemed to know what was about to happen as he did not sleep much the night before. When we went down to pre-op and they took him to go to the operating room, he started to cry like he knew we were not going with him.

To say that it broke my heart is not strong enough to express what I was feeling. We packed into the waiting room, all 14 of us. The three hours of waiting seemed to crawl by, before the heart surgeon came out and told us that he was done and it all went well. We waited for what seemed like an eternity before my husband and I could see him.

In the room of the cardiac recovery unit, our little guy was hooked up to numerous IVs and tubes were everywhere. The room was small, and we spent the night sleeping in chairs to be close to him. His recovery went blessedly well and we went home ten short days later.

We were able to be at home living our lives together as a family, going to LOTS of doctors' appointments and changing or emptying ostomy bags. Dreading the leaks in the bags that always seemed to occur at the worst times, my husband and I were often telling the other that it was their turn to vent the bag or dump the vile contents from inside. We were also still doing the dilatations - I got the morning one and my husband would do the evening one. As time passed after his pull through surgery, the dilatations became routine and easier for all of us.

Finally, on March 6, 2020 the reconnection surgery was scheduled. At last, no more stinky bag!

The surgeon that we'd been with since his very first surgery at two days old had left, and so we had a new one. We arrived the morning of the surgery and pre-op went well, and after three hours the surgeon came out. She told us that the surgery had gone well. A short time later we got to see him and he looked good! Only a small bandage where the ostomy had been. Johnny could have clear fluids in recovery and later went to a regular room. Apart from a fever, everything was going so well, until Saturday. They had us start feeding him regular bottles which he vomited after drinking. This isn't unusual after reconnection surgery and they inserted an NG tube hooked to suction.

While waiting for him to start pooping, the nurse said we were going to get a private room. After moving, the new nurse said that his abdomen looked swollen and measured it. The NG tube wasn't suctioning correctly and so they changed it. As soon as the new one reached his stomach, the contents had so much pressure behind it that it shot out of the NG tube diagonally across the crib. Of course, I was standing in the line of fire and was also sprayed. However, his stomach continued to increase in size. We were moved again, this time to the PICU. The Resident that was on staff for the night told us he suspected a leak in his intestines and that he would need a second surgery.

The next morning, we asked the surgeon what time she would be performing the surgery on Johnny. She explained that he did not need one, that he had some air in his abdomen that was causing the distention and that the Resident was in trouble for causing us undue worry. That night Johnny's abdomen grew larger and the next day they decided they would insert a drain to relieve the pressure. But there was no anaesthesiologist available so it would be the following day.

That night while changing his poopy diaper he pooped again. I asked my husband to hold his feet up so I could get the mess cleaned. Johnny was crying and I could hear it trailing off, his oxygen started dropping and he started turning blue. My husband ran out into the hallway and alerted the nurse who ran in and bagged him. We thought it was odd. We thought that since his heart was fixed the oxygen issue was behind us.

Something had to be wrong. Johnny was sent to imaging so they could place the drain, because by this time his belly was extremely distended. My strong fighter looked so beaten and tired. We were in the waiting room for about 45 minutes when the Doctor came in. His abdominal cavity was full of fluid and he needed surgery, and as he was already sedated they were just waiting on an operating room. After what seemed like forever, we asked what was going on, but no one knew.

Luckily, one of the staff kept calling for information and she found him. He had already gone to the OR and we needed to go to a different waiting room. By the time we got there, we were told that they were closing and the surgeon would soon be out. It had only taken 30 minutes. She came out and told us he did have a leak and she'd stitched it up, checking to make sure it was holding and not leaking any more. We returned to the PICU for a couple of days. He was STILL having fevers and they were monitoring his drainage.

We were moved to a regular room for about four days and then discharged home. Two days after going home, I called the surgeon's office as Johnny was still running fevers, but I was told it was not surgery related and advised to call his paediatrician. I said that he had been having fevers since the colostomy reversal, but they insisted that it wasn't related to his surgery and to just call the paediatrician.

The paediatrician ordered an x-ray and labs. As soon as the results came in, she called and sent us straight to the ER. His inflammatory markers were extremely high. We decided that we did not want to go back to the hospital that his surgeon was at and went to a different one; the one where he'd had his heart surgery. This was in March 2020 when Covid-19 had started, so my husband was not allowed in with us. They ran a bunch of tests to find out his abdomen was full of abscesses extending all the way up over his liver.

Once again, they needed to go in and clean the cavity out, but this surgeon needed to make a new and larger opening to be able to get to everything and make sure that it was thoroughly cleaned. She also wanted to put his colostomy back in place to give him time to heal and recover. He was very sick, and our little boy needed to have this surgery right away. I was beside myself and afraid that I was going to lose him, and so the hospital generously made an exception to allow my husband to come and sit with me during surgery.

A few hours later they came and told us it went well and they would come get us when we could see him. We waited for hours and went to see if they just forgot to come and get us after getting him settled. Apparently he had a bad inflammatory response and was crashing! Thankfully they were able to get him stabilised and we were able to go and see him. His official diagnosis was acute sepsis and peritonitis.

Before the surgery while we were home, Johnny wasn't his normal self. He was normally a happy, wiggly and full of life boy. Now, after a couple of days our boy was back to smiling and more like his normal self. However, his inflammatory markers were still high. He was on two different IV antibiotics. He needed time to heal. A month in the hospital and his numbers were finally down and we were able to go home.

Life was back to our normal. We went to his follow-up appointment with his surgeon but she was no longer there, so we ended up being seen by the head paediatric surgeon. He wanted to give Johnny plenty of time to heal before we gave the reconnect surgery another shot at the end of August. The plan was to admit him a day before the surgery so that they could get him good and cleaned out, then they would do it once more when he was under for surgery. The doctor was frank with us about being unsure how long the next surgery would take, due to the presence of scar tissue that he would have to remove.

This time we would be updated through phone calls so that we knew what was going on. Three hours later, everything had gone as planned. Johnny needed to pass gas or poop before he could have clear fluids, which was the next day. That night he was able to have his regular diet back and his appetite was back too.

Four days later he was discharged to go home. We spent the next few days changing diaper after diaper. Then Sunday night Johnny started getting fussy and throwing up almost every hour. I called the surgeon's office Monday morning and they wanted us to take him to the ER to get him checked and given fluids.

He was admitted and X-rays showed he was backed up. He was given MiraLAX mixed with Pedialyte every two hours and a suppository, which was good because the poop had stopped.

 The next day everything started moving again until he was cleaned out. Another X-ray that was clear and we were sent home with a bowel regimen.

While we have had some bumps in the road and medication changes, as of right now it is working for him, other than a raw bottom from being exposed to faeces for the first time.

Johnny is now 16 months old, five weeks post-surgery and doing great! No signs of infection and he can take daily baths without the worry of changing his bag.

22. Hitting the Jackpot - AJ's Story, Jessica (USA)

They said the feeling was like to hitting the jackpot.

At 38 weeks pregnant, my AJ was ready to make an entrance into this world. We were fully prepared. All prenatal and ultrasound checks looked well. My quad screening reading, which checks for abnormalities was negative, and I was told to expect a healthy well-developed baby. My little family of three - would soon become four!

My written birth plan called to labour in the tub in the hospital room. We got lucky enough to get assigned to the one patient room that had a tub in it. The labour was a short one, and AJ soon made his entrance. He was immediately placed on me, where skin-to-skin was given for a few minutes.

They said the feeling was like to hitting the jackpot.

He was then pulled away to get cleaned up, and that's when the whispers began.

Oh, they must be admiring how precious he is.

The whispers then called for my midwife to come to my bedside with a different look on her face than I had ever seen in all my years of knowing her. "Mom, your baby is precious, isn't he?" As she held him near me. I nodded my head in agreement. She then flips him over ever so gently, so that I see his bottom side. "He is the most perfect baby, and he's perfect for you, but I want you to see that in examining him, we realize he doesn't have an exit hole."

As she's talking to me, she shows me his bum, and sure enough, his bottom side looked just like a Ken Barbie doll, where there was no exit hole. "What does this mean? Why did this happen? Is he okay?" I asked.

She eventually tells me he will need to be examined sooner than later by a paediatrician as our little AJ also has characteristics of Down syndrome.

The paediatrician wasn't as nice as the midwife was, but eventually it was in fact confirmed that AJ had Down syndrome and a rare condition known as an Anorectal Malformation (ARM), also known as an Imperforate Anus (IA). We didn't know what any of this meant immediately after delivery, however we'd learn more about the conditions as time allowed us to.

Prior to having AJ, I had worked with the disabled community, and now I'd be sitting on the other side of the table, although initially that wasn't something I was proud about.

There are stages of grief that parents may go through, as we mourn the loss we had envisioned in our head.

By kindergarten, AJ would have eight surgeries with most revolving around the ARM condition. He would eventually have a few more, and now at seven years old he's had twelve surgeries.

We have come to the realization AJ will have lifelong conditions that will require extra steps than a nondisabled individual, however this doesn't limit his ability nor does it limit the value he brings to this world.

AJ has helped us look at life through a different lens than we had before. He's given us purpose.

I am now an advocate for the differently abled and assist parents in navigating through the special education process.

We are very proud to have been chosen.

They said the feeling was like to hitting the jackpot. That it is.

Chapter 4 - Parents/Family with Toddler (2-4 Years Old)

23. IA/ARM Through My Eyes as a Parent, Levi's Story – Tahlia West (Australia)

Levi Ronald West came into the world on the 17 July 2018, twelve days after the due date. It was not a fairy tale birth, but it is special in its own way. Levi was born by an emergency c-section after a long induction and eighteen hours of trying. The normal fairy tale goes that the baby is brought over to you after being cut out and having those first moments. But for me, those first moments were laying on the operating table wondering if he was breathing after just seeing a little foot.

They told us he was stunned and was not breathing great. I waited for him to be brought to me, but that never happened. As I lay there wondering why I had not been given my baby boy, my husband Leigh told me he was being taken back to the nursery. He was whisked away so quickly I did not even get the opportunity to either see or touch him. Leigh followed them as he had no idea knowing what was going on either. I was exhausted from such a long labour and c-section and could not fully process what was happening.

I was taken back to my room, waiting for when I could see my beautiful baby boy, when Leigh came in and sat with me. After we shared the news with the family that Levi had been born, Leigh gave me the news that the medical team were on the phone to P.I.P.E.R. (Paediatric Infant Perinatal Emergency Retrieval.) I knew what that meant but Leigh did not. My heart sank and I demanded to see Levi, but was told he was still breathing rapidly, and as it had not eased he needed to be monitored closely.

He was air lifted to a hospital in Melbourne at 11.30pm. I finally got to hold my baby for the first time for less than five minutes before they took him away again. He was put on the paediatric patient's trolley screaming and wheeled out, while I was taken back to my room and told I would be advised when he had safely arrived at the hospital.

Leigh went down to Melbourne the following day while I recovered in Echuca (three hours away). They told us that Levi had a simple infection in the chest and the talk was that Levi would be transferred to a larger rural hospital closer to our home the next day. It was such an overwhelming relief.

As I waited to see my husband back in Echuca at the hospital, he received a call saying Levi's tummy had distended and he had not passed any meconium. He was then told that Levi was being transferred to the Royal Children's Hospital in Melbourne and a team would contact me about what was going on. We were both in shock and had no idea what was happening, as we waited patiently for this phone call.

At 10.30pm the phone rang, and it was from the amazing Assoc. Prof. Sebastian King, who is a paediatric colorectal surgeon. From memory he explained that Levi did not have an anus and that he would require urgent surgery. That was the beginning of our adventure.

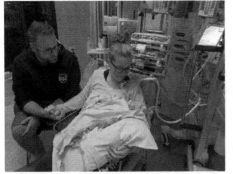

On Friday the 20th July, three excruciating days since I briefly first saw him, I arrived in the Butterfly NICU ward of the Royal Children's Hospital and walked into the room where my baby boy was lying in a bed with tubes and machines everywhere. It was very overwhelming. In the room with Levi were some lovely nurses who explained a tiny bit about what was going on. They immediately contacted Sebastian to say we had arrived and wanted to touch base.

Sebastian met us to give a tiny explanation about what Levi's condition was and that was the first time we heard the true meaning of the words, 'Anorectal Malformation and Imperforate Anus.' He told us that he would only drip feed information to us, as we needed it, which to this day I am so grateful for. I was still recovering and was not processing things like Leigh, but I heard a few words which included more tests, surgery and a stoma.

Being a first-time mum and with no clue, honestly it was scary. We did our best to stay away from Dr Google, but I did use the information Sebastian gave us about the ONE in 5000 Foundation, which was all about IA/ARM, to get as informed as I could on the condition.

Levi was in NICU and HDU for a total of fifteen days. In that time, it was an ongoing lesson for me. Going from being a mum with a newborn, to a mum who had never had a night with her newborn and then having to deal with changing a stoma bag and learning what IA/ARM is. Levi passed all other tests with flying colours to rule out VACTERL association. We were sent home and followed up with other tests to understand if the fistula was attached to the bladder or not. Levi in my eyes was such a champ, as he fell asleep while he had a catheter put in and one hour of tests. The results showed that Levi's were stuck side by side, which was a positive, as it lessens his chances for incontinence issues in the future.

The date of the surgery for the pull through was the 19th of November 2018, to create his bottom opening. It was the longest day, just waiting and waiting. Once the surgery was completed, Sebastian told us the wonderful news that it had gone as planned and it was a success.

He recovered like a little strong boy would. When poo appeared in his nappy, I was as shocked and as excited as any parent could be, and even though it was left over from when he was born, it was still a good sign.

That week I was lucky enough to also be in Melbourne at the RCH (Royal Children's Hospital) at the same time as the ONE in 5000 Foundation was holding a weekend seminar at the hospital. It gave me a lot of information about IA/ ARM as well as hearing from IA adults themselves and other parents.

The next part was the part I did struggle with, even though I thought it would be easy and told myself that over and over. This was the anal dilation stage of the process. When it came to go to

Melbourne again to learn how to do the dilation it was bigger than I thought. As much as Sebastian tried to warn Leigh and I, I always told me self it would not be a big deal, but it was.

The first time Levi was given a dilation it was under a local anaesthetic. We were shown how to do it to help his bottom to allow poo to pass through more naturally. He was motionless but I told myself it must be done to help improve Levi's life.

The first time I had to do it at home with him awake, I cried and he cried and I am not sure whether that was from him seeing how I was, or if it did hurt him. It sticks in my head to this day. Some days were better than others and I just had to tell myself it is for the best for Levi and his future.

The 1st April 2019 was the day for the stoma reversal and a semi big step to see what would happen for Levi's future. If there are no complications great, if there are, well we will manage it as a team.

We still battle with change in diet and worry whether he has pooed enough, is in pain, or drinks enough for his age. This never leaves my mind. The one thing especially that never leaves my mind is other kids knowing. I wonder how they will react when he is older and what problems we might face with toilet training and more. But as much as that sits in my head, I see this beautiful boy grow and I will forever help him and support him. Even if I might not know the answers, I will answer them as best I can.

The most amazing part of all of this, apart from having a pretty kick ass kid, is that we are a part of the amazing ONE in 5000 family. I am so proud that this wonderful foundation was created in our home state and country and it has created something that cannot be described in words. It means the world to me because it has created a support network for IA/ARM people and their families. You cannot get any more solid support than having a family who understands and helps with any questions you have.

24. A Grandmothers Story - Roslyn, Levi's Grandmother (Australia)

Our IA/ARM journey began in July 2018 when our grandson Levi was born. He is our second grandchild, and we were excited and overjoyed. Within a few hours, Levi was airlifted from Echuca Regional Health to the Mercy Hospital in Melbourne with breathing problems. Little did we know that forty-eight hours later Levi would be diagnosed with ARM and would have to undergo major surgery to save his life.

Levi had not passed Meconium in forty-eight hours and while at the Mercy Hospital his stomach had become distended. They did an X-Ray and found that he was missing part of his bowel and it was not connected to his anus. Levi was airlifted to the Royal Children's Hospital for life saving surgery.

My husband and I did not get to meet Levi or see him before he left Echuca and we were very worried about him and also the impact this would have on our daughter Tahlia and son in law Leigh. Levi was born twelve days over his due date and quite a big baby when he was born. Tahlia had gone through an eighteen-hour labor, only to have a Cesarean section.

Tahlia was unable to travel for three days, which was hard on her because all she wanted was to be with her precious baby Levi, whom she had not yet held or bonded with. Leigh went to Melbourne the day after Levi was airlifted and was able to hold him and feed with some expressed breast milk.

We spent as much time as we could with Tahlia in hospital and were there when Leigh phoned to say that Levi has IA/ARM. He explained that he had to have surgery and he would have a colostomy. That Thursday night I sat with Tahlia in the hospital holding her hand and praying that the surgery would be successful.

At about eleven pm we got a phone call from Dr. Sebastian King who gave us an update on Levi and his surgery. We were able to rest a little easier, knowing that he had made it through the surgery, but he still had a long way to go. On the Friday Tahlia and Leigh went to Melbourne and that was the beginning of them living at the hospital and then in Ronald Macdonald house for two weeks.

We finally got to meet Levi on Saturday in the Neonatal Butterfly ward. He was attached to a lot of machines and we had to be careful with hand hygiene and not touch him too much. Tahlia and Leigh were very tired and stressed but remained positive.

Everyday Levi slowly improved and a week later we finally got to hold him and have our first cuddles with him at the hospital. After learning how to manage his colostomy they were able to come home. They did not tell anyone that they were being discharged and they surprised us when they arrived home. It was good to be able to start bonding with Levi.

Then in November Levi had his second operation, which was his pull-through and I was privileged to be able to support Tahlia, Leigh and Levi at this time. Leigh had work commitments and was only able to be in Melbourne for the day of Levi's operation and another day during the week. I had booked a self-contained unit not far from the RCH for a week and Leigh and I tagged team so that Tahlia and Levi had someone with them for the whole week. I cooked meals and would take them over to the hospital and we would eat them together.

I spent time playing with Levi and trying to keep him entertained while he recovered from his surgery. His favorite nursery rhyme is "Twinkle Twinkle Little Star" which calmed him down and it is still his favorite nursery rhyme now. He even sings it to his little sister Angie when she is upset.

The highlight of the week was attending the IA/ARM seminar that was held at the RCH. This was organised by Greg Ryan and I learnt so much from the panel of professional speakers. I was also able to network with other parents and grandparents of children with IA/ARM. Tahlia found this day so rewarding and gained so much information that she has grown to be able to help other parents with children who are diagnosed with IA/ARM.

On the Monday Levi was discharged and we had survived the second round of surgery. Tahlia and Leigh had to go to Melbourne to learn how to dilate their brave little boy for the next five months. Sometimes I had to help her do this.

As Levi got older, he would sometime struggle and resist having this done. This upset Tahlia and she would cry because she thought she was hurting him.

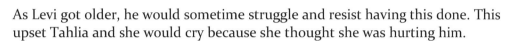

The next operation Levi had was the reversal of his colostomy in April 2019 and this time Leigh was able stay in Melbourne the whole time. We did go and visit and gave them time to go out and have breakfast together. They spend the afternoon out of the hospital and were able to have time together.

Levi has not looked back and is such a loving, caring boy. We know that he will have his challenges, but he will take them in his stride and overcome them to the best of his ability. He will always have the support of his parents and grandparents who be there for him as long as we can.

I have worked in the medical profession for over 35 years and had never heard of IA/ARM before and I was amazed at how IA/ ARM affected so many organs in the body and the levels of IA/ARM.

Levi will always our brave Lion.

25. Holly's Story - SRH (USA)

Ms Holly was born with a traumatic beginning. After a peaceful labour she did not drop as I moved into transition. She worked with me as I pushed her down, and the doctor blind cut and clamped the tight cord around her neck, that was impeding her birth. She was out safely, and she started breathing on her own, but soon after her newborn assessment and a hard delivery of the after birth, the doctor told me she had to be taken to an NICU two hours away because she had been born with Imperforate Anus.

I had never heard of such a thing, I thought I was being punched after the scary delivery we had had. She was rushed to the NICU with dad in tow. I arrived a day later, once they made sure I did not lose too much blood and after five days in the NICU we were allowed to go home. My babe is healthy and happy, born perfectly, though pooping in the wrong area.

We navigated the first few months with dilators, we shopped around for doctors and kept landing with the wrong one. Her first anoplasty surgery (supposed to be the only one) was successful, with good muscle placement, but terrible healing protocols. A week later we were still in the hospital for a redo and to pull up the colostomy.

We made it out of the hospital just in time for Christmas and for my husband to make it to his brother's funeral. Everyone says 2020 is terrible but 2019 was the worst for us.

Our sweet girl keeps us on our toes! We have learned how to double diaper with cloth and have FINALLY found the right doctor to take proper care of her! She went through multiple tests and moved up in dilators, until she was ready for the reversal! Her reversal was successful! Now our life is ALL about poop, how much, what colour, when, where and soooo much clean up!

We are so thrilled she has been thriving since her take down. Our sweet girl is an absolute joy to this world, and we are so thankful to have her, regardless of all the challenges we have faced. Knowing that the IA life is forever, we are ready and willing to face any new challenges head on.

26. Amazing Grace – T.C. (Romania)

An amazing 38-week pregnancy came to an end in a beautiful spring in 2018. Nothing prepared us for the days, weeks, months and years that were to come. Our daughter was born. She looked beautiful, delicate and healthy, exactly as we expected! In the Eastern European country where we live, it is still common to separate new-borns from their mothers, so that I was only allowed to see and breastfeed her for about fifteen minutes every three hours.

During this time everything seemed just fine, except her poor appetite, but new-borns are not very good eaters anyway, I thought to myself. However, I really enjoyed the short time spent I with my little bundle of joy. I was counting the minutes until the next meeting with her and I was the last mom who was leaving the room at the end of the time given. I just could not wait to take her home, to be together all the time and to spend precious moments as a family.

The day came. We were ready to go home. She seemed a little fussy and I heard a few noises coming out from her belly during the last breastfeeding session, but this is not very uncommon for babies and I did not think too much about it. Just before leaving the hospital, the doctors had become worried for the first time. They noticed a distended abdomen and begun to order different tests, such as ultrasounds and X-rays.

Our positive emotions changed to fearful ones in an instant...and the results confirmed our fears: bowel obstruction – a medical emergency. She needed to be transferred to a paediatric surgery unit right away. By the time we were told this, her belly had become extremely distended. They put her on antibiotic therapy and stopped any milk intake. This long-awaited day was filed with countless tears, with despair, with intense sorrowfulness and the fear that we might lose her.

During the next week, her condition was kept stable with the help of a rectal tube, but there was no clear diagnosis, and nobody knew what to do. We were only allowed to see her five minutes per day. Our whole world was upside down! It was so hard to get a diagnosis because she had a recto-perineal fistula. This is a very catchy diagnosis as everything looks pretty normal even to a doctor. They wanted to take her to the operating room for a rectum and sigmoid colon removal, without having any idea what blockage was causing them to be so dilated.

We are grateful that an incredible dedicated neonatologist came into our lives at the right moment and taught us to ask for a colostomy instead. When they refused, we immediately took the decision to change the hospital and this was the first step in improving the care for our daughter and a sign of God's love for us, that we treasure so much in our memory.

As soon as we arrived in the new neonatal intensive care unit, she was checked from head to toe and not only did they find the correct diagnosis, but also some other issues related to her spine and spinal cord. At this point we had the feeling and the fear that more investigations would bring along other problems.

Our baby underwent colostomy surgery at the age of two weeks old, but the medical team admitted, that in our country the likely repair of her malformation, as well as for her tethered cord, anterior meningocele and presacral teratoma was dangerously low.

It was not easy to see her suffering after her unexpected first surgery and during the entire stay in the hospital: one month and a half. Only a mother's heart that has experienced such distress can understand the painful feelings that cross your mind, soul and body seeing your tiny precious one in such sufferings. However, in the new neonatal intensive care unit we had the great opportunity to be able to stay next to her twenty-four hours per day and this was a huge blessing and relief!

Time passed and we finally got home. Her crib that had waited for her for so long, had suddenly come to life when she was gracefully smiling, kicking her legs and even sleeping peacefully. A worthful spectacle to our eyes!

Raising a baby with a colostomy bag can be challenging sometimes, not only regarding the leaks and detachments of the bag that often occurs, but also being constantly alert concerning the possible complications that can arise, such as severe rash, occlusion, prolapse or bleeding. Besides, her anterior sacral meningocele was still in place and this was a huge anxiety for us as it could have led to meningitis, in the event of a common enterocolitis.

However, this time was so valuable for us and we truly treasured every single moment with her, as we witnessed blessings that we would only have dreamed of when she was hospitalised. Life without numerous wires coming out of her seemed unreal in our first day at home. Yes, being able to move around while holding her, to visit grandparents and to take a walk in the park were activities we did not take for granted.

Also, seeing our baby girl being able to finish her sleep without being interrupted every single time by medical staff, watching her in the peaceful process of waking up in the morning, stretching and yawning and not in the painful routine of morning pokes made us grateful beyond measure and enjoy to the maximum this time in between our surgeries.

The decision to continue her treatment in a prestigious Center for Colorectal and Pelvic Reconstruction in Columbus, Ohio, United States of America was the second step in improving the care for our daughter. Again, a clear sign of God's love for us. as so many hearts helped us raise the enormous amount of money that we needed.

After eight months spent at home in the still and peace of our house, we began our next journey into the unknown.

Her repair surgery ended up being much more complicated than the doctors expected, and they needed a neurosurgery team in the operating room as well. It turned out that her meningocele was attached to her rectum. We looked back in time and praised the Lord for His guidance towards us when her first surgeon from our country wanted to remove her rectum without the proper investigations. This could have been a scenario we refuse to imagine.

Her recovery was difficult as well, as we dealt with the effects of a cerebrospinal fluid leak. Although it was something they expected, the source of the liquid was not clear until the lab results were ready. In the meantime, our daughter suffered not only uncontrollable pain but also headaches, dizziness and vomiting. We continued to keep her lying down for a period and things improved gradually.

Until the next set of surgeries, we had to undergo another common challenge for anorectal malformations: dilations. Yes, it was a hard thing to do at the beginning. All three of us were already overwhelmed by the recent events, but eventually we found the strength to go over it.

After three months we were back in Ohio for the tethered cord release and colostomy closure surgeries, two major interventions only six days apart and only one day outpatient in between.

We made the long trip from Romania to Ohio, USA twice in a matter on three months, first in March and then again in July. It was a massive commitment for our family, but we were determined to get our daughter the best care and treatment possible.

Regarding our daughter's anorectal malformation surgeries, there are no words to describe our gratitude for Dr. Marc Levitt, Dr. Richard Wood and Dr. Alessandra Gasior, as well as the entire colorectal team from Nationwide Children's Hospital - Center for Colorectal and Pelvic Reconstruction. As children with complex and various types of malformations is a very sensitive subject and specialised area, there are only a limited number of specialists across the world.

We greatly appreciate all the effort, energy, research and commitment that these doctors put in their work and studies so that we can benefit from all of it. We also received great care from Dr. Leonard Jeffrey and his team in the neurosurgery department.

After the reversal things completely changed for us. Without a bag it became even more complicated as we were constantly wondering whether she had completely evacuated her colon or if her laxative dose was enough, or maybe too much.

Ever after her diagnosis was clear to us, we have never stopped wondering about her future. Lots of thoughts cross our minds, but we have learned to take each step at a time, focus on each day, gather precious memories together and enjoy this unique period of our lives to the fullest!

Today, five months after her second birthday, she is a happy and social toddler, very compassionate and ready to share love with everyone around her. She brings so much joy into our lives and she is our delightful treasure!

However, problems have not forgotten us yet. She still has headaches caused, most probably, by her cerebrospinal fluid leak, potty training is not accomplished yet, and we have routine check-ups for her sacral teratoma. Nevertheless, we go ahead trusting in The One who held the rein of our boat throughout this journey.

These pages would not be enough to write down all the experiences and emotions we have experienced but I have tried to share the main events, the way that we perceived them and most importantly, Divine providence.

A poem dear to our hearts called "Light Shining Out of Darkness", by William Cowper (1778 – 1858), inspires hope for the believer through their troubles. Hopefully it may also help others just at the beginning of their journey, to get through their trial as positively as possible. Please take the time, dear reader, to find, read and ponder it for yourself.

This article is dedicated to my beloved and brave daughter, to my loving and helpful husband and to everyone who shares a similar trial.

27. Wait and See – Emma Quinones Roberts (USA)

The words complications or chromosomal abnormalities never quite describe the moment one finds out by scientific terms "the child is not perfect"

The opening missing seems so minor and insignificant.

It is the start of series of events no one can ignore in medical aspects.

The child is different. But different is good right?

Sure it is, don't mind the financial burden, the constant fear of maybe today will be the day I can't go.

Sitting on a toilet somewhere pondering about laxatives and stool softeners or perhaps more surgeries.

While so many sit on a toilet to let natural bodily functions take its course and think about pleasant things.

But not I, I never forget that saying "it's a repair not a fix".

We shall wait and see.

28. Bailey's Story – Chantelle (Australia)

My name is Chantelle, and I am a mum of two boys, Bentley and Bailey and I want to tell you what it is like for me to have a child with a medical condition. When you decide to have a baby, you do not really think that you will end up having a baby born with medical issues, or with a disability, it is just not on your mind. But my Bailey was born with a medical condition called VACTERL.

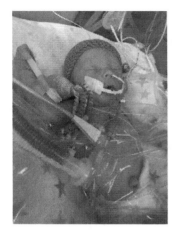

Bailey was born with multi cystic kidneys hemivertebrae with possible tethering of the spinal-cord and an imperforate anus, which was classed as high, along with a fistula and a few other issues. My medical journey with Bailey has been incredible. It has been eye-opening, and it makes me appreciate things from a different perspective.

Bailey is now eighteen months old and I was on this journey, even before he was born. At my twelve week scan the doctors advised me that my unborn baby had multi cystic kidneys. They had a concern, but told me that he should be fine, and they would check it out again at the twenty-week scan. When I had that scan, it showed that his kidneys were not that great and then we were referred to a specialist.

While I was pregnant, we saw the specialist and they were not that worried and said all this is common with boys and he will go on to live a normal life. They did not know that there were other health complications going on, which were not identifiable at the time.

I am sitting here writing this now and it is making me so anxious, as I am reliving the most traumatic experience of my life. I will never ever forget the moment where my newborn baby momentarily 'died in my arms.'

Bailey was delivered by Caesarean, and as I was cradling him in my arms, an hour after he was born, his little face suddenly changed colour, and he went purple! I said to my step-mum who was the only one in the room with me at the time (my partner Luke had just left the room to go outside) that something is wrong, he has gone purple. She immediately grabbed him off me and started doing CPR. I could not even reach the buzzer. When Luke walked back in my step-mum said, 'Go out there and scream for help!'

The next thing I knew, Bailey was ripped out of her arms and about thirty doctors came running out of nowhere. All I remember is hearing over the PA system 'code blue... code ... maternity... code blue... code blue...'

The next hour felt like a lifetime, as I was hopelessly sobbing my heart out, waiting to see what had happened with my son. I could not even move as I had had a Caesarean. What was even worse, I had convinced myself I had killed my baby while I had him on my breast. I thought I had suffocated him.

The doctors finally came back in and said that Bailey was on life support and that he would require surgery within twenty-four hours. They had discovered he had an imperforate anus and they needed to run some investigations and medical tests to see what was going on. I could not believe it, I had no idea what that even meant, I did not even know if my son was going to make it through. Plus, they could not explain why he had stopped breathing, which was extremely concerning. All they said was that they had resuscitated him for three minutes.

All I wanted to do was to hold my baby and I could not. I remember trying to get into a wheelchair, but I could not move, and I cried, and I cried, and I cried. I have never cried so much in my life. Finally, the nurses were nice enough to wheel my bed into the NICU, where for a tiny, short minute a lovely nurse let me hold Bailey. I got to hold him for one minute, just one minute. I was told when I could and could not hold my baby, as it was crucial that he was put back in the incubator.

So, after a minute I got wheeled back to the room where I lay crying my heart out. After several hours had passed, I manage to get in a wheelchair, and I was able to sit at Bailey's bedside. Within twenty-four hours of being born, he had his first surgery where his stoma was created. I was now learning something completely new and I had no idea that they made colostomy bags tiny enough for a little baby, who was only five pounds. It was crazy.

The next fourteen days were horrific because I was not allowed to stay overnight with him. It was horrible travelling back and forth to the hospital, being there all day and leaving each night. For me, leaving my newborn baby in a hospital bed, while I had to go home, was absolutely heart-breaking and I hated every second of it. I live forty-five minutes away from the hospital and I remember leaving and sobbing all the way home.

A few weeks went by and a few more tests were conducted. It was discovered that there was a fistula causing Bailey to wee poo, which was greatly distressing as you can imagine. We then had a meeting with the paediatric surgeon in Hobart and he said because of the complexity of Bailey's condition and that the gap, which was 3.2 cm, was too high for him to deal with. He referred us to Associate Professor Sebastian King at The Royal Children's Hospital Melbourne, who specialised in complex conditions such as Bailey's.

When Bailey was three months old, we flew from Hobart to Melbourne (a one-hour flight) and we had a consultation appointment with Sebastian. He then ran through what the next stage of life would be for Bailey and at four months old Bailey had major surgery, which was called a PSARP and we were in the hospital for a week.

We went home after his discharge, but had to return two weeks later, to be shown how to do the dilations. I will never forget the first time Sebastian showed us how to do it. I was so scared. I had thought to myself there is no way I would ever be able to do this, to have to stick something up my son's bottom! Every fibre of my body was telling me that doing this to our son was not normal, but it was the reality for us and to help Bailey, this had to become our new normal.

Let me tell you dilations are horrible, the most horrible thing I have ever had to do or overcome. I never thought I would ever be okay with this process, as it is so overwhelming and scary. I mean you are sticking a metal rod up your up your son's bottom! It was so confronting, and no parent ever imagines that they would have to do that. But we did, and we are still doing it and it is horrible, but I know at the end of the day it is to help him.

We travelled back and forth for a couple of months as we progressed in size and we would have short, two-day visits in Melbourne. This is our journey and so we are doing what he needs to get him to where he needs to be.

We eventually progressed through the dilation rod sizes, and although there were hiccups along the way, we have finally progressed to size twelve. When I noticed Bailey was crying every time, I was doing it, and he started peeing pus, that is when I knew something else was going on. He had an MRI and it showed that he had a cyst located behind where the fistula was at the back of the urethra. It was causing a lot of discomfort during the dilations and needed to be fixed before we could proceed to the next size and stage.

We had to go back to size nine and ten dilations after the MRI, until Bailey could have surgery on the cyst. However, because of COVID-19, it was put on hold and we had to slow down, to stop causing him so much discomfort. We did not have that surgery until July, which was in the middle of the pandemic here in Melbourne.

Travelling interstate in the middle of a pandemic has caused us to be Covid swabbed, Covid tested, and to self-isolate at home. Then after the hospital visits in Melbourne, we had to wait for approval to go home. Being away so many times and not being able to have any support has been crazy.

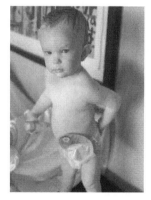

In July 2020, we went back to the RCH Melbourne for a series of tests and procedures which included: an exploratory laparotomy to find the bleeding, (which they didn't find), the division of fistula, a cystoscopy for the cyst near his pee and sperm line which took them two and a half hours to dissect and an orchiopexy, which is stage one of the dropping of his testicle.

I mean sure it would be hard given the circumstances, but in the middle of a worldwide pandemic it was even harder. I also have to leave my son Bentley at home, who is seven and even though he understands a little bit, he wants to come every time we have to travel to Melbourne.

He struggles with me being away and has issues of his own, as he feels really left out. It is horrible and I hate that he feels like this. I try my absolute best to reassure him every time.

We had to travel back to Melbourne again and on 29th October 2020 Bailey had his stoma closure surgery. I had never felt so many mixed emotions about this surgery, and when Bailey woke up it and the next 24-48 hours were so extremely difficult. He cried so much, and I don't know if it's because he knew things were changing or if it was pain or if it was just a mixture of everything but what I didn't realise was how different I was going to feel about this.

But, on 1st November 2020, after 18 months of having the colostomy bag on Bailey did his very first poo using his bottom. I couldn't believe that he was using his bum for the first time. I was so happy, but also a little sad that we said goodbye to the colostomy bag, only because I knew things were changing. Who thought I would get so many mixed emotions about poo?

I could not have done this without the amazing support from the RCH and the amazing medical team of Sebastian King and his wonderful team.

I feel like I owe them a thousand life's and so many more for making this happen for my little boy. I could not have asked for any better medical team to care and support Bailey through this. I know his journey is not over yet and it never will be, but I know he is in the right hands.

I was also very blessed to have met Greg Ryan on this special trip to Melbourne, and I'm thankful he will be a part of our lives now and we will have someone else who will help support us through this.

29. Eliza Jade's Story – Christina (USA)

Everything leading up to the birth of Eliza seemed normal. Nothing out of the ordinary on the ultrasounds, my labour was normal and, after 12 hours of contractions, Eliza was born on December 7th, 2018. The nurse did her check list and I did mine. She had 10 fingers and 10 toes. She was breathing and she was healthy. I held her for a long time and stared into her eyes. She was perfect to me. We were moved to our overnight room and everything still felt okay. I knew that you were supposed keep them in their own bed but, as I have always been extra protective, I immediately moved her to my own bed.

She was such a good baby that first night. She slept most of the time and I changed every diaper. I started to notice however, every time I tried to feed her she would immediately spit up. When I mentioned that to my nurses though, they would say it was normal. It would take time for her to eat, but to me it didn't seem normal. I mentioned it again, still receiving the same answer. The next day a paediatrician came to check her out and he said everything was normal, giving us the okay to leave.

I immediately thought it was weird because she hadn't pooped yet, and I remembered with my son that they waited for him to poop before they let us leave. I mentioned this to the nurse and she had told me that Eliza had indeed already pooped, but I knew this wasn't true because I had held her all night. While the overnight nurse had written that she had, I made it very clear she had not. Between her spitting up and her not pooping, I knew something was wrong.

The nurse talked to the paediatrician and he recommended an enema. The nurses then came in with the supplies to do the enema only to discover Eliza did not have an anus. They seemed surprised by this and immediately looked at me and said, "There is no hole". I asked, "What does that mean?". I had never even thought such a thing was possible. Immediately Eliza was being wheeled down to the NICU and I couldn't even begin to grasp what was going on.

All I remember is our paediatric surgeon telling us that Eliza was full of stool, she had no anus and needed emergency surgery. I was crying and my husband was crying, but we agreed to get her into surgery immediately. The surgeon told us she had an Imperforate Anus and that it would require a series of surgeries and recovery. I was so shocked and tired that I could not comprehend what it all meant.

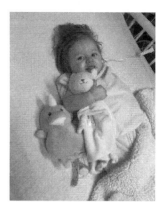

Two hours later Eliza was out of surgery, hooked up to every tube and wire you could think of. It broke my heart to see her like that. The fact that I couldn't hold her made it even worse. Immediately we noticed her stoma, which was where her stool would come out. Since she had no anus, she would need a colostomy bag.

We stayed a week in the NICU and learned the proper care for her and how to change a colostomy bag. I remember crying a lot, mostly because of the uncertainty facing us and the fact that I had little knowledge about her condition. No one had ever warned me this might happen and I felt so lost and alone. Once we mastered the care of her colostomy bag and her stoma, we were able to go home. This was such a relief.

Once home, we were able to start the healing process, but the moment we arrived I started to feel anxious. No longer did we have the help of the nurses or care of the NICU. We were all alone. The colostomy bag seemed to be a bigger problem than we thought.

My husband worked night shifts so, most nights, I was alone to get up and care for Eliza. This seemed to be the time her colostomy bag wanted to leak and needed to be changed. It was possible to do with only one person but was easier with two. Trying to gather all the supplies and get the bag on before she would poop again was hard.

Many times, it would take me forty-five minutes to an hour to get it on and, by that time, Eliza and I were both tired. Besides the frustration of getting the bag to stay on, she was doing great. She was a baby with regular baby problems, but just with the added complication of a colostomy bag.

I didn't tell many people what was going on with her because I wanted to leave it up to her, as she grew older, who she would tell and how much. It was always a little awkward when someone asked to hold her and they could feel her bag. I would tell them kind of what went on with her when she was born, but then leave it at that. When she was three months old she had her PSARP surgery. This was when they created her anus and it was a big surgery which took a few hours.

When Eliza came out of her surgery, she was very swollen and in and out of sleep for twelve hours. It seemed like she was in pain but, besides giving her pain medication, all we could do was hold her. Luckily after a day she started feeling better, and we were able to go home and start the second part of her healing process. We also started dilations at this time. Dilators were sticks made to help stretch the anus to prepare for poop. It seemed pretty invasive and scary at first but, over time, she barely seemed to notice when I was doing it.

When she was six months old she had her colostomy closure. This surgery was what they said would be "the big one". They told us her pain levels could be high and that recovery could sometimes be rough. I felt so much stress and anxiety and barely slept the week leading up to it. After her surgery she seemed to be doing okay. She had a fever which went down after a few hours, but we weren't allowed to leave until she pooped. We also had cream and powder that we had to apply generously on her butt. This was to help with the rash that they said would occur since her skin was not used to having poop on it.

On the second day in the hospital, she finally pooped. Just a little bit of poop, but there was poop! Never in a million years did I think I would cry over poop. It was such a strange experience. I felt the weight of months of worry carried on my shoulders start to lift. I felt like I could finally see the light at the end of the tunnel for her. I could start to see her future although a lot of work still needed to be done.

Making sure she was pooping enough and she didn't have a rash felt like a fulltime job. But straight up I noticed she was not pooping a lot at all. We had just started her on baby food and stayed away from things that could be constipating. Our doctor recommended pear or prune juice. That seemed to work for a bit but then she started getting backed up again. After numerous doctors' appointments we finally agreed to use MiraLAX and enemas to get her all cleared out. Because she was staying so backed up, we did this every day as well as going to the doctor weekly to get X-rays done.

Finally, after a couple of months we got her cleared out. Our next step was to put her on Senna. We gave her the chocolate squares and they worked great. Enemas were needed from time to time and we still had to give her MiraLAX too. When she was 20 months old, she went into a surgery for three hernias on her belly button and above. This was a quick surgery and she was able to go home the same day.

Throughout this whole process I have learned how strong Eliza is. The amount of pain and procedures she has endured in the first two years of her life is just crazy. She is such a happy girl though. Every time we think something is going to hold her back, she surprises us with her strength and perseverance.

I think this will leave a bigger mental scar on me and her father than it will on her. She knows her doctors well and is always excited to see them. Even when she's in pain she still smiles and laughs. That usually makes it easier on us when most of the time I feel helpless or like there is more I should be doing.

When we first got her diagnosis of Imperforate Anus, we had no idea what it was or how to deal with it. I had never heard of anyone ever having it and I felt so alone. Even when people would ask what was wrong, I didn't know how exactly to describe it. I didn't want to get the facts wrong or share too much of Eliza's personal story.

I felt myself going back and forth between wanting to shed light on something that happens to 1 in 5000 babies and letting Eliza have her privacy. This happens a lot more than is talked about and it's time to raise more awareness. I want to help new parents who hear this diagnosis and feel doomed.

I don't think I would have managed as well if I didn't find the IA page on Facebook. This page helped us through our journey so much and I finally felt like I had people to talk to that understood what we were going through. A community that understood crying over a leaking colostomy bag or our kid's first poop!

Eliza isn't even two yet so I know we still have a lot to learn. As life continues, I'm so glad we have the support of the IA community and her amazing doctors.

We will continue to work to make sure she can achieve anything she wants in life and to wear her diagnosis as a badge of strength and honour.

30. Our Son's Story – Katie (USA)

Our son was born with Imperforate Anus with a rectoperineal fistula in October 2013. He is our first child, and because he had been born by c-section and was having trouble nursing, we were in the hospital for five days. During that time, he was examined by many paediatricians and nurses. Because of the fistula, he was passing meconium normally and his condition went under our radar. One of the paediatricians who examined him during that time told us his anus did not look normal and threw out the words 'Imperforate Anus.' However, they did not explain to us what this meant, or how this condition could affect our new baby, who seemed to us to be one hundred percent normal.

My husband googled the condition, and it seemed to mean a birth defect, where a child was born without an anus or could not pass any stool. What we did know was that it seemed terrifying, but since our son had an opening, we decided not to worry. When we were discharged from the hospital, we were told specifically to ask our paediatrician about it.

We pointed it out to her on our first visit and even brought it up at follow up visits after that. However, she never seemed worried. She acknowledged his anal opening did seem to be out of place, but since he was stooling without any trouble she was not concerned and assured us that she would keep an eye on it.

After about nine weeks, our son had developed an umbilical granuloma that was not being successfully treated. We were referred to a gastroenterologist specialist (GI) at the local Children's Hospital.

January 2014
Three days after PSARP

I will never forget the GI doctor completing the exam for my son and start to prod me with questions. 'What's going on with his anus? What did his paediatrician say about it?' I sort of stammered in shock since this was not why we were there, while I tried to remember exactly what the paediatrician had said. The GI explained to me that my son had IA, would require surgery, and that even though he was stooling normally, now, we would have big problems when he started on solids. He informed us of the need for additional testing as many kids born with IA can have other issues.

Our son's surgery was scheduled for three weeks later. Our world was shattered. We were so angry and confused that it had taken nine weeks, to learn that our son indeed had a birth defect that could affect the rest of his life.

During our son's post-op appointments, the GI warned us that our son would deal with constipation issues. He said if we were very lucky, we could manage them with diet, but that some kids needed daily enemas. As my son was not even eating solids yet, this of course was information we tucked away under the 'to worry about later' category. The doctor told us to call his office every year to check-in.

I will never forget the first time I called in. The woman who answered the phone questioned me in a way that suggested she had no idea why I was calling, or what kind of message to give to the doctor. I felt very dismissed and silly about the whole thing, so I did not call back the following year.

Our son grew up as a fairly normal toddler, but with lots and lots of diaper changes and rashes. We learned how to manage his condition as best we could, and we continued to hope for the best. We started trying to potty train him when we started thinking about pre-school. However, he seemed to be constantly stooling, so it was extremely frustrating for all of us. We had no idea how to even begin to potty train a child and just assumed that because he was stooling so much, that he was not constipated.

I called his surgeon's office in an act of desperation to see if we could get some direction or help. The woman who answered the phone once again made us feel dismissed and silly for calling. She asked, 'This is your first-time potty training, right?' and said we should check with our paediatrician for ideas first. She told us it was totally normal for a little boy of his age to not be fully potty trained yet. She suggested we call them the following year if he was still having issues. I never called them back, assuming that if they had the resources to help us, she would have let us know.

We felt so alone and confused. No one told us how to deal with my son's IA during the toddler and pre-school years. We had no idea what our options were or who to turn to. We had tried to rely on our paediatrician and the GI office, but they did not seem to have any special advice or direction for us. We took all of the bad advice that was thrown at us by well-meaning friends and family; we were so desperate for a solution. I am ashamed to say following this bad advice only led to a lot of raw emotions and tension around 'potty time,' which was only damaging our son.

Because we did not understand how to advocate for our son to get the medical help he so desperately needed, we also did not understand how to get the support we needed within the school system. We were left begging with pre-school teachers to help clean up dirty diapers and trying to explain about a condition that we did not fully understand ourselves.

In June of 2018 everything changed. Some close friends of ours had a son also born with IA. His was not detected until his second day of life when his mother noticed he had not had a dirty diaper yet. Their son was rushed off to the Children's Hospital Colorado for a colostomy.

By this time, Dr. Pena and Dr. Bischoff had joined the Children's Hospital Colorado and the International Centre for Colorectal and Urogenital Care had been established. Our friends knew of our son's medical issue and potty-training problems and asked Dr. Bischoff if she could help us. The answer was YES!

We made our first appointment in August 2018. Dr. Bischoff noticed that the lower portion of our son's spine had never been imaged. After a subsequent x-ray she told us his lower spine had not formed normally and explained that he could not feel when he needed to poop. She explained that we would need a bowel management plan to help him stay socially continent. Once again, our world was shattered.

We finally understood how our son would be affected by IA for the rest of his life. We felt so betrayed that we had been left to struggle and suffer on our own for so long, and that the GI's office had been so dismissive of our potty-training issues. I felt particularly angry at myself for not advocating for our son properly, for not pushing for more appointments or better answers, and definitely angry for all the frustration and stress we had caused our family over our unrealistic expectations of potty training him. It was an incredibly difficult time for our family. But after some of the initial shock wore off, we realized that our son had a brighter future because, finally, we had support to help us understand and manage his condition in a productive way.

By October 2018 we were attending Bowel Management Week and learning what care would look like for our son. We spent the week learning about enemas, getting x-rays, and trying to find our new normal. We were also connected with an online support group via Facebook. And even though this transition was one of the hardest things we have had to accept, it started to change our lives for the better.

We are so fortunate that overall, our son did really well with his daily enema regime. We had our share of bad days, tears (his and ours), temper tantrums, and dirty laundry, however, there were also the days we decided to go out without any diapering supplies, or I would look at the calendar and realize that it had been weeks since the school had sent home any soiled clothes. We started to celebrate our small victories! Our son started kindergarten in August 2019, and that school year was different because we had the support and language, we needed to properly advocate for him.

In August 2020, our son got a Malone procedure done. It has completely changed our lives. Our morning routine is cleaner, faster and less stressful for all of us. We are teaching our son to be more independent, and how to do his flush by himself. We are starting to consider overnights with grandma, camping, and travelling.

The awareness that the IA community is raising around the condition, the need for transitional care from childhood to adulthood, and mental health awareness, makes us optimistic for his future. I am so grateful for the healthcare specialists and people affected by IA that have made helping families like ours their passion. Having support from people that have travelled this road before us has made a big difference for us, and we hope we can do our part and do the same for others.

31. Our Warrior (USA)

Perhaps it was merely what I needed to see in our son's bright little eyes at that very moment, but when I received the first images of our Warrior from my husband, just hours after he had been born, all I could hear was, 'Mom, stop all that worrying, I've got this.'

There was a calmness about his demeanor and a wisdom, that pierced through the camera, as he looked directly into the lens for his very first photo. Warrior is a twin, born just twenty minutes after his brother who was down the hall struggling with lung complications, and due to a diligent OR team, Warrior's imperforate anus was discovered just moments after his birth.

Warrior and my husband were taken by ambulance to a children's hospital, a few miles away, and I did not get to see or touch him for the next four days. Those pictures, the ones where he spoke to me with his eyes, they were what made me believe that 'we,' as a fierce little team, would get through all the battles that were to come.

Warrior spent the first ten days of his life in the NICU, far fewer days than many, yet it still felt like an eternity. He was born at a meager four pounds and struggled to regulate his own body temperature and keep on weight. More than anything I wanted to hold him, but I was simultaneously terrified to do so. He had a 'unicorn' IV in the vein on top of his head and he looked so fragile and so strong all at the same time.

I would never wish such a low birth weight upon any child, but it ended up being a blessing. It bought us the time we needed to research his condition and find the best team for his care. Had he been a few pounds heavier, the general surgeon would have performed his PSARP just hours after him being born. He instead received a colostomy and my husband and I gritted our teeth through the learning curve that is that process. There just is not enough real estate on a four-pound body to securely attach a bag.

The hospital was guiding us along, but there was no central person connecting all the varying pieces, to help us figure out what Warrior would need and when. At first, we were told there was a fistula, but then assured there was not. It was explained that it would likely heal itself, but our research led us to believe that was extremely unlikely. Just as Warrior was about to have his distal colostogram, the tech looked at me and asked me which hole he was supposed to put the tube into, for the procedure. So. Many. Red. Flags.

I was nursing twins at the time, so I did not have much time for sleep, but it did leave a whole lot of time for me to scroll the internet and research the heck out of the VACTERL checklist. I did not know where we were going to go, but I did know we were not going to stay there. I felt as though I researched every corner of the world, joining every virtual group I could and sending blind messages to anyone I could find in my area who also had a child born with IA.

But as it turns out I just needed to look eight miles from where we were. Warrior was born roughly thirty minutes away from the Children's Hospital of Colorado, where one of the world's leading Colorectal Center's is located. Not a single person at either of the two hospitals he first went to, ever informed us of that, because it would have taken us and our money out of their health system.

Within twenty-four hours after reaching out to the International Center for Colorectal Care at the Children's Colorado we were seen by Dr. Bischoff and the entire team. The experience was so night and day different, than the one we had previously had. We of course still have to advocate for Warrior but being in a place that understands all of the factors associated with IA makes all the difference.

Warrior had four surgeries before his first birthday and his team is optimistic that he will not need any more in the future. Only time will tell. There were times that it all seemed so overwhelming and exhausting, but now that nearly a year has passed since his last surgery, the edges seem to have rounded themselves out.

We are still early in our journey and recognize our path has not taken the sharp turns that so many others have. We are on the cusp of starting toilet training and I think constantly about what new bumps that endeavor may throw at our IA journey. I know that we will most likely always have new obstacles related to Warrior's IA as he grows, but I also know what I saw in those bright little eyes the day he was born.

He is a Warrior. WE'VE got this.

32. Jaxson's Story – Rebecca (USA)

When I was around six or seven years old, I had this overwhelming feeling that I was going to have a boy someday. It was not just me feeling this way because I wanted a boy. No, quite the opposite. I remember feeling disappointed and trying to convince myself it was just my imagination. I wanted girls! I did not want a boy! No matter how hard I tried, I just could not shake that feeling. Years later, my mother would also tell me that she had always felt I was meant to have a boy.

When I gave birth to our second daughter while struggling with infertility, I thought, 'God must have changed his mind!' After all, we struggled to have our two girls and a third just was not on the cards, even if we had wanted another child. However, when my doctor said, 'You have a time frame of about two months where you might be able to get pregnant. After that, you will not be able to have more.'

My husband, Joe, looked at me and said, 'Well, three might be fun!' So, there we were, one month later, pregnant with our third (and final!) child. As soon as I got that positive test, I knew this was my boy. This was the boy God told me I would have. And I was over the moon!

I had a normal pregnancy and a normal delivery. On September 26th, 2018, Jaxson Carter-Thomas Vickrey was born. The nurses looked over his perfect little body, wrapped him up and handed him to me. He was beautiful! Over the next day in the hospital, Jaxson was refusing to eat and would spit up everything he did take. His nurses kept trying to force him to eat, while giving us reasons why he may be having trouble. None of it was a concern, as it was not completely out of the ordinary to have some issue at first. Jaxson's paediatrician Dr Jeff Brand MD, came in to do his routine newborn check. I remember like it was yesterday. 'I don't think he has an anal opening.' The next thing I knew, Jaxson was being whisked away to the NICU while Joe and I sat, completely scared, and confused. No anal opening? Is that even possible?

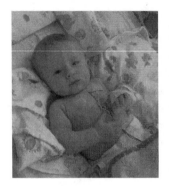

Jaxson would have his first surgery that day. We were told to expect him to come out of surgery with a colostomy, but we would not know the extent of his anorectal problems until they could open him up. This was devastating. It was all I could do to keep myself together. I cried almost constantly. My baby was one day old, and we had been getting ready to take a healthy baby home less than a day ago. Now, he is in surgery and we do not even completely understand why!

Jaxson came out of surgery with a colostomy. He had an imperforate anus, but nobody knew what type or how severe it was. We were told that nothing else was expected to be wrong, but with the imperforate anus came routine protocols that meant he needed to undergo many other tests, to rule out other issues. Over the next two weeks we were bombarded with doctors, specialists, and therapists.

Before every test, every MRI, every ultrasound, and Xray, we were told not to worry. They did not think anything else was wrong, though nobody ever specified what they were looking for. But after every test, MRI, ultrasound and Xray came something new that was wrong with our son.

Jaxson had a tethered spinal cord. He was missing his coccyx. He had two holes in his heart. He had hydronephrosis of his left kidney. We were told he may lose kidney function; he might develop a neurogenic bladder and need to be catheterized every day for the rest of his life. We were told his tethered spinal cord was not an issue that needed to be addressed now. We could wait two years to even have it looked at and they might not ever want to do surgery to untether because it would just re-tether and that we should just 'wait and see' what happens. Eventually, Jaxson was diagnosed with VACTERL Association. He had four of the letters in the acronym. Vertebral, Anorectal, Cardiac, and Renal. We would also learn that Jaxson's imperforate anus was one of the rarest types and he has little chance of being bowel continent. He has a high imperforate anus with a recto-bladderneck fistula.

We were in what I can only describe as a 'fog'. We walked through the halls of the hospital dazed and red-faced from crying. I remember, after learning about Jaxson's kidney issues, we left to get lunch at the Village Inn. The waiter noticed our NICU badges and our red eyes. He too had been a NICU parent. He paid for our meal and only said, 'Us NICU families stick together.' I will never forget that.

In the hospital, we had to learn how to change a colostomy bag. This was something that Joe did, not me. Looking back, I do not really know why. I suspect I was not handling things well and I just could not bring myself to do it. The biggest issue with it was that nobody really knew how to do it. It is something we do not see much of in Alaska. The nurses just had minimal training in school and never really had to practice on the job. They showed us the basics, but ostomy parents know it is anything but basic.

Jaxson was discharged on October 10, 2018. He was doing well, considering everything he had just gone through. We were set up with an ostomy nurse in Anchorage and an ostomy supply company out of state. We had our follow up appointments and a binder full of paperwork, specialists, diagnoses and medical jargon. The next fourteen months would prove to be some of the hardest of our lives.

Jaxson's colostomy bag leaked constantly. We have a handful of ostomy nurses here, none of them having experience with infants, so we had little help. Jaxson was a unique case. His surgeon had accidentally reversed the stoma and mucous fistula during surgery. The stoma was the raised 'raspberry' that is supposed to protrude from the abdomen while the fistula is flat and acts as a sort of valve for excess mucous in the intestine. However, in Jaxson, stool flowed out of the flat fistula instead. This caused many problems with leakage, as stool could easily get under the sticky wafer and cause the entire bag to come loose. We were going through a new bag every couple of hours. Jaxson's skin would break down, peel off and bleed.

While at a postpartum checkup, I was talking to my doctor about Jaxson. She asked me something I had not even thought of. Had we considered going out of state for a second opinion for Jaxson's colorectal issues? Living in Alaska, our medical options are limited. She suggested maybe seeking a specialist would be beneficial. I brought this up with Dr Brand and he agreed and suggested also seeing a paediatric neurosurgeon, as the neurosurgeon that saw Jaxson admitted he had never treated infants, nor had he seen this type of cord tethering. I was soon on my way to Seattle with Jaxson for a consultation.

This is what I consider to be the turning point. In Seattle, we saw a surgeon who specialised in colorectal issues like Jaxson's and she also trained under the famed pediatric colorectal specialist, Dr. Levitt. The surgeon was wonderful and scheduled Jaxson for his next surgery, the PSARP, when he would be four months old. This would correct his anorectal malformation, though his future for bowel continence would still be unknown. Our new surgeon would also re-do Jaxson's ostomy, fixing the mistake made by his previous surgeon and switching the stoma and mucous fistula back the way they should be.

We then saw a Paediatric Neurosurgeon. After reviewing all of Jaxson's imaging, he told us our local neurosurgeon had misdiagnosed his tethered spinal cord. It was something that needed to be taken care of now, but it would not re-tether. If we had waited like we were originally advised, Jaxson would have suffered irreversible damage to his spine, and he may never have crawled or walked. Surgery was scheduled for three months after the PSARP. Jaxson would be just seven months old during his third surgery.

Both surgeries went well. We were finally on a track where we could see some light at the end of the tunnel. Jaxson was scheduled three months later for his colostomy reversal. Our boy would finally be able to poop like a 'normal' kid and we would not have to change colostomy bags! The day finally came, August 14, 2019. Jaxson was ten months old. For some reason, this one scared me more than the others. But when he finally came out of surgery without the bag, I thought it was over. Five days later, Jaxson woke up screaming. I kept pleading for help saying something was wrong with my son, but I was brushed off. Our regular surgeon was not in that day, but the other doctors on her team just kept telling me he was fine. No amount of arguing could convince them otherwise, but they did some X-rays anyway. There was no blockage, he seemed fine from a medical standpoint.

At nine PM that night, Jaxson was rushed into emergency surgery. His intestine had come apart inside his abdomen and he was leaking infection and intestinal fluid into his tiny belly. He would need the colostomy again. Three more months. Each doctor on the team came to me and personally apologized. They should have listened; a mother's intuition is a powerful thing. His next colostomy reversal went without a hitch, though it was by far the most terrifying. We could only worry about reliving the last time. It took a long time for us to finally relax after his successful colostomy reversal. He was fourteen months old during his sixth surgery.

Jaxson turned two years old this year. The holes in his heart closed on their own. We were told he would need to be followed his entire childhood by urology for his kidney and bladder.

During his last exam, it was found that his kidney has completely healed, and his bladder is healthy and working properly. He was released by urology. We were told he would need to be followed by neurology his entire childhood because of his tethered cord, missing coccyx and his overall VACTERL diagnosis. He was also released from neurology.

He is symmetrically strong, showing no signs of muscle weakness or any signs that he ever had spinal abnormalities. The part of his spine that he is missing is not affecting him at all.

Our little miracle is healing, and his doctors are astounded. The only obstacle now is potty training. Jaxson will need bowel management for the rest of his life, but at the rate he is going, I am hopeful this too will prove minimal.

Our little warrior wears a smile constantly and has a laugh that lights up a room. He steals hearts everywhere we go, and my three babies are best friends. His sisters love him more than life itself and he adores them the same. He was meant to be here; he was meant to be ours and he was meant to do big things in this life!

Watch out world, this boy is unstoppable!

Portrait by Michelle Collins

33. Madison's Story – Aimee (New Zealand)

Madi was born at 3.20am on Monday 4th February. She was a tiny 6lb 3oz baby, but she was the most perfect human I had ever laid my eyes on. She was a very quiet, sleepy baby. At 4.00am the next day I was woken to feed Madison. I changed her nappy in an attempt to rouse her so she was awake enough to feed. In that moment, I never expected our life was about to make another massive turn after having become parents for the first time.

Madison had had a bowel motion but it was all up her front, to the point that they had to remove the clamp from her umbilical cord. The midwife and I investigated further, as the words "Has that come from where I think it has?" came out of my mouth. Sure enough, it had. Madi had no anus opening and, before I knew it, there was a paediatrician racing into the room as I was trying to wake up Madi's dad to tell him what was going on.

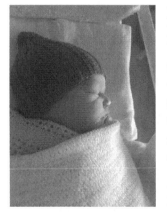

Madi was whisked away to the neonatal unit and I was left to wonder what had just happened. We pulled ourselves together and went to see our tiny baby who now had lines in her arm and down her nose. As we walked in, the nurses told us to prepare to be medivacked out to a city that could help us, so we went home to pack. We rang grandmothers to prepare them and the family and returned to our hospital. But luckily there was a paediatric-trained Urologist doing a year's work in the hospital, so we were saved a medivac trip and Madi was to stay in the neonatal unit until a surgeon could come to see us the next Friday.

Friday arrived and we were all eager to hear what this surgeon had to say. He met us around 3.00pm and said that Madison was ok and they'd look at creating her stoma when she turns three months old. We were also given the diagnosis of "Imperforate anus with rectovestibular fistula" and told that her fistula was open and that it was all looking "good".

We finally got to take our tiny human home! Saturday came and Madi had gone back to sleeping a lot and being hard to rouse. She had thrown up some random looking gunk on her sheet which concerned me so I saved it for the midwife visit. The midwife came and I voiced my concerns about how she seemed to have gone backwards, and then showed her the sheet. She said it was fine and it should clear up in 48 hours, but I was concerned and wanted to call the neonatal unit.

My mum instincts were screaming at me that something was not right, that my baby wasn't ok. When I spoke to Madi's dad he said to listen to the midwife, "She knows what she's talking about". I tried to let it go and set an alarm to feed Madi every four hours.

Sunday morning rolled around and I was so excited to have a lazy Sunday in bed as a family for the first time ever! I got Madi out of her bassinet and hopped into bed with her. I put my knees up to lay Madison against them and she projectile vomited the same stuff as the day before but on much larger scale. I freaked out and said I was calling the hospital because something was not right. Madi's dad said, "The midwife said give it 48 hours", but I lay Madison with him and walked out of the room. I rang NNU and explained what had happened and was told a doctor would be consulted and I would get a call back.

Only five minutes had passed when I got the call back and was told to get down there as fast as possible and pack to be admitted. So, forty-five minutes later I was taking my very sick baby in to be seen and it was so much worse than I could have imagined. Her fistula had closed and she was aspirating, so essentially her poo was coming out her mouth.

Thank goodness the urologist was in Invercargill as they managed to decompress her and arrange a commercial flight the next day, to Christchurch, for surgery to create a stoma. By the time we arrived in Christchurch at lunch time on the Monday, Madi's stomach had ballooned up and she was screaming. The child who never made a peep was now inconsolable.

That evening she was decompressed again in the paediatric HDU by two surgeons and a bunch of nurses. They got well over a litre of stool out of our tiny, tiny baby and she was much more content after that.

Madison was booked in for emergency surgery on the Tuesday afternoon and had her colostomy formed.

I wish I could say it was all smooth sailing from there, but it really wasn't. At three months old, Madison's colostomy needed a review as it had sunken in and wasn't working. She was bypassing through the fistula, so it was a good thing she still had it.

At six months old she had the pull through surgery done but it turned into a nightmare. She required two emergency surgeries afterwards due to her body trying to use the new opening instead of her colostomy, so they had to detach the distal bowel and then a few days later her mucus fistula got so infected it fell into her stomach which also required surgery. I praise her surgical team as this kid always seemed to make things super hard, but they always managed to kick butt at sorting her out.

At nine months old her colostomy decided to stop working for no apparent reason for a couple of weeks, which landed us back in Christchurch for a week. We got no answers but it eventually it started to work again on its own.

During this whole time Madi was so resilient. Most doctors never believed there was anything wrong with her because she always played, smiled, gooed and gahhed at everyone. Again, another reason why I am grateful for her team as the main surgeon always knew that Madison would be Madison regardless of how she felt or what was going on.

We, as parents, have learnt a lot about strength and how to push on with this little girl, because if she can, we can!

At 13 months old Madi had her reversal done. Out of all her surgeries and hospital admissions this one was the hardest. It really took a toll on her and most of the time she just wanted to go and be herself but, obviously very sore, would lay down and rest a lot more than usual.

It didn't help that it was the beginning of the Covid-19 pandemic here in New Zealand, so tensions were high in the hospital and life in general. Once she started to bounce back it was all on! She was trying to run out of the hospital ward every chance she got and trying to do rounds with all the nurses.

She had a few issues with infection and bleeding once we returned to Invercargill, but we managed to keep her out of hospital.

We also still have a lot of "out of the ordinary" things going on with her bowel and stuff, but we just persevere as much as we can.

Madi doesn't know anything different and nothing ever holds her back. She is tiny but fierce. She is the most amazing learner. She has a great sense of humour and an awesome imagination. She has a stubbornness that not many kids her age would know, and I truly believe that without IA (ARM) she wouldn't have a lot of these traits.

It's been a hard road and there is still a long way to go, but we wouldn't have it any other way because she is the best.

34. Florian's Story - Renate & Oliver (Austria)

On 17.07.2018 at ten am, it was time. We were off to the car as our son Florian was in a hurry and wanted to get out! At about eleven a.m. there was an ultrasound examination with the statement: 'Today he is still coming!'

At 11.58a.m. Florian, a healthy boy, saw the light of day. He was 52cm, 3490g and had ten fingers and ten toes, all perfect! For about fifteen to twenty minutes that is. Then the midwife, a nice student said to me that we are still looking for the first stool. Well, ten fingers, ten toes, but there is no butt hole!

About ten minutes later there were: two discoveries:
1. No one had seen this condition before in the hospital!
2. Our son needs surgery today!

An hour later, I sat with my two-hour-old son in the rescue car, as we headed to Vienna to a different hospital where they were able to provide the expert care Florian required. My wife had to stay in the hospital where she had given birth for an examination and she was then later transferred to the hospital where our son and I were. I think every mother can imagine how she felt in those hours.

To our great happiness, which we were not aware of at the time, the surgeon was extremely helpful. She had an excellent discussion with me about my son's anorectal malformation and operated on him a few hours later.

I think many parents are not lucky enough to have an internationally experienced surgeon by their side, so soon after finding their child had been diagnosed with Anal Atresia. At about eleven-thirty pm on the same evening after the Stoma OP, my wife and I were able to greet our son together for the first time and shower him with love and affection.

It was, at the same time, the most beautiful and the most 'frightening' moment in my life! In total we spent eight days in the hospital and four days were in the intensive care unit. During this time, I began to realize how lucky we were that Florian 'only' has Anal Atresia without secondary diseases. After we learned how to handle and care for a stoma, we went home.
We had agreed with our surgeon to perform the second surgery in December of the same year. After that came a rather turbulent time for us, as there were unfortunately hospital policy inconsistencies. With a retrospective view, I am very shocked that in our progressive Western world, hospital policy matters are being played out behind the backs of patients, even when it comes to patients in infancy!

After expressing my displeasure with this situation, the reaction to it was zero, so we promptly looked for another doctor to treat our son. I think that was one of the best decisions in our lives! We were lucky to be able to find Dr. Carlos Reck-Burneo in Vienna, who became our treating doctor for our Florian. Dr. Reck is still Florian's 'body doctor' and hopefully he will stay!

On March 1st, Florian had pull-through surgery and three months later the re-transfer. In August 2019, he had a small correction of the anus.

The stoma began a new challenge for us. After initial difficulties with the skin, the whole thing worked out relatively well for a few weeks – except that we had to wrap between ten and twenty times a day. Unfortunately, Florian's skin did not play along anymore, and it did not want to heal.

Together with Dr. Reck, the decision was taken to rinse Florian. Again, we had some initial difficulties. As of today, the rinsing works without any problems. Florian is up to forty-eight hours stool-free and leads the life of a toddler without great restrictions. We hope it stays that way!

However, the big challenges lie ahead. We wonder how his condition will affect his future when he starts kindergarten and school and then puberty. These are the things we are not yet aware of!

I would like to take the opportunity to offer some personal words.

'Dear Dr. Reck, thank you very much for being Florian's doctor and thank you for the friendly relationship.

Likewise, Greg Ryan thank you for your education on anorectal malformations and thank you for giving me the opportunity to contribute the story of our son, so that we can break the taboos about anorectal malformations in our society!"

35. A Story of Hope - August and Mariki (South Africa)

Hope is an optimistic state of mind based on the expectation of positive outcomes.

It's 18 September 2020, my son Leonhard's second birthday, and I'm sitting in my office with tears running down my face. The "Doc" just called to give me wonderful news regarding Leonhard's condition. It caught me off guard and I find myself reflecting on what we've been through, what we have to be thankful for and the hope we now have for the future.

Rewind two years to 17 September 2018. It was a normal day, except my wife was 37 weeks pregnant. Leonhard was showing little movement the past 24 hours so the doctors decided to keep my wife under observation for the evening. It appeared that Leonhard was under stress and may have to come early. The next morning, they decided to deliver him by c-section that night. We were not too phased by this because we are not the type of people to overthink things. Later that afternoon we sat in the maternity ward, contemplating the difference a second child would make to our lives. Our firstborn was three years old and we were confident that since we handled everything well with him we would be able to do so again, unaware of the extraordinary challenges about to face us in the next couple of hours.

The delivery went smoothly and I joined the paediatrician for his routine check on my son. I thought something looked strange as he glanced past his anus and he continued with his examination. About thirty seconds later he stopped and said "Wait!", swinging back to his anus only to find no opening. At this moment everything stopped, joy being replaced by worry in an instant. My head said it would be fine but my gut said there would be no easy way out of this situation. The paediatrician started telling me some terms such as "imperforated anus" and I wanted all the facts at once, but it was probably better that I didn't as it could have driven me crazy. He handed me my child and said he would need to be transferred. But why? I started to worry but managed to keep my composure as I took my son over to his mother. They had a moment together and then we left. My wife remembers trying to listen to us as she was being closed up, knowing something was wrong as she waited for what felt like hours to be with Leonhard. What was supposed to be one of the best moments ever became the worst.

The paediatrician said that my son had an imperforated anus, explaining that the anus wasn't formed and would require several procedures to correct. These procedures could not be done at the private hospital in our hometown.

There was only one specialist in South Africa who could do this, the "Doc", at a hospital in Pretoria 230km away. It was imperative they transfer him there immediately. I phoned my parents who are both medical doctors and they immediately understood that the road ahead would not be as we had imagined.

After I had sat with my son for about thirty minutes before they moved him to NICU, my wife emerged from surgery but I had nothing more to tell her. It was hard having no information. All I knew was that our "normal" was about to change quickly. My wife was not allowed in NICU and she was also not allowed to travel to Pretoria for two days. This must have been hell for her!
I sat with Leonhard all night and felt his calmness and strength. My wife made her way to NICU and saw Leonhard properly for the first time. She held his hand and prayed over him until it was time to transfer. At 5am they started prepping him for the transfer to Pretoria.

The NICU transfer ambulance arrived, loaded him and I drove the long journey behind. He arrived at the Pretoria NICU safely and the procedure was to be done urgently. My wife stayed behind in Klerksdorp, so I was in charge of keeping an eye on Leonhard, completing paperwork, gathering information and providing updates to everyone.

It was determined that Leonhard had a high IA. Shortly after learning this I met the "Doc", a big man with a quiet, gentle manner. He looked like he had the weight of the world on his shoulders, or at least the weight of the whole neonatal ward. He was the Paediatric Surgeon, a professional of note, who specialised in Imperforated Anus. By now I had figured out that with IA, the biggest long-term issue would be continence. The "Doc" and I had a quick discussion, very direct and to the point, and I was told that high IA does not have as good a prognosis as low IA and that the chances of long-term continence were 50:50. He explained that my son would have a surgical procedure later that day called a colostomy and he would have a colostomy bag for at least nine months.

Leonhard Shortly after his colostomy surgery

At only twenty hours old, Leonhard was taken away for surgery. Meanwhile, I sat outside trying to put together a message that everyone would understand to explain what his issues were and the way forward.

When I next saw him, I could see the red of his intestine covered by the colostomy bag. He was so unaware of what was happening and what lay ahead, and I felt so sad that his life would not be normal.

The next day was filled with tests as I learned more about the condition and the possibility of secondary issues. It appeared however, even though he had high IA, he did not have any other issues after all. I was taught the art of changing a colostomy bag and Leonhard seemed quite unfazed by the whole process even though I imagined it was painful.

My wife arrived later that day and was shocked to see our little boy with tubes and a colostomy bag. She spent some time with him, finally having the opportunity to process all that had happened and what would be needed.

Leonhard spent a week in NICU, our memory of it being a blur of juggling breastfeeding, recovering, splitting time between Leonhard and his brother Werner, no sleep and constant worry. The day we went home was the first time Werner got to meet Leonhard, after months of waiting and then still not being able see him the first week. He is very loving and protective of his little brother.

At home, finding a new normal was challenging. Knowing nothing and trying to come to grips with the reality of a week-old baby with a colostomy bag was tough.

Mother and child reunited after two days apart

That first week was the hardest. On the first night my wife woke me at 4am because the colostomy bag had come loose. As we struggled to fix it, Leonhard was screaming so intensely that he woke his brother. After a while, he seemed to pass out either from exhaustion or pain or both. Tears ran down my wife's cheeks as she tried to comfort Leonhard, with Werner also crying and clinging to her leg. That bag change took an hour and was a very rude awakening for us all, leaving us scared and exhausted. Later that morning the search was on to find colostomy bags. We had used the only one given to us by the hospital and all the local pharmacies gave us the same answer of "Sorry, we don't stock colostomy care products". Midway through the morning, Leonhard's colostomy bag became loose and was leaking. We went to our local wound care practice and had the bag replaced, with Leonhard again crying uncontrollably. My mother is a doctor and had access to a medical supplier, and so she was at least able to find some bags which, although not the same, would do. They were delivered to her practice about 900km away and then couriered to us. At last, we had bags and we could breathe again, if only for just a moment.

Three weeks in, we started to come to grips with the fact that this was now our "normal". Unaware of the colostomy bag lying beneath our baby's clothes, people presumed all was fine. But unlike most parents, our average nappy bag was the size of a car boot because of all the supplies we needed on hand. Challenges kept popping up - getting enough bags, getting the right bags, bags coming loose early in the morning and the relentless cries of our son every time a bag had to be changed. No one could babysit because no one else could change a bag. Some days, as many as four or five bag changes had to be done. And the costs involved kept creeping up. We felt like zombies every day, just waiting for the next step or challenge to arrive, over and over again.

Diarrhoea is tough at the best of times but trying to manage it with a colostomy bag is a nightmare! At five months old, Leonhard had such severe diarrhoea and that he was admitted to hospital. It was scary realising how little everyone knew about IA. His skin had first degree burns from stomach fluids and we tried various methods to protect it. Every time anything touched his skin he'd scream in pain. We soon learned some useful things though, such as using a double diaper as a quick fix for a leaking colostomy bag. This would buy us time, when shopping or visiting, until we got home.

The second major step in Leonhard's IA story was the pull-through surgery. He was nine weeks old and had to weigh at least five kilograms. This was the biggest of the three operations that he would receive and entailed connecting the underdeveloped caecum to the anus, and then opening the anus. The colostomy bag would remain for another couple of months.

If the operation and recovery went well, with no infection, he would be out of the NICU in less than seven days. The operation was to take three hours, but after four hours I started worrying and at five hours the "Doc" finally came out. He said that because of the high IA, Leonhard's intestine was short and it had been a struggle to get it attached. It was one of the toughest ones he had ever done, but he was happy with the results.

The first day post-op went well. I went to the Cape on business as things were under control and my wife was coping. The next week however, my wife called and said an infection was settling in and Leonhard was to be rushed back to theatre. I caught a flight back to Johannesburg, arriving after the operation was done, but the fight against the infection was far from over. He ended up spending six weeks in the NICU.

It is heart-breaking to experience problems that seem insurmountable. Our time in NICU, however, made us grateful to the Lord that we could at least hold our child and finally walk out with him, after witnessing so many parents leaving with nothing. Leonhard was named baby of the year in NICU for his beautiful smile that stole the hearts of all the staff. He even melted the heart of the "Doc". His utter joy for life made his problems seem small and kept on giving hope to all who witnessed it. They even held a going away party for him.

The whole family leaving the hospital after six weeks in NICU

In December we went home and Leonhard still had a catheter for the next week. We decided we needed some backup and would spend the festive season with family. The days were filled with disinfecting wounds (three times daily), fixing bags and worrying about bladder control, as the prolonged catheter use had created some new issues which eventually completely resolved.

A new addition to the routine was that of dilatations which, in my opinion, is the worst part of being an IA parent. After the first two dilatations the emotional strain was too much for my wife and the responsibility for it then became mine. The emotion and pain of this dreadful procedure will stay with me for a long time.

Leonhard was developing more personality daily. As the strength of his character grew, we knew it would still be tough for him in the future. But he already showed that he had what it takes to overcome anything.

Dealing with colostomy bags became quite normal for us, figuring out what worked for us, learning some tricks to make life easier and even coming up with new ones ourselves. We even have some funny memories, like accidentally staining Leonhard with gentian violet antiseptic.

A captivating shot my wife did summing up the challenges faced with IA

It became so normal in fact that we were afraid of the next step, which was the closing of the colostomy. It was the fear of having to face the unknown again, after having become used to our current "normal".

Leonhard's colostomy closure was scheduled for eight months of age. He was a normal eight-month-old and showed no ill-effects from the supposedly debilitating colostomy bag, or IA for that matter. The procedure went well and when Leonhard had his first dirty diaper he could go home. We were overjoyed at being able to change that dirty diaper, something most parents take for granted but we'd had to wait for so long. The biggest challenge post-op was keeping an eight-month-old boy, scared of nothing, in his hospital bed. A few days later we were out and had a whole new set of challenges ahead.

If I could give one piece of advice to all IA parents it would be to start buying diapers the day your baby is born, to be ready for the day the colostomy is closed. A normal eight-month-old toddler will use about eight diapers a day, but we discovered that between twenty and twenty-five diapers a day were needed to cope with the endless poop. It seemed impossible to keep up with it and stay on top of the inevitable diaper rash, which always got really bad before it got better. We finally found a barrier cream that seemed to help, but the rash was so bad we ended up ordering a "special mix of creams" from a pharmacy several towns away. This cream was both magic and affordable.

All the while we still had to manage dilatations. It was a real struggle, however the benefits soon became apparent as a new "normal" set in. There were no more bags so we could hold our child normally, and Leonhard adjusted so quickly it was as if it had never been there.

Things continued to get better as the number of diapers slowly decreased, the constipation management became easier and more normal, and the bum rash disappeared as if it was never there. Leonhard even started to point out when he wanted to go to the toilet. He is the same as all his friends at the creche, wearing diapers just like they do. He is smart, strong and fast, and most people presume he is now normal, oblivious to the potential lifelong struggles he may yet face.

At twenty-two months old, IA was just a normal part of everyday life and my wife was a machine when it came to managing his tummy. The "Doc" performed a short routine follow-up procedure under anaesthesia to check dilatation size. All was normal and so another hurdle was checked-off.

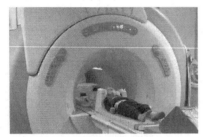

We took Leonhard for a routine MRI to check for secondary issues such as tethered cord syndrome, which came back negative. The "Doc" called me at work, on Leonhard's second birthday, to tell me there were slight indications of spina bifida occulta, a mild malformation of his sacrum which is common in children with high IA but could have been much worse as some can have no sacrum at all.

Leonhard going for a MRI

The best news was that Leonhard was likely, with a 99% probability, to one day have control and continence. It brought tears to my eyes, making every second of the last two years worthwhile. I left the office with hope in my heart to celebrate my perfect son's second birthday.

It is hard not to overthink the problems one might be facing when hearing bad news. It can take your mind to a dark place. But by just taking one day at a time instead, it is easier to cope with the present tasks at hand. The worst outcomes that could have been imagined may never actually happen anyway. We were fortunate to discover that Leonhard's problems were not as complicated as they could have been and he was able to reach the usual milestones, like walking, as most children do. No matter the circumstances, a child is a blessing, and we believe that God will never give us more than we can handle.

We might not know for sure what the future holds, but we know God will continue to be with us every step of the way. I have an exceptional wife and together we will give Leonhard the best opportunities he can possibly have in life. He has shown us what it means to be tough and that there is joy to be found in every situation. He has given me hope. He is perfect in every way, and I love him.

Me with the boys having fun

36. Nazier's Story – Niyah (USA)

This is my son Nazier's story. He was born August 08, 2018.

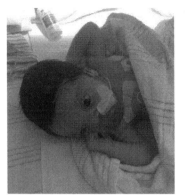

When he was born we were told that he had no anal opening, this was all a surprise to everyone. At the time I was 20 years old and he was my first child, so things were really scary.

He was then transferred to a Hospital in Washington DC where he remained in the NICU for nearly three weeks. That's when I was told by the doctors that there were a list of things going on with Nazier.

I honestly heard nothing but bells ringing while the doctors were talking. He was born with an Imperforate Anus, Tethered Spinal Cord, Hydronephrosis (after surgery to place the stoma his kidneys were okay). He also has a hole in his heart, but that has gotten smaller over time.

Nazier continues to amaze me every day. I didn't know what to think or expect and at times I have felt so lost.

Thankfully, I found out about the support groups on Facebook and I must say they have helped with so much.

Nazier "smokes" and has the biggest heart. I pray that all moms in this situation find light in their paths, it does get better eventually.

37. Arthur's Story – Kirsty (Northern Ireland)

I want to tell everyone Arthur's story. I want to fill every parent with hope and strength to get through this if it should ever happen to them. I don't want this to be a sad story. I want this story to inspire every single person who reads it and for my Arthur to change the world like I always tell him he will. He is one very strong, special little boy who has fought a big battle and I want to tell you all about it.

July 2018 was a month we will never forget. I was due to give birth to my beautiful baby boy, who was prayed for and longed for so very much. After a long labour, he was born absolutely perfect in every way. I felt like my whole world had just been completed and he was everything I had ever dreamed of. A little while later we were taken down to the ward and left to settle in. He had his first bath and first nappy change, but things just weren't right. Arthur didn't have any interest in his milk. Every time he had a bottle he threw it back up again, and violently at that.

Overnight the same thing occurred and by the next morning he looked like he had been on a two-week holiday he was so jaundiced. We were being asked constantly if he'd had any dirty nappies, but as you can imagine he hadn't. It was 30 hours after Arthur was born when the midwife started to question this. She moved his legs like he was cycling a bike and noticed that he had no bum hole, or as we now know it, he had an imperforate anus. He was taken away from me and rushed to have a cannula put in his tiny arm. I was told to ring whoever I needed. I rang his daddy, almost unable to explain what was happening. We had a quick cuddle with him before he was rushed off to surgery, and I still have the picture of the three of us taken right before he went in.

After what felt like forever, we finally got word that he was out of surgery and in intensive care. We could see him. As you can imagine we raced down there, but what we saw when we arrived was a sight I'll never forget. Our tiny baby was covered in tubes, with lights all around him and little glasses covering his eyes. It was the first time we had seen his little body with a colostomy bag, a sight no parent ever wants to see.

As the days passed, he went from strength to strength. After a few hours he was breathing without support, then on day three he was transferred to the city Children's Hospital where he spent the next four days and would return to for his further surgeries. I could never thank the surgeons, nurses and doctors enough for everything they have done for our boy.

On day four I was allowed to feed him his bottle. This was the first time, as he had been fed via a tube before that. I think the first bottle is something so taken for granted when you become a mummy. It was something I waited to do for so long and I was finally able to do it. From then on, he went from strength to strength and on day seven he was discharged with all our stoma bags, special scissors, sprays, gauzes and sticks to prevent breakouts around the stoma.

After numerous tests, Arthur returned to the hospital in September and had his pull through surgery which gave him his designer bum. Unfortunately, they nicked the bladder and a catheter had to be kept in for two weeks. After four days we were discharged and returned again two weeks later. It was then we got his catheter out and were given the rods and jelly to begin dilating his bum hole, to prepare it for when he would get rid of his colostomy bag.

For the next few months, we continued with bag changes and dilatations in preparation for surgery number three.

Throughout all of this however, I was determined that nothing would stop Arthur and he could do anything he wanted. Boy, did he do just that! From five months he was doing his swimming lessons and going under the water. We were told his milestones were likely to be delayed due to his condition but that was far from the truth for Arthur. He never let his colostomy bag stop him from rolling over, crawling, swimming, weaning, sitting up or lying on his belly. At his first-year assessment we were told he was way ahead for his age and we couldn't have been any prouder of him.

In August 2019, Arthur was ready for his colostomy bag reversal. All we had ever known was coming to an end. No more bag changes and no more dilating, but as one journey was ending a new one was just beginning. After around two hours in surgery, he was out. He was in a lot of pain and for the first time in his life he had no colostomy bag. He was on morphine for the pain as well as paracetamol and ibuprofen. He was allowed fluids, but until he'd done his first poo he wasn't allowed any solid food. He had the surgery on the Friday and then did his first poo on the Sunday. As most parents know, it's the best feeling ever to see that first dirty nappy. Monday morning came and he was discharged with all his medicine and bum creams.

Arthur is now just over two years of age. When people knew he was getting his colostomy bag reversed, the most common phrase we were greeted with was "That's great, he's all better now" but that couldn't have been further from the truth. Due to the positioning of Arthur's imperforate anus, he is on two different laxatives. His feeding isn't at its best and he attends a feeding clinic and dietician for that. As you well know, input affects output and as we need Arthur to poop every day this has become very tricky. He is weighed often, either at the hospital or via the community nurse.

I don't want this to scare parents however, or make them wonder if this will be them, as every imperforate anus child is different. We have many obstacles still ahead such as potty training, but as long as we do it a little bit at a time and together, we will get through.

Arthur has an amazing support system from his family and without them we wouldn't have made it through. As I say, Arthur is now just over two. He plays football, goes to swimming lessons, never stops talking, loves animals and soft play (in fact, he went three weeks after surgery being number three - he is a little warrior).

He has an absolute love for life, he laughs at everything and never lets anything get him down.

I want his story to be one of hope and when people read it to smile and think "Wow, what an amazing little boy" just like we all do. From the day he was diagnosed we knew he had an imperforate anus, but he never let it have him.

38. GKHS - Parents of an Amazing IA baby! (Scotland)

In 2019 I gave birth to our baby boy "H" and we were absolutely over the moon. During my pregnancy my growth scans were fine but, due to this being my first baby, I was very anxious and couldn't wait for him to be out and safe in our arms. So, when baby was born and he got the okay from the nurses and doctors, we were blissfully happy!

Very soon however, things started to go downhill. Baby H wouldn't feed, he was foaming at the mouth and vomiting, and it just didn't seem right. We then spent the next forty-eight hours asking every midwife that came into our room why he wasn't eating and was it normal for him to vomit like that? Everyone told me he was fine and that every new baby was different. My partner and I had also noticed that his poo was coming out like a string of spaghetti and we couldn't clean it off his bum properly.

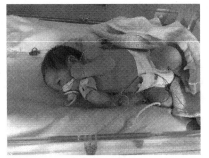

It appeared to us that his anus looked different too, but we couldn't figure out what made it seem so unusual. We asked for the doctor to come check H over a second time and specifically mentioned that his anus didn't look right and we couldn't work out why. We were assured that "baby is fine, his anus is in the right place, so stop worrying and enjoy your new baby".

Well, no thanks to that doctor, less than 24 hours later H was being blue-lighted to the neonatal unit at another hospital, as he was vomiting bile, his abdomen was hugely distended and his other organs were shutting down. His bowel almost perforated.

It wasn't until this point that we learned our son had an imperforate anus. His anus had not formed properly and he had a fistula where his anus should be. For forty-eight hours no one had picked this up and H had rapidly and seriously deteriorated despite our questioning and requests for help. We were absolutely devastated. We didn't know what this condition was. We had never heard of it. We knew nothing of the prognosis, options, complications – we knew nothing at all. It was terrifying. I had got myself so upset at this point because I was scared I was going to go home without a baby.

We got to the new hospital and H was getting taken away for an anoplasty operation to help form an anus ASAP. That heart-wrenching feeling of helplessness as we watched our baby being taken away to theatre will stick with us forever. Those two hours felt like two days.

Luckily, he came out of it okay and we moved on to the recovery part. We spent a further five days in the hospital getting scans and tests to rule out VACTERL, a condition that IA can be associated with. Baby H endured head, neck, and spine scans, blood tests, kidney ultrasounds, an echo of the heart and an ECG, as well as constant monitoring, pain relief, medication and creams.

That entire week, from when I gave birth up to when we got discharged, was hell on earth and really took its toll on us as a family. It was the hardest time I've ever experienced in my life. It felt like forever, but at least we came home as a family. Every year from then on, for that same week of the year, we plan to take time off work, normal routine etc and do something fun as a family. It's our way of trying to turn it all into a positive!

Life for the first few months, though, was very difficult, filled with constant cleaning of the wound, creams and nappy changes. We had anal dilators that had to be used twice a day for nine months. Trying to insert a dilator into a crawling, kicking, screaming baby is not anyone's idea of fun.

There were many tears shed from all participants and I can only be hopeful that, as H was so young, the dilations won't be remembered. H also suffered from severe constipation, which took months of doctors' visits, health visitor appointments and an A+E visit before we got the right medication to help.

Even after all that, there can still be times now where he cries and screams from constipation. He'll go red and become sweaty from pushing and sometimes suppositories are needed. We encourage every bowel movement and celebrate every dirty nappy with him though. There was one point we didn't know if H would have the ability to push, so every unassisted poop is a bonus.

H is now only 18 months old so we are still at the start of our IA journey. We have the odd episode of constipation but it's pretty well controlled. We get annual hospital check-ups and at the moment things seem okay.

We are hopeful that it will continue positively, but we do remain apprehensive. We worry about his future, continence, potty training, explaining IA to him when he is older and teaching him to manage his condition. As parents, we have attended many counselling appointments and are slowly building up to hopefully having another child in the future.

Please advocate for your babies if you feel something isn't right! It has taken this long to come to terms with what happened and accept that maybe it could happen again. It's a scary thought but we'll get through it. We are so thankful that we have our beautiful little boy at home with us and we love him beyond belief. He is such a fun, happy and wild wee thing. His laugh is intoxicating and he lights up the room.

We wouldn't change our IA baby for the world!

39. Five Survival Tips from a Proud New Parent of a Baby with IA (France)

1) Separation:

I was separated from my daughter for four days immediately after birth. I stayed in the maternity ward listening to the sounds of happy new parents with their healthy babies. I had a rough labour and needed a lot of medical attention, before I was able to be discharged and go to the hospital where my daughter was. This separation, during the first surgery was devastating.

Simple things could have made this a little easier for me:

i.) Having the name of the hospital, surgeon and contact details given to me immediately.

ii.) Getting updates by my medical team (or a support team) on my daughter throughout the day/night

iii.) Having someone who had been in my shoes, listen. I was lucky to have discovered the Facebook group and hear words of wisdom from others.

2) Breastfeeding:

As our babies do not eat right away (my daughter had a feeding tube for her first seven weeks), we must start pumping immediately. My surgeon made it clear that breastmilk would be best for her, as she also had 'Colonic Atresia' and breastmilk would be easiest for her to digest. This placed an enormous amount of pressure on me to produce and be successful for my daughter's health. I luckily had a great support system in France for this and was given a schedule which I stuck to religiously. Having a breast-feeding midwife/consultant to help new moms is critical, as these babies benefit so much from a mother's milk. For me this was something I could physically do for my daughter in the first weeks, before our real time together could begin.

3) Family Support:

The family foundation is shaken, and a new foundation needs to slowly be built. From speaking with adults living with IA, and other moms of babies with IA, I quickly recognized the psychological impact that this would have, not only on my daughter, but on our entire family. We as a family, chose to make psychological care as important as physical care. The biggest obstacle for us is time. I found an online counsellor through 'Better help', and I thought, w it would be wonderful if there were a few 'Better Help' counsellors or psychologists available on skype, who are ready to take on IA families, and who understand deeply the short and long-term effects of this diagnosis. With medical costs in certain countries, I realize this is a luxury and a blessing for some. We are lucky enough to live in a country where my daughter's care is free, so we can afford to pay a monthly fee for counselling. At five months in, we are focusing on self-care in our marriage, so when my daughter reaches some rough paths, we are a solid foundation, and we hope to have techniques in place to help teach her to work through the bad, and cope.

4) Community:

For me I have tried to connect with other Moms with IA babies born in 2017 through Facebook. My hope is that we can keep in contact like pen pals, and when our kids are older they will know they are not alone. I hear repeatedly from Adults living with IA that community has been such a powerful and healing part of their journey. I also love speaking with adults living with IA who give their knowledge on how to survive. I remember one man saying he wished his Mom had bought two of everything for school clothes so when he soiled himself, he could change, and no one would notice. This small comment meant the world to me as a mother. Because, like his undoubtedly strong and amazing Mom, I may have never thought of this on my own. I will never walk in my daughter's shoes, and her journey will be different from mine. I need teachers to help me learn.

5) Academic Research:

This may be particular to me, and my coping, but I will read any book, and article and blog with the words 'Imperforate Anus'. I keep everything as a resource for my daughter as she ages. Knowledge makes me feel stronger, better equipped and less overwhelmed.

40. Leo's Story - by Lucy Macbeth (England)

Leo-George Greenhough was born on the 30th August 2017.

The first few days after Leo was born, he was not drinking much milk, and when he did, he could not tolerate it and he would bring it straight back up with green 'vomit and phlegm.'

Five days after he was born, he was seen by his health visitor who noticed he had swollen feet and prescribed antibiotics, but by the time he had finished that course he was back in hospital again and diagnosed with a viral infection.

We noticed early on that he had hardly any poo in his nappy and he would continually scream. The only way we could soothe him was to bathe him, and then he would pass his motions, which were a very greenish colour, and worrying. We took him to the doctors many times as he was poorly, and I was concerned about his bowel issues.

But they kept on telling us it was a reaction to his milk, or because of the medication he was on, as he was always poorly. At one very scary time after being prescribed, he developed a very severe rash, and we were so worried that we had to call an ambulance for him.

He was admitted to hospital and the doctors suspected he potentially may have had sepsis or meningitis, and they did the relevant tests, but thankfully he was given all clear and we were able to take him home.

Not long after, we had to take him back to hospital, as he was once again unwell, but as we were waiting in the waiting room, Leo passed wind which made an almighty sound, and had the doctors and the nurse actually come to ask what the noise was. For myself and Leo's dad it was not a big deal, as this sound was very familiar to us by then.

By this stage, I had been feeling like a complete failure as a mum for months. I knew deep down something was not right with my beautiful little boy as he continued to be poorly. After six months I was still being told that it was either his diet, milk, or the many antibiotics he has been on.

I kept on taking him to hospital and doctor for many months and no-one could figure out why, but I knew something was not right as he struggled to poo and seemed to be always in pain. It was really affecting my mental health at this stage, as it had become relentless and frustrating as Leo was not showing any improvement, and I was not getting any answers.

But on the ninth of April 2018, we once again took Leo to the doctors, and insisted that he get a thorough examination. I explained that his poo was still dark green, and it seemed to get stuck in his 'tunnel', which was my way of describing how he was having trouble passing his poo and I was concerned he was constipated.

Thankfully, the doctor agreed to have a look at his bottom and within a minute of doing a close examination, he turned to me and said the words that I will never forget, 'You need to urgently take Leo to Birmingham Children's Hospital, as he has an issue with his anus which will require immediate surgery.' He went on to explain to me that Leo's bottom was very swollen, just like a baboon, and this is because it was full of poo awaiting to escape.

The doctor then rang the hospital and in a total haze of wondering what was happening, all I heard him say on the phone was, 'I have a young boy here who hasn't got an anus.' He then gave me some paperwork and advised I leave for the hospital asap.

I instantly rang Leo's dad and told him what had happened, and he left work straight away and got his parents to pick us up and we headed straight to the hospital.

Even though I was heartbroken for Leo about what was happening, I actually felt a sense of relief, as finally a doctor had listened to me. After seven months and countless medical appointments, my motherly instincts that there was something wrong with my baby had been vindicated.

Once we got Leo to the hospital, over the next few hours he was seen by many different doctors, surgeons and consultants. As we waited patiently Leo's Dad and I had no understanding of what was really going on or how to process anything. All we knew at that stage was Leo didn't have an anus and emergency surgery.

Finally, we were called into a meeting and advised that Leo would be having surgery the next morning for a condition called 'Imperforate Anus', which neither of us had ever heard of. The doctors explained to us that it is a condition where a baby's anal opening is either missing, too small or in the incorrect position, which should have been identified the day Leo was born. In Leo's case it was advised that he had a very small hole which had the shape of a triangle under his testicles.

They explained that in the surgery Leo would be given a colostomy bag, so his poo would go straight into the bag from his tummy. After a few months, he would have a further surgery to make his anal opening the right size, and then another surgery to remove the bag and allow him to have a functioning anus and be able to poo through his bottom

I stayed with Leo that night and the next morning Leo's dad was going to come in as he was going into the theatre, but unfortunately, he was delayed. I had to go to the theatre with Leo and watch my baby lie on the bed, surrounded by the medical team, as they put him to sleep.

I remember vividly not being able to breathe, my heart slowing, tears flowing down my face and feeling very hot. I had to run out of the room as I needed air and I instantly saw Leo's dad and just totally broke down.

The wait for surgery to be over seemed to go for an eternity, but nothing could prepare us for what would happen next, as we walked into the recovery room and saw Leo lying there. All we wanted was to take away the pain we knew he was enduring.

The next few days after his surgery were a steep learning curve for us, as we learned how to change his bag. We watched every moment of how the nurse would do it and we asked a lot of questions. They were fantastic and showed us how to do the changes, so we could be prepared when we took Leo home.

It meant extra to me, as I had been really letdown by the medical system since Leo had been born, and I still carried a lot of anger and frustration that Leo was not diagnosed for seven months. But I had no time to think about that, as my focus was on Leo and caring for him.

When I was allowed to hold Leo after the surgery, I didn't know how to hold him. I was concerned I would hurt him, as he looked so vulnerable and fragile. I will never forget the moment when the nurse placed him on me, it was such an amazing feeling holding him again, and I instantly fell asleep with him in my arms. It was the best sleep I had had in days.

Later, Leo's dad held him, and Leo was smiling and looked so happy, it was like he had not been through the surgery. It was now our turn to do the bag changes and under the guidance of the nurses we were smashing it. We were then told you are ready to take him home and he only had to have a final consultation with the stoma nurse, who would be seeing Leo for ongoing care.

That stoma nurse was Gail Fitzpatrick, and she has been the most amazing person, not only has she provided absolutely incredible care for our son, but also has become my biggest support network.

She never fails to go above and beyond, and as much as Leo's family and friends know about Leo's issues and have supported us tremendously, it has been hard to talk to people who cannot give us the answers, but Gail has supplied those answers!

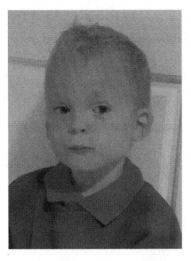

Leo was a little fighter throughout the period of the surgeries, and he carried on like nothing had ever happened to him. He has been so incredible throughout it all, especially when it came to me having to perform the anal dilatations on his new anus, which is such a traumatic experience.

We would not have been able to get through all the difficult years without the support of all of Leo's family, as they have been a pillar of strength and support throughout and have seen how distressing it was for us when Leo was unwell for many years.

Leo is now fighting fit and just like any other child his age, apart from taking meds every day to help him with his everyday life.

I would also like to mention how important it was for me to come across Greg Ryan on Facebook and his ONE in 5000 Foundation pages, which have both been a massive support and comfort to me. It has been so comforting knowing that we are not alone dealing with this rare congenital condition.

It is an incredibly special community. Leo has gained an extra special family which we are so proud he is a part of, and I am passionate about spreading awareness of IA.

Finally, ours is a cautionary tale as well for the medical community. By sharing, it is my hope that no other family will have to endure what we did for seven months, due to a misdiagnosis at birth.

NB: When I notified Leo's health visitor of his diagnosis and surgeries, she was extremely apologetic.

41. I am Sharing Leo with You - Kerry Macbeth, Leo's Aunt (England)

On the day my sister Lucy phoned me and told me that she had just taken Leo to the doctor yet again, but this time was advised they had to take him straight to hospital to have emergency surgery. We didn't know what was happening. All Lucy knew was that he had a problem with his anus.

My husband rushed down to Lucy's house to pick up her daughter Kaizha and her belongings, as she needed to come stay with us while Lucy took Leo to hospital. Lucy kept in touch with us throughout the whole hospital stay and we tried to do research as much as we could on Imperforate Anus. There was not a lot of information, but what we did read was difficult to read and understand and had us all concerned for Leo.

When they eventually came home and were getting to the new normal for him, it was hard to see. We had to have these weekly meet ups with Leo's wonderful Stoma Nurse, Gail, who would help train us to change and empty the bag, so that we could assist and support Lucy. It never got easier to do, but eventually it just became our normal.

There were only certain foods Leo would eat, which made things hard, and he would only tolerate his liquids through a syringe, even when he was offered a bottle. Michael got him to eat cold custard, to get some sort of milk into him. He was able to teach him to squeeze the bottle so the liquid would shoot into his mouth like a syringe, then Leo eventually started drinking more from a bottle.

As time went on and Leo had his second and third operations, he was slowly hitting his milestones. As Lucy had to continue to work, Michael's care and relationship with Leo really was crucial to Leo's wellbeing. As we have our own children it was hard work, but we all got through. Leo has such a wonderful connection with his baby cousin who he dotes on, and who has pretty much been at the same developmental level as him.

Throughout the whole process Leo has been clingy to his mum and the only other person who was able to settle him was his Uncle Michael. Leo is really shy to do things and try new things, but his uncle brings out the best in him and gets him to do things that all the other kids will do naturally.

42. Yasmine's Story – Israa (Saudi Arabia)

Hello everyone, I am Israa from Jordan, although we now live in Saudi Arabia.

My daughter Yasmine who is two years old was born with a low type of anorectal malformation which is called perineal fistula.

She was delivered via c-section and we were discharged from the hospital after four days without any problem. When I changed her diaper for the first time, I thought something was abnormal, as the area between the anus and vagina looked strange as it was thin and red coloured skin.

After one week, we went to the paediatrician for the one-week check-up and I asked the doctor to check it. He said that it was normal and gave me an ointment. We went back home, where I used my phone flashlight to check it again. I was sure there was something wrong.

After one week, we went to another paediatrician who was an older man who after he had checked her said, 'Yes, it's very close to her vagina' and referred us to a paediatric surgeon. Our first paediatric surgeon said that it was an anterior ectopic anus. We were so shocked. What was he talking about? He then advised that we wait for two months to see if the anus would go back to its normal place.

I started googling about it and I kept crying day and night, as I was so desperate for information and felt helpless. I fortunately was able to find an online IA/ARM support group which was very helpful, and I found out so much information which I desperately needed, as well as find people who were very supportive.

As I was not satisfied with the answers, I had received from the first paediatric surgeon and because Yasmine was still having difficulty, we travelled to Jordan to get her examined again. This time she was seen by two surgeons and one of them checked her anus with an anus electric stimulator, and they assured us that there was no need for any surgery.

After six months, she started eating solids and I kept an eye on her to check if she was struggling passing any hard stools, but thankfully she was okay.
However, as a mother I knew she just wasn't right. I made contact with Dr. Andrea Bischoff (Colorado Children's Hospital, USA) by email and she ordered a lot of scans and tests to help us.

With the results of the tests, we went to another surgeon and he did the x-ray for her abdomen and the x-ray showed that her colon was full of stool. I lost my mind and kept thinking how I am going to persuade the surgeons that she needs help.

Then we went to another surgeon and when he was examining her, he said that as she was passing stool, she was good. I asked him to please put your finger here under the hole, and I showed him the exact place where her muscles in her anus were contracting, which I had been noticing for a while.

He agreed with me that she needed surgery, but he did not want to do anything. He said just to wait another two months to book the surgery and to keep her colon full of stool for these two months.

By that stage I was incredibly frustrated, and I refused to wait anymore, so we went to get another surgeon. Thankfully this surgeon performed the surgery within two weeks, and he told us everything had gone well.

We went back home, but she then started to pass stools all the time and we had to change her diaper every five minutes. We lived in the bathroom literally

Then we asked the surgeon to give her laxatives and he refused. That was when I decided to stop listening to these surgeons and listen to my mom's gut and to the Facebook group members. I started giving her laxatives and she began to get better.

But when I looked at her tummy, I saw it was distended all the time, so I asked her surgeon to do an x-ray and he kept on refusing.

I kept looking for a surgeon who was interested in the paediatric colorectal field, but I could not find one in the whole Arab World. Then I contacted an administrator in the IA Facebook group, and she was a big help to me and gave me Greg Ryan's contact details.

I contacted Greg and he is the one who saved my daughter's life. He told me he would make some inquires, as he knew a lot of doctors from around the world and he was hopeful he could find a surgeon in Saudi Arabia for us.

Greg then came back to me and gave me the name of a surgeon in Saudi Arabia who was experienced in anorectal malformation and had trained with Dr Alberto Peña himself.

I thought I was dreaming!! Finally, we are going to be seen by a surgeon who is knowledgeable and interested in IA. Her name is Dr. Jamila Al Maary, and I contacted her immediately and within a week had an appointment with her.

She was very knowledgeable and helpful. Yes, now we have a bowel management program in KSA! She adjusted the laxatives dose for Yasmine and gave us a schedule to fill in with all the details about her bowel movements and with daily x-rays to make sure it was the suitable dose for her.

And now I can contact her if I have any question or problem and she is welcoming us every time. We are so glad to find a surgeon like her in our Arab world and specifically in Saudi Arabia.

A big thanks to our inspirational Greg for the efforts that he made and still does for my daughter and the whole IA community.

43. Faye's Story – Nicole Chamberlen (England)

Faye was born on the 8th May 2018 weighing 5lb 9oz. I had never heard of anyone being born without an anus. but an hour after my little girl had been born that is exactly what we were being told about our baby.

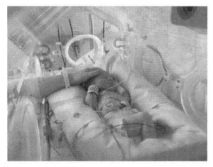

That night is still a blur, while I was taken to theatre to remove my stubborn placenta, Faye was whisked off to the NICU. The following morning my husband and I made our way over to see her and she looked so tiny, but perfect.

During that first day, we met her surgeon and several other paediatric doctors who advised us they had done scans to check for other conditions. They had detected that Faye had a small hole in her heart, but her spine was good.

Her surgeon discussed her condition with us, and that is when we learned about Imperforate Anus for the first time. He explained she would need three surgeries, the first to create a stoma, the second a few months later to create an anus, and then finally the last to reconnect her bowels so that she could start to use her new anus.

The first surgery was scheduled for the very next day, when she was just two days old. I cannot describe how terrifying that was and the wait for that beeper to go off seemed to take forever. The surgery took around three hours and we were advised that all had gone as planned and was successful.

 Instead of taking our baby home, we had to stay and learn how to look after a stoma and how to change the bag. After ten days we were able to take our precious baby home. It can seem so daunting at the start, especially when you have days when the stoma bag just will not stay put, but you soon get into a routine and learn what works for you.

Faye was six months old when we finally got a date for her second surgery, it was scheduled to take five hours, but it actually took eight and a half. After this operation, we were advised that Faye was also born with a vaginal septum that would not be corrected until she is older.

She recovered from this operation really quickly and we got sent home with anal dilators which we had to do twice a day. This was the part I really struggled with and had to get my head round the fact I was doing it for her, not to her!

We had to take her to the hospital every week for her surgeon to see how the dilations were progressing and then plan for her final surgery.

This last surgery was going to be the hardest for Faye and for us too, as everything we had gotten used to over the past year was now about to change. At one year old the reversal surgery took place. I really wish the doctors and nurses had a better understanding of her condition and the implications of having a functioning bowel opening. The aftercare was not really explained fully and unfortunately this caused us to have many issues.

We were sent home after four days with olive oil and Vaseline whilst Faye's skin on her bottom was already starting to break down. Those next couple of weeks were the hardest as she was so uncomfortable and just not herself.

Luckily, we have a fantastic community nurse and team who did lots of research and got us a prescription for ilex and flaminal hydro gel, which worked a treat.

Faye is now two years old, but unfortunately, she is still soiling twenty-four-seven and will need extra measures to keep her clean. At her last appointment her surgeon was discussing anal wash outs so that could be our next step.

Whatever the future holds for Faye I am sure it will be just as amazing as she is, she will continue to cope with the ups and downs of her condition as she has from the day she was born... with a smile

44. Solomon's Story – Kristyn and Jake (USA)

October 22, 2017. A day that has forever changed our lives. After a long and gruelling labour, our beautiful, healthy baby boy Solomon was finally here. As with any new parents, my husband and I began navigating the world of diaper changes, breastfeeding and figuring out how to be a Mom and Dad. It felt as though our life was complete.

The nurses would come in often, asking if he had had his first bowel movement yet and did not seem concerned that he had not. They responded by saying sometimes babies are stubborn and they do not get worried until after they are twenty-four hours old. Fast forward to two am, Solomon was now twenty-four hours old and I was awoken by a nurse asking if he had finally pooped. Since he had not, she said that she would try to stimulate him with the thermometer, to see if that could get him to go. As I was anxiously watching her, she looked confused and remarked that the thermometer would not go in.

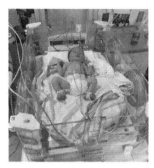 I frantically woke up my husband, telling him they were going to get a doctor and we began to panic, knowing something was wrong. The doctor came in and examined him and then had to call the on call paediatric surgeon. At this point, there were multiple doctors and nurses all hovering around our baby. The surgeon began to examine him and informed us he would most likely need to have surgery tomorrow and be given a colostomy. We were in complete shock. A colostomy? What do you mean? At every scan and every doctor's appointment he was completely healthy.

At this point, all I could do was cry and fall into the arms of my husband, who was trying to comfort me. The surgeon took a dilator and was able to 'pop' a membrane that had been blocking his anus. I have never seen so much poop in my entire life, let alone coming out of a seven-pound baby.

The next morning a team of doctors came in and informed us he would have to be taken to the NICU for more tests. We were sleep deprived, confused, worried, heartbroken and had no time to process any of our feelings. His first test was an echocardiogram on his heart, and this took the longest. My husband had gone with him. because I had been pumping when they took him away for the test. It felt like they were gone for an eternity. I had just given birth and now my baby was away from me and I had no idea if he was scared or aware what was happening in his brand-new world.

The next tests were ultrasounds and X-rays of his kidneys, bladder and spine. We were not allowed in the room and had to wait in the hall, which felt like we were miles away. He was crying and hooked up to all kinds of wires and monitors and we could not do anything to comfort him. At the same time, the head surgeon was telling us that our son had what was called, Imperforate Anus. Imperforate what?

We had no idea what he was talking about, as neither of us had ever heard of such a thing. He said that there are often other issues associated with the condition and they had to do something called a VACTERL work up, which tests for: vertebral defects, anal atresia, cardia defects, trachea-esophageal fistula, renal abnormalities, and limb abnormalities.

To say we were in shock was an understatement. When you go for nine months having ultrasounds and scans that are normal, to a baby in the NICU with something wrong, is unimaginable and so difficult to process. We waited in agony for the test results and began researching on our phones what exactly Imperforate Anus was. We started learning that more times than not, babies born with Imperforate Anus have other issues associated with the condition and our hearts sank. We also learned that Imperforate Anus is a rare birth defect that only affects 1 in 5,000 people. That is only a 0.0002 percent chance that this occurs.

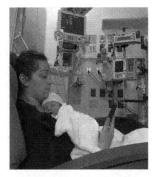

Finally, the results were in. Every single test came back normal! The surgeon could not believe it and said Solomon was so lucky to have nothing else associated with his Imperforate Anus. At this point he also started to discuss what the future would look like for him. Many times, the anus can be completely absent and luckily since he had a formed anus, the surgeon stated he did not need a colostomy. At this moment I thought we were out of the woods, but little did I know we still had a long road ahead.

He said his anus was smaller than normal and that he would need surgery around three months old and we would need to start dilations. Dilations. To this day, I do not even like to utter the word. He explained we needed to stretch the anus with dilators to help make it bigger and easier for him to poop. He showed us how to complete this and that we needed to start with three sizes, twice a day. I felt my heart sink again into my stomach and could not help but cry. I could not stop crying and could not understand why this was happening. The surgeons made sure we knew how to do the dilations correctly, and soon after, we were sent home. Every time we had to complete the dilations my heart broke into a million pieces. Solomon would cry as we tried to comfort him, and I would have to hold back my tears so that I could try to be strong for him. Afterward I would scoop him up, hold him close and profusely apologize that we had to do this.

There were days I was so furious that this had happened to him, and I was worried we were going to scar him emotionally for life, since he could not understand why this was happening. This process lasted for eight long months. I will never forget the moment at the appointment when the surgeon said we could finally stop doing dilations. I remember asking, 'For good?!' as I tried to hold back my tears, but this time they were happy tears filled with joy.

When Solomon was just shy of three months old, we had to take him in for his anoplasty surgery. I remember us in the waiting room, already so nervous to have our couple of months old baby going under anaesthesia for surgery, they were running behind, he was hungry, and we were ready to have this behind us. There was one anaesthesiologist I will never forget for the rest of my life. He came in to take Solomon away and could see how frightened and worried we were. Solomon had never left our side. He scooped Solomon into his arms, instead of wheeling him in the crib, so that he could comfort him while taking him back into the operating room. He probably has no idea how much peace he gave us on such a stressful day. We were given a pager and received updates throughout the surgery, which seemed to take all day. The surgeon pulled us aside and stated everything went great, that they had to reposition and make his anus bigger and that they tested his muscles and they seemed to have good function.

One of the other unknowns of Imperforate Anus is whether the child will have the feeling to know when they have to poop. I do not think we could have rushed faster back to our baby, who was still so groggy and sedated, and we lifted him up immediately. We were lucky as he only required this one surgery, because often times multiple surgeries are needed. On our way out we ran into our amazing anaesthesiologist and I asked him for a hug, and he gave me the biggest, tightest hug that I had never needed more.

Solomon faced the most hurdles over the first year and a half of his life. When we started introducing him to solids, he had been exclusively breastfed until this point and needed no meds to help him poop. The first problem was around seven months and he went five days without pooping. We did not know at that time that it is imperative that people with IA have a bowel movement every day to prevent back-ups, which can cause major issues like impaction. This was the start of numerous X-rays a year to see if he is staying cleaned out and the start of nightly Senna (a natural laxative to help people poop).

Every person with IA has different control and function of their bowels, so it is only by trial and error that you find a dose that works. For the most part Senna was working great to help push the poop out, until we had our first experience with Senna burn. This is something that can happen when the poop becomes so acidic it actually burned his little bum, until it blistered. This happened to him a couple of times and we ended up needing to add fibre powder, twice a day, to help bulk his poop and prevent this from happening again. After a few months of good visits with the surgeon and clear x-rays, we ran into our next hiccup.

We heard the dreaded words, that he had gotten backed up, and we needed to complete enemas twice daily for a week to make sure he was cleaned out, before upping his Senna dose. It brought me right back to our time of doing dilations and wondering if he was going to understand or be scared. Solomon was so brave and handled it so well, especially for someone who was not yet two years old at the time.

Today, our son has just turned three years old and is thriving, happy, bright, brave and so resilient. In his short life, he has faced more obstacles than most people I know, and he has no idea how strong he is.

He inspires us daily with how well he handles doctor appointments, tests and daily medications. He has been doing so well, having clean x-rays and managing his IA. What many do not understand, is that this is an everyday battle for people with Imperforate Anus. The course of action can change, you need to constantly monitor your bowel movements, making sure they are the right consistency and amount, so you do not risk getting backed up.

With our son being so little, we also worry about him feeling alone with this, as he gets older and understands more about it.

We worry if he will come into contact with misinformed, ignorant people, as we have, who will not be understanding or tolerant of his congenital condition.

Our wish is for the world to be educated on Imperforate Anus so those who suffer from it can get proper treatment, have the best support systems and do not have to feel alone.

45. Luke's Story – Bianca (Luxembourg)

At 2.20pm on July 31st, 2017, I gave birth to my little boy named Luke.

It was a very easy pregnancy without any indication that there might be something wrong with him.. After he was born everything seemed fine, that was, until around ten pm that evening. When a nurse came to check his temperature and she noticed that Luke did not have an anal opening.

She called the paediatrician, who then talked to a doctor from the neonatal unit from the children's hospital and they decided that Luke would be transferred the next day to the children's hospital.

When we arrived at the hospital, I was told that Luke was born with thirteen pairs of ribs, they mentioned Tethered Cord, a 4mm Ventricular Septal Defect (VSD) and Imperforate Anus.

They already had everything prepared for the colostomy surgery and we spent the next eight days in the neonatal unit before going home. When Luke was about four months old, he had his PSARP surgery which took about six hours. Fortunately, it was a very easy recovery and after a four-day hospital stay we were released.

Two weeks after the PSARP surgery we started dilatations once a week. Honestly, I am very happy that they were always done by one of our surgeons, because from the very beginning Luke did not support them and he always cried and fought against it.

I always felt bad after the dilatations because I had to hold him so that the surgeon was able to perform them. It was so difficult for me, as I felt like I was contributing to my son's pain.

Luke with his Great-Grandma

When Luke was six months old he had his stoma reversal and had an easy recovery, but he did suffer from horrible diaper rash and he was also still having the dilatations.

By that stage they had gone from once a week, to every other week, and then once a month. The diaper rash was so bad that Luke started bleeding and I tried everything, but nothing worked.

Then I remembered that I had once read a post from another IA mother that corn starch would work, and it worked miracles. After three days the diaper rash was gone.

When Luke was about a year old his VSD had closed on its own. Then at eighteen months Luke had to have another surgery because he had a rectal prolapse and his neo anus had narrowed.

Fast forward to five am on the 22nd May 2020 when Luke woke me up saying to me, 'Momma my tummy is aching.' I answered, 'Come here, I'll give you a massage' and then my not yet three-year-old, IA son said, 'No momma I have to go to the toilet, I have to pee and poo.' It was such a wonderful moment for us, after everything he had been through.

Luke now does not need enemas, medicine or any other sort of bowel management. I just watch what he eats and honestly, he can eat everything and is a happy little boy who is going to preschool. He knows his numbers up to twenty, some letters of the alphabet and we could not be prouder of him.

46. VACTERL: A Mother's Perspective – Anne Elizabeth (USA)

I had never visited a hospital or ER before my husband and I decided to have children. My first hospital stay was for a D&C (Dilation and Curettage) when we lost our first child. My second was for the delivery of my son.

My pregnancy was fairly routine, except for some panic-inducing bleeding. After a visit to my OB-GYN and her confirmation of my son's heartbeat, she indicated I should not be worried. But having a previous miscarriage meant a little more anxiety for this mama. I was pregnant during a hot and humid summer, and major conditions included heartburn and swollen feet. My labour and delivery were textbook, besides being four weeks before my due date. My labour progressed naturally, and I delivered my son naturally. Once he was born, however, our journey truly started.

We had no indication of any complications pre-birth. Only two ultrasounds were done, one at eight weeks and one at twenty weeks, and no issues were detected. When he was born, though, the doctor and nurses knew right away something was abnormal. I was unable to hear or understand, as my placenta did not detach as it should, and I was losing a lot of blood. The attending doctor finally was able to dispel the placenta. I was weak and could not walk on my own for many hours after.

My son was whisked to the NICU, where he was hooked up to wires and monitors. I was not able to see him for hours after he was born. My husband and I were able to hold him for about half an hour before the survival flight crew came and took him away in their helicopter. Our hospital was not equipped to handle his issues, so he was flown to a bigger hospital. We made the agonizing decision to have my husband stay with me, so that I could leave when discharged, instead of him going with our son. The next day, we left the hospital emptyhanded, and drove to our new home for the next two and a half weeks.

My lack of medical experience was immediately apparent. I had no idea how to be a mother, nor how to handle a child with higher medical needs. I was trying to figure out pumping (since he was so premature, they had to measure his intake) and also wrap my mind around this new acronym I had never heard of: VACTERL. The doctors seemed unsure of the diagnosis at first. My son had an imperforate anus and required a colostomy procedure when he was eighteen hours old. We were not even there when they first took him to the OR, because I was not yet discharged from our original hospital. He also had a solitary kidney, which led to the VACTERL diagnosis.

Because of his diagnosis, we had to see more doctors than I could count during our stay. They had to rule out every other possible complication that came with VACTERL. We were blessed in that almost everything else was considered normal (he does have an innocent heart murmur but that was cleared by cardiology). Our son is technically vActeRl, with only anal and renal abnormalities.

We almost lost him on his second night on earth. The nurses who attended our little boy were certainly angels. They were calm, collected, and sure of their steps. They relegated us to the corner of the room while the Code Blue was activated, and all the available nurses in the NICU rushed in to help. I cannot accurately describe the feeling of helplessness as you sit in the corner and medical professionals surround your day-old son, doing their best to help him breathe again. After a few seconds, but what felt like ten years, he did. He has never had a problem with his lungs, before or after that moment.

Our little man was the giant on the NICU floor, born 6 lbs. 1 oz. Seeing the other children, so tiny, with so many more machines, wires, monitors, and tests, was a true shock and gave me some perspective. Watching the other parents' haggard faces and tired eyes as they sat with and encouraged their little babies to fight for life, is a truly humbling experience. The tears cried, both happy and sad, soaked the floor with both sorrow and hope. Sorrow for limitations on functionality (physical, mental, or both), lost time, and the dreams and expectations of 'normal' shattered; hope for successful surgeries, developmental progress, and eventually going home.

I had planned on staying home after his birth, but now I had no choice. My son had a colostomy bag, was on antibiotics daily to prevent infections, and needed special care. I grew to hate those bags. Sometimes we would change four in an hour because we just could not get a good seal. I cried while using the scissors to cut the holes for his colostomy, tears blurring my vision as I questioned again and again why us? Why my son?

One time our medical supplies were not delivered in time. The colostomy was high, so a diaper would not cover it. I made do with some samples, but my poor son's skin was so red and irritated by the time the supplies arrived one night after eight pm. I did not care; I needed to help my son feel better.

My role as advocate and warrior blossomed as I learned how to communicate with nurses and doctors (different methods for each, for optimum effectiveness). I researched the condition, what causes it (nothing), how to prevent it (you cannot), and treatment options in the future. I went to all follow up visits and surgeries, watching as the doctors and anaesthesiologists took my son away from me to an OR where I was not allowed. I sat in the lobby/waiting area for over twelve hours during reconstruction surgery, desperately watching the surgery update screen.

If you want to know what strength looks like, visit the lobby of a children's hospital.

I despaired as my son stopped gaining weight, despite eating the same amount. I took him to weekly weigh ins at the paediatrician for months, before they finally decided he was on his own growth curve. I stuck a metal rod up his newly formed anus daily so it would not close up. It was easier when he was little; once he grew bigger and stronger, it took a team of us to hold him down to perform dilations. (I was grateful sometimes our hospital is a university hospital, so we had medical students to help keep him still during exams.)

I knew when we decided to have children that there would be a lot of poop talk, but I had not bargained for how much!

In my son's first year of life, he spent twenty-eight days in the hospital, had seven surgeries, and attended thirty additional doctor's appointments. In the years since, those numbers have decreased. Now, he is four years old, and we are working on potty training. He takes MiraLAX, fibre, and Senna daily, and poops almost every time he goes to the bathroom. But we are seeing progress. He has a functioning anus. I am hopeful he will progress and have a remarkably close-to-normal life.

I know there will be other unique challenges as he grows. We do not know if he will have any continence, sexual, or other challenges related to his condition. We will have to take those as they come and continue to draw on God's strength. At the end of the day, my little boy walks and talks and laughs and drives us crazy like most toddlers. He has a few extra challenges, but so far, he has proven there is nothing he cannot handle. He is truly my superhero.

I will never forget the moments of panic, fear, relief, grace, and utter awe at my son's courage and resilience. Every day I am amazed God chose me to be his mama. This is not my journey, it is his. But I hope as he grows, I can provide some perspective for him on events he will not remember. And I pray he will always have the confidence that I will be with him, will fight for him, and will support him through it all.

This is not what we signed up for. But if this is what needs to happen for my son to light up our lives, it is worth it every time.

47. Hamish's Story – Marjory (Scotland)

We had no idea that Hamish had any health issues when he was born. I did not realise that the midwife had noticed straight away that something was wrong. Thankfully, I was given the chance to give him a wee feed and he had a lovely snuggle and snooze before the head midwife came in to do another check. They acted as if this was normal, so I had no idea anything was wrong. They introduced the idea that something was different and said that there was a wee dimple in his bum and they would get a Paediatric Nurse in to check.

I still was blissfully unaware and managed to have a shower while he slept and his daddy watched him. We had organised for his big sister Veronica to come up to see him with her cousins. Then it all got very scary, the nurse came in and said that something was wrong with his bum and that she needed to run as it was the weekend. The doctor that needed to check him was about to leave and she left me with the midwife. I then had to call my sister to say not to bring Veronica up as she was only three and we did not want her to be scared. I could not get through and had to leave a voicemail saying what was happening.

The consultant then came in and I will remember the feeling of sheer terror that my perfect wee bundle was going to die, as he explained to me that he did not have an anus. It is not just the Imperforate Anus; it is also the news that this prognosis does not usually come on its own. They had to tell me about all the health issues they would be checking for. My other memory of this, is that my sister was desperately trying to get through on my phone and as it was across the room I could not answer it. Everything was out of my control. My sister is a midwife in the hospital and it was her team that was dealing with Hamish's birth, which must have made it very difficult for them, as they had all been excited about her niece or nephew being born with them.

Again, the team were amazing and gave us ten minutes to have another cuddle before they took him to intensive care. I felt a lot of guilt as my partner went to speak to my sister on the phone and Hamish was taken away before he got back.

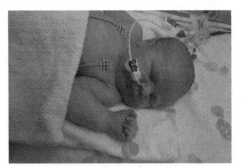
Our 1st photo of Hamish

We then had a frantic hour and a half as my partner sat with Hamish once he was settled and I had to try and get myself discharged so I could go in the ambulance with him when he was transferred.

The staff kept us calm until we left on our journey to a Children's Hospital in Glasgow.

When we arrived, Hamish was taken immediately for tests and my partner was with me by the time the doctors came back, to say that he needed a colostomy immediately and that the surgeon was on his way.

We were completely in shock with all this information. It was comforting that they would check his major organs while operating to see if there were any other obvious issues. Again, they were kind and gave us a wee half hour with him and I was allowed to go down to theatre with him. It is absolutely gut wrenching to watch your brand-new baby being wheeled away and knowing that he is so desperately ill that this is your only option.

We had a horrible wait, but fortunately the surgeon phoned to say that all his organs seemed ok and they would make the stomas and have him back with us ASAP. I was desperate to get back to my baby and it was amazing when we were finally allowed to see him. I was exhausted after giving birth (he was 10lb 13oz) but I wanted to stay with him and after an hour or so I went to the relatives room where we stayed for two days.

Over the next two weeks we felt so lucky because every test came back clear. He did not even have a fistula between his bowel and bladder. What seemed to be the worst thing that could happen very quickly became a blessing, as we were surrounded by babies that were always going to have health issues or had huge battles ahead of them and my wee boy just kept going from strength to strength. I found the colostomy care quite easy; the nurses were very good at letting me watch them and answered my questions and let me ease into the care. I started by emptying the bag of air, then faeces and then I was talked through the colostomy bag application and stoma care by Maggi the fabulous stoma nurse. I had nurses watch me for the first few times to gain confidence and then it started to become a new normal. It soon became just as routine as nappy changing had been with Veronica. A bit more preparation and fiddly but it was the wonderful thing that kept my wee boy alive and thriving.

Once home it was easy as the stoma nurse, the district nurses and the health visitors were always there for us and kept a close eye on him. The only drama we had was with his inactive stoma/mucous fistula. I woke one day and he was passing a bloody foul-smelling discharge so I took him to A&E. They could not find any cause for alarm and thought that maybe he had a virus and this was his body reacting to it.

However, over the next ten days it became worse and every second day the same thing would happen. Luckily, Maggi listened to me and we were able to get him back into hospital for IV antibiotics and they taught me how to flush it out with a catheter and saline. It was scary the first time but again became routine before the first week was out.

PSARP surgery

I was expecting him to really suffer after his PSARP, but he treated it like a walk in the park. He was moving about the next day and was even allowed to go home that night. My wee Hamish was proving to be a true warrior. He was a wee trouper with his anal dilations that we did every day, a couple of weeks post-surgery and after a quick cuddle each time he would be off playing. This was probably the hardest time for me because as a mummy the last thing I wanted to do was distress my child, but in the back of my head I was able to repeat to myself that this was the best thing for him. I was helping him to a life where hopefully he would be able to poo on his own, with no complications.

Unfortunately, the Coronavirus lockdown happened the week he was ready for his reversal, which meant that we continued with the dilations having no idea when the end would happen. The stoma nurse was an amazing comfort at this point and so were all the other medical staff who helped us. Knowing that we could chat with them was a godsend and I will always be so grateful for them making our journey so much easier.

Reversal surgery

Thankfully, we did not have to wait too long for his reversal. We went in on the Sunday and Hamish had his surgery first thing on the Monday. I felt so thankful that I was able to be with him while his anaesthetic was administered, the NHS staff really tried their best to make the impact of COVID-19 as small as possible.

Hamish was in pain the next day, so he had an extra day of morphine, which meant an extra day on fluids, as his appetite was not t great. But he was happy as long as he could have a cuddle.

Amazingly he was home on the Thursday (after running about the ward playing football) and it blew my mind that we could have a lovely walk on the Saturday at a local park. I had to keep reminding myself that he had just undergone major surgery, as he was back to normal, and even better, was pooing away.

We were the fortunate ones that Hamish's skin on his bottom coped very well post-surgery and he did not have any redness or sores. I had been prepping his skin by rubbing poo on it and leaving it for as long as possible for two weeks pre-surgery, but ever since he has been a baby, every few weeks I would rub poo on his bum for fifteen minutes or so to make sure it would not hurt. I don't know if it made a difference, but I was still breastfeeding him and maybe that also helped to make his poo less irritating to his skin.

Now two months on he is absolutely fantastic. He squats to poo, lets me know that he has pumped or pooed and is so happy. His wee scar on his side healed well and hopefully for him it will all be a story that I tell him. However, this experience has taught me that we will deal with anything that life throws at us. He is a wee fighter that will not let anything get him down and I will support and love him every day.

The other important thing in all this, is family and friends. My sister embraced his diagnosis straight away, did some research and when she came to see him in hospital had wee colostomy bag covers, a fantastic wee Babygro with 'Poo? It's in the bag' on it. He was a wee Star Wars baby born on May the fourth so he had a cracking nickname of Stoma Trooper. Between my partner and my family, his sister Veronica was well looked after so I could concentrate on him for the first few weeks.

His big sister Veronica has always been involved in his care. We explained what was happening and why he was ill in hospital and she has embraced helping look after her wee brother.

Holding his hands while I changed his bag (he loved a good scratch at his stomas if given half the chance), she chatted and sang to him during his dilations and was always there to visit him in hospital and love him all the time.

If you have other kids include them, I think it really helped Veronica to be a part of Hamish's care. I am so glad that we were open about his condition. I have received nothing but love, support and compassion from everyone who has known Hamish.

Hamish and Veronica

48. Our Story – S.M. (Iraq)

My name is S.M. and I want to share my daughter's story who was born with Anorectal Malformation (cloaca). She is now two and a half and I am married with another daughter who is eight and we are from Iraq - Kurdistan region.

I want to start with my pregnancy which was a healthy pregnancy and everything was showing normal until I reached the seventh month, when my doctor told me that her abdominal circumference was showing it was bigger than her age. I went and had ultrasounds almost every week and it was always the same. It was then they said she might have imperforate anus, which was not a familiar word to me until that time and I was praying for a miracle to happen.

They decided to do a C-section for me at the thirty-eighth week of pregnancy. That day I was so excited that I was going to see my baby for the first time and nervous, at the same time, as I did not know what was going to happen. When she was born they checked her and I asked my doctor what was going on and she said, 'We were right, she has an imperforate anus and they have to take her to another hospital which has an NICU'. It was such a hard moment, and I cannot actually describe my feelings at that time. They brought her to me, I kissed her and she was the most adorable baby girl ever.

She stayed at the NICU for three days and it was the most difficult three days of my life, because I could not go to see her. She had her colostomy done one day after she was born. It was such a relief when the doctor said that I could finally see her and I totally forgot about my surgery pain when I heard that. I went to the hospital and held my baby for the first time and nursed her, it was the most beautiful feeling in the world. We took her home two days after her surgery.

The first two weeks I could not clean her at all, so my mom always did it for her. Anytime she started cleaning her, I started crying because the whole thing was new and strange to me. Before my daughter was born, I had never heard of a colostomy or anorectal malformation. As we live in Iraqi Kurdistan, colostomy bags for babies are not available here, but we managed it with two diapers and we also put a clean cotton cloth on the colostomy area.

After two weeks I decided that I had to be strong for my baby girl, who was depending on me, because I knew being a weak, crying mom did not help her at all. I had to stand strong for her so she could take strength from me. Yes, it is true that sometimes I was screaming from inside, but I had to show myself as strong. I will never forget those nights when my husband and I cried, knowing nothing about what was going to happen tomorrow, or the day after.

I have to mention that due to the economic and political crisis in the Kurdistan region of Iraq, hospital services are affected greatly, and our experience was not a pleasant one. It would be difficult for people to understand, unless you have experienced it.

I witnessed some very distressing incidents while at the hospital, due to this situation. On one occasion the parents of babies in NICU were told to take their babies home due to the lack of staff. It was incredibly challenging and made me feel like I needed to seek alternative care for my daughter, as she required further treatment.

The day that my daughter had her colostomy surgery there were not any heaters working in the hospital (it was February), because there was no gas for it and as I have already said, colostomy bags for babies are not available.

Generally, when you go to a government hospital the care and treatment is not at the same level as a private hospital, due to the lack of staffing and equipment. Even then, there are still issues in private hospitals.

My reason for explaining this, is when you have a child with a health issue, it is really tough for parents and as you can imagine, living in a country like this, makes it worse.

After she came home from hospital, we decided that we would not let her next surgeries be done in Iraq. We did a lot of research and we found a good hospital in Dusseldorf, Germany. So, we started the process to take her there and we eventually got confirmation from the hospital that they would treat our daughter and they sent an invitation for the four of us.

But after we applied for the visa, we were contacted by the German embassy, who informed us that only one of the parents and the baby could be approved for a visa. It was a tough decision we had to make because we did not want to risk having her next surgery, which was her PSARP done in Iraq. If we decided to take her to Germany, I was the only one who could go with her.

My oldest daughter was only six years old at the time and she had never been away from me. It was very distressing for my husband, as well, because he did not want to be thousands of miles away from us when our daughter was having such a big surgery. But in the end, we decided the most important thing was our baby's health.

When she was four months old, I travelled with her to Germany. I cannot describe that early morning before I left for the airport, when I kissed my oldest daughter goodbye while she was sleeping. I felt like I could not breathe and I could not stop crying.

We arrived in Düsseldorf, Germany safely and everything went to plan for the next five days, leading up to her PSARP surgery. Despite all of my sadness, the treatment and behaviour of the hospital staff and her surgeon in Dusseldorf was very nice and they made me feel at home among family. I saw a big difference compared to what was available in my own country.

On the day of her surgery, they took her to the surgery room at seven am, but the surgeon came out to me after two to three hours to tell me that the surgery plan had changed. She told me that they would have to do the PSARP and the colostomy closure, at the same time, due to complications they had found. It then got to eight hours since they had started, and I began to doubt what they were telling me. The doctors kept updating me and saying it was going along fine. I was sitting all alone on the floor, in front of the surgery room, convinced that she had died and that they were lying to me.

As my husband was so worried about the surgery, I told him that it was supposed to start at four pm (nine hours after it had started). He was contacting me for updates and because I did not want to add to his worries, I had to lie to him and pretend everything was fine, which made it even harder for me.

Finally, after thirteen hours, the surgeon came out to tell me that her surgery was over and that she had come through it well. What an incredible relief and I immediately let my husband know the good news.

We stayed in hospital for fifteen days and she received very good care. We then had to stay for another three months in Germany, so that she could be seen weekly by her surgeon, until it was decided that she was fine and we could go home.

It is important to say that the ARM community (there are some groups in Facebook) supported me so well during these three months, when I was alone in Germany. I am thankful to Greg Ryan, as he connected me with a mother in Germany, who I could talk to and he supported me a lot and introduced me to many parents online with ARM kids. Talking with them made me feel strong and I felt like I was not alone.

Those three months saved my baby's life and made her healthier but at the same time, it impacted negatively on my oldest daughter. It does not matter how much she loves her sister and how much she wanted her to get well, she still feels that I do not love her as much as her little sister because I left her for that long time.

She does not understand what a visa is and why they did not give one to her. I tried to explain it to her in a simple way by telling her, 'Honey, I cannot take you with me because there are only two seats left in the plane and your sister needs to have surgery, so I have to take her.' Even now, whenever we talk about travelling, she says, 'Is there a seat for me on the plane? 'which breaks my heart.

After we came back to Iraq, I started work again, and my baby was better than before. We decided that we should hire a nanny for her, because we did not want to take her to a nursery school, because she needed good care, especially for cleaning time and diaper change and she cannot get that special care in nursery schools.

My daughter is fine now thank God, but being born with ARM needs regular medical care and checks, which we cannot get, in the way we should, in Iraq. So, we are thinking of leaving here and moving to a country where she can get the care she deserves. It is not easy but we do our best just to provide a better life for her.

There is an important thing I have to talk about. Since I am from an eastern society, it is very hard to share my daughter's story, as people's attitudes here are so strange. That is why I do not share much information regarding her health with anyone, and if someone asks, I say she is fine and everything is normal now.

A girl who has a health issue does not have an easy future to look forward to in this country. When people talk about it they show pity for her and this can lead to her having a weak and a broken personality (I have seen many examples like that), but this is not what we want for our child and that is why we want to take her away from this society.

We want to give her a good life and a bright future. We want to prove that she is as normal as any other child. God created her with a health issue, but at the same time, he gave her many blessings. At the end I want to say I am so thankful and grateful to have her in my life, despites the ups and downs we have been through.

She is so valuable to me. It is because of her, I am a stronger person. I am very proud of myself, because when she was born, I told myself that I have two choices, either I choose to be a weak, collapsed person, who cries all the time and makes her child's life worse, or I stand strong and steady and give strength to my child. I wanted her to feel that she is no different from any other person. Luckily I made the second choice and I am so proud of that!

I want to send a message to every mom who has a child like mine, or any other health issue. You are strong and you are blessed. God asked you to go through this because he knew you could get through it. Your baby is the best teacher for your life as s\he teaches you to be strong and independent S\he helps you find your real self, discover who your real friends are, who really loves you and who supports you during hard times.

49. D's and My Story – Katie (England)

My name is Katie, and I gave birth to my beautiful son D in June 2017. He arrived in the world three weeks early, via emergency caesarean section, due to me developing pre-eclampsia and becoming unwell, very quickly. It was scary but I knew I was in good hands and would soon be holding my healthy baby boy.

Within 24 hours of being admitted I was able to hold and feed my newborn D. He was simply perfect. He latched on immediately and fed from the breast for about 30 minutes. It was incredible as I had really struggled to feed his big sister for the first few days, so nothing was going to stop me this time!

D was checked over and placed in a 'hot cot' as he was struggling to keep his temperature up, but I was not concerned. The focus was on my health, as I was still seriously unwell. I knew that D was okay, and he had his daddy with him to keep him company, while I tried to rest. We stayed in the delivery suite for 24 hours while I was medicated and then moved onto the maternity ward where luckily, we had a side room, so it was just the three of us.

D's big sister came to visit that evening with my parents and sisters, and we had a lovely hour together, taking photos and all having squishy new baby cuddles. All the while, I knew that something was not right with D. He was refusing feeds and was barely making noises or opening his eyes.

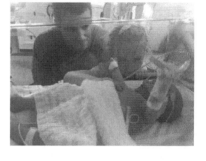

I kept wondering and asking if things were ok and kept being reassured that it was normal for c-section babies to take longer to 'wake up' due to the drugs administered and the lack of being squeezed out of the birth canal. We tried to feed him with syringes, bottles and the breast but he just clenched his little mouth shut. I was so tired and starting to really worry. I just wanted to take him home, but without him pooing and me still feeling unwell it was not looking possible.

Later that night I heard D straining and got really excited thinking that he was doing a poo and we would be able to go home the next day! But to my horror, upon looking inside his nappy, he did not have a bum.

He was taken from me and wheeled down to the Special Care Baby Unit where he would stay until the next morning and be taken via a special neonatal ambulance to the Neonatal Intensive Care Unit in Bristol, more than fifty miles away from me.

By the time he got to Bristol his rectum had perforated and he was critically sick. They had taken so long to transfer him that his tiny tummy just could not handle it any longer. He was rushed to theatre for emergency surgery and he had a stoma created.

I was stuck in Swindon, as I was too poorly to travel, according to the private transport used by the hospital. Lucky for me my mum is a midwife and so she discharged me. She wheeled me down to the car and we raced to Bristol to be by his side. I did not know if he was going to survive; it was the worst moment of my life.

That being said, D is now three years old and he is healthy and happy. He goes to pre-school and has lots of friends, he loves Lego, singing and cars and is an absolute whirlwind of a boy!

Three years passed and I still could not seem to move on from the first two weeks of D's life, spent in the NICU. Every night I would lay in bed, struggling to breathe, replaying moments of those days over and over in my head. I decided I could not carry on like this anymore.

I had been in and out of mental health care since he was born and felt as though nothing, or nobody could help me. I was on the highest dose of two different types of anti-depressants and felt like I was spiralling out of control.

Until one day I referred myself to a self-help scheme and was referred to Oxford University for a research trial of online PTSD therapy. It was daunting starting something that is brand new, not knowing if it would work or if I would be wasting twelve weeks of my life!

But actually, it was life changing. I was assigned a therapist called Alice, who would become my rock, my voice of reason, and who never made me feel like I was crazy or losing the plot! She taught me to love myself again and that I had not done anything wrong. I focussed on the 'hotspots' of the trauma – the most frequent memories – and broke them down piece by piece, filling in the gaps and ending them with positive thoughts. I was learning to process the trauma and three years later the puzzle was beginning to be complete and I was not fixating on the same few moments.

I re-wrote my story and after every negative experience I explained to myself why it happened and what the outcome was, I filled my traumatic two weeks with hope and positivity.

I reclaimed my life and was able to think about our time in hospital without suffocating, without fear but with gratitude and pride. I even revisited the hospital during a follow up appointment. Whilst there I recorded videos of D running, hopping, singing, and holding my hand, all of the things we could not do when he was born.

I was learning to replace the old, traumatic memories with new, fun, exciting memories. It was not easy and I had to face a lot of triggers, but I knew that I needed to do this, not just for me, but for D, his siblings and my husband.

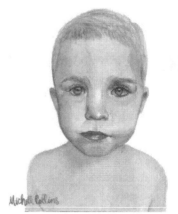

Portrait by Michelle Collins

The following things were the most important things that I learnt over those twelve weeks:

- Be kind to yourself, you did nothing wrong. Everything that happened was to help both you and your child.
- Focus on the 'Here and Now'. When your mind drifts off to those scary, traumatic moments, just draw yourself back to the here and now and remind yourself of what is different, right now, in this exact moment in time.
- With every negative memory that you cannot seem to remove from your thoughts, replace it with a positive outcome of that memory.
- Do not block the traumatic memories. You would not try to stop a train at the station by jumping in front of it, so do not try to stop your thoughts by jumping in front of them. Acknowledge them and allow them to pass through that station and wave them goodbye. Process them.
- Try to pinpoint your triggers and face them head on, remembering to focus on the here and now!
- Imagine that a friend or family member had experienced what you did. What would you say to them to support them? Now sit down with yourself and tell yourself what you would say to your friend. Do not be hard on yourself.
- You are not a bad person, you are a brilliant parent, your child is cared for and loved and no matter what you have all been through, they love you and need you.

50. Our Young Man's Story – Rachel (Australia)

Our young man is now four years old, doing very well medically, but what a rollercoaster ride the first few years of his life were!

With no indication from any of my pregnancy ultrasounds, it was a shock after his birth to find that our beautiful little boy had a somewhat crooked bottom and a skin tag (just to begin with). Our first of many appointments at our capital city's Children's Hospital was at the age of ten and a half weeks. It was a routine paediatric appointment, resulting in an x-ray of his lower spine and followed up with a consultation with a surgeon.

The X-ray was fairly uninformative and it was decided he required a cocooning MRI. An MRI was performed while he slept, wrapped up in an inflated blanket to keep him still. The only problem was he kept waking up and they couldn't perform the MRI. Thankfully, there'd been a cancellation for the next day and it was decided, as he was only a couple of days from being three months old, that they'd give him an MRI under anaesthetic instead. This was the first of many anaesthetics he'd have over the following years and the results of which wouldn't be known to us for another five months.

In March the following year however, at around the age of five months, our stress levels as parents soared even higher. Having begun eating solids, it seemed as though his bowel motions were coming out like spaghetti. A nappy full of silly string was what he had. That was disturbing enough, let alone the monumental efforts he had to endure each time he used his bowels. Sometimes it was just lots of breath-holding, exertion or grunting. Most times though, it was LOTS of crying, with the occasional bleeding and screaming as well.

The worst of it was at five and a half months, when he didn't or couldn't use his bowels for over three and a half weeks. The stress by this time was being felt by the whole family. Following multiple visits to our local GP, he finally told us to take him to an ER in our capital city. We waited from 9:30am until 4pm, just to be told he'd probably experience this his whole life and we were to double his Lactulose (stool softener) dose.

Returning home exhausted, we did as we were instructed, but sadly to no avail. Our GP then told us to take him to a regional city ER an hour from home where there were local paediatricians. Several days later, after giving him an ever-increasing dose of medication, he finally used his bowels. This was, however, to be an ongoing problem right up until nearly his first birthday.

At eight months of age, we headed back to the Children's Hospital for appointments regarding his MRI results. He was given both a Neural Tube Defect Clinic appointment, which meant nothing to us, and an equally baffling neurosurgeon appointment. After an hour of answering questions during his first NTDC appointment, we had to interrupt the doctors to tell them that we really had no idea what they were talking about, as we'd not been told what was wrong with him yet.

They patiently spent the next hour and a half explaining his condition, what life more immediately would or could look like and his life prospects. His diagnosis, in the early years, was spinal dysraphism. In the years that followed, after more MRI's, it was clarified as sacral dysgenesis and spina bifida.

This didn't, however, give us any explanation as to why his bowel motions were as they were. By now I was telling any and every doctor we saw about his spaghetti poos, still looking for answers, along with experimenting with different ways to try and help him pass his motions with as little difficulty as possible - from lying him on his back with his knees together pushed up towards his chest, to putting him on a potty facing away from me, with my hands on his tummy gently applying some pressure for him to push against. And lots and lots of hugs and kisses both afterwards and during, with many tears shed.

It was after an especially difficult episode of nearly one and a half hours, where he sat on the potty pushing and crying to the point of screaming and passing nearly nothing each time, and then falling asleep in between times, that we finally got the help we needed. After several conversations with a stomal nurse from the Children's Hospital, we arrived at the best way of helping him. It literally took two people, one having to hold his knees pulled towards his head and the other gently applying pressure around his anal opening. This pressure helped give him something to push down against and became the way he used his bowels for quite some time to follow.

To say that life was stressful would be an understatement. I didn't feel like I could leave home at all as I didn't want to burden any of our other children with having to be the ones to help him. He was now able to pass poo more easily but that's not to say it was easy for him to pass. He still often bled and remembering how much he cried from the discomfort still brings tears to my eyes. Enduring his pain and pleading cries was agonising as a parent and was felt by our entire family. Many a time we had to pull the car over while travelling and lay him across our lap in the front seat to help him. Life was incredibly stressful and awkward.

Our real breakthrough came via three different avenues. Firstly, after seeing a local paediatrician for the first time, we were finally being heard. Once again, I detailed his toileting difficulties and he immediately forwarded his concern onto our son's specialists. Secondly, his stomal nurse was also instrumental in raising awareness amongst his doctors, and thirdly, my husband took the initiative of repeatedly ringing until he spoke to the initial surgeon we saw at ten weeks old. We were now at just under ten months of age and finally on the way to a diagnosis.

This surgeon booked him in for an EUA (examination under anaesthetic) immediately following his return from holidays. It was discovered in about five seconds that when an electric probe was used to stimulate the area around his anus, his rectal muscle contracted elsewhere from where his opening was actually located.

Diagnosis: Anorectal malformation (ARM) with a perineal fistula. This meant a misplaced anal passage that is often narrowed, along with a perineal fistula which was the abnormal anal opening located outside the sphincter muscle complex.

It didn't come as a complete shock, as now that he was bigger everything was easier to see and I'd mentioned to my husband just the week before that there appeared to be a dimple in that exact area. But it was a complete shock, nevertheless, having never heard of anything like it. His grandmother, a nurse for many years but now retired, hadn't ever heard or come across it before either.

What was to follow five weeks later, with an initial consultation with a colorectal surgeon, was the answer to all our questioning. He would perform PSARP surgery (posterior sagittal anorectoplasty) and give our young man a functioning bottom. But first he needed laparotomy surgery for the formation of a colostomy - a surgery that brings the colon to the surface of the skin where a bag can be fitted to collect all the faecal matter.

PSARP Surgery - December 2017

Because he'd been so severely constipated for such an extended period of time, his body needed time for his colon to decompress back to the size of an eleven-month-old. This surgery kept us in hospital for six days and the stomal nurses helped to train us in how to apply and change the colostomy bags before we left for home.

The colostomy bag was changed every second day and was made easier if combined with a bath. Preparation was everything, as once bath time was over it was a very busy time. This involved getting everything needed and having it all at hand. Change mat, wipes, stuff to remove the bag with, something to put it all in and everything ready for the new bag to be applied, along with patience - lots of patience - and an extra pair of helping hands. Cutting out the replacement flange, the part the bag attached to, was one such task. My husband made this way simpler for me by making up a template to use, computer skills at their handiest. That way, all I had to do was trace the stoma shape onto the flange so that it could be cut out to exactly the right size and position and fit perfectly every time. That turned out to be a real life and time saver.

His PSARP (pull-through) surgery happened when he was fourteen months old. Now his rectum and sphincter muscle were finally aligned. This turned out to be an eight day stay in hospital as he developed an infection around his newly created anus. Twenty-five days later we headed back to hospital for another EUA to decide whether the healing was complete enough to start dilatations. It was determined that he needed another week's healing before that could begin. So, we headed back there yet again to be taught how to do dilatations, and many times afterwards to check how they were progressing.

Dilatation at fifteen and a half months turned out to be yet another stressful period. It involved inserting a lubricated stainless-steel rod about 7 to 8 cm long into his anal cavity for a short time. To warm up the rod, I'd put it down the front of my bra beforehand for several minutes. I wasn't coping very well with doing this for our son, so my husband offered to do it instead. He managed to have our son laughing throughout the whole dilatation process, which helped me realise that it was more my stress than the act itself that caused our son to cry. Dilatation times became much better as I managed my stress better.

Having said that, each time an increase in the size of the rod occurred there was still some pain. But it didn't last long and, after a few goes into using it, things settled down again. Due to his late diagnosis (with a condition usually discovered at birth) we had to do dilatations for five months. We had to go through several sized rods to increase his sphincter muscle and anal canal size until it was appropriate for his age.

Having recorded his final stoma bag change to show him what his life looked like when he was too young to remember, we went back to hospital. At twenty months of age, with his anal passage realigned and increased in size, he was finally prepped for his colostomy reversal surgery exactly nine months to the day from its creation. A week in hospital and a bottom that now pooped properly, we were sent home yet again. It took some getting used to, him using his bowels without any ordeal and having to change dirty nappies once again.

By this time, we'd made fourteen trips to the Children's Hospital. With home being over four hours away, we were often exhausted as most appointments involved overnight or multiple-night stays away from our other children. We've had many, many specialist appointments, multiple tests, ultrasounds, MRIs and anaesthetics, as well as the difficult days that often followed them. But on the brighter side, our son now has a functioning bottom that he's gained enough control over to be toilet-trained these past nine months.

He's a really happy young man who's faced a lot in his four short years, and who may face more difficulties and trials in life to come. But what a blessing it is to call him "Son" and to walk beside him on this journey called life.

51. Lexter's Story – Lerma Decena (Philippines)

I am Lerma Decena and I have a son born with congenital defects (Imperforate Anus with Rectovesical Fistula). He had a colostomy bag for two years, with his reversal surgery then being performed last October. Unfortunately, we are living in a remote province of the Philippines where ostomy supplies are very difficult to acquire.

Due to the poor availability of ostomy supplies, I created an improvised bag out of a plastic bag and tape to protect his stoma and catch his bowel motions. Truly, his ostomy journey was not an easy challenge for us.

His first surgery was the colostomy procedure and was done twenty-four hours after he was born. I didn't really have any knowledge about the colostomy or my son's health issue, so I researched ostomy groups. I joined the very first one I came across which was the Imperforate Anus International Support Group. This group is amazing.

His second surgery was a PSARP procedure, done when he was seven months old, and it was successful.

His third surgery was the colostomy closure, or reversal, done as a free surgery by a different doctor. This surgery failed however and caused so many complications. Worst of all, instead of just three surgeries, my baby would have another three more.

I know people will wonder why I took my son to another doctor, and why the closure failed. I'm going to answer that honestly.

When my son Lexter had his first surgery, it was an emergency, and I did not have the choice of a better hospital. Later, I brought him to a Regional Hospital because our hospital here in our province of Mati, Davao Oriental doesn't do the surgery. This hospital was public, and the surgery is almost free.

The surgery was performed only by a resident doctor who advised me to bring Lexter again for the PSARP procedure after he reached 10 kilos. We stayed at the hospital for a month which really affected us, especially my two children left at our house.

After that, I followed the doctor's advice to wait for Lexter to gained weight, but sadly it was difficult for him to reach 10 kilos in six months. Even now at two years old, his weight is only eight kilos. So, we knew someone else with the same condition as Lexter and they recommended us to a particular private surgeon and consultant.

So, I visited his clinic. He was disappointed because the created colostomy was wrong and instead of transverse colostomy, what the resident doctor had done was a loop colostomy. The doctor told me it was not true that we needed to wait for him to reach 10 kilos first before having his second surgery.

He explained that Lexter should have his PSARP surgery (the second surgery) while he was still a baby so he would develop his reflexes early.

At that time, we still had enough savings for Lexter's surgery. The doctor asked us for P95,000 (pesos) to cover his doctor's fee, and P100,000 for the hospital fee; a total of almost P200,000. Lexter's surgery would not be free because the doctor was a private doctor. So, it was done and Lexter was ready for closure after three months.

The reason why I decided to bring Lexter back for a free surgery and take a risk (for his third surgery) was because I had no more savings to bring him again to the private doctor.

I lost my twelve-year-old son to suicide last year which financially drained us due to his funeral expenses. I am very distressed about what happened to my children. I have sold all my things and used all my savings. I didn't really have a choice. The worst thing is though, that Lexter's closure was a failure.

Out of desperation and feeling helpless, I tried to reach out again to the group I mentioned. There I meet Greg Ryan, who is such an amazing person. He has guided me with advice on what to do and I am really thankful for his emotional support. I have also met some IA warrior parents who have helped me to raise funds for Lexter to have another surgery.

The private doctor performed another colostomy surgery on Lexter as he was having very bad infections as a result of the failed surgery. He actually almost lost his life.

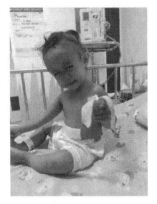

Nothing was ever easy as Lexter developed complications that needed to be fixed. His fifth surgery was performed just last January 2020, and finally his closure just last October 2020.
I really thought it would be impossible for us to save Lexter from this struggle. I am very thankful for all the people who have helped us to raise funds for his surgeries.

Now, Lexter is recovering and doing well. He still has a constant output, but it is slowly becoming manageable. His body is still adjusting and I'm hopeful he will be able to achieve good output soon.

As a mother, seeing Lexter free from the colostomy bag and being happy is a great achievement. The happiness is priceless. Some parents would think negatively about their child's situation, being an IA warrior, but my advice is please do not lose hope. Everything will be fine as long as we are not giving up.

To all our earth angels who also never give up on helping us, my heartfelt thank you. You did not only save Lexter, but my entire family, from this nightmare.

Why? Because I already lost my twelve-year-old son, and if I also lost Lexter last year I might have felt like ending my life too because of depression and desperation. Then my family would be even more lost and broken.

Thank you so much. I owe all of this to all the people who helped us.

To God Be The Glory...

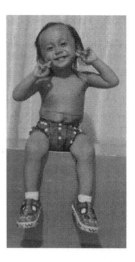

52. Ervin's Story – Tabitha (USA)

I finally became being pregnant again with my second child, after years of struggling and five miscarriages. I started doing the normal pregnancy routine of check-ups, until one day they found hydronephrosis (swelling) of the kidneys. From then on, I had to have check-ups every week, so I anticipated kidney problems at birth.

When my baby boy was born everything seemed so perfect. His dad, Ervin Snr was there, and his sister came to visit as well, but once it was time for her to leave the hospital, he left also to take her across town to stay with family.

While he was gone, the nurse came in and asked if my baby had had any poops. I told her no and asked her to help me into the bed with my baby. I also asked her why he was only sleeping and not eating, and why he hadn't cried. She said, "Well, let me take him to the nursery and check him over again".

I was sitting in the bed, waiting and waiting for my baby to return, when his dad came back. I asked him to go see where my baby was because by that stage it had been quite a while and I was starting to worry.

At that moment a nurse called the room phone and started explaining something about my baby needing to be in the NICU, which really shocked me and the next thing I knew was a nurse had appeared with a wheelchair for me. Before I could ask any questions, the nurse said, "Well, he was born without an anal opening and will need surgery to get a colostomy bag". I was in complete shock and couldn't comprehend what was happening. It was then that we were first told of the medical term Imperforate Anus.

Once we arrived in the NICU, I remember the nurses asking me what his name was, and I instantly said Ervin. It wasn't supposed to be Ervin, but it came naturally as they asked. It was all so heart breaking, so I called my mom and she drove in the snow over an hour away to come to the hospital to comfort us.

It was so hard knowing our little guy was to have surgery the next morning. I had just had a C-section, so I had to stay in my room. It was awful - how do you breast feed your baby who's in another unit and how do you comfort your brand new baby while you're forced to be in a bed to heal? It was absolutely devastating.

Once I was released, I went up to be with him round the clock, pumping and feeding and learning all about the bag and how to keep it on. Our family came and sometimes we stayed at the Ronald McDonald House so we could shower, rest and eat if we had time. We spent about twenty-one days in the NICU.

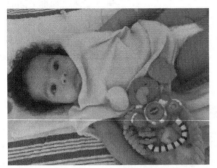

It was nice to have my grandparents and dad come all the way here, to Iowa from South Carolina, and be with us and our new baby boy.

At first it was hard. I was emotional and exhausted, dealing with breast pumping, doctors and monitors, and more doctors and nurses and room service. There was all kinds of testing and it was just chaos.

I had to learn to work with a lady who was called an ostomy nurse. I found it difficult connecting with her. I'm not sure if it was my hormones or the fact she was the one who had to teach me how to take care of my baby's new anatomy (mucus fistula and ostomy).

Finally, the day came when we found the right steps and the right bag and mom was a pro! That was, until I got home and realised the bag was off - arrgghhhhhhh! I had all these supplies and diagrams but guess what, no scissors to cut the tiny little hole! Frantic, I sent my partner to the store and he came back with scissors, but they were too big, and it was impossible to cut the bag.
So back to the hospital we go, this time admitted to the PICU. After days of fighting insurance, we finally got approved to take the tiny little ostomy scissors home from the hospital and it was then we finally got to stay home for a while.

I started to do research online and found an imperforate anus support group on Facebook. I'm not sure how the universe lined all that up, but I was ever so desperate to find out how to deal with this new way of life and where to start. How do I do this and who is there to help me? Once I left the hospital I was on my own! I had to figure it all out myself.

Through this group I found out about a colorectal centre in Ohio that specialised in IA patients. I knew that Ervin had to have a PSARP surgery soon and I wanted to find the best care possible for him, so I made the relevant inquiries.

After persuading our insurance that he needed this specialised surgery in Ohio and doing all the paperwork and working with miracle flights, we finally got approval. So, Ervin Snr, little baby Ervin at just three months old and I were on our way to Ohio for Ervin's PSARP, which was a success.

We went back for the colostomy closure surgery a few months later, but this time I went with the baby alone.

After a while, Ervin started to become very agitated and would scream all the time. I had no idea what was happening. Every time I took him to a local doctor, they had no answers which would make me so frustrated. I really started to doubt myself and wonder if I hadn't done the right number of dilations.

I finally found a doctor who gave him a full examination and I was told that Ervin had a rectal prolapse. I knew his bottom looked different, but I just assumed it was because of his IA and the surgeries he'd had.

Dr Pena and Ervin

By that stage I had separated from Ervin Snr and was a single mom with two kids, one with special needs. It was an extremely difficult period in my life. I had limited family support where I lived, and I felt like I was failing my kids as a parent.

I reached out once again to the IA support group and was able to receive wonderful support and important advice. It then became clear that I once again needed to seek specialised treatment for Ervin for his prolapse.

It was at this time that I was given the contact details of Dr Alberto Pena in Colorado. I was able to contact him and he was wonderful. He asked me to send Ervin's medical records to him and I also sent him some photos of Ervin's prolapse, which by this stage had become very noticeable.

It took me well over a year fighting with insurance before I was finally able to get approval for Ervin's prolapse surgery. There were endless phone calls and emails which tested me emotionally along with endless enemas to keep him regular.

It was incredibly difficult seeing my son in so much distress when I wasn't able to get him the treatment he required.

Once I got the approval, I was able to book Ervin's surgery with Dr Pena, and my dad, daughter, Ervin and myself drove to Denver.

The treatment and care we received from Dr Pena and his team was amazing. We were in Colorado for 24 days.

Ervin is now running around and playing like any other four-year-old boy and you wouldn't know of the tummy problems he still has to deal with. He also now has a little baby brother who he absolutely adores.

Unfortunately, I still am dealing with constant issues with insurance about coverage for his medical supplies and treatments, but I will always advocate for my son.

53. My Super Logan (USA)

From the minute Logan was born, our lives changed drastically. We went from being a regular mom and dad, to a special needs mom and dad. We had no advance notice. It is like a switch was flipped and suddenly, we were these new people. Having a special needs child shows you new things about yourself, almost daily.

For one, you find a strength you never knew you had. You become familiar with medical terms and procedures that would have sounded foreign to you just months or even days before. Most importantly, you discover a deep aching love that you did not know existed.

My husband and I had been parents for almost two years when Logan was born. We knew that our hearts would double in size the moment we met him, just as they had when his brother was born. But adding in his imperforate anus diagnosis and the journey that followed, showed us new depths to what it means to love someone.

Logan is now four years old and a stubborn, opinionated four-year-old at that! The 'lows' we have experienced over the past four years have been numerous. I will never forget the day the doctors told us that Logan needed to start daily enemas. We had tried MiraLAX and senna, but the result was about a dozen bowel movements a day causing awful rashes. In my head, I knew that enemas were the best way to keep him from getting constipated and to prevent rashes. However, my heart broke, having to put him through the process every single day.

We have called Logan our super baby since he was born, which is very fitting given that he was named after Wolverine. He proved his superhero strength, when we started those enemas over two years ago. Of course, there are bad days, but overall, he does not mind. To him, it is an hour he gets to spend on his tablet watching YouTube videos.

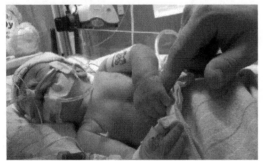

NICU

One of the worst days we ever experienced with Logan was when he was about three days old.

We were emotionally raw from finding out his diagnosis, having him transferred to another hospital, and seeing him through his first of three surgeries.

On this particular day, we had some hope though. We were being moved to the 'step down unit' which meant the doctors thought he was almost ready to go home! Unfortunately, what no one realised is that he was not as awake from the anaesthesia as we all thought. Everyone thought he was handling the post-op pain so well, when really, he just was not feeling it, yet.

Almost immediately after moving to our new room, Logan started to feel that pain. My sister was holding him when suddenly, all these alarms started going off. A nurse came in, put him on the bed, and tried waking him up. More nurses came in. Doctors came in. An oxygen mask was put over his face. My baby had stopped breathing. I stood there with my sister and husband, watching them work for what felt like hours. In reality, it was probably less than five minutes. They got him breathing again and moved him back to the other side of the NICU.

He had two more episodes like that, over the next 24 hours. That night was the first and only time I ever saw my husband cry. That day is forever a reminder to us of how bad it can get, and how grateful we should be for the days we have now.

A recent 'low' we experienced happened at a baseball game. Logan had just wrapped up his first ever season playing t-ball! But about halfway through the season, we were at one of his games when disaster struck. I was helping in the dugout, making sure the kids got to where they needed to go with the right equipment. The game was almost over and Logan came up to me and said he needed to go potty. I assumed he had to pee, because we had done his enema earlier that day, so that he would not need to poop. I asked if he could hold it because he was the next player to bat. He replied yes!

After he batted and made it back to the dugout, my husband took him to the bathroom. They were gone awhile, and Logan ended up missing the last inning of the game. He made it back just in time to run onto the field for the last few minutes. As he ran past me, I saw it: the stain on his white baseball pants. He had had an accident, and it leaked out of his pullup and stained his pants. I looked at my husband wide-eyed, and he told me that Logan must not have gotten all of his enema out, which happens sometimes. I held my breath, hoping none of the other kids would notice his pants, and thankfully they did not. Logan, as per usual, had zero cares in the world and was just happy to be around his team.

While my husband helped Logan get packed up, I headed to another field where my oldest son was playing. On the way, I had to stop because I could not hold back the sobs anymore. I just stood in the middle of the park crying. This was my fault. I should have let him go to the bathroom as soon as he asked. For a split second, I forgot I was a special needs mom. I was just a baseball mom making sure her son went to bat when he was supposed to. The guilt was so strong, I could not breathe. But the most important lesson here was that Logan did not care. He was not hurt or upset. He was just enjoying his post-game snacks. Reminding myself that it is ok to mess up sometimes and that I will not always be the perfect special needs mom, is a daily struggle. One I am trying to get better at every day.

I might have painted a grim picture of life with IA with these examples. While this is an honest glimpse into our lives, it is not the whole picture. For every low, there have been a dozen highs. The day we found out enemas would be part of our daily routine, also meant that Logan would attend preschool without worrying about having a poop accident. He gets to spend the night at his grandparents' house, have playdates with friends, go to Awanas at church, and play baseball without us worrying that he will poop every couple of hours. The peace of mind enemas gives us, is worth the time they take and the temporary discomfort they put Logan in.

Logan's first run scored

The awful guilt I felt at the baseball game I mentioned, was nothing compared to the overwhelming joy I had when Logan wore his uniform for the first time, scored his first run, hit his first coach pitch, or was awarded the game ball from his coach. I do not think Logan is going to get called up to the Majors anytime soon, but just seeing him play a sport feels like a miracle.

Through the first year or so of his life, my husband and I did not talk about the future like we did with our first son. With our oldest, we talked about his first day of school, when we would buy his first baseball glove, his first time going to the movies, or having a sleepover at a friend's house. All the fun milestones we had always pictured with our future kids.

But after Logan was born, we felt that discussing those kinds of things was tempting fate. We were always (and still are sometimes) in 'wait and see' mode. We did not want to imagine watching him playing sports in case that day never came. But it did come, and the pride we felt could barely be contained.

Even though we did not talk about future milestones with Logan, we definitely celebrated the ones that did come along! The worst day of our lives, when we watched Logan stop breathing, taught us to celebrate every single win, no matter how small. Doing that has made us appreciate everything Logan accomplishes, at a whole new level.

The first time he sat up on his own, felt like a miracle! Swimming in a pool for the first time will forever be one of my favourite days! His first day of preschool! The only way I could express the pride I felt, was through tears. Every time he goes through an x-ray, ultrasound, or doctor's visit without complaint, I feel like the luckiest mom in the world. The nights when he crawls into my lap and says, 'Mommy can I snuggle with you?' are a precious gift that I would never have fully appreciated, without everything that came before.

Life with IA is hard for Logan and for us, but it has given our lives more meaning and filled us with a deep never-ending love.

54. Jano's Journey – Mariska (South Africa)

Our journey started on the 18th December 2017, when our son Jano was born. I had never heard of children who are born without an anus and was quite shocked when the paediatrician told us that he would have to be admitted to high care, because he had no anus. His last scan, before his birth, showed his kidneys were a little bigger than expected, but never in our wildest dreams did we know how this would change our lives.

Further tests again revealed his enlarged kidneys and with the imperforate anus he was sent to another hospital later that same day. The next morning doctors and surgeons came to see us to discuss his condition. That same morning our one-day old baby went into theatre. A couple of days later we went home. My new baby had a stoma and a mucous fistula.

It was quite an emotional roller coaster ride, not knowing what to expect and what the future would hold for us. It was a struggle to fit the stoma bag at first, as it always leaked, and the mucous fistula always seemed in the way. I was often saddened by the fact that I had to remove this sticky bag from my newborn baby's delicate skin, but we eventually got the hang of it.

I think at that stage we still did not realise what this all meant. I remember telling my boss in mid-January 2018 that by the time Jano turns one, it will all be over. However, when the doctors told me that this is a life-long condition, I had to face reality and realised that this is part of our 'new normal.' I often felt upset, because I assumed that my son would never have a normal life. That he will need bowl washes every day for the rest of his life, that he will never be able to have sleepovers at a friend's house, play sport or attend a mainstream school.

Since then, I have learned from other parents who have faced these same challenges that our children are stronger that we think and maybe he will be able to do all those things. I have learned to take it one day at a time.

Jano had his pull through at five months old. This was the most challenging of all of his operations. It was the hardest hospital stay for us, because there was a twist in his small intestines, which caused him to vomit and he cried a lot. He went back to theatre to correct it. Once that was sorted out, it went much better and he recovered quickly. Jano then had an anal prolapse which was corrected when he was seven months old.

At ten months he had his stoma reversal. We were so excited; I could not wait for him to just poo 'normally.' Jano's normal will never be normal, but at this stage with stool laxatives and medication he is doing well. Our new challenge will come when we have to start bowel washouts, but we will stay positive and take it one day at a time.

At the moment, we are spending more time in hospital dealing with bladder and kidney related issues. Kidney reflux is just one of his other challenges. It caused a lot of damage to his ureters and kidneys. He had a ureteral reimplantation in August 2020 and currently has stents to help his kidneys drain into his bladder.

We trust that once they remove it in October, Jano's kidneys will do better. Our main concerns are that he will have to go through kidney dialysis or need a kidney transplant but will cross that bridge if we ever get there.

We are so thankful for the IA/ARM International support group. It helps knowing people are going through the same things or have already been through it and can give us advice and show us that even if our children are unique, they can still live productive lives, play sports, attend school and just be children.

55. Daniel's Story Through His Parents Eyes - Alex, Father (Spain)

Egocentrism of the 21st century. For me, it appears as the titan Saturn, devouring his children from Francisco Goya's painting. Likewise, our humankind, with bulging eyes and endless looped, dimensionless consumption devours everything that surrounds us. Global warming, viruses, environmental contamination and wars are its direct consequences.

However, egocentrism is a part of our nature and for centuries it has been limited through religion and culture. In the 21st century, when religion no longer plays a significant role anymore, when it has been replaced by consumerism, the human ego has started to become a centre of the universe.

Just check out Instagram or TikTok, the two most popular social networks. What are the main messages there? "I want to show you what I have". "Look how awesome I am". "Look what places I visited...what I have consumed just now...how sexily I can move, yeah!" And thousands of followers, who 200 years ago would have listened to the shepherd's sermons about the deeds of the saints and would have been inspired by them to improve their actions, are now looking at Instagram and their desire is growing. The desire to repeat what they see or at least have those good things in order to have good feelings. I bought a new car and a month later I saw my neighbour's BMW and I wanted the same. I bought a BMW, but my friend is already driving a Porsche, such a shame and so on. On the one hand, desire rules the world and gives the main drive to business and the economy. On the other hand, it is obvious that in global terms it is destroying us.

Is there a way to find a balance? Is there a way to stop the triumphant march of egocentrism and what destructive consumerism can overwhelm? It seems to me that one thing is definitely capable - it is a human empathy. In other words, it is caring for others, switching a person's attention from his own ego to other people. In many ways, culture is already helping us in this, because a huge amount of literature, movies and works of art carry this meaning. And of course, the largest part of any religion is empathy and charity.

I would like to tell you about how our son Daniel helps me to cope with my ego. Over the past four to five years, my perception of reality has been changing and many things that worried and distressed me earlier do not have such an impact on me today. But let me tell you the story first.

My son Daniel was born with VACTERL syndrome in April 2016. Today he is four and half years old. We went through eight hospitalizations and five operations. He was born with Imperforate Anus (IA). Today we went to the playground and Daniel was pooing almost the whole time, so my wife had to clean his pants six or seven times during our walk. He is our second kid. Our first is Sofia, a 13-year-old girl who was born with no conditions and has always been a very calm and kind child. She was born when I was quite young, but it took us many years to have a second child.

Five years of continuous attempts to achieve pregnancy again had marked us significantly. My wife had an ectopic pregnancy in 2011, so she had to go urgently to hospital for surgery. We were so scared for her life this time because such cases are high risk.

In 2015 we unfortunately lost our unborn baby in a later stage of pregnancy. Due to major complications, the doctor recommended that we terminate the pregnancy. We made the extremely difficult decision to follow the doctor's advice. This decision, and the act itself, had a great psychological impact on both of us.

I remember that I supported my wife during that first half a year. I forbade to myself have any feelings or even thoughts about our loss and trauma. We decided to continue our attempts to have a child, because we thought that the birth of a healthy kid would help us to get over this crisis. Six months later it happened and my wife was pregnant again. For me, during those days, she looked fine. I mean, she didn't tell me anything nor did she mention our lost baby and somewhere deep inside I felt that she had overcome the crisis.

Unfortunately, that was a kind of signal to my psyche that it could relax and fail. I had huge panic attacks and was very afraid about the life of my daughter and my wife, about the lives of my parents and sometimes about people that I barely knew. Actually, I was very scared to lose what I loved and what was important for me. I started to dig inside myself to resolve it, but the more I dug the worse it got. The whole thing I wanted to solve was, what is wrong with me, how can I feel better?

I was 32 years old and had come back to Prague, from half a year working in South Africa, to support my wife in her pregnancy. The nine months of pregnancy was the worst time in my entire life. The psychological problems I experienced such as panic attacks and anxiety were almost killing me. Sometimes I was not even able to talk to people and it took me tremendous effort to even have a meaningful conversation with someone. I was looking for a solution to get rid of it, but almost nothing helped. I went out every day to nature, did sports several times a week, I started my second business just to keep very busy with work, I travelled, but nothing really worked or helped much. I think this was a taste of a real deep depression combined with anxiety. The doctor said that I had developed a form of obsessive-compulsive disorder (OCD).

On 29th of April 2016, my son was born. It was late at night and we were alone in the hospital. I remember very well the anxiety that I had during the last two hours - I was not able to breath, I was crying alone while sitting in the hall of the hospital and was praying to all gods that exist or don't exist to give a life to my baby. Then I suddenly heard a baby crying. So, he is alive. I went to see him when the doctor invited me to enter, but I understood that something was not right. The doctor told me that my son was born without an anus and that he must go immediately to Prague's main hospital to have surgery. That night I cried as I have never cried in my life. It was unstoppable and I felt sorry for myself and for our baby.

That situation was stressful for me. My wife was in the hospital for the next two days, but I had to run early morning to the main city hospital to sign all the papers for the surgery and to talk to the doctors. Ironically, this was the day when my anxiety disappeared for several years. Immediately all my fears and non-existent problems were replaced by the real challenge. A disabled child.

The birth of Daniel changed my life quite significantly. It is better to say that it changed my perception of life and it continues to change. From the moment that he was born, I started to recognise when my egocentrism tries to control my behaviour and when it wins or when I beat it.

Half a year ago, I bought Greg's book "A Secret Life" and I was not able to read more than one page at time. I started to cry on almost each page. The first 14 pages took me almost two weeks to read. The first two pages I read in a cafe and it must have been a strange sight to see an almost 40-year-old man crying when reading a book. Yes, I did. I saw my son in almost everything that Greg described. And you know what, I always feel better after reading the book and after crying. Empathising with an author gave me the strength to live and to continue.

Now I have five years of experience bringing up a disabled kid and this is the same amount of time that people study in University. My wife became almost an expert in many aspects of VACTERL diagnosis and IA and can talk with doctors in the same language that they do. Often, we must explain to them what our Daniel has. Also, as we spent quite a long time together in hospital with our kid during his first two years of life, I saw many different children whose fight, I think, is a real fight when I compare it to ours. I saw children who will never walk or even talk.

All this gave me a very strong belief that my egoistic wishes are not the most important things in the world. There are other things that I really care about. I care about the health of my family and, not only this, I also care about how I communicate with other people. Someone said, "be polite to all people, you don't know what the person is fighting right now". This exactly defines how I feel.

During the last five years of my life, I have become much less prejudiced and judgmental in general. I now consider are you from a different nation, different gender, different race, different sexuality, have a disability or disorder? Now I am trying to understand what is behind these layers and who you really are. Before, I was pretending to do this, as still the main aim was my point of view. I can say that I am now much more advanced in listening to people.

When the Covid19 crisis came and we had to spend three months at home in Spain, nothing actually changed for us. We had been at home or at hospital with Daniel for over two years. I work from home a lot of the time anyway, because my IT business does not require my physical presence somewhere. For me, the best way to survive in lockdown was to care about other people - make food, play games with kids, read them books, talk to my wife and of course leave some space for the things that my ego likes, such as playing guitar, reading and watching movies. But I found that the first part is much more important, and I feel better when everyone around me is happy.

I must admit that it's not easy to listen and actually hear someone. You need to put in effort. The same effort as if you are running 10km. To start running your mind should say "hey man, run, don't be lazy". So, you go and run. And you need to push your mind to work same way, and say "hey buddy, stop thinking about the things that you are worrying about, just listen and understand the person right now". And very often, the effort to run even 20km is not a problem for people but seems impossible to make an effort for a ten minute conversation with a person about things that he or she really cares about.

I am pretty sure there is a role for all people with disability in society to help other people develop their empathy. The co-feeling, to become more open to others and to control and manage the self and the all-destroying ego.

My wife started focusing her artwork to bring attention to VACTERL and IA kids, and I think this art and cultural message is a truly needed message for the 21st century.

56. Daniel's Story Through His Parents' Eyes - Daria, Mother (Spain)

What is your wish?

A few days ago, I read a book with my 4-year-old son who was born with VACTERL and Anal Atresia (IA). In the book, one boy saved the fairy and as a gift he could make a cherished wish. I asked my son if he has a cherished wish? "I want to stop pooping forever", he said. In his answer, you could feel all the deepest emotions and experience he is going through.

I had no complications during my pregnancy with him. When our son was born, it was a shock for us to find out that he had Anal Atresia and other birth defects. It turned out to be very difficult to find information and communities of people in languages other than English.

We had really a tough experience. The first two years were the hardest. Our only desire was to talk to someone who had already gone through this and who would tell us that everything would be fine.

I am an artist and I decided to dedicate all my work to spreading awareness, educating people through visual images, through painting, to let them feel what children and adults with rare birth defects live through.

We speak so little in society about what we have to go through: surgeries, incontinence, constipation, medications, accidents, feelings of shame, unpleasant odors, physical and emotional pain, enemas, procedures, refusal from favourite activities, loneliness, bullying etc. It is not accepted to discuss this in society.

All of this can be expressed through art, to teach people to understand and accept. And this is what I want to speak about and will do for my son and for all of us.

My cherished wish is to be heard. What is yours?

These are my portraits of Daniel, and of a stoma/colostomy, as my tribute to all IA children who have had this surgery.

You can view my artwork on my Instagram page @dariavis_art (Daria Vishnyakova)

57. This Mama's Prayer - Summer Barzcak (USA)

My hand on

your back,
your heart

beating so.

A heart I never dreamed
I'd know.

I lay in your bed and watch you
drift slow.

This day has been long,
I fold my

hands,

then bow my head
low.

And

thank the One who
spared your

sweet

little

soul.

By a mama of four children, two who have been affected by IA and/ or Currarino Syndrome.

Chapter 5 - Parents/Family - Cloaca

58. Taylor's Story – Ange and Trent (Australia)

After having a lot of trouble falling pregnant with our identical twin boys, we were surprised to fall pregnant just nine months later with our third child. Our boys were IVF babies and born prematurely with emergency surgery; we thought that journey was tough enough. We were not prepared for what was about to unfold.

After a troublesome pregnancy, scans showed at thirty weeks a large black mass in our baby's abdomen, which was terrifying. Ange was flown from our regional hometown to a city hospital for further investigation. After days of much concern, we were then told to drive another hospital for a second opinion. Specialists were again inconclusive about what the mass was. Ange was advised to relocate to the city near a tertiary hospital to monitor our baby. Taylor's kidneys were under severe distress. Keeping her inside to grow for as long as possible was the plan because surgery on a baby as close to full term was the best hope for her survival.

We took the advice and Ange stayed with family in the city and relocated for a further two weeks to Ronald McDonald House. At the same time, I continued to look after our twins, work and drive over every weekend to Ange for quality family time. It's impossible to describe how tough this was on our young family.

During the time Ange was in the city pre-Taylor's birth, a surgical professor mentioned to us that our baby possibly has a condition known as Cloaca. In short, he said she could be born with no bottom hole and possibly a multitude of other issues that can be associated with this condition. Being born without a bottom hole was not something we had ever heard of, or ever conceived could occur.

We were told our baby would need lifesaving surgery on the first day of life. We waited out the next couple of weeks with this on our minds and what it all meant for our baby. The professor mentioned he was a leader in this field, although he would not be at the birth due to annual leave, he assured us that we would be in capable hands. Our experiences since Taylor's birth have shown us that this was indeed not the case.

At thirty-seven weeks doctors at the Hospital booked a date for a C-section. On the day, the Neonatal Intensive Care Unit (NICU) did not have enough beds or staff. We were bumped off the list until the next day, adding to our stress and anxiety. Early the next morning Ange could not feel our baby, we rushed to the hospital. Taylor was in distress; it was now an emergency instead of a planned delivery. The NICU was still understaffed and under pressure. In the end though, our baby just had to be delivered and was done so in an unprepared theatre.

Our fears were realised when our daughter was born. Taylor was born with no bottom hole. Although this was not her worst issue at this time. She was born with immature lungs; emergency action was required. They could barely stabilise Taylor as staff waited for the drugs for her lungs to arrive. She was stabilised just enough to be rushed off immediately for surgery.

It was not until twelve hours later a surgeon spoke to us and confirmed that our daughter Taylor was born with a condition called Cloaca. This is where a female is born with one opening instead of three. This condition causes all sorts of bowel, urological and gynaecological issues and they were unsure of her internal anatomy or if she had any other issues. During the surgery, a colostomy was formed for Taylor to poo from and there was a tube inserted in her stomach to drain urine. This would not be the last surgery for Taylor.

Taylor spent the next six weeks in NICU which was the most confronting, emotional, and challenging time we have been ever been through. Staff at the Hospital were not equipped to deal with the complexity of her condition. Taylor was on breathing equipment and a multitude of drugs to keep her alive. We had to accept and then learn about her colostomy and mucus fistula care. She underwent test after test and surgery after surgery to try and stabilise her little body.

She nearly died several times due to the stress on her body, especially her kidneys from failed surgeries and infection. I can still remember an NICU nurse looking after Taylor asking if I would like a wipe for her bottom (which did not have a hole!), which really highlighted our concern over her care.

When we eventually brought our Taylor home, she came home with four stomas. This included a colostomy for poo and a mucus fistula. There was a total of thirty-five centimetres of bowel exposed on the outside of her body. She had two more stomas to drain urine from her little body a vesicostomy and a vaginostomy. All her connections inside were mixed up. This was how Taylor would live for the coming months. What sort of way is this to live? It was a very fast learning curve to ensure Taylor maintained her health.

Usually these are the weeks, months where you focus on bonding your new baby with your family. This time for us was spent researching. We researched Cloaca and where the best place to treat this condition was. We knew that this condition needed specialist treatment so we began to research online.

Our research led us to email Nationwide Children's Hospital in Columbus, Ohio which had a Colorectal Centre that specialised in ARM patients. We sent an email via their contact page pleading for help for our daughter. Little did we know that this email would change the trajectory for our Taylor's long-term outcome and quality of life. Within forty-eight hours we had a phone call from Dr. Sebastian King here in Australia. He had trained with the best in this field over in the US and was now a surgeon in Australia at the Royal Children's Hospital, Melbourne.

We met with Sebastian soon after and immediately felt comfortable. We knew he would be the one to perform the reconstruction surgery Taylor required to make her internal connections as normal as possible. This involved among other things creating the missing openings including her bottom hole and urethra, diverting connections and closing stomas. Sebastian performed lead up investigations and led a team of specialists for each system (bowel, urological and gynaecological).

The surgery was twelve hours long. It was a collaborative approach to gain the best outcome, with the hope of limiting the number of surgeries required in the future. This approach is how complicated conditions like Taylor's should be treated. Trusting someone with your child for twelve hours is indescribable, however everything leading up to this was calculated and dealt with in the most professional manner which gave us some peace.

Three months after the reconstruction had healed enough, Taylor had her colostomy reversed. All this in the first nine months of her life took a toll on our family physically and especially mentally. This period was not without its ups and downs, but Sebastian thankfully remained accessible for us to seek advice on many different situations and issues that arose. We could not simply go to our local hospital or GP, for help. They had never seen a baby with a stoma, let alone the other complexities associated with Taylor's condition.

These surgeries and procedures, (there have been nine of them in Taylor's short life) by no means have made Taylor 'normal'. This condition and conditions like Taylor's are chronic and lifelong. Her bottom hole and bowel do not work like ours. She requires a stringent diet and daily concoction of laxatives, to manage her bowel as best as possible.

There will be further surgeries to allow her to be 'socially continent' and to assist her maintain her mental state of mind. She will have a small hole in her stomach to allow top-down flushing instead of the trauma associated with rectal enemas.

She currently has a stoma under her belly button to wee, her vesicostomy. It constantly drips and we have had to get custom made underwear for her. Without these she would wet through her clothes all day long. She will have surgery in the future which will allow her to catheterise for wee. This will mean another hole in her abdomen to catheterise from.

We have tried as best as possible to not let this condition hold our little girl back. We sent her to day care one to two days a week to experience socialising and learning with other children. However, we had to remove Taylor and her brothers from day care, due to the negative effects on the management of her condition, her privacy and her health as she was constantly getting sick from the poor hygiene in day cares. More recently as she has grown, and she has been able to gain more control over her bowels, she has been attending preschool and loving it. Nothing really holds her back these days, she is active, sassy and is growing like a weed. You would not know that this little girl has gone through what she has, when you look at her.

All we want is for our little girl to live a happy normal life. To do this Taylor and children like her need the right care. Her condition is complex and requires specialised treatment. These children deserve more than a surgical fix up and a follow up in an outpatient clinic. They need ongoing care and support, for their entire life. This includes mental health, regardless of age these issues are real.

In addition, the families need support; the emotional and financial burden is immense. We cannot even begin to fathom what a condition like this does to a person's mental state. As parents thinking of this scares us. It is so private that people with this condition suffer in silence and hide it from the world for fear of ridicule. No one should live like that.

We have been lucky enough to have had Sebastian care for our daughter. If Sebastian was involved from the start, Taylor and our young family would have been better off. My wife Ange has recently begun attending sessions to help her deal with the post-traumatic stress she has suffered as a result of this whole experience.

We are lucky there is someone like Sebastian here in Australia who wants to dedicate his life to support and care for these children to achieve a better quality of life and their families as well. We are equally passionate about advocating for kids like Taylor, and families like ours who have had to endure so much trauma due to the lack of awareness and understanding of ARM in not only the general public, but also the medical community.

We are part of several private social media networks, both locally and internationally and realise that we are far from alone in this situation. Although every family's story is different, we are still all walking the same path.

Despite the challenging parts of our journey, we have found that in great adversity, comes opportunities. Due to the ongoing issues, we have had regarding Taylor's incontinence, we have now established a business offering specialised incontinence underwear for children with bladder and bowel incontinence.

We are also proudly actively involved in the ONE in 5000 Foundation, as we strive to advocate for kids like our beautiful daughter who continues to amaze us every day.

59. Peyton's Story – Laura (USA)

Our beautiful daughter Peyton was born at 9.35pm via emergency C-section on a cold winter evening. She came a few days before her due date, determined to splash into this world on her own terms and in her own time. It is almost nine years later, and nothing has changed. She is a force to be reckoned with, determined, independent, energetic and sweet.

We knew early on that Peyton would have some challenges. At our twenty-week ultrasound the radiologist noticed a growth on one of Peyton's kidneys. One kidney was also smaller than it should be.

They referred us to the doctors who run the Special Delivery Unit at the Children's Hospital in our state.

Extensive testing concluded that Peyton would be born with an anorectal malformation called Cloaca. She would have to come via C-section to protect her and me. She would also have to have a bunch of surgeries and she would be in the NICU for a while.

We were devastated by the news and it took a while to wrap our heads around what it would mean for our family.

Questions swirled. How would we manage Peyton at the hospital and her three big brothers at home, how many surgeries would she need, how will we make ends meet while trying to care for our baby, who will take the boys to school while we were at the hospital, just to name a few.

As it turns out, we were blessed with many family and friends who offered to help in any way we needed. Hundreds of people reached out to see what they could do. Quite frankly we could not have done it without them. We had our army behind us, arrangements were made for our boys to be taken care of and we just had to wait for the big day to arrive.

As we got closer, I was overwhelmed with the thoughts of keeping everyone in the loop about what was happening with our family. We were getting phone calls and texts all day long from our army and I wanted to answer every single person, but it was impossible to keep up.

A friend suggested a website called Caringbridge.org. It was a space where I could keep our friends and family, our volunteer army, updated. It was also a space where I could write down what was going on in my head, a way to decompress. I loved the idea that I could keep everything in one place, and I hope to share what was written with Peyton when she is older.

This is a blog post from the day I was discharged from the Special Delivery Unit. I think all mothers with a baby who cannot come home with them can relate to this.

Feeling Disconnected

"Hello Friends: We are home. It was a long day and it felt like forever for us to be discharged from the hospital, but they kicked us out of the Special Delivery Unit. It was an emotional day for me. I have been feeling a bit disconnected this entire time. I felt the pains of labor but was knocked out for the C-section before reaping the benefits of having a baby swept up and placed in my arms during that first few minutes after 'the great push. '

I missed the chance to feed her for the first time at birth and the first time I saw her she had tubes everywhere. I could not hold her when I first saw her because I was too sick from the anaesthesia. Finally, on the first full night we were in the hospital I held her in my arms, and she was so beautiful, in spite of all of those tubes. She looked at me briefly and fell back to sleep.

I could only hold her for twenty minutes because she had to get back under the UV lights to help her bilirubin levels. She went for her surgery the next morning and the staff in the NICU although nice are not very good at communicating. They came and got her before we had a chance to see her in the morning.

We agonised for three hours, waiting for news and finally Peyton's surgeon arrived to give us the news that we were prepared to hear from the beginning. She came through fine and she is a trooper, but she has a complicated case, and she will have a hard road ahead. Hopefully, her father and I will bear the brunt of that road and she will not remember much.

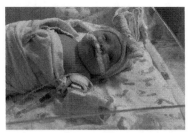 We got to see her after the surgery. It was a shock to the system. She was in pain...you could tell. She had a belly full of tubes and a few extra cuts where they used an instrument. It was a mother's worse nightmare--a child crying and no way to help them.

To me she looked terrible and the only thing I could do was stand there and cry, stroke her head and sing "Jehovah God is My Shepherd" to her in hopes that she remembers hearing me sing that to Weston, at night while she was in my belly. I just want to hold her, and I cannot. The nurse gives her an extra dose of pain meds and she calms down. Now I just need something to calm me down.

I go back to my room and try to pump, and nothing comes. For three and a half days nothing comes. Maybe it is this disconnected feeling that I have, or I am just not used to pumping this early after giving birth. I pray that something happens soon because it is the only thing I can do for my daughter. I've even resorted to drinking a disgusting can of beer with the hopes it will help with lactation.

And now we are home, but a piece of us is still missing, lying in a small little bed forty-five minutes away, unaware of the big splash she made into this world. Unaware of how crazy she has made me from day one, but hopefully she already knows she is loved, not only by her mommy and daddy and big brothers, but her extended family and friends too.

I am signing off now to finish this awful beer, pump and put these poor swollen elephant trunk feet to bed. An early day tomorrow back down to the hospital with some news of how the ultrasound she had today went. Hopefully some more news tomorrow.

Our love to all of you out there. Thank you for the support and kind words here in the blog and phone calls as well."

Chapter 6 - Parents/Family with Pre-school/School Child (5-12 Years)

60. Nate-Lewis' Story – Kirsty Malkin (England)

It was an unusually hot May, yet the heating was still roaring in the Intensive Care Baby Unit where my baby boy was laying, covered in wires and tubes. He had graced the Earth with his presence just twenty-nine hours earlier, surrounded by doctors and nurses, I named him Nate-Lewis.

'Everything is fine, he is a perfect baby boy,' were the midwife's words after his physical examination. The words I had dreamt of hearing since my first scan, where I was told there was an abnormality. I was told I could terminate my pregnancy, but I declined and so these words came as a huge relief. Little did we know, this was going to be far from the dream.

The doctors came to do their morning rounds on the ward, where Nate-Lewis had another physical examination. Removing his nappy to check his bottom, the doctor covered him up and hurried away, stating she just wanted her superior's opinion. The next thing I knew I was running after my baby as he was rushed into the Special Care Baby Unit. His bowels were so full they were beginning to crush his tiny organs. He was being transferred to a Children's Hospital immediately. A twenty-one year old, single mum, with no idea what was going on; my world was spinning out of control.

Anorectal Malformation, low grade, with no other complications was the diagnosis. So, at just 30 hours old Nate-Lewis underwent anoplasty surgery, where the doctors created an anus opening for him. Everything went well, the doctors were happy and after six days in the ICU we were able to go home.

I had to learn how to dilate Nate-Lewis, to keep his anus from closing, because it was scar tissue. It was heart breaking to do and my parents helped by reminding me that this was not forever, and it was in his best interest, when I just could not put my baby through this pain anymore.

Over the next two years, Nate-Lewis had numerous medications. We went from one extreme to the next, screaming on the floor trying to poo, to then having thirty nappy changes a day. His consultant explained that his low grade was the worst he had under his care. More often than not it was the constipation we had to deal with. We were constantly at the hospital, enema after enema, suppository after suppository. Then these turned into emergency surgeries for manual extractions, where he was put under general anaesthetic so the doctors could empty his bowels by hand. Each time I held his hand, watching him drift off to sleep and every time it got harder. I was told he may have nerve damage, that he could never be fixed, that it could get better as he got older. But the older he got, the worse it got and I needed to be prepared for my son to start primary school, still wearing nappies.

By this point Nate-Lewis was starting to understand what was going on around him and he knew what he would have to endure whenever we had to go to hospital. That is when the night terrors started. He would scream out through the night, shouting in his sleep for them to stop hurting him. He would cry hysterically, saying he did not want to go to the hospital anymore, all while his eyes were shut and he was physically asleep, but his mental state was traumatically wide awake. I was exhausted from lack of sleep, as I spent all night sitting by Nate-Lewis' bed trying to console him. After everything he had been through, he now suffered from this form of traumatic stress due to the pain and procedures he had experienced. Getting him to let the doctors and surgeons anywhere near him, became just another impossible, heart-breaking task to overcome.

It was just after Nate-Lewis had been admitted to hospital again, this time having a nasogastric tube (NG) fitted, that I stumbled upon some information about a procedure called an ACE that a lot of children in the USA were having, to help with the complications he was suffering from. I researched it over and over again and then began to question the consultant about the procedure.

I remember sitting in his office with my dad and Nate-Lewis who was playing with the toys in the corner. He was nearly three years old now, with more than seventeen hospital admissions under his belt and all medications available to us had been exhausted, and still he was no better off. I began again asking the consultant about the ACE procedure, but he was not having any of it. Nate-Lewis was too young and they would not do the ACE in the UK until he was at least nine years old.

He would not understand what it meant to have a button on his belly, it would not be beneficial to him. He left that room in my dad's arms, while I cried, and my dad reassured me that we would keep pushing, that we would do everything we could to help our little soldier.

Nearly a year passed, with more and more hospital admissions and more emergency surgeries. My partner moved in with us and with his help, my parents and my partner's parents, we really began to apply the pressure about finding a longer-term solution for the constant pain and suffering that Nate-Lewis was dealing with every day. He was in Foundation at school (the class before starting Primary here in the UK) and his condition was affecting him more than ever.

When we dropped him off at school in the morning he would latch onto my leg, he never played with the other children, he did not even speak to them. He was petrified of going anywhere if he was having a bad time with his condition and had to wear a nappy. We had all had enough of the suffering our little boy was going through by this point.

It was during another hospital visit, where we spoke to one of the surgeons who had regularly operated on Nate-Lewis over the years. We explained to her all the reasons we were desperate for the ACE procedure to be considered. It was the first time we really felt like we were being listened to and she herself put forward our argument of the ACE to the consultant. We heard nothing.

We were getting on with our lives, stumbling through, taking the good days with the bad for Nate-Lewis. We were all exhausted, we were up through the night with him in agony, worrying all through the days that he actually made it to school, and nobody really knew what the future held. He was four now and still had to wear a nappy on the days when he was uncontrollably leaking. He had just started year one in primary school when I received a letter through the post. Reading it, I was confused. It was from the hospital for Nate-Lewis and it made no sense. It mentioned that he was booked in for an operation in two weeks' time, but we had no idea what operation. It had only been around three weeks since his last emergency surgery and we had not heard anything from his consultant.

My partner called the hospital to ask them to explain what the letter was about, and his mouth dropped open. The letter was referring to the ACE procedure. We cried and we smiled, we rang all our family to tell them the news, we had finally done it, Nate-Lewis, at four years old was getting a Mini Button.

 The day soon came around, it was a chilly October and my dad dropped myself, my partner and Nate-Lewis at the Children's Hospital. Again, I watched him drift off to sleep in the anaesthetic room and then we waited. At six pm he was brought back onto the ward.

He awoke groggily, and as usual after every operation we presented him with an array of snacks. He clumsily ate his cheese sandwich and cried in pain.

We slowly got him dressed into some fresh pyjamas and that is when we all got a look at his new mini button, it was sore, red and bloody, but we had hope that this was a new beginning.

It did not take long for Nate-Lewis to get used to his new addition but the first time we had to do his wash out was a whole new story! His button goes into his large intestine which requires us to do a wash out procedure every day, to flush his bowels. We use an enema solution and salt-water through his button, he stays on the toilet for around one hour while the solutions do their magic and clear his bowels for him. The first time the nurse came to show us how to carry this out was quite an experience. Myself, my partner, the nurse, and Nate-Lewis were all squashed into the bathroom. Nate-Lewis did not like it one bit, his button was only around four days old, still sore and he flinched and cried when we had to touch it to attach his tube and bag and still to this day he tells us how horrible it tastes when he has his flush out!

It has been two years now and we have not had one hospital admission since his ACE procedure. Nate-Lewis is out of nappies, out of pain, he no longer gets constipated, nor does it leak out uncontrollably. His superhero button, as he calls it, has literally changed his life. He enjoys going to school, has many friends, playing football, is on his scooter, motorbike and quad, is amazing in his swimming lessons (maybe because my parents buy him fish and chips every week after his lesson!) and he loves chasing the beagles around the garden at my partners parents' house!

Nate-Lewis no longer holds onto me in the playground, he is off running around with his friends, laughing and playing like a six-year-old should, and the night terrors have finally phased out. He does not let his button stop him from doing anything, the world is literally his oyster.

The first four years of his life were heart breaking for everyone around Nate-Lewis, but most people were understanding and helpful with the situation. Occasionally there was a person who found it funny that my son was born with no anus, but we continue to raise him to be proud of his experiences and his condition (he's always showing off his magic button!). I was a young single mum with my parents as my support and it has now extended to my partner and his family too. Life is finally good; we are currently waiting to hear about the next steps in the process for my partner to adopt Nate-Lewis too.

We don't know what lies ahead long term for him, maybe he will regain control of his bowel and he can have his button removed or maybe he will have it for life, but either way we are confident he will grow up to be a very special, charming, young man.

He may be one in 5000, but to us he is our one in a million.

61. Monroe's Story - Emily Virginia (USA)

My husband and I were very excited to be expecting our second child, a daughter. I started having contractions at 35 weeks and she was born that weekend. Shortly after delivery, a nurse came into the room and asked us if we had been told that something could be wrong with our daughter. We were both taken aback by the question and said no. It was then that we were told something that no parent wants to hear. She was born with an imperforate anus, meaning no anal opening.

They told us that she would need immediate surgery and that she would be transferred to another hospital which was only five minutes from our house. We got to go up to the NICU later that morning to see her and hold her.

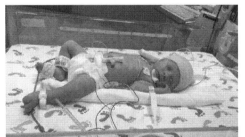

At some point during that first day, she passed some meconium which was great news! That meant that she did not need immediate surgery or a colostomy. Initially, they thought she would need a colostomy to be able to have bowel movements until her corrective surgery.

A lot of babies, like Monroe, need a colostomy right away but we were lucky because she had a fistula, a tiny opening in her vaginal canal, that she was able to pass stool from. I had to dilate it each day to make sure it stayed open until her corrective surgery.

She would need to stay in the NICU for several days for jaundice. The doctors said I could nurse her that evening. Thankfully, she nursed liked a champ and since we lived so close to the hospital, I was able to go up there and nurse her every three hours. She had a few setbacks with the jaundice, but after a week we were able to bring her home at 4lbs 13oz.

Life went on as well as it could considering the circumstances. When she was four months, she had her first major surgery to create her anal opening on August 20, 2015. It is called a PSARP (Posterior Sagittal Anorectoplasty). I was so nervous about caring for her after this surgery. We spent five days in the hospital, but thankfully it was only five minutes from our house, so her dad and brother were able to come visit often.

A few weeks after her surgery the surgeons instructed me to start dilating her new opening. This made me so nervous because of all the stitches and Monroe would really stiffen up when she knew it was time to dilate. I had to do this twice a day for about a year. It was the hardest thing I had to do, but the consequences of not doing it would have been far worse.

In January of 2016 she started having fevers off and on with no other symptoms. I kept taking her to the Paediatrician and never got answers until about the third trip when he decided to check for a UTI (urinary tract infection) and that is exactly what it was. So, she started a round of antibiotics. A few days after finishing the medicine she started having a fever again. Another UTI! So, we were referred to a paediatric urologist.

The urologist scheduled her for a test called a VCUG (voiding cystourethrogram). They would put her to sleep and inject some dyes into her kidney to look for reflux. This means her urine would flow back up into her kidneys from her bladder and ureters. Sure enough, she did have the reflux. She was put on prophylactic antibiotics, low dose, to help prevent future UTI's. This is a condition that sometimes corrects itself as children grow. She got another UTI about 6-8 months later. This time we decided to correct her reflux by having the doctor perform a Deflux which is where he adds a little gel to the flap between the kidneys and ureter to prevent backflow.

She was free from UTI's for over a year when they started returning. She was also stooling non-stop and none of her doctors could tell us why. Her paediatrician suggested I give her Imodium, so we did that for over a year, but it did not help much. She would go so frequently that as soon as I could change her, she would go again. She also had bleeding sores on her bottom from all the stooling. I took her to the Paediatrician, her surgeon, Dermatologist, Infectious Disease, and Wound Care. Nothing helped! I tried nearly every OTC booty cream and well over ten prescription creams. The obvious answer was to get her to stop stooling but how? During this time, we moved from Louisiana to Texas and I found an amazing support group for families and people with an Imperforate Anus. I found out so much information that no doctor had mentioned to me previously.

I was all set up to take her to a hospital in Ohio where there are doctors that specialise in IA. That is when I found out about a local surgeon that trained with the doctors in Ohio and he was opening an ARM (Anorectal Malformation) Clinic in downtown Houston. This hospital is only 35 miles from our house! I knew it was God that brought us down here to get real help for our sweet girl. I immediately called and got her in to see this doctor. He scheduled an exam under anaesthesia to ensure her PSARP had been performed correctly.

Many times, kids have to have them redone because general paediatric surgeons are not knowledgeable in this procedure. The good news is that Monroe's PSARP was done correctly. He also did a contrast enema to check for abnormalities in Monroe's colon. He found that she was the most impacted child that he had ever seen! Thank goodness for this doctor. After this procedure she stooled and then she stooled for days! It was a mess, but I was so happy to have some answers and relief for her. I felt terrible that she had been so impacted, we had no idea and I had been giving her Imodium which only made it worse.

She was then put on daily laxatives to help her go. People with IA do not just have a birth defect, but it also affects how the colon and intestines works. Their muscles do not work well, if at all, so they need laxatives or enemas daily to give their colon a push to empty. With the laxatives she also takes fibre to help bulk up her stools, so it is not as runny. This is not an exact science and two years later I am still trying to help her find the right balance. The IA Surgeon also ordered an MRI to check for a tethered spinal cord. This is another condition common with IA and can also affect the bladder and bowels.

When the results came back, we were referred to a Neurosurgeon who confirmed she does have a tethered cord. Back to the urological aspect, once in Texas and after her UTI's came back, I got her in to see a Urologist at another hospital. This urologist scheduled a called Urodynamics. This test studies how the bladder and urethra perform their job of storing and releasing urine. Everything looked fairly good with this test, but it did show that she does not fully empty her bladder after going, which could be another reason for the UTI's. She was put back on a prophylactic antibiotic to prevent any more UTI's.

This brings us to March 2019 when she had a fever and had check for a UTI. I was right, she had another one. About a month or so later she ended up with another UTI. This time the test showed she was resistant to most antibiotics and her urologist referred us to Infectious Disease to figure out what is going on. Each time she is on an antibiotic she becomes resistant, so with this current UTI she has two oral antibiotics that could get rid of it and if she becomes resistant then the only thing left is IV antibiotics.

In May 2019, I took her downtown to see her IA Surgeon, a new Urologist who is supposed to be one of the best, and paediatric gynaecology. Urology wanted me to try some behavioural bladder control and timed voiding. The problem is that she mostly refuses to sit on the potty. Then in June she had another UTI. Another round of antibiotics and she was put back on a prophylactic. We saw the downtown Urologist in July and they wanted to do another VCUG and Urodynamics test which was scheduled for August. Based on this test she was diagnosed with a neurogenic bladder. Also, her reflux was back and worse than it was originally. She had another UTI during this test. The urologist did not want to do anything but continue to wait and monitor.

After encouragement from friends, I decided to take her for a second opinion to a urologist in another state, who also knows a lot about IA. He instructed me to immediately start cathing Monroe every three hours. This was terrifying but a relief because I felt like we were finally getting Monroe some help. I knew something had to be going on because she could not potty train and needed to urinate more than other kids. Monroe was not receptive to the cathing, so I got her a bunch of small gifts and she could pick one each time she cooperated with a cath. After about two weeks she realized that it did not hurt and became very cooperative.

In January 2020, Monroe began hating the chocolates laxatives again. It would take hours to get her to put it in her mouth and then she would keep it in her mouth for up to three hours. Her stooling was all over the place and she was getting giant, fluid filled blisters on her bottom. I told her we were going to have to start doing enemas if she does not take her medicine. I got everything set up for an enema and she was getting nervous. She allowed me to insert the catheter and then she said, 'Well that didn't hurt'. Since then, we have been doing enemas every night. It is also not an exact science and takes time getting the formula right. She has gotten backed up twice, but the last few days have been going well.

Also, in January I took her back to the Urologist for another Urodynamics test so that he could see how her bladder and reflux were doing since the cathing. He was pleased and said things are coming along as he would expect. She still has reflux, but it should heal, and the neurogenic bladder is likely for life. We will be cathing forever, but she has been wanting to help take it out.

It has been a year since we started intermittently catheterizing and Monroe has been UTI free and her VUR (bladder reflux) has healed!

62. Estelle's Story – Coralie (Australia)

Estelle Marie Fraser was born on Valentine's Day in 2015. Estelle was not born in my hometown. We had to go to the city as we already knew before she was welcomed into the world that she had a condition called dextrocardia, which means her heart was on the right side, not the left. When she came out screaming, I was so relieved.

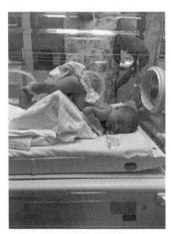

When a child with a heart condition comes into the world all you want is to hear that cry. Knowing this we had a team of doctors, come rushing in to check her over and after ten minutes a lovely doctor came over, and said calmly they had seen this lots before. He said that Estelle had no anal opening and needed to go to special care and may need surgery. We were told by our surgeon, either she may come out with a colostomy or they might make her anus and do a reconnect.

She came out of surgery, a day old with a colostomy and we spent the next two weeks finding out more about the complexities of Estelle's condition (VACTERL association) and learning how to look after her at home and manage her bag.

A few weeks later, we came back to get her test results. We walked into a very daunting situation with our surgeon, who was very off putting. He pushed his chair out arrogantly, put his notes on his lap and did not speak and then slammed his notes on the table. He then looked up and said that even though Estelle may live to an old age, life would not be easy.

In that meeting he went on to say she would live a sheltered life and was trying to say she would not have a sex life even though she was not even one years old yet. He said we needed to move to the city and buy a house near a school so that if she had accidents, she could come home and shower.

He said we should not talk to anyone about her condition so that she would not get bullied at school. The meeting was heart wrenching and left us dumb founded that a professional would speak to us so rudely. I honestly felt that he was blaming us for her complex issues.

I have decided to make this story short and sweet, as I honestly could write a full book of Estelle's journey and she is only five, soon to be six. The journey has been an absolute rollercoaster, but we would not have her any other way. We live in very rural Australia in the middle of nowhere and we travel for specialist care, which is a six hour drive every time. Estelle, now at age of five, has had close to forty surgeries, and that does not include the awful tests and appointments.

The date we will always remember is her first birthday where she was taken for emergency surgery, after a surgery break down went wrong and her little body was going into septic shock. Looking back that was one of the hardest moments. I cried so hard the night before when the fever started, I was worried I would lose her, and I felt out of control.

Another story is just before my wedding with Estelle's dad, Jake She was hospitalised with a blood infection and being rural we were told we may need to fly to the city and miss the wedding, that would be hard because I was technically the main event.

Well, we persevered, and she got better, but then the vomiting started. Our doctor had given us gastro from the boy next door and two days before the wedding she was still in hospital with this nightmare. On the wedding day things were looking better as Estelle was going to be released. But then I started to vomit, yes, I had gastro on my wedding day.

A week later we went to the city for a surgery for Estelle. Our honeymoon was spent in the city in Ronald MacDonald house. Well, as if it could not get any worse, it did. There were complications and Estelle's bladder stopped working and we were down there for five weeks.

There are so many stories to tell, so many days when we have all felt like we wanted to give up, especially the tests where they held her down to stick tubes everywhere.

We have changed surgeons and thankfully we are so incredibly happy and grateful for our new surgeon, who we have a much better relationship with. In the last year things took a huge step back, I was hoping Estelle would be finished with surgeries before school, unfortunately she is going to big school with a colostomy bag, but she does not mind. She loves herself anyway.

But my god our little girl is amazing, she's so resilient and confident and she has no fear and has such a personality. We would not have her any other way; her scars tell a story and remind us of what she has endured and how far we have come.

We are unbelievably proud of her.

I hope one day she can stand up tall and tell everyone about her bravery.

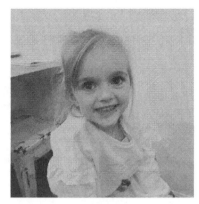

63. My Son's Story – Chloe (Northern Ireland)

My baby boy was born just over five years ago with high IA. I was only 19 at the time and he was my first child. I was already nervous and then had a dramatic labour, as his heart rate dropped and loads of doctors rushed in.

Not long after my son was born, during the post birth check over, I noticed all the doctors went quiet and suddenly loads of other doctors were coming and going. I still had not held my baby boy at this point and I was wondering what was going on.

Then one doctor came over to me and said that your son has no anal opening. In the hospital where I gave birth, they had never seen this before, so loads of doctors came and went. They then took him away to the neonatal unit and he was then transferred to the royal hospital further out, which had dealt with cases like this before.

I felt so lonely spending my first night as a mother in hospital with all these crying babies, while mine was in a different hospital to me. I had nurses coming to check on my baby then to realise I was actually alone. I just remember crying the whole night, it was awful.

He had surgery on day two and got his colostomy bag. At first, I felt so ashamed and blamed myself and I constantly searched to see what I had done wrong in my pregnancy for my baby to have to go through all this pain. I felt like a bad person.

I managed reasonably with the bag, but I did not know any different, as he was my first child. I still felt like I could not talk to others about it, as it was all so unusual. Having a baby who has to have this bag on his belly, was difficult but I managed.

We got threw the dilations phase which was very hard because I had to physically restrain his wee legs in a 'frog like' position, and again that made me feel like the worst mum in the world. Why did I have to be the one to put my baby through all this? His daddy could not handle doing it, so I felt like all the pressure was on me. It was the only way of giving him a sort of normal life.

Fast forward to four years later and he has no colostomy bag, but still has no bowel control. Some days are better than others and it affects his mental health. I see this every day and it tears me apart, because there is nothing I can physically do to take that away from him.

He is the strongest, most determined little boy I have met. I know there is a long road ahead for both of us but especially for my boy. I just hope we can get to the stage where he is comfortably clean and can enjoy life as a child, without having to worry about 'accidents' that he is not aware of.

It must be so hard for him to deal with and I just wish I could do more for him!

64. Sarah Morton - 5 Year Old Son (England)

When I think back to when my son was born, I felt so much happiness, but that was quickly replaced with fear and sadness. I did not understand what was happening at the time they took my baby away from me to a different hospital. All I remember is surgeons and doctors talking to me, explaining everything, but I did not take any of it in. It was all just a blur.

He was diagnosed with low Imperforate Anus and at two days old he had his first operation to have a stoma, which at the time I did not even understand what it was. I was so scared and worried, and it was so hard, and I cried so many tears. I am a single mum and I did not know how I was going to cope on my own. I knew that I had to be brave and try to find strength which I did not know I had. I am just so grateful I had my mum's support group.

I remember sitting on the NSU ward for hours and I would look at my tiny baby and feel terrified, wondering what his future would hold. He then had his PSARP operation at five months and then his reversal a few months later. Thankfully, it all went really well, and his surgeon was happy.

However, we have had to deal with ongoing issues with constipation and at times getting very backed up, so we started him on Sodium picosulfate and Movicol. It has taken a while to get the right amount that works for him, but in the past six months he has gone from having no control of his bowels to now starting to get some 'feeling' and learning to recognise when he needs to go to the toilet. He has recently stopped wearing pull up nappies and the only problem he has right now, is sometimes when he needs to go, he has to get to a toilet fast.

He is now five years old and he is doing amazingly and he makes me so proud every day. Life has not been easy for him but he is such a happy boy and he is my real-life superhero. I have spent the past five years worrying and thinking that he will never have control of his bowels.

I know that every child is different, but I hope my son gives some of you some hope for the future.

65. Our L's Story - Keith and Jess (Canada)

Our little L was born in November 2015. Our fourth child, planned and anticipated, prayed over and prepared for, he promptly arrived on his due date and we were smitten. His warm little body snuggled against mine; we savoured those first few minutes of meeting our newest little family member. We took pictures, our big smiles showing we had no clue that our world would change so very quickly.

I (Mom) am a special education teacher and have worked with many children with a variety of disabilities and differences over the years. Two of our older children have hearing loss and wear hearing aids. When my husband and I found out we were expecting our fourth child, we started praying for good health and particularly that this baby would pass his hearing test. And while baby L did later pass his hearing test (hallelujah!), we discovered shortly after his arrival that he had a host of other medical problems that we had simply never heard of and didn't know existed.

Savouring the thrill of having just met our new child, we waited eagerly as our family doctor checked L over. Our doctor came over to us and, as gently as he could, broke the news that little L had no anal opening and would need surgery today or tomorrow. We would be transferred to the local Children's Hospital. I was not allowed to breastfeed him yet. Time stopped as we tried to take this all in. A paediatrician came to assess him. We were in shock, blindsided by all the new information. The paediatrician thought there were a few more small abnormalities and perhaps our son had a type of syndrome, but later we found out that some of her observations were incorrect!

We bravely, yet still excitedly, phoned our parents to tell them of our son's arrival. The phone call to my mom and dad stands frozen in time. "We have a new baby! A boy! His name is L and he was born today." There was much joy and congratulating and then a pause. It was a pause that stands still in my mind as I knew that what I was about to say next would weigh heavily and hit hard. "There is a problem though, he, well, has no bum hole".

Sometimes life makes your heart break, and my heart broke with a scar that might not fully heal until heaven. What did "no bum hole" mean for our child? Besides being scared, we were grappling with the awkwardness of what to tell family and friends. If I had been born with an imperforate anus (a new term we quickly learned), would I want my parents to tell everyone? We simply did not know and a world of unknowns was just beginning. Soon our sweet baby boy was whisked away in an ambulance and we left the hospital with empty arms. We quickly packed additional items at home and then sped to the Children's Hospital to be with our son.

Entering the NICU (Neonatal Intensive Care Unit) was like entering another little world of its own. Rigorously washing-up before entering, we were then met with the curious looks from other parents and staff who were already professionals at navigating this new place. Along with the constant beeping of monitors, there was a maze of screens, drips, poles and cords around each baby's station. Seeing the little incubators nestling tiny babies, we quickly noted that "Little L" was "big beefy L" compared to the premature babies delicately being cared for here.

Baby L was being checked over thoroughly when we arrived. His heart was good. The cardiologist happily introduced herself, only to wryly add that she hoped we would never need to meet again.

More check-ups and tests followed and then, in a blur, our baby L went for surgery to have a colostomy placed. A newborn with a colostomy. It seemed so foreign. When can I hold my baby? When can I breastfeed him? Where can I lay down and let my post-delivery body rest?

We spent a week in the NICU. More check-ups, medication for L's pain and recovery, holding him at last, pumping breast milk, breastfeeding at last, beeping monitors, visitors, learning how to change L's colostomy bag and crying our eyes out at Starbucks. These things all filled that week. We were eager yet nervous to go home. We missed our other kids, although thankful that family could help with watching them while we were with L. We longed for finding a new normal back home with four kids, whatever that might look while juggling a colostomy. Yet the hospital felt safe with having staff on hand. Could we really manage the colostomy bag at home? Was breastfeeding really established? Was he really getting enough nutrients for his post-op little body? Was he for sure gaining weight?

Life did settle into somewhat of a routine, albeit stressful. L's skin didn't seem to like the colostomy sticker too much and we had many, many bag leakages; so often they seemed timed for 3:00am. At first it was a team effort (from both Mom and Dad), but with my husband's return to work I needed to find a way to conquer this on my own and I did. We managed. But then other things began happening and soon we discovered what seemed to be urinary tract infections - repeatedly. Several rounds of antibiotics later, little L was actually still little. Weight gain was such a battle. Why was it so hard to grow?

More testing was done and, after too many trips to the emergency room for infections, his medical team concluded that he had a fistula, though its location and implication were vague. The hope was that at his next surgery, aimed for six months of age, an anus would be constructed and the pull down of the bowel would block off any problematic plumbing.

We limped along, trying to navigate the winding path of L's health. We certainly celebrated milestones such as smiling, reaching for toys, mid-lining and rolling over. Despite trying times, we found many moments of joy and could count our blessings. But as the infections and medical care continued, we accepted the news that unfortunately our son had significant bladder problems too. The diagnosis of neurogenic bladder was added to his file and we again shed tears of worry and sadness for our sweet boy. Soon he went for surgery for a supra-pubic catheter to be put in. We learned how to manage this new intervention and thankfully his infections decreased. But bladder spasms then became an added problem, sadly causing many sleepless nights for L (and us as parents) due to so much discomfort from the catheter.

L turned six months of age and went for his anal reconstruction surgery. At this time, his bladder was also on trial as we spent the week in hospital. While his bum cooperated, his bladder would not, so as both his medical team and parents, we were left with no other choice than to go ahead with a vesicostomy for L. (With hindsight, this was a good decision and his bladder has been healthy ever since, with nearly no infections! The downside of course is that generally there are then few options left, meaning that L, who is now four years old, still has a vesicostomy and the plan is for him to have a Mitrofanoff within the next year or so.)

L then turned nine months of age and had his colostomy reversal surgery. No more bag. It was surreal. Victorious, right? Not totally. He struggled with a severe bum rash for the next ten long months. It finally cleared however, and I can only conclude that it must have been the many probiotics that I finally rigidly prioritised after trying many other remedies. We certainly tried them all, from various kinds of creams and ointments to various "old wives tales".

And then life settled into a quiet rhythm, for a brief while. No more surgeries loomed for now. We watched our beautiful son grow and thrive and then, at age two, become a big brother! We were unexpectedly blessed with a fifth child, which was a joy but also added to the busyness of life! A new rhythm came, but this time it was "just" the zoo of life with a newborn and becoming a family of seven!

Time trekked along then suddenly kindergarten appeared on the horizon.

While we had become fairly used to L's situation by this time and had been blessed with a lot of support from family, friends, church and babysitters, it still felt scary for our little boy to enter the school system.

L also started to ask more questions. While this was good and appropriate, my heart ached when he would blink his long eyelashes at me and ask, "Why do I have a broken bum?".

How could we, as parents, give him the right attitude to accept and be comfortable with the bum and bladder that he was given? We tried to answer as age appropriately as possible, telling him that his bum was indeed tricky, but that was alright and with the help from amazing doctors he would be ok. We focussed on the positives and the bigger picture, reminding him that he could run fast and jump high and write his name and be a good friend. We still remind him of those things today (he is nearly five years old), and as parents we remind ourselves of this too and try to keep perspective.

We don't know what L's future holds, though we know God holds his future. We are thankful for L's amazing medical team in Vancouver, Canada. As mentioned, he will likely get a Mitrofanoff. We are also in discussions with his medical team to have a cecostomy done. Many children with imperforate anus have successful continence stories to tell but, so far, we do not. But this does not need to define him. And it's not where his story ends. L is brave, smiley, goofy and athletic. He learned to ride a bike early (two-wheeler at age three) and has a special softness for animals (we have a dog and a bunny).

He loves to whisper at bedtime "Guess what I'm going to say?" and when we pretend to not know, he says, "I love you!" and giggles. He loves to give "lovey hugs", a name he gives for extra tight hugs that include a kiss on the cheek.

He has started kindergarten now and has a wonderful Educational Aide who changes his diaper three times a day (or as needed) at school. He loves school and has many friends there. He really has been blessed with a wonderful life.

If you have a child who is similar to L, feel free to send me a message to our email address keithjess@gmail.com

One of the most powerful things for us was to find other parents in the same boat as us. You are not alone.

Like us, perhaps you've joined a club that you didn't know existed. Despite the ups and downs, there is still much joy here.

66. You Are My Sunshine When Skies Are Grey - By Anonymous

On my son's second day of life, while still in the hospital, I asked the nurse on duty, "So, will I be able to go home if I don't do a Number Two?"

"Will our son, Joshua, be able to go home if he doesn't do a Number Two?" my husband wisely and thankfully interrupted.

"What? He hasn't gone yet?" the nurse questioned perplexedly.

Soon thereafter many confused nurses and doctors peeked in, inspected and quietly left our room. Something was up. My heart raced. Uncontrollable tears streamed down my face.

I witnessed the nurses look at and weigh every diaper since Joshua's first breath. Had they not paid attention to this potentially fatal error, even after the inspecting doctor hadn't caught my son's missing anus?

My experience with ARM (Anorectal Malformation) had just begun. Although I was in a fog, I remember doctors telling my husband and I very early on that due to the position of the join in our son's ureter and rectum (being closer towards the bladder) plus lack of muscle development near his anus, Joshua (among other health concerns) would be highly prone to faecal incontinence.

As if this invisible but ever-present condition wasn't enough, there was a possibility that Joshua may have other associated abnormalities that we had not yet been made aware of. Thus, a VACTERL test was done. In a nutshell, this is an assessment done on babies to determine whether or not there are any other accompanying conditions that may be present. While we were most fortunate to not have any other irregularities, life for our family was still vastly altered.

I was completely unprepared for how to navigate raising a son with this rare condition, which occurs only "One in 5000". I felt clueless and completely out of my league.

Although it was terrifying at first, we were offered a community care nurse to come and support us after coming home from the hospital. She managed to ease my nerves somewhat and over time I managed to change Joshua's colostomy bag without becoming a nervous wreck. I had learned, despite the severe rashes and leaking pouches, that Joshua would be okay. Nonetheless, I was still discouraged. Why him?

As time went on, I gradually became more familiar with Joshua's condition. Although I was becoming more well-versed in it and could ask more relevant questions during check-ups, specialist appointments and nurse visits, I still didn't seem to get any straight answers to most of what I asked. Mostly, what I heard seemed to be comments like:

"It depends."
"We'll wait and see."
"Perhaps, overtime he'll have more sensation"
"We are hopeful..."
"I am encouraged that..."
"We need to be careful that...etc."

As far as what was really going on inside his body, it was far too complicated to get a straight answer, made all the more complex given that no two people with ARM have the same road map of life. Oftentimes, it has been a lonely and bumpy road trying to figure out what is best for Joshua, both physically and emotionally.

Fast forward - Joshua is now five years old. There continues to be a daily urgency of his digestive tract. Consequently, I too have a pressing importance to step in and give him a hand cleaning up. Sometimes however, I struggle... Do I continue to jump in every time offering my support and teach him to respond appropriately? Rather, do I wait it out a little longer and just delay the deafening moans, groans and frequent meltdowns that inevitably come from being told that it's time to go to the washroom as he understands this will result in a prolonged amount of time. Simply reminding Joshua that his body is telling him that it is time to go; giving reminders of what his doctors have suggested to him; offering stickers towards a preferred activity; or the promise of being awarded added screen time do absolutely nothing to entice Joshua to go without EXTREME hesitation. The following response has become repetitive and somewhat exhaustive:

"No, I hate the washroom!"
"I don't want to!"
"I never want to go to the washroom again!" and, most recently,
"I hate food!" (for he knows this will result in solid waste).
Being reminded that he could get a rash, or have bleeding due to his avoidance is frequently met with,
"I DON'T CARE!".

Regardless, great patience is needed. During these moments, I have nothing better for coping than to just breathe slower, deeper and with compassion.

I desperately wish I had the magic words, non-invasive procedure, or better yet, cure to make it easier on all of us. I am fully aware that Joshua is not trying to be difficult. Instead, he is frustrated and would far prefer to be doing something more exciting and less time consuming than wait for his body to even partially eliminate - something others take for granted each day.

My husband and I consistently and faithfully do what we need to, in as supportive a manner as we can, in an effort to ensure that Joshua doesn't feel at all burdensome. This is when I hear the teachings, "Patience is a virtue" and "There are people who have far more complicated conditions" and "we are fortunate".

I am so grateful to Joshua's surgeon. He will forever hold a place in my heart for he gave my son an "opening". As well, I am thankful for Joshua's nurses especially his nurse practitioner, who not only gave my husband and I quality education about ARM and ostomy care, but for her peaceful aura and listening ears during our scariest of days. Being able to send Joshua to a nurturing school with caring teachers and caregivers has been a huge relief. I have gratitude for Joshua's paediatrician, for her support, dedication and willingness to learn alongside us, as well as the friendly and inviting manner in which she greets Joshua at every visit. As well, a private online network reminds me that our family is not alone. Here we have learned about webinars run by specialised health experts and have received advice from families like ours. I am comforted by members of the ARM community who have been brave enough to tell their stories. I have been given perspective, suggestions, warmth and kindness. For the prayer warriors out there, words can't express my appreciation.

Finally, I continue to find comfort from the support of my understanding family and very close friends. They not only remind me that I can have a shoulder to cry on when I get down and need more encouragement but also advise me to continue to be hopeful that there are bright days ahead.

Joshua is our most precious gift and we continue to advocate for him while we can. We continue to be determined to make him aware that he can do and become anything he wants. Each day, we pray for his continued healing. It is our hope that proper attention, empathy, medical advice and solutions surrounding quality of life will be offered in the near future both for him and the many others who are faced with ARM.

Joshua will always continue to be the sunshine when skies are sometimes grey.

7. Zachary's Story (New Zealand)

This is my son Zachary's story and I believe it is his to tell when he has his own voice and can fully understand how his body works, but I would like to briefly share my perspective.

I was absolutely stunned when the doctor told me that there were some problems when my baby was born. He was subsequently diagnosed with Imperforate Anus, which I had no idea of, and did not think was even possible. He was diagnosed with other issues. They were a hole in his heart, ventricular septum defect and he did not have an appendix.

It was a real struggle for our family in the early years, because we had surgeons say totally different things to us. This caused great frustration. And I just could not understand why there was not a consistent diagnosis and knowledge of IA.

When we finally got comfortable with a surgeon, inevitability they would leave, and I would have to start all over again. I got so sick of repeating my son's story every six months to a new person.

I have learnt so much in the seven years since my son was born and I honestly feel like I could be a doctor myself now. I had always hoped that his bowel issue would magically fix itself and he would be able to go on his own, but I now get that was just wishful thinking.

When he was four years old, we chose to go down the path of having further surgery and he was given a Malone where he could have his flushes through his tummy.

Initially it was a battle for him to adjust to having the flush, but he slowly adjusted to it and now is pretty accepting. He has struggled at times with a bit of growth under the Chait button, pushing it out and then it catches on things and bleeds.

As he continues to grow, we have had to change his button each year, but it is a relatively minor procedure and he has it done without any sedation. He is such an incredibly brave boy.

We have settled into a regime of having his flush every second day and fortunately he has been able to remain clean in between, which has been a definite relief for his schooling.

As much as it has improved his quality of life, he wants to change the times he has his flush and sometimes just cannot be bothered. So, I have to keep explaining to him that it is something he has to do even though it is not what he wants to do. My hope is that as he gets older, he will fully accept and understand why it is so important to keep a consistent regimen.

My great hope is one day Zachary will get to the stage where we can try and get him on a laxative only regime, and he will not need to use the Malone.

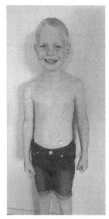

Zachary has had to deal with so much in his seven years, he has had to endure countless hospital visits and medical appointments. He has had twelve surgeries and even more tests and invasive procedures due to his many complications. Thankfully, his cardiac issues were able to be addressed through surgery when he was a baby, and he has not had to deal with any long-term problems.

I have been told by the surgeons that his IA is a completely random occurrence, but I feel like there must be some sort of explanation, it is frustrating.

After having so many issues with his medical care, we are now fortunate that Zachary has been able to establish a very close bond with his paediatric surgeon who he really trusts. He really helps him with his button changes and his ongoing care and treatment.

As he has grown up spending so much time in hospitals and now has such a special relationship with his surgeon, he is now telling us when he grows up, he wants to be a surgeon, which is just so precious.

68. Nico's Story - Rhett Tanner, Nico's Dad (USA)

After three solid years of "practicing "and lots of fertility, we were blessed with a handsome baby boy that came with his own set rules. From day one he was ready to forge his own path. Everything we had planned had to be adjusted. Nico decided he was on his own schedule!!

Of course, our initial response was what do we do, how do we proceed!! With many sleepless nights and soooo many questions, Nico endured surgeries every three months for the first two years of his life.

He is a ROCKSTAR. Through it all, he has had the best outlook and attitude. Nico continues to be a strong, caring, and courageous little athlete. The day after his biggest surgery he was outside in the courtyard of the hospital playing baseball with his physical therapist and Occupational therapist. I'm not so sure it was advised by his doctor but the occupational therapist said it was ok. This is just one example of Nico's perseverance and love for sports.

I love you, little man!! Keep on crushing!!

69. Nico's Story - Hailey Tanner, Nico's Mom (USA)

My name is Hailey and when I was 33 years old, Rhett and I became parents to a beautiful baby boy on Thanksgiving Day, November 22, 2012, at 9:31 AM. The doctor's initial report confirmed his heart murmur but other than that he looked good. My husband asked if they looked at the base of the spine in which they replied no. They re-examined Nicholas, returned, and gave us the news that he did not have an opening at his anus. That is the moment our journey with IA began.

I cannot lie. The first few years were full of challenges and many times where the rare and unexplainable became the norm. To this day, my eyes fill with tears every time I allow myself to go there as he did not deserve the card he was dealt. No one does!

What I didn't realize was that Nico was born a Rockstar of epic proportions. He had surgery every three months until the age of 18 months, a total of eleven to date, and each and every time we were amazed by his healing. Nothing can get this kid down for long.

In search of answers to the millions of questions we had, we found a support group called the Pull-Thru Network. In the summer of 2016, we attended their biannual conference and THIS is where our world changed for the better. I will never forget the overwhelming feeling of walking into that conference room and knowing that everyone there, "got it." To talk with other parents and for Nico and his sister to meet other IA kids and siblings is so powerful. PTN also brings the best doctors to this conference and this is where we met Dr. Alam.

With this knowledge, Nico was able to see the best urologist, Dr. Alam, and in turn, got him to a healthy place in life. Nico is active in all sports, loves school, playing in the pool, and being with friends.

These days, in October 2020, he is about to turn eight years old. His Malone and Mitrofanoff have done wonders for his quality of life and I don't think he's seen the doctor for anything but a urine culture in the past two years.

For now, he is on a good track and we are so grateful. He's our warrior!

70. Nico's Story - Emilie Cox (Hailey's Mom), Nico's Nana (USA)

Almost eight years ago, when our grandson, Nicholas Tanner was born and our entire immediate family was there. All 11 of us and Steven (Rhett's best friend and the best man in their wedding)! We came to Charleston to Hailey and Rhett's for Thanksgiving since our daughter, Hailey, couldn't travel being weeks away from delivery.

To our surprise, Hailey had to have an emergency c-section due to her blood pressure that morning. We were prepared Nico could have heart problems but nothing prepared any of us for the imperforate anus diagnosis! Rhett actually found it! How hard this was for him is incomprehensible. How the staff missed it was shocking. We didn't even know there was such a thing.

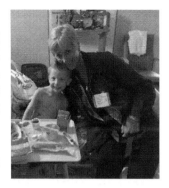

By the next day, our precious baby had a colostomy. Through the following months, we learned how to care for Nico. His fraternal grandmother and I became very close since our "kids" were hard-working caterers at the time. We babysat together many a weekend so they could work. We were there for his many surgeries. We learned how important hygiene is to prevent infection and how to do the procedures he needed daily.

We were there for our little warrior and his wonderful parents. I couldn't be more proud of Hailey and Rhett. God gave Nico exceptional parents!!

All the while, as a mother, it was so very hard for me to see how hard this was on Hailey and Rhett. Then one day Hailey came home with a sign she immediately hung. It said, "If God brings you to it, he'll bring you through it."

There was a lot of internet searching going on. Fortunately, Hailey and Rhett found the Pull-Thru Network! Their support is immeasurable! In the summer of 2016, Hailey and Rhett met Dr. Alam at the Pull-Thru Network conference. He has been Nico's doctor ever since, and a lifesaver for Nico. We all had so many unanswered questions.

We read Greg Ryan's book "A Secret Life" that opened our eyes even more as to what these children can go through. Then I met Greg at a Pull-Thru Network conference in Arizona in 2018. By then, Hailey and Rhett had reached out to him and we all gathered together to get to know each other better. Support and knowledge are key for the children and their families. Greg was trying to get ONE in 5000 off the ground. We all donated a bit and hoped it would help. Our families need support on so many levels. This organization can be so enlightening and informative. These kids have a rare disorder that isn't understood by the public. That needs to change.

Just as parents, grandparents, aunts, uncles etc. we want everyone to understand what we tell them, they cannot understand that it is a condition that is managed, not cured. Greg is opening up this source for us. We are thankful to this wonderful man.

71. Nico's Story - Barbara Thomas (Rhett's Mom), Nico's Grandma (USA)

How to describe my precious grandson, Nicholas. He's got the most wonderful smile, that warms my heart. He's loving, caring, energetic, brave, has a great sense of humour and occasionally is a little bit mischievous. In other words, he's a normal, almost eight-year-old, well-rounded, boy.

On that Thanksgiving morning, he was born, the majority of his family was at the hospital waiting to welcome him into the world. We are so thankful that it was a world that he would meet with toughness, courage, and perseverance as Nicholas was born with VACTERL Association which resulted in him needing numerous surgeries. During his surgeries and recoveries, he's amazed us with his strength. He never let his condition hold him back.

It's obvious that he gets his strength from his parents, Hailey and Rhett. Through all their anxiety, worry, and concern, they hold on to their faith that Nicholas can overcome the obstacles his condition presents. They've encouraged him to be open about his condition and he shares his uniqueness with his family and friends.

Looking into the future, how will I describe my precious grandson, Nicholas. I see him as a compassionate, responsible, generous, kind, loving, young man who doesn't let his medical condition hold him back as he continues to meet the world with toughness, courage, and perseverance.

72. Nico's Story - Kim, Nico's Aunt (USA)

In being a part of Nico's life and watching him grow up, I've been impressed with his ability to make the best out of every situation and look on the Sunny Side of Life. He's an inspiration and I think much of this comes from the personality he was born with, as well as his parents and extended families belief that he is strong and capable of being anything he wants to be.

All people have different limitations. Nicholas's limitations haven't stopped him from making relationships, being curious about the world, learning, growing and helping others. The IA community and the Pull-Thru Network have made a huge difference. It's amazing how parents, siblings, and patience can lift each other up, support each other, and provide information both Medical and practical, that enhance the lives of all involved.

I see Nicholas as an inspiration and believe he has the ability to make a big difference in the world. He loves with his whole heart and makes you feel special. He has my heart.

73. Nico's Story - Molly, Family Friend (USA)

Nico has been like a family member to us since he was three years old. Our two families first met when our infant daughters became day care best friends at Montessori school. The girls grew so close, in fact, that their teacher invited Nico's mom Hailey and I to school one day, convinced that we had to meet. Hailey and I soon grew as close as the girls. It was the same with our husbands. Relationships between families like that are few and far between and must be treated like gold. Coincidentally we also both had two older boys who were also the same age. Truly, it was and continues to be a match made in heaven. Not only did our daughters, Maisie and Kylie continue to be joined at the hip, but Nico and our son, Jonah quickly because fast friends as well.

We started all spending a lot of time together and it wasn't long before we also began taking trips together. I remember when our two families decided to travel to Black Mountain, North Carolina together to attend a family-friendly music festival called The Leaf Festival. The children were still quite little. The girls were maybe two-three-years old and the boys were five. We camped together for a few nights and truly had the time of our lives. Our kids were all inseparable and the layout of the festival made it so they could run around the campground freely. Watching them play outside all day, dance around to live music, giggle, get muddy and cuddle together by the fire at night are memories that I will cherish forever.

I tried hard but I wasn't able to adequately take pictures and capture all the moments I would have wanted. There were simply too many. One memory from that weekend that I will always cherish and did manage to get a photo of is all four of our kids, dressed in their warm fleece pyjamas, gathered around Nico while he sat on a small, plastic travel potty during his daily flush. He had a blanket draped over his lap for modesty and all the other kids were gathered around him. They were watching cartoons on an iPad and giggling together. The kids all knew what was happening.... They just didn't care. All they cared about was that their friend got to have an iPad and they wanted in!

Seeing them all so happy together was great. I smiled.... But I remember the moment bringing Hailey to tears. I hadn't considered up until that moment how frightening it must be to have a child with special needs and having to step back and let them be vulnerable in front of other kids. Being a mom is hard no matter what and we hold our kids emotions like fragile glass eggs. Letting go is scary for all of us but all the more so for Hailey and other mothers whose children might be considered "different".

But it was clear that all that was happening in that tent was love and laughing and having fun. I was so proud of all of them. My kids for naturally seeing Nico as a whole, wonderful human being and friend who they loved and not someone with a condition that made him separate or different. And Nico for trusting all of them enough to allow himself to be seen versus being ashamed or hiding.

As these children have grown up, they have changed and matured yet the level of respect, love and understanding that we witnessed inside the tent that morning has never changed.

Portrait by Michelle Collins

We have spent lots of time with Nico and the Tanners since then. Nico has spent the night at our house multiple times, and we have done his drains. He has patiently walked me, as the mom, through the process reassuring me that I'm doing everything correctly.

My kids see all this and don't bat an eye. Nico has taught them that different is nothing to be ashamed or fearful of. I am grateful to him that, just by being his wonderful self, he has engrained this truth into them since they were tiny.

We love that kid like a son and are so grateful to have him in our life. I can't wait to see what wonderful things are in store for him!

74. Matthew's Story - Sinèad Switzer (Ireland)

Matthew was born on June 29th, 2013 and my pregnancy was normal. He was a healthy 7lbs 11ozs, but as soon as he was lifted off me to be checked by the doctor, I knew immediately that something was wrong with his bottom. It just looked a bit unusual and I was informed by the doctor that he was born with no back passage and would need an operation in the coming days to correct it. I did not know then what that would entail. In fact, I had never heard of imperforate anus. It was a big shock, and I was utterly devastated for my little boy.

He was transferred to another hospital at twelve hours old and they were amazing! They still are to this day! He had surgery to give him a stoma at three days old. It was then the doctors realized Matthew was allergic to strong painkillers, as he would swell up like a balloon and his little eyes would be swollen shut. So, every operation he had after that one, he only had ordinary paracetamol as pain relief. He truly has the highest pain threshold even now and never complains when he is sick.

At seven months old Matthew had his surgery to create his back passage and due to a poor recovery from his anaesthetic, he spent a night in intensive care. However, he was soon well enough to be discharged and then we had to do dilatations to stretch his anus and get it to the size needed for his stoma reversal. He had his reversal at thirteen months old and it went really well. His first poo was emotional, but odd, as I was not used to changing a dirty nappy and I was so slow that Matty kept weeing on me! But I soon got used to it!

Everything went really well for Matthew and I until he was nineteen months, when he unexpectedly got extremely ill. At first doctors thought it was a bad stomach bug, but thanks to a very observant nurse who smelt faeces on Matthew's breath, it was quickly realized his bowel had become blocked due to scarring from previous surgeries. He had an emergency operation to fix it. I will never forget that time...my heart was broken as we had come so far. But my little warrior was soon back to his smiling self and life returned to normal!

Matthew started playschool, but I had a huge amount of difficulty potty training him. As he has not got functioning sphincter muscles in his bottom, he would end up soiling himself constantly. Things deteriorated quite badly then for Matthew as he would get horrendous constipation which would lead to overflow, and his skin on his bottom would become red raw.

Just before he started primary school, I rang the hospital in tears as I could not imagine him going to school the way things were. At this point my poor boy was pooping twenty-four hours a day, every nappy change he was soiled, and he could not wear pants like his peers.

However, a wonderful nurse changed Matthew's life forever when she suggested he would be a good candidate for bowel washouts. I was taught by her one rainy afternoon over two years ago and even after the first one Matt did not soil himself. In fact, the next day we went to buy underwear for him! He loved picking out ones with buses on!

Since then, Matthew has thrived! We do washout together every night and it has become a lovely time with us talking or reading while we wait for his bowel to be clear. He loves the freedom it gives him!

Anorectal malformation is a journey of ups and downs, but it has never stopped my boy! He loves buses, science, maths, ballet and animals, especially our dog! He runs with his friends and you would never know what he has been through! He is a warrior and ARM has given him a huge inner strength. As a parent I have learned so much too! The early days were scary, but I would never change it! It has made Matthew who he is, and our bond is incredibly strong for it.

75. Kaden's Story - Suzie Schultz (USA)

After almost 24 hours of labour and several hours of pushing, our baby finally arrived. But instead of being handed over to me, a swarm of medical staff surrounded our baby, and no one was talking to us. Finally, they took my husband aside, and explained things to him. They let him convey the news to me. Imperforate anus? What did that even mean? Surgery? When? What? How? It did not make sense; we had never even heard of it. What were we going to do now?

After surgery the following morning to create a colostomy for Kaden, we got to visit him in the NICU. The nurses showed us the colostomy bag and we learned we would be getting lessons on how to change it. However, our son's skin reacted horribly to the stool that was gathering on the slivers of opening around the patch. The colostomy bag was off again less than a day or so later and it never went back on. Instead, we learned the unperfected art of double diapering an infant.

When we shared the news about our Kaden's birth, we only included vague information about staying in the NICU. With already mounting trepidation about both our son's condition and the potential social implications of such a diagnosis, we did not share openly except among family members and a few close friends. However, I did have one sorority sister who responded privately about my general Facebook post to gently inquire about the reason for my son's stay in the NICU. Only God can answer why she was the only person to ask for more details.

But it was not long after my candid response that she quickly replied, 'I think that is the same condition one of my husband's co-worker's son was born with.' And our first connection to another 1 in 5000 was made. I will be forever grateful for the over an hour phone call with Saree while she sat Robbie's bedside where he was recovering from yet another surgery. She shared hope, empathy, advice and the name of an expert, Dr. Levitt, who would soon become our son's surgeon too.

After about a week in the NICU, even though he was not yet gaining weight, the doctor made the blessed decision to release him, hoping he would gain better at home. He did! We figured out how to make things work with double diapering. We learned how to laugh, even in the challenging moments. When a child is stooling through a colostomy, they are almost always stooling. Having a baby boy pee during a diaper change is not fun but having a poop fountain through the colostomy was worse. We learned early on to keep the colostomy covered.

Also trying to double diaper is a sure recipe for frequent accidents, which resulted in a lot of clothes changes. This reminds me of a onesie our son wore that had small monkeys all over it. Quite often it would look like one monkey had pooped on the monkey below him, because the double diapers had leaked. Another particularly memorable time happened during a night-time feed when I could feel warm liquid starting to touch my own skin. Ew! We laughed. Dad cleaned up baby. Mom took a shower in the middle of the night. We carried on.

During the first six months of our son's life, we made three trips to Cincinnati, Ohio from our home in South Dakota to see Dr. Levitt. He had his PSARP surgery when he was three months old and his colostomy reversal at six months. We had planned his colostomy reversal shortly before Christmas, as I would have some time off from work for us to be in Ohio for the surgery. Kaden had a rather quick recovery and we were able to still make it back to Nebraska to celebrate Christmas with family.

The days are long, but the years are short, definitely rang true for us.

We managed his stooling with an incredibly strict diet. 'White' foods were simply banished from our house. There were only a handful of times he ever showed signs of constipation. But the stooling was frequent, and we finally realized we really were not going to be able to achieve potty training on our own.

We had heard about the bowel management program when we had been out to Ohio when he was an infant, but we were reluctant to take over a week off to return to Ohio.

By this point in time, we were in Kansas City and reached out to our local hospital. We were connected with a Gastroenterologist (GI) who seemed familiar with Kaden's condition and knew about Dr. Levitt and his work. We were excited to find local support to help us start our son on an enema routine.

However, it was not working. When our son was four and a half, we finally resigned ourselves to go to a bowel management program in Ohio. Dr. Levitt had moved to Nationwide Children's hospital by that time, so we headed to Columbus instead of Cincinnati. Our son had been having worse and worse stooling, until he was almost pooping constantly. The enemas did not seem to be helping at all.

Our bowel management trip was one crazy roller coaster ride. Both of our sons got sick on the way to Ohio. I went to the opening orientation by myself since my husband stayed back at the Ronald McDonald House with our sick children. In the short couple of hours of the orientation I quickly realized I had learned more about my son's condition and how to properly handle bowel management than the GI doctor had known. That same evening, I had the chance to meet a mother and her daughter who were also attending the bowel management boot camp. It was her daughter's birthday. What a way to celebrate, huh? We formed an instant connection, but I did not realize then how amazing a friend Michelle would become.

156

While we were there, Dr. Levitt ordered a stool test and our son was diagnosed with C.Diff. which is a bacterium that can cause symptoms ranging from diarrhea to life-threatening inflammation of the colon.

He had had surgery in January where he had likely contracted it, even though he was on antibiotics. I too had surgery in February for a deviated septum and had also been on antibiotics. I quickly suspected C. Diff., got tested, and it was confirmed. While we were still in Ohio, our youngest developed yet another ear infection from his illness, requiring a visit to urgent care, and resulting in more antibiotics. We braced for yet another family member to contract C.Diff.

We did have a chance to meet with other families with a child with anorectal malformation at a gathering in the Ronald McDonald House over the weekend. One of the little boys had a Malone. Before we had come to boot camp, one of the nurses had talked to me about a Malone being an option for my son. However, at the time, I was absolutely appalled at the suggestion of making a hole in my son's belly button to allow a catheter to go in for a top-down enema. I do not know what I imagined, but I certainly did not realize it would be invisible.

However, hearing another family talking about it as, 'the best decision ever,' almost instantly changed my perspective and I became eager to explore this option for my son. However, with my his ongoing illness and being on antibiotics, the hospital decided that the bowel management program would not be effective, and they sent us home early. We had officially failed bowel management boot camp.

However, what we learned while we were there, allowed us to figure out the right recipe for our son's daily flush and once the antibiotics took care of the C.Diff, he started to stay clean regularly for the first time ever. We also got on the schedule as soon as possible for a return trip to Ohio for a surgery to create the Malone. It just so happened that the surgery was scheduled just a few days before his birthday.

As I will readily tell our ARM community, we got our son a Malone for his fifth birthday and it was the best birthday gift he will probably ever get.

The night before we were supposed to fly back to Ohio to have the tube removed from the newly formed Malone site, the tube fell out. We did not know what to do and it took a few hours to hear back from the doctor. However, I did hear promptly from my good friend Michelle who told me in no uncertain terms that I had to get the tube back in before the site closed up. We had already put the boys to bed, so we woke up our son, managed to reinsert the tube and taped it in place. When I spoke with the doctor later, he said that 'If we were able to get the tube back in on our own, we wouldn't have to go back to see them.' It made me laugh to hear him say 'if'. Michelle had not said it was optional. She told me to do it and so we did!

It has been over four years since Kaden had his Malone. In the meantime, Dr. Rentea, who worked with Dr. Levitt, came to Kansas City and now provides us with exceptional local care. We are so thankful for her and the staff at Children's Mercy. We continue to have our ups and downs, our triumphs and our trials. There was the time his Malone opening closed up so much we had to go to the ER to have it reinserted. Under anaesthesia, they put in a Chait tube to keep it open. It fell out in the pool three days later. He has had to have a couple of additional minor surgeries. I think about the quote, 'It doesn't get easier; you get stronger.' And I am so thankful for the ways God has strengthened us through the trials. We have met amazing individuals and families who have encouraged and inspired us and helped us to carry our burden. We are so thankful for our ARM community.

I have also thought a lot lately of an analogy Bob McHardy once shared from his work with medical professionals. He asked them what it meant when a patient reacts to a drug. They said it meant negative side effects. He asked what it meant when a patient responds to a drug. They said it meant efficacy, essentially accomplishing what it was intended to do. I think the concept of response vs. reaction can also be applied in our own daily lives, particularly when we consider the extreme challenges that life often throws our way. Reacting may be our first tendency, but we also have an opportunity to respond.

I know my son's medical condition will shape him and his life in many ways. I hope we are intentional in how we respond to the challenges and opportunities that come our way, as we search for the silver lining, laugh through our tears, and find joy in the great moments, as well as the hard ones.

We want to seek opportunities to grow and learn, to develop greater empathy and compassion, to allow others to help carry our burdens, and to help carry the burdens of others as well. It is amazing how when we help lift the burdens of others, somehow our load seems to lighten a little as well.

76. A is for Austin. B is for Blake. C is for Colostomy. – Amanda Marszalik (USA)

This is the story of Blake. My sweet, kind, sassy, and goofy IA warrior. To understand Blake's journey, we have to start before he was born because Blake, is a "not-so-identical", identical twin. When I was around eight weeks pregnant, my doctor, said "Let me show you what I'm looking at here." She turned the screen, and there they were. Two little babies. Two tiny heartbeats.

Around 16 weeks, we learned that baby A and baby B were boys, and that they were starting to show a discordance in size. At 20 weeks, the official diagnosis was in. The boys had twin-to-twin transfusion syndrome, a rare and serious condition that occurs when twins share a placenta. Abnormal blood vessel connections had formed, and Baby B (Blake), the donor, was sending his fluid and nutrients to Baby A (Austin), the recipient.

At 27 weeks, concerns were growing about Blake. He was much smaller than his brother was. Anything over a 20% size discrepancy is extremely dangerous for both babies. "Did you know you are having contractions?" the sonographer asked? I looked at her surprised. "Uuuuhhhhh, I'm having what?" I assumed that contractions were the kind of thing that sent women into fits of screaming rage, or at the very least, caused one to stop in their tracks and think, "Hey, this isn't right." My abdomen felt tight. Uncomfortable. I assumed it was just normal.

They had me go to another room to monitor the contractions. Everyone seemed shocked that I didn't feel anything, and when my doctor viewed the report, I was sent immediately to the hospital.

After three days of intense medications, no food and little sleep, the maternal foetal specialist came to check on us. Within a few minutes, she said it was time. Blake's heart rate had dropped dangerously low. The babies needed to come out. Less than thirty minutes later, two itty-bitty munchkins entered the world. The nurses whisked both boys to another room where they began to resuscitate them. Austin came out first. He was in a plastic box, an isolette. He was 2 lbs. 9 oz. (1162 grams) and was breathing on his own with the aid of a CPAP machine.

Labour and delivery comments for little Blake indicate that he was born at 2 lb. 3 oz. (982 grams), and say things like "no initial resp effort," "became apnoeic when attempted to place on CPAP prongs," "copious hypopharyngeal secretions suctioned," and "sluggish response to initial intubation." While it felt like it took a lifetime for all of this to occur, I imagine it was all less than 15 minutes. Blake's APGAR score increased from one to 3 to 9 in a span of ten minutes, and he was wheeled away in his little plastic box.

Blake at 7 days old

For the next week, I watched the boys in their isolettes. They looked like tiny, plucked chickens with strawberry blonde hair and red skin. So many machines. Constant beeps and alarms. Nurses whizzing by. Hearts racing. Sighs of relief.

On day seven, everything changed again. When we called to check on the boys before heading to the hospital, the nurse explained that something was wrong with Blake. He had not yet passed stool. The nurse attempted a glycerine suppository and was unable to pass a rectal probe. The nurse used phrases like "there was nowhere for the probe to go," "rectal dimple," and "lack of anal opening."

I had NEVER heard of this, but it was the second time, in a week, that my life would change forever. I had no idea what this meant, and for the first time in ten days, I cried uncontrollably.

When we arrived at the hospital, doctors confirmed that Blake had an imperforate anus. They could not say much more. He would have to be transferred to a different Hospital down the street. A special ambulance, the Teddy Bear Transport, showed up within the hour.

The team consisted of neonatal nurses, paramedics and respiratory therapists. They carefully unhooked Blake from all of his current machines and reconnected him to their own. I stood there completely helpless as I watched everything they were doing and looked over at Austin "safe" in his own isolette. My mind was spinning with despair. How would I be a good mommy to two babies in different hospitals?

At nine days old, Blake had his first surgery, and the paediatric general surgeon was unable to locate a fistula, or abnormal passage. While it was obvious that Blake had no anus and that his rectum was not going to the right place, they couldn't identify with confidence where it was going. Blake was just too small for a safe repair, and he was given a colostomy.

"Are you ready to hold Blake?" the nurse asked?   "HECK YA!!!"

My tiny tot was 12 days old and two days post-op. The nurses and respiratory therapist helped to move Blake into my arms, onto my chest and down into my shirt. Just like a baby kangaroo in its mother's pouch, he snuggled up against my beating heart.

For a little while, all was right in the world. I softly sang a little song that I made up right there, and that I still sing to him today.

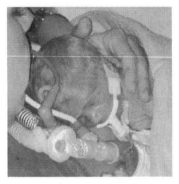

You're my little Blake.
You're as sweet as a piece of cake.
And I love you. Yes, I love you
You're my baby boy.
You bring momma so much joy.
And I love you. Yes, I love you.

First time I got to hold Blake in my arm at 12 days old

Blake joined his brother at home after 81 days in the NICU. While navigating being a first-time mom to twins, I also became a colostomy nurse. I had researched all the tricks and tips to keep Blake's skin healthy and to create a good seal on the pouch, but if it was going to leak, it never failed to do so in the middle of the night. Baths in the dark at 2:00 am followed by new attempts at getting the colostomy pouch to stick were commonplace.

At six months old, Blake weighed enough for his PSARP surgery. When we met with the surgeon afterwards, we learned that Blake has high IA. His rectum was attached to his urethra, and there was almost no muscle tone or nerve response. This was the first time that we heard the term "worst case scenario." The surgeon explained that Blake would likely never have bowel control and might have urinary issues.

For three months, I would do daily rectal dilations to help stretch the anal opening that his surgeon created. It is amazing the things you learn to do as an IA parent that you did not know even existed before this became your life. At nine months old, Blake had his colostomy take down. I can still hear his little screams from the first time he had a bowel movement. I was both horrified and overjoyed. We were entering a new phase of this journey.

Once Blake could poop, that is basically ALL he did. Unlike many IA warriors who battle constipation, Blake is hypermobile. He just kept pooping. I would go through 15 to 20 diapers a day trying to keep his skin clean and dry, but he still ended up with horrific rashes and wounds. I had to make my own wipes with only water because even the "all natural" and sensitive brands, would lead to a blood curdling scream when I tried to wipe him. We started seeing wound care specialists who helped me find special skin barriers and ointments to protect his degrading skin. Blake also developed a mucosal prolapse that served to amplify the skin irritations. He had an anoplasty done at about 18 months old to repair the prolapse, and thankfully, he has yet to have problems with this again.

When the boys were two years old, we moved to the Rio Grande Valley in south Texas. One of the most impoverished communities in the nation, it is nearly impossible to find any paediatric specialists, let alone doctors who are experts at treating this type of condition. I settled on a paediatric gastroenterologist who knew little about IA and chose to put Blake on Imodium for his hypermobility. While this helped, tremendously, it was only a Band-Aid for his problems. When he was three years old, the doctor had the nerve to lecture me that he was not potty-trained, yet her solution to his condition was that he would simply wear diapers for the rest of his life. Extremely frustrated, we walked out and never went back.

After researching other options, I decided on a hospital closer to our new home. Although it was a six-hour round trip drive it was far preferable to being alone with two toddlers waiting three hours in an overcrowded waiting room of a doctor who had shown no real interest in helping Blake. At the new hospital, we saw a wonderful gastroenterologist. Unfortunately, she still had little experience in treating children like Blake. She recommended an amazing physical therapist who specializes in helping children cope with bowel and bladder issues.

Although Blake loved to visit and play with his new therapist, it took him over a year to allow her to place electrodes on his bottom and belly so that he could practice using his muscles through a "video game."

She taught him different tricks to help him on the potty and suggested that we see one of the physician's assistant in urology who was treating children with IA using a special enema system called "Peristeen".

Blake at 3 years old

Everything drastically changed once we started seeing someone new in urology. Blake had MRIs, urodynamic studies, kidney ultrasounds, abdominal x-rays, and barium enema x-rays. Although the hospital frowned upon it, Austin came along to every appointment for moral support. He was Blake's cheerleader when it came time for a blood draw or the "jelly belly."

It took Blake months to recover from the emotional trauma of the barium enema x-ray. I almost wish I had it recorded because my little boy turned into the Incredible Hulk once they inserted the enema catheter and taped it to his skin. We needed six adults to hold him down to the table while he screamed and cried, wind milling his arms through the air.

The MRI and examination revealed that Blake had a tethered spinal cord with fatty lipoma as well as an undescended testicle. At four years, Blake had his sixth surgery, an orchiopexy to repair the testicle. At this time, the neurosurgeon overseeing Blake's case was not recommending that we repair the tethered spinal cord because he was asymptomatic.

The idea of waiting for Blake to show symptoms related to the tethered cord that may be irreversible did not sit well. He was starting to have more bladder accidents at school plus leg pains, and I sought out a second opinion.

Mom, Blake & Austin supporting
ONE in 5000 Foundation

During spring break of his kindergarten year, Blake had a laminoplasty to release the tethered cord. He stayed in the hospital for four days and was home from school for three weeks. It was very difficult for him to be away from his brother, teacher, and friends for so long.

Currently, Blake is an active, second grader who is a member of a youth triathlon team as well as the local swim club. He does high volume enemas every 24 to 36 hours to stay clean and takes medication for bladder control.

He is finally out of Pull-Ups and wears special underwear. (Sometimes he throws them away which drives mommy crazy!) He has good days and bad and days that he refuses to do his washout. He is encouraged to advocate for himself, and his treatment is always up to him.

My greatest concern for Blake is not medical but knowing that he will always have this condition as both a financial and emotional burden. For now, those burdens are mostly mine to bear.

Blake Dylan, you are our hero. Because of you, I believe in miracles.

77. Austin Story, Blake's Brother - Words and Art (USA)

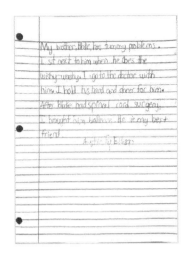

"My brother Blake has tummy problems.

I sit next to him when he does the wishy-washy.

I go to the doctor with him.

I hold his hand and cheer for him.

After Blake had spinal cord surgery,

 I brought him balloons.

He is my best friend."

Austin Ty Ellison

78. Xavier's Story - Natalie (Canada)

As a first-time mother you are filled with joy, excitement, and anxiety. You pray for a healthy baby with ten toes and fingers, a great heartbeat and a smooth delivery. So, the day that your water breaks or the doctor tells you it is time, you are overjoyed to meet the little life or lives that you have been housing for months.

Fifteen minutes after midnight on May 13, 2013, my waters broke. I was scared, nervous, excited and ready to meet my little boy. My contractions were close together, so we got to the hospital as fast as we could. Everything moved so quickly that night and all I kept thinking was "I hope this doesn't hurt too much". Once we got settled into the hospital, I was told I had tested positive for GBS and that I needed to be given antibiotics during labour.

I was dilating very quickly however and was unable to get the shot that I needed to ensure that it wasn't passed on to the baby. A paediatric doctor was called down to assess the baby once he was born. My delivery room was filled with doctors and nurses, and I was exhausted from pushing for over an hour. When Xavier finally arrived, he was 5lbs and 7oz. Hearing his voice for the first time melted my heart and I was filled with so much love and joy.

The doctors took Xavier, cleaned him up and did their checks. He was cleared and given to me to bond with and have skin to skin time. We were held in the hospital for 36 hours after his birth because his blood sugar levels were low and they wanted to observe him. The nurses only came to check his sugar levels and neither bathed him nor confirmed if he had his first bowel movement.

Upon being discharged from the hospital, the nurse changed Xavier and we noticed a very small amount of black stool at the front of his diaper. When I asked the nurse about it, she stated that sometimes the poo can shoot up to the front of the diaper. Being a first-time mom, I didn't question her but thought it was very strange. We were released from the hospital, super excited to bring our brand-new baby boy home. Adjusting to our new life was easy, as Xavier was a good baby. He ate, he slept and he barely cried.

I noticed, however, that every time I changed Xavier's diaper a strange discharge was coming from his penis. Being concerned about this, I brought him to my family doctor for his three-day check-up (Thursday, May 16, 2013) and enquired about the discharge. He examined Xavier and sent us to get some tests done as he was unsure of what it could be. He asked if the hospital had completed the mandatory birth examination, in which they are supposed to check that his anal canal is open. I advised him that I was unsure as there were so many people in the room at his birth, but that there was a doctor who examined him in the room due to my testing positive for GBS. We were unable to get the test done that day as our appointment ended late and the test facility had been closed.

The next day (Friday, May 17, 2013), Xavier seemed to be sluggish and not himself, so we went to a walk-in clinic to see another doctor. We explained to the doctor what was going on and he examined him, only to tell us that he was fine. He stated that the discharge from his penis was normal because the skin around his penis had not formed correctly (we later found out that Xavier also had hypospadias). Although it didn't seem right to me, I believed him as he was a doctor.
The following day, Xavier was very lethargic and spitting up green bile, so we rushed him to a hospital emergency room where a doctor thoroughly examined him and told us Xavier was born without an anal opening.

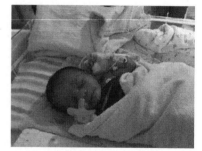

We were then rushed to a major children's hospital immediately where Xavier underwent emergency surgery to remove all the waste that his body was collecting and storing and given a colostomy.

I have been through a lot of things in my life, but nothing could have prepared me for the rush of emotions and fear I felt. I was powerless. I couldn't protect my son from his pain. I couldn't make it better. I couldn't understand this. I went numb.

Xavier at a week old in NICU

Although I was able to keep myself together on the outside, I was falling apart on the inside. My pregnancy was normal, there weren't any complications or abnormalities and all the tests and ultrasounds had been clear. According to the doctor there had been nothing to be worried about. I was not prepared to digest this news, but I couldn't break down. I had a newborn baby that needed me.

Xavier spent a week and a half in the NICU. The excellent staff at the hospital informed us that he was born with an Imperforate Anus and educated us on the steps that would follow. We were provided a home care nurse that would assist and teach me how to care for Xavier's stoma. We were told that he would have all three surgeries within the first year of his life and everything would be over before he turned one.

But that was not the case as there were other unforeseen obstacles. We had two surgery dates cancelled on us and two surgery dates postponed, one because he was sick and the other because his haemoglobin levels were very low. We were sent to the haematology floor of the hospital to determine why Xavier's haemoglobin levels were low. It was determined that he had smaller red blood cells due to genetics and was put on iron supplements to bring up his levels.

We were able to adjust to our new normal as my happy baby didn't know that he was different. However, I found myself internalising my feelings. The best way I can put it is that I felt like a functioning zombie. I thought about what his life would be like growing up "different" and the challenges he would have to overcome. I didn't talk to anyone about how I was feeling and found myself constantly praying for strength and patience.

I limited our outings because it was difficult changing an ostomy bag in public bathrooms that didn't have the changing table in the stalls. People would stare and look at you with either pity or confusion. I didn't like it and I didn't want to have to explain it. I was not ashamed of my son or his condition, but I didn't want people feeling sorry for us. Deep down inside I knew we would adapt and overcome anything thrown our way. My thought process was that there are so many people in this world dealing with the worst, and I am so blessed to have a healthy baby.

Xavier was just under 18 months old when he had his second surgery to create the anal canal and repair his hypospadias, on October 30, 2014. It was a difficult time for us because he was older than the normal age to receive the second surgery. His body had developed without knowing the sensation of a mass bowel movement.

I was very concerned about how this would affect his development once he had his final surgery. It was clear that what we see as the normal stages of childhood development would look very different for Xavier. Processing all of those thoughts and dealing with the new plan of care for him after the second surgery took its toll on me.

The hospital showed me how to dilate the new anal canal so that his body wouldn't heal itself, but it was something I couldn't stomach. At the time I had no help at home to help do the dilation every night, as Xavier's father was at work. Since he was now 18 months old, he was bigger and stronger and put up a fight with everything.

Honestly, I couldn't blame him. I totally empathised with him and wished that I didn't have to contribute to his pain. There were many nights I sat in sadness, unable to cry because I didn't know if I would be able to stop once I started. I tried my hardest not to ask God "Why me?", "Why us?", "How did this happen?", but rather focussed on being positive for Xavier.

The dilation of his anal opening was extremely difficult, so when the hospital offered to assist me weekly I jumped on their offer to help. Xavier still fought the process, but I had help and could comfort him rather than be the source of his pain. He continued to grow into a happy boy that loved to laugh and make new friends. He attended a home day-care, so all his friends loved and accepted him for him.

The great thing about being around people that love and support you is that Xavier didn't think he was different in any way. The potty training was easy for him, as he was only concerned with doing number ones. He was put on a high fibre, low sugar diet and was hitting his growth milestones. There were a few scares when his stoma would bleed for hours but, for the most part, things were moving along as normally as could be.

Xavier was almost three years old when he had his final surgery on March 6, 2016. Although we were happy that the three major surgeries were over and done with, and we didn't have to worry about buying ostomy bags, a bleeding stoma or skin irritation, it was a difficult healing process for us. It took almost three years for a process that we were told should have been completed in the first year of his life. I believe that the delay created more obstacles for him to develop and adjust to living with IA.

Xavier getting ready for his final surgery

Before his final surgery, Xavier associated pooping with his ostomy bags and had never felt the sensation of having to go naturally. This made potty training more difficult as he wasn't able to identify the sensation of a mass bowel movement or control his bowel movements. Also, the skin on his bottom developed without having built up a resistance to having poop on it, which created a huge unforeseen problem with diaper rash.

Since Xavier was eating regular food and his waste was more acidic, he developed a very bad case of diaper rash for over eight months. The skin around his new anal opening and surrounding skin was totally stripped away. It was red and raw all over his bum. He hated pooping, diaper changes and even sitting, as he was in so much pain. Every diaper change was a battle because he was so strong and cleaning the area caused him pain. The rash was so bad that we had to go into the hospital for weekly check-ups as the doctors had never seen a diaper rash that bad before. Eventually, we were able to get the rash under control by using stoma barrier powder and spray to protect his skin.

Xavier is now seven years old and I have watched him go through the realisation that he is different. When he started school, I was so concerned about how he would adapt and how the other kids would treat him. The doctors explained that the main goal for him going to school was to try and make sure he was socially clean. We tried to develop a bowel movement schedule with laxatives to clean him out and put him on a diet that wouldn't constipate him, but the movements of the human body are hard to predict, and we struggled with trying to find that balance. He had accidents at school and he was very self-conscience about the way he smelt.

I slowly watched the once bright light in him every so slowly dim. He started to internalise his limitations and get frustrated quickly when he couldn't control his bowel movements. I also noticed that the instances of negative self-talk increased. He started to realise he was different, not "normal", and it broke my heart.

I remember his first in-class incident when another classmate made fun of him for wearing pull-ups. He was devastated. As the teacher explained the way Xavier cried and how she could feel his pain, I couldn't stop the tears from falling from my eyes. No matter how much you try to prepare yourself for the possible challenges that will come your way, you still can't help but feel powerless when you cannot protect your child from feeling pain.

The older he gets the more he realises he has more limitations than the other kids. Something as simple as going swimming takes time and preparation. Kids at this age just want to have fun and do whatever their friends are doing. I so want that for him as well. I hoped that once he had all the surgeries, his body would just magically figure it out and he would be able to live free from worrying about using the washroom. I know it is naïve of me, but I just don't want Xavier to feel like he is not a regular kid, because he is.

2020 has been a very strange year for us all, but this is the year that Xavier wanted to share his story with the world and bring awareness to others about IA. We created an Instagram page just for him @xcie_xbox_dix

People ask me why I waited so long to share our story and I have told them that it was Xavier's story to tell. I didn't want people to label him or pity him before they got to know the incredible kid he is. Since starting this page, I have seen his confidence levels go up. He is not ashamed or hiding. He has taken control of his story and how he wants to tell it. Watching him make new friends and becoming comfortable with who he is has also helped me to deal with some of the things I have suppressed.

The thing about being a functioning zombie is that you forget to allow yourself to feel or deal with the weight that is on your shoulders. I have been so focussed on making sure that Xavier is taken care of that I forgot to take care of myself. As a mother you just deal with it, no matter what it is. Your child or children come first and nothing else matters.

All these years I have operated under the assumption that if my child sees how strong I am, he will be strong too. Xavier is strong and we are stronger together. I have cried with him many times and I have reassured him that we would get through this together. I thank God that we have a good support system around us and that we can overcome each challenge together. This year Xavier will start visiting a new bowel movement clinic, which will help us determine whether or not he needs any more procedures.

I know we still have a long journey ahead of us, but we are positive that we can handle it.

79. My Daughter X's Story (England)

X's adjustment after surgeries:

Blessed with patience, a background in Personal Development, a great Tier 1 Hospital and a willing community nurse, we soon learnt to adapt to the new post pull through surgery life. As X was so young, the impact on her is hard to gauge. For me, I felt trapped. I was a single parent with no support system to help provide childcare for X's siblings while I cared for her needs after surgery.

Our hospital gave me lots of information on support groups for my child's condition - VACTERL and IA. I found it utterly depressing. I joined the Facebook groups but swiftly left, as I needed hope and it wasn't to be found there (until I met Greg online). In the interim years, I just soldiered on.

Human ability to adapt is a blessing. We had no choice but to face the curtailment in our freedoms that X's surgery brought about. What this meant for X was lying on a changing mat with a nappy off for most of the day so we could have easy access to her bottom. I found this challenging after a while. At the time, we were living in rented accommodation with cream carpets so letting her run around was not really possible without incurring a massive bill to replace them. Also, the hygiene factor for X's siblings was always a concern, even when I allowed this in the garden.

It also meant we couldn't go out as I was continually changing X's nappies. I know parents say this, but it really was a continuous flow of poo for the first few weeks, and gradually it became less although it seemed like it went on for many weeks.

Also, as the skin in that area was not used to poo on it, it would burn, so I just couldn't leave X in a nappy as the burns to her skin would be too great.

We got through it. Our community nurse was fabulous, finding all sorts of tips to help X's skin like porridge oats in a sock in a bath, cleaning the area with medical grade olive oil and cotton wool balls, dabbing not wiping, strange ointments and potions. I recall Orabase being effective, and also leaving X's nappy off overnight to allow as much air as possible to stave off the broken skin that would otherwise happen.

The biggest adjustment for me really was handling the relentless flow of poo, whilst simultaneously dodging the relentless flow of negativity I directed at myself - Bad mother! I should be able to do this better! Why hadn't I got a better support structure? etc. I hated that I had so little time to be a mum. I felt like a robot administering care but pulled in every direction and doing nothing really well.

I kept saying things like 'this too will pass', 'this will make me stronger', 'everything is always working out for me' and all the other stuff friends would say to get me through. Most of the time I didn't believe a word of it. There was no escape, nobody was coming to help, we just had to get through it and focus on moving forward. Fortunately, I'm not house proud, so I just decided to applaud myself every time we made it through the day fed, relatively clean and not losing anyone.

School - how we've continually got the care needed through the school system:

Unlike many other parents I've personally met with an IA child, we've been extremely fortunate in the care and support provided by nursery, lower and middle school (the three-tier system). I don't believe our experience is normal though, from discussions with others.

In trying to understand why this is, I've narrowed it down to a handful of reasons. I honestly believe we are blessed to have had the people we did and I just prayed and trusted it would be ok (Personal Development background - what you focus on you get). But I was also blessed by having teachers in the family who could see the challenges a school setting may pose for an IA child, as well as the resource issues it may have on the school.

Being able to stand in others' shoes, to appreciate the challenges they may face in implementing a care plan, was really instrumental in being clear about what X needed and how we communicated with each school. So, very early on before we started at each institution, a letter would be drafted to the school. We met with the Head Teacher at least a term and a half before X joining. I think there were a series of meetings with nursery and lots of training from our community nurse, and a key person was appointed in nursery to provide care for X.

Then moving to lower school, the choice of school was based on ability to care for X as well as being a good school (based on criteria like, does the Head smile? Are the teachers happy? versus how high up the league tables the school ranks). We repeated this selection criteria at middle school. It was never about the league tables but more about the pastoral care programmes.

I think a key thing here for us was not to go into school with a sense of entitlement, but rather to understand the pressures the schools were under and be cognisant of that in all communication. I think being respectful in how we spoke to them and how we listened really supported our cause. I also created a sense of partnership with the TA's (Teaching Assistants) involved. Our community nurse was also proactive and would join me at school meetings well ahead of time, then go off to train the staff in the ongoing care of X.

I think people skills and communication skills were, and continue to be, key in getting all the care we had with no EHCP (Education, Health and Care Plan – UK only).

Other issues we focussed on at school were for the child to feel the same as part of the peer group, so she felt neither different nor differently treated in any way. So, whilst separate bathrooms were available, X would never use them herself and hated it if teachers told her to use the disabled loo.

We made sure that a secret code was understood by the all the staff in the case of emergency when X needed the loo. So, unlike other children, X could present the keyword in class and be excused immediately. This was really essential for X's dignity.

As X was not continent until Year 3 (about seven years old), Teaching Assistant support was needed and that was given in a separate bathroom. X hated this. It invariably raised questions among her peer group and made her different.

My goal was to make X independent so she no longer needed TA support. This was achieved one summer holiday from school. We went cold turkey and removed nappies and pads, and X was fine during the day with no accidents. At night-time, pads are still needed. This was a big step forward for X and the school.

This increase in independence thwarted our EHCP application, as no support was given from the school around toileting and the social and emotional needs not deemed serious enough to affect access to education. I disagreed, but knew we stood very little chance of getting it.

X was excluded from swimming lessons on the grounds of there being no resource to care for her, even though I had offered to be that support. I was not allowed to provide this and I was furious. After questioning how this could be fair given the Equality Act, and the fact other parents were assisting, I was then allowed to help. But X only attended two lessons and missed out on certificates for swimming.

Another thing which was an issue for X and I was the fact she never won a 100 per cent attendance award at the end of each term at the school service. This was because she had to go to hospital for surgery and was not eligible for the award having missed days at school, even though she hadn't missed other days due to sickness. It took me four years of fighting for her and other children to be included in this award if the days missed were due to hospital appointments or surgery.

X was a keen musician and regularly asked to be the soloist at the school shows in lower school. She rarely got to perform in the concert though and was excluded from Music because of bad behaviour. The behaviour was nearly always linked to her being asked to work hard on a piece during term time, which she did, but then not being allowed to perform which was a huge disappointment. The behaviour was definitely linked to that disappointment. In her eyes, it was a feeling of injustice and also feeling annoyed at working so hard for a whole term for nothing.

Self-esteem, emotional and behaviour issues, and the impact on siblings:

This is by far the biggest challenge we face and where most of my focus goes. I have ultimate faith in all the surgeons, consultants and nurses, but the biggest need for us was access to support for these aspects of X's life. Every time I sought support, I was told they couldn't deal with the emotional aspects until X was continent. This made no sense to me, given we'd been told X may never ever be continent.

I fought for years for this and went to every parenting course available, but to be honest none of them worked with X. They worked well for the siblings but were just not appropriate for X.

PDA (Pathological Demand Avoidance) and ODD (Oppositional Defiant Disorder) were terms bandied about by two professionals in trying to understand her behaviour, but no official diagnosis was made. Basically, X has no control over her rage sometimes. She manages it at school but at home, with me, it can be scary. I sought help everywhere but nobody could give it.

The impact on her siblings has been huge. Growing up with a child who is physically frail but emotionally dominant caused issues for them. Also, her behaviour at school, because she was smaller and frail, was a source of embarrassment to her siblings. At home, they give in to her for a quiet life. They put her needs before their own which in tween years is now causing issues with their own self-esteem and self-worth.

Two things which made a massive difference were the Positive Discipline book by Jane Nelson and the FAMILIES IN FOCUS (FIF) group who provide strategies and training to help parents who care for children with additional needs. They also recognise the impact on siblings and provide courses, run by play therapists, to help siblings learn coping strategies.

X has written to FIF to complain about the courses her siblings go on. She insisted that she has her own course because she needs it, and that they improve the course her siblings go on because it's not helping them!

She is the first person to do this.

Finally, I have to acknowledge Greg Ryan who responded to a post of mine in another Facebook group about how to handle the challenging behaviour that goes with IA. Greg connected with me outside the group through Messenger. He was the first adult I had access to who could give me an experience of X's anxiety and emotional state behind the behaviour. His messages were pivotal in my acceptance and compassion of X's behaviour. He allowed me to stand in her shoes and at least glimpse what she was feeling. This lifted a heavy burden from my shoulders and enabled me to connect with my child's sense of despair, lack of control and many other complex emotions that she was feeling.

The battle that had raged before quickly subsided. It still flares up without warning, but I'm much better equipped at soothing X. Previously, I was trying to stop the rage, but it was like a state of combat. After those initial chats with Greg and many tears, I began to understand what X may be feeling. Being with her with that new understanding, my responses to the rage were driven by love. The rage melts away quickly now.

Greg gave me access into X's world, and I think that has been the biggest lesson and defining moment in supporting X and her challenging behaviour.

Other resources are <u>Families in Focus</u> and their <u>Siblings First Programme</u>, Greg's book and the Positive Discipline by Jane Nelson.

80. Nicola's Story (Canada)

It was a peaceful winter evening on January sixth when we welcomed our beautiful baby boy, Nicola, just three days before his due date. He was the most beautiful baby we had ever seen. He was angelic and he immediately stole our heart. We called in the paediatrician to come and check our baby, as we were told when I was five months along that he would be born with a birth defect called hypospadias. I was, at that point, prepared for everything we needed to do, as I had done all of my required research on this birth defect.

The news I received after the paediatrician checked our baby was more than I was mentally prepared for. I asked if he in fact had hypospadias and she said that he did, however, that was not our main concern right now. She turned Nicola onto his stomach and ran her finger down his bottom. She showed me that he had no bottom hole and that I should refrain from breast feeding him right now, as he would have trouble passing the stool. She told me he was born with an anorectal malformation called imperforate anus. The medical term at that point was very confusing and odd to me and those words of not being able to feed my baby and form that bond I had been waiting for, crushed me.

Within thirty minutes of having my baby, Nicola was whisked away from me to another room and immediately hooked up to machines. I had no idea what was next, except that they were making a call to a hospital in Toronto, to transfer him there for emergency surgery. In less than an hour Nicola and my husband were taken in the ambulance to the hospital and would meet the surgeon in the morning.

I spent the night with my mom in the hospital crying because I could not be with my baby and I was afraid of the unknown. However, I was determined to get a good night's sleep and I demanded to be discharged in the morning. I needed to be with my baby and my husband and to meet with the surgeon and discuss our next steps. Six hours after delivering Nicola I was discharged and rushed to the new hospital where we met with our surgeon.

I remember being in the NICU talking to the doctors and all of them looking at me like I had taken some sort of drug. I was very alert and determined and they kept asking me to sit down, as I had delivered my baby less than twelve hours ago. In my mind, all I could think of was that it was up to me, Nicola's mother, to take care of him and advocate for him. This feeling and determination has never gone away.

After Nicola's first surgery at just one day old, I saw how special and strong this baby boy was and would continue to be. His first surgery was to create his colostomy so that he would be able to pass stool, until his anus was created and working properly. After his surgery we waited in the NICU for test results on things I did not ever imagine we would have to check. That was one of the scariest times I have ever experienced. I kept looking at my baby boy in the incubator and thinking how all this could be happening. He looked so perfect and he was.

The doctors were so proud of how he bounced back after surgery. The nurses everyday kept telling me that he was the healthiest boy in the neonatal intensive care unit. Again, he continued to show me his courage just like he had shown as a little newborn. Another nurse said to me the words I will never forget. She said that if someone says to me that this could be worse, remember that this is my worst and I have every right to be sad, mad and everything else I was feeling. This was my baby and my family who was going through these scary times. She told me this was a little bump in the road and Nicola would be just fine.

After four days in the NICU we were moved onto the general surgery floor, into a ward with nurses caring for five babies at a time. Nicola was now in a crib and I had a rocking chair where I could finally nurse him. I stayed with him all day and night and left when he went to bed. I called the nurses' desk every morning at three am to make sure he had had his overnight feed and had done well. I was back at the hospital every morning when he woke up for his morning feed. While at the hospital my husband and I were taught how to change the colostomy bag and care for our baby. We were ready to take him home nine days after he was born.

At home, we were provided with a nurse, who came once a day to help with the colostomy bag changes and overall care of Nicola. She was so kind and sweet and quickly became a shoulder to cry on when things were too much. One of the hardest things about being home was that I felt so alone, even though I was surrounded by all of the people I love and care for. This condition was so rare that

I did not know anyone who had gone through this. Although Nicola and I had so much help and care from my extended family, they still could not help me with Nicola fully.

I had a two-year-old that wanted mommy all the time, but Nicola needed me constantly too. Bag leaks started very quickly and as Nicola grew older and the weather warmed up, we wanted to get out and enjoy the sunshine. We had been cooped up inside a hospital and then our house in the winter and the sun was exactly what we needed to lift our spirits. We would go on walks and even take trips to the mall, but soon this became so stressful, because we experienced bag leaks constantly. The bags would just not stay on and the skin around his colostomy became oozy and sore to look at. The only time things went smoothly was when Nicola was in his baby chair. This made me sad that we could barely hold him or take him on regular trips. When we finally got the hang of his bag changes and finally treated his skin around the colostomy, it was time for surgery number two.

At around six months old Nicola was back at the hospital for his anoplasty surgery. This surgery involved pulling the rectum down to the anus where a new anal opening was created. Luckily, Nicola had everything in place internally, so the doctors told us it was a simple procedure. After eight hours of waiting, Nicola was out and happy. I remember driving home and my other son who was two years old loved One Direction. We played the album in the car on our way home and Nicola began kicking his feet to the beat. It was amazing to see and the courage in such a little boy was evident once again.

The second surgery was complete, but our work was not done. The doctors taught us to size the anal opening by inserting a metal instrument into his anus and then using a different size each week. Once the anus was at the preferred size, we would be able to perform his last surgery. In the meantime, the colostomy remained so that Nicola would continue passing stool through the bag. Sizing the anus was very disturbing for Nicola, as well as my husband and me. Nicola would yell so loud it broke our heart. We knew this was something necessary, but it still did not make it easier and this procedure never got easier, for any of us. What felt like a never ending three months, brought us to his final surgery.

We arrived at the hospital bright and early for Nicola's colostomy closure. Nicola's surgery was completed in under four hours. After surgery, we stayed in the hospital for a few days waiting for 'poop.' I never thought I would be so excited to see poop come out of his anus. While we were in the hospital, I met a boy and his mom who had gone through the same procedures. The boy was eight, at this point, and he had just had his Mace procedure done. I spoke to the mom regularly and we exchanged emails to stay in touch. I remember being so relieved to have met someone, who lived close by to me and who knew what we were going through.

Everything was smooth and Nicola was passing stool regularly, so we were able to go home. Nicola's life as an infant was pretty much the same as any other infant. He began eating solids, met all of his milestones and loved laughing and playing with his older brother. His stools were more or less normal with the few issues of constipation. He stayed on a bowel regime of stool softeners, probiotics and a healthy diet.

As time passed and Nicola grew into a beautiful toddler it was time for him to start school. He was potty trained to pee in no time but pooping in the toilet was more of a challenge. He was doing well, and on a great bowel regime, taking both stool softeners as well as some natural supplements. We were nervous for his wellbeing at school, so we decided to start him with pull ups. We agreed that if he had an accident, he was to call me, and I would help him change the pullup.

This never happened because, as a full-time working mom of two, I was not always aware of what was happening at school. This was especially true because the school failed to understand the importance of Nicola using the toilet. The school always saw it as just a constipation issue. He did not look like he had a disability, so they failed to see it as one. It became evident after about a month that Nicola was holding his poop during school. Once he held it for so long, his body was unable to pass stool properly and effectively without pain.

One night he was in major pain and crying hysterically. We rushed him to the hospital where he was given an enema and he filled six diapers in less than ten minutes. He was completely backed up and it was very traumatic for all of us. That day I left my full-time job to be there fully for Nicola and my family.

Me being home and communicating effectively with the school, ensured that Nicola did very well. By his second year at school, he was pull up free. He had a few accidents, but our main trouble was that he still did not want to use the toilet. Even at home it was a fight to use the toilet and we would always have to play a game and make the toilet 'fun' in order for him to agree to use it.
By the time Nicola was six years old the surgeons were talking about the next procedure that was available to us. Our surgeon mentioned the Mace procedure. That procedure was very much in my mind ever since I met the little boy who had had it done when Nicola had his last surgery. I remember the surgeon saying that this is the next step for these kids. After much thought and research, I chose to wait it out.

Nicola is now eight years old and doing so well. He is a smart, energetic and loving boy. Although he still suffers constipation issues from time to time, Nicola thrives more and more each year. He is more aware of his body and what he puts into it, which helps greatly with keeping his bowels moving regularly.

I feel like the best thing we could have ever done for Nicola was to never give up on him and we never will. We try to understand his feelings and thoughts, just as much as we pay attention to his symptoms. We feel that keeping a calm, loving and happy environment is key for his emotional, mental and physical well-being.

Nicola is not afraid to tell others about his journey as a baby and his ongoing journey with his condition. He is proud to show his courage and confidence to others and is enthusiastic to help others in any way possible. I say he is going to be a doctor one day. He says he is going to be a rock star. I tell him all the time that he already is!!!!

81. Aaron's Story - Katcha and Daniel Fowler (USA)

On April 9, 2012, we received a call for an eight-month-old little boy who had just been taken into custody by Child Protective Services. We rushed to get this little boy and were immediately connected to his big, blue eyes. Daniel and I had never been parents and became parents with only forty-five minutes notice.

After having Aaron for five days, we became increasingly concerned that his bowel movements were irregular and strained. His belly was bloated and his blue eyes were sunken. We took him to the hospital for continued vomiting and lethargy. We were then told we would be going to a Children's Hospital because Aaron was suffering from a complete bowel obstruction.

We did not know at this time that he had had surgery as an infant for IA. We knew no medical history at all! Once at the Children's Hospital, we were in a whirlwind of learning about the life of IA patients. On day eight of the hospital stay, the doctors called in his birth mother because they did not think Aaron would make it through the night. He was septic and his tiny, thirteen-pound body was struggling.

Miraculously, he made it through and we were taught all the things to do to keep Aaron healthy. Learning about the life of an IA child is overwhelming at times. We were conversing about poop on a daily basis! Aaron was getting more and more healthy and we continued to learn about all his various medical diagnoses. He eventually returned to his birth mother.
After eleven months of being gone from our home, he came back into custody and we started the IA journey again! We were back in the hospital, but a much shorter stay this time. We made sure to get him back on daily medications and enemas as needed. We continued this plan of treatment for a while and it was starting not to work. We researched and met with specialists constantly. We were determined to find the best way to help Aaron. We found a doctor that introduced us to the Pull-Thru Network and we learned about the Malone.

After years of time in foster care with us, we were able to adopt Aaron and now we could concentrate on surgery. We met with the team in Texas and determined that the Malone would be best for Aaron. We have been so thrilled with the outcome and how independent it has allowed him to be in school.

He started kindergarten in diapers because of the constant bowel movements and leaks. Now, he is in 4th grade, and able to confidently go to school without the help of anyone in the bathroom. It has been life changing!

Along the way, we have met and communicated with so many wonderful people in the world of IA. This is not a journey we would want to travel alone!

Aaron is our miracle from Heaven and we thank God daily for allowing us to be his parents.

IA is a large part of our lives, and it makes our baby special, and we would not change that for anything in this world!

82. Troy's Story – Angelica and Sergio (USA)

Our son Troy was born at 28 weeks weighing 2 lbs 6 oz - a tiny little guy. I was waking up after the emergency c-section surgery when doctors were telling my husband and I that he was born with VATER syndrome, one of the characteristics of this being a congenital malformation called Imperforate Anus. I had never heard of it!

After only 24 hours of being born he had colostomy surgery. We were very concerned and I never prayed more in my life!

Troy was in the hospital for 104 days. The wonderful nurses taught us how to clean him up and change his colostomy bag. I was nervous at first to change his bag. I didn't want to hurt him. The nurses were always so patient with us though and guided us every step of the way.

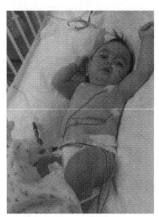

He was discharged from the hospital on December 17. It was a true Christmas miracle for our family. His big sister Ashlyn, who was four years old, was so happy to bring him home. We had so much to be grateful for.

Eight months later, he had his first reconstruction surgery to create his anal opening. He did great!

It was a difficult process to prepare him for his next surgery. We had to do anal dilation every day and it was so heart wrenching to do. I did it as gently as possible. He was uncomfortable but, we had to remind ourselves, it was just for a short couple of months and it had to be done for a successful outcome. I still cried over it.

A couple of months later was his pull-through reconstruction surgery.

Then, a couple of days later he POOPED through his new anus!! It was the most exciting sight! I never thought we would be so happy to celebrate a first POOP. We were all giving each other high fives!!!

The doctors did an AMAZING job.

Once Troy turned four, we had to start potty training and we used enemas to help him. It was difficult at first but, after a lot of patience, trial and error and messiness we learned what worked for him.

When he started school, we made sure he had extra clothes and wipes in case of an accident. He didn't have them often since he had an enema every night but, once in a while we would get a call from the school nurse. Troy would handle it like a pro. He cleaned himself up and go back to class. His friends never even noticed. I think I was more worried about his friends making fun of him then he was.

As he gets older, he does worry about his friends making fun of him. He always makes sure that his extra clothes are hidden deep in his backpack so his friends won't see them. He gets scared they won't want to be his friend anymore and of them calling him names.

Sometimes he says his body isn't working properly and that he is a failure. He asks, "Why did God make me this way?" This breaks my heart to a million pieces. He has faced so many challenges.

We tell him God made him PERFECT and that he is so special, and God knew he can handle it like a CHAMP! A STRONG WARRIOR!!

Troy is a happy boy. He loves playing video games, bike riding, hanging out with his friends, and football. He has such a big heart and is smart and caring. He drives me crazy at times too!! LOL

We don't know what the future holds, but we know one thing for sure, that we trust and have faith in Our Father God! He has big plans for Troy and he will do amazing things.

He makes us proud every day and we will always encourage him, love him and walk with him every step of the way!!

83. Pauline's Story – Lana (Australia)

I was expecting my second child, a baby girl. I was very happy and full of dreams. The whole nine months of pregnancy were absolutely normal, with all tests being clear and showing no problems.

Somehow during those nine months, I had a very strange feeling. It was like a sign of my worry, something which I felt deeply in my heart, like a little bell that was making me not feel confident. I remember I kept repeating to myself, all those days, that I hoped the baby would be okay and that her health would be alright.

My daughter Pauline was born a week after I was due, by a late-planned C-section. She was very loud, cried a lot and her face reminded me of the face of a very old lady. She was a big sized baby, weighing 4.25kg with a length of 55cm.

As soon I saw her, I thought she looked absolutely gorgeous, with her thatch of thick black hair immediately reminding me of my husband Andrei's grandmother who was of Chinese heritage.

But even after her birth, I still had a heavy feeling which was not relief.

An hour later, Andrei came to me with a doctor and told me that Pauline had a birth defect. I had no idea what it could be, but inside I had a thought that yes, my worries are coming now. I knew I was about to find out something that would shock me.

So, Pauline was born IA and her anus was closed. I cried and almost screamed in shock because she was immediately being taken away to a major children's hospital for her first surgery.

She had four surgeries in total. Because the 3rd wasn't successful, it needed to be repeated. I stayed with Pauline all the time, trying to comfort her every day with everything I could. I loved everything about her so much. But it was a feeling of love mixed with fears and stress.

I guess all parents who have been through this will understand my pain and fears. The first year was almost a "black" year for me and I wasn't prepared for it. All I wanted was to be with her, I was so scared of losing her. Looking back now makes me feel like crying, and I feel like my nervous system is changed forever.

I thought that after the surgeries had been completed everything would be normal for Pauline and we would forget about it all, as if it had been a bad dream. But I discovered I was mistaken, as another problem appeared later and developed badly.

I began to feel a form of depression which was mostly was a massive sense of sadness, and I also lost a lot of weight. I was in a constant state of tiredness because I was balancing a very busy full-time job as well as managing Pauline's constant health battles. It was like my life and these circumstances were too overwhelming.

This then led to issues in our marriage and Andrei and I got divorced.

After many ups and downs after our divorce, we decided to get back together because of Pauline. We both knew that I couldn't do everything myself, and alone I wasn't emotionally strong enough for her.

I look back now with great pride that, despite everything going on in my life, I never let it affect my work performance and I was given many plaudits by my employer for the high standards I achieved in my job.

Thanks to God, things are better now, and we are all together and all okay.

Pauline is almost eleven years old now and is well, but we still have to deal with problems with her constipation. After countless doctor appointments, I came to the realisation that she may not be able to go to the toilet normally and will always have problems.

The options we were given included rectal washouts, surgery (mace) or laxatives. I could not accept having to put her through further surgery for the mace procedure. We are instead concentrating on using laxatives at the moment, as the washouts are not an option because of the traumatic impact they had on both of us.

I believe in God and I hope He will look after both her and I. We need His blessing so much. I started praying every morning and night for her health. The praying helps greatly by enabling me to feel calm.

The laxatives are not perfect, and she still has soiling issues, with both good days and bad days. It is always a challenge. I have learned how to hide my tears now, as I don't want to show them to my girl. But some days when she sees my puffy face she knows why and just hugs me back. We are both learning how to deal and live with it, and we will never give up.

Apart from her IA issues, Pauline is a perfect kid who loves activities and to play sport. She loves her music and is in Year 3 at a music academy. She is a very happy child and I hope she will be a happy person for the rest of her life.

I am so proud of my darling daughter. She is adorable and is everything to me. It warms my heart when she says to me "Mum, what would I do without you?" I am glad to share our story, but I hope it doesn't appear like I'm complaining too much.

The Facebook group for parents and IA kids is very helpful and continues to assist me with my questions. I am very happy when I see that someone with IA has managed the problem better and I always try to learn new ways to help my daughter. The IA life is now about sharing experiences and keeping strong and our spirits up.

My hope is for our IA kids to be strong enough to manage their lives by themselves one day and be independent. Amen.

Portrait by Michelle Collins

Best of luck and kind regards,

Lana

84. Birgit Risan (Norway)

Finally, the day came when I would give birth to my fourth child. It was a planned caesarian section, and my now ex-husband and I walked excited into the hospital. Our beautiful boy was born at quarter past twelve, and the doctors congratulated us, saying he was all healthy.

After an hour or so, the midwife and my ex came with my son to me, but they did not smile. I found it scary. For a second I thought he was dead. They put my beautiful baby on my chest, and I was relieved to see him breathing.

What is wrong I asked? – Why aren`t you smiling?

We had to take him to another hospital. He needed to be checked by a specialist. I had to wait until the evening before I was taken by an ambulance to the same hospital as my son. I do not normally pray, but this afternoon the same sentences kept running in my head. Please, please, let him live. I will manage whatever comes, just please let him live.

The hours I waited, with little to no information was the longest ever. When I finally got to hold him again, the nurses told me he had Analatresi (Anorectal Malformation). I remember I answered that maybe one day I will be able to pronounce this word, but at the moment it meant nothing. Never had I heard about this condition, and I had no idea what it would mean for him and for us.

The next day he had his first of several surgeries. I was terrified. Every parent who ever had to leave their child in the care of surgeons knows that we feel powerless. It can be so hard to have faith in doctors you do not know, but still, you have no other options.

A friend called me asking how I was doing, and my reply was that I knew I was going to learn a lot from this, but that I was sad my son would have to go through so much pain. The rest of my emotions I could not put into words until years later.

I felt guilt. Had I done something wrong that gave him this condition? I felt guilt over my other children who I had left home in my mother's care. I felt guilt that my mother had to take care of them all. I was worried sick over the future. What would this mean for us as a family? Would we be living in a hospital for long? My world was turned upside down in a second and I had no clue how life would be.

Most of all I was afraid of losing my son. When he woke up from his surgery, he was so peaceful, compared with his first day of life when he seemed tense. It was as if he was released from pain.

Tomorrow is his 10th birthday. Most of the worries I had, I am glad to say were a waste of time.

Things I did not worry about, on the other hand, did happen. He has for instance broken his arm twice. Thing is, kids with analatresi can also break their arms if they fall, they can have tantrums, they can be happy, sad, with friends or without. The point is people with analatresi are first and foremost people.

180

They are not their condition. They live with a condition, and so do their family.

We live in Norway, where we are so lucky to have a good health care system, and even though we are only five million people we have an organization for children with Analatresi in our country, who have the opportunity to meet others. It is such a gift, both for the children and adults. Most of us felt lonely until we joined this group, feeling that nobody could understand what we were going through.

To share our stories and learn from each other gives us strength to face our daily challenges. We are not alone. You are not alone.

This is my story, not my sons. One day he might share his own story, or not, that will be his choice.

85. Veniamin's Story - Nadejda (Russia)

This is our story about the life of my IA son. He was our first child who was born in 2011, when I was 30. During the pregnancy my husband and I prayed for a healthy child. All ultrasounds we had showed that nothing was wrong.

After a very long, painful and hard delivery I was shocked to learn that my newborn baby had IA and hypospadias. I had never even heard these words before. I did not know, what would happen with him, with us, or would he even survive.

They did not put my boy in my arms. They did not show me his face, they just showed me his genitals. He was born at 10.45 pm (Moscow, Russia).

In the morning he was taken in the emergency car to the major Children's Hospital in Moscow, and I was only allowed to hold him for a few seconds.

He was baptized on that day and at the end of his first twenty-four hours of life the first surgery was done. It was awful, with so many questions and fears. They also found that he had some heart issues.

When I got home (Veniamin was one week old), I began to search for information in Russian and I found nothing encouraging. But in English I found a site of one mother (I do not remember her name but her first son was born with IA and they were from Latin America).

I learned that we are not alone and that there are many IA children and adults. I began to believe that my son would survive.

I had many difficulties with breastfeeding my son. Because he could not suck at the beginning, we fed him from the bottle with expressed breast milk, then formula because of the Staphylococcus aureus in my milk, which caused him to vomit. Then we returned to expressed breast milk. After his PSARP surgery at the age of three months, he had a cystostomy because of hypospadias.

My son had a colostomy from his first twenty-four hours until eight and a half months and a cystostomy from three months until he was fifteen months. After his PSARP surgery he spent six weeks in the hospital and his tongue-tie was corrected at three months.

We thought it was a miracle when he came home at four months old, refused the bottle and began breastfeeding. I breastfed him for two years and eight months. His third surgery – the reversal of the stoma occurred when he was eight and a half months.

At fifteen months, he had his fourth surgery because of hypospadias. And after that his cystostomy was closed.

All that time from his birth he also had pyelectasis in one kidney and at the age of two years and ten months my son had to go through his fifth surgery, angiography and we learned that he has pyelectasis in one kidney because of extra vessel. He has had five surgeries, nine narcosis, and he was admitted to hospital many times during his first fifteen months of life.

Also, we have a smaller daughter without this issue (IA). We lived in Moscow, but when my son was six years old, we moved to a small town because of my husband's work. As we live in small town, we have protected our son's health issues very tightly.

My IA son is nine years now. He is in third grade at school and in the music school he plays piano. He went to school with 'clean' medical documents with no mention of IA, which means nobody at his school is aware of his issue. He is clean most of the time and we are able to achieve this by closely monitoring his diet, but also, he takes some laxatives and rarely does he need an enema.

The biggest issue we have now is not the physical aspects of IA, but the psychological issues. We fear there are problems ahead because I see that due to the tough beginning of his life, all pain and fear and separation from me in the hospital has influenced him. It is even harder to cope now, than when I had to change his colostomy bags when he was a baby.

I think both of us carry this trauma and that we have psychological issues. He does not even know about IA yet. He just knows that he has had surgery to save his life and he has asked about the scar on his belly.

I found that there was an online conference for IA children in Moscow recently, and I learned much new information. We cannot go to Moscow to visit the bowel management centre because of the virus now. I hope that I can find out how I can support my son in his future.

86. Heidi's Story – Nicola (England)

We would like to share Heidi's journey with you. We are very proud of the strong girl she is. She was born on the 10th October 2010 and she was born with High Imperforate Anus. At eleven days old she had her stoma/colostomy made.

She had this for around one year, while growing up it was a constant struggle to get her to have her enemas and this caused her lots of problems and ended up with a lot of hospital visits. Her struggles caused embarrassment at school too.

Two years ago, Heidi had the ACE and it has changed her life for the better. It is not always easy, as it takes an hour a day for her washouts and even though Heidi is still so young, she is now clean every day and has control of her bowels.

Heidi is a proud member of a girls' football team and before her ACE she would not have had the confidence for this. We are so proud of her.

87. My Son's Story – Roxana (Romania)

Hello, my story is not yet a happy story

It all began with a desire to have a child...a very loved and wanted child! I had a quasi-normal pregnancy where in the last trimester I had a uterus-muscle hypertonia, but no doctor could identify what the problem was. So, I said to myself, it is going to be ok at the end.

But the gift of having a baby was overshadowed by the doctor's words that the baby could not pass any meconium and had to be transferred to another hospital for more investigation. He was operated on the next day. I had no idea that this was the beginning of a lots of tears!

My baby boy, I found out later, had been diagnosed with a high anorectal malformation, with prostatic fistula and he also had an associated renal issue.

The first year was exceedingly difficult, because he had to have three operations and he spent many more days in hospital dealing with many renal infections.

We have had wonderful support, which enabled us to travel to other countries (Hungary, Vienna and Austria) for more specialised investigations. He has also had more surgeries and a reconstruction.

In the subsequent years he has had to deal with faecal incontinence, which is a continual frustration and it really tests our patience. We are still trying to find doctors here in Romania to help our son who specialise in his rare conditions, as they are so little known here.

My son is now eleven and he has grown up to be a very handsome, intelligent, and talented young man. He plays piano and violin, and we are so very proud of him and the way he deals with his condition.

My hope is that many people are able to understand the condition in this country and most importantly that doctors are educated and are able to provide the right care and treatment for my son, so he that can lead a more normal and happy life from now on.

88. The Story of My Son, Diego – Gena (USA)

Diego was born via c-section in 2009. It was discovered, during his first bath, that he had imperforate anus. I was in my hospital room when this happened, so my poor husband had to go through several hours of uncertainty surrounding the health of his newborn first child, alone. I was blissfully unaware, and because this was my first baby, I did not know what to expect anyway. It was not until about three hours after the birth that I asked my nurse where the baby was because he would probably need to be fed again. When she said, 'Oh, I don't think the doctor will want you to feed him,' I knew something was wrong. My husband tried to sugar coat things for me over the phone and say that Diego was just being checked over for a few abnormalities.

Finally, I was wheeled into the NICU and saw my poor baby all hooked up to wires and tubes. It was shocking, as he had seemed perfectly normal at birth and had even breastfed once. The doctor explained that my son did not have an anal opening, just a dimple and that several tests would need to be done to determine where his colon was in his little body and if there were any other complications. He would need to be transferred to another hospital in our town with a better NICU. I demanded to go with him, so we were put into separate ambulances that evening and reunited in the new hospital's NICU. So much drama for what was supposed to be the happiest day of my life!

Once all the tests and scans were done, it was determined that Diego had high-type IA, and he would need a colostomy for several months until he grew big enough to have an anus surgically created. So that was his first surgery, at two days old. Once that was over, he had to learn how to breastfeed (not so easy for a baby with post-operative pain), and we had to learn how to care for his colostomy. The days after his surgery were spent by getting myself from my room to the NICU for a thirty-minute feed, then back to my room to pump my breasts to stimulate my much needed milk production, and lastly sleep as much as I could until the process started all over again. It was a continuous three-hour loop, day and night, for several days. Absolutely exhausting. We spent a total of six days in the hospital, which I now know is not that long at all.

We perfected Diego's colostomy care all on our own. We did not have any of the IA resources that are available now. Eventually we got really comfortable with the colostomy, and I was glad I did not have to change poopy diapers. On good days, I would just empty the bag neatly into a diaper once or twice.

Diego had his anoplasty done when he was eight months old. We had to let that heal for six weeks and then the colostomy was reversed at about ten months old. It felt like such an achievement to have those three surgeries behind us. One thing we did not anticipate was how horrible the initial diaper rash would be. Since Diego's little butt had not ever been in contact with stool before, and he had small bowel movements several times a day, his little booty was on fire for months. I am not sure if there is any way it could have been avoided, but he eventually got over it with the help of a combo of antifungal cream and zinc oxide powder.

With Diego's new bowel pattern of several small bowel movements a day, it was like having a normal newborn, except he was bigger and crawling. I knew that he would potty train later than most American boys (around three years). He went to day-care, and I took any advice I could on potty training, but none of it worked because he continued to have stools that looked like what I can only describe as skinny cat poops. How can you potty train a kid who has to go all day long? It was very hard to know what he could feel or control.

When he was around four years old, I took him to his surgeon to beg for help with potty training. He asked me if Diego had ever been checked for "Tethered Cord". I had never heard of it, and the surgeon described it as an abnormality that often comes along with imperforate anus. We took Diego in for an MRI, and he did in fact have a thick fatty ligament that was tethering his spinal cord to his vertebrae. Having a neurosurgeon cut into my baby's spine was so much scarier than the previous surgeries on his GI tract. The recovery was a bit different than the previous bowel surgeries, but Diego did great and we were home in a couple of days.

After that, because we were having so much trouble getting him to the potty in time to not soil his pants, we had his surgeon do a couple of surgical adjustments to his man-made anus. The intestinal tissue had prolapsed a bit, making his anus look a little like a colostomy stoma. We thought this might be impairing his sensation or the function of the sphincters, so we let the surgeon do a couple adjustments, but it did not help his sensation or elimination. He was still wearing disposable training pants to kindergarten and the kids were starting to notice and get mean. Luckily that winter, our surgeon told us that he was not sure what to do next for our son and referred us to two of the best paediatric colorectal specialists in the US. They both looked into Diego's case and came up with the same plan.

We decided to go to Nationwide Children's Hospital in Columbus, Ohio to have Dr. Marc Levitt work on Diego. They have a renowned colorectal practice that many patients travel long distances for. Their social work team was wonderful in helping us secure lodging at the Ronald McDonald House and even airfare assistance from American Airlines.

Since our surgeon had been with us so long (almost six years at that point), he came up to Ohio to attend the surgery.

He received all the follow up care instructions from Dr. Levitt so that he could be our post-op doctor back in Texas. This was the only surgery we travelled for, and it was pretty daunting to arrange. It took several months, but everything worked out so well, that we knew we were doing the right thing.

Dr. Levitt recreated Diego's anus and preformed a Malone procedure. We would run 500-800ml of saline with a prescribed amount of glycerine through Diego's Malone every day, and he could finally have one large bowel movement and no accidents.

Our sweet boy was able to start first grade in underwear! had his daily 'flushies' for almost five years. It took about an hour a day. He decided this year that he wanted to get that hour back, so we started working with a new surgeon (our first one retired) who is starting a bowel management program with several of his patients. He coached us through trying different laxatives and diet changes and checked the progress, using regular X rays.

Diego has not used the Malone in months now. He takes laxatives at night and has a few bowel movements in the morning. I still think the size of his stools are a little small, and he could probably benefit from dilations (under sedation) or another surgery, but he is old enough now to have a say in what he wants to do with his body. He is not just along for the ride anymore!
Diego is eleven now and for the most part is just like any other kid his age, but he has a maturity that shines through. He does not remember all of his surgeries, but the knowledge that he has been under the knife more times than many adults gives him confidence, grit and empathy. My kid is tough.

He has handled a lot of painful procedures and his experience with dozens of health care professionals has given him the ability to talk to grown-ups from a young age.

I am probably most proud of the way he shows up for his friends and family when they are in pain. He has supported a friend through his medical journey and even a cousin with the death of his mother, by drawing on the strength he has gained through years of struggle.

He has had to work hard to achieve a level of normalcy that most people take for granted. In doing so, my son has strengthened the warrior inside.

89. A Little Child Growing Up and Attending School with Incontinence (England)

Children who can't walk get the support of a wheelchair to use in daily living. These children perhaps get more support from school staff, as well as a care plan to support their day at school. Children who can't feed themselves probably get the support of a staff member to feed them or to set up their intravenous feeding. Children who cannot physically groom or wash themselves would usually get assistance to do this. Most of these children would have outward signs that would encourage others to understand and have compassion towards them. The staff at the school would possibly have specialised training in teaching children living with these disabilities, as well as providing wheelchair support, lifting and handling, intravenous feeding, physio and other assistance.

What about the child that cannot use the toilet in the way that society thinks they should? What about the child that lives with incontinence? What about the child that poos themselves? Poo - society recoils when there is anything associated with poo. It is a subject most people would not want to discuss at any time, never mind around the dinner table. People's faces would turn in disgust at the mention, sight and smell of poo. There is no compassion towards those people who cannot 'poo' normally, no training, no understanding and very little support.

So how does a little girl or boy of six years old feel when they witness this or, even worse, become the topic of everyone's jokes. That little girl or boy has possibly already been through numerous surgeries and procedures, as well as having lived with the physical demand of bowel disease every day such as fatigue, nausea and pain. That little girl or boy has most probably missed out on many simple joys of everyday life, like going to the park, as they need to stay in close proximity of toilets. That little girl or boy will feel damaged and struggle with their identity. That little girl or boy will become confused as to who is there to help them and who isn't.

I won't discuss here about my child diagnoses, surgeries, procedures or how we coped with changing colostomy bags. I will instead focus on when my child was five to eleven years old, which I believe was when her real-life struggles occurred. In preschool, my daughter was happy and confident. Despite her numerous hospitalisations she would happily talk to people and sing at the top of her voice. On her first day of school, she went in without looking back. There were no tears, just excitement. As time went on however, this changed. She grew to be a child that screamed and refused to do anything at home. Why? The reason was because her peers were singing poo songs about her. They played tag with her but called it 'poo, don't touch Emma'. At first my daughter played along with it, desperately trying to fit in.

The teachers and headmaster ignored our pleas to stop these games and behaviour. We were told the children were just being children playing innocent games! We were told our daughter was lying and, when it was finally proven through my records and witnesses, the headmaster simply said, "We cannot see everything that is going on in the school". The SENCO (Special Educational Needs Co-ordinator) even told us that my daughter used her condition (of pooing herself) to her advantage!

Staff could not see her embarrassment, shame and humiliation, even saying to me they forget she has a disability as she is not in a wheelchair. My daughter was not picked for any sports or outside school activities. After raising the issue with the school, she was picked for the school choir, but we received a letter that she was not to attend any out of school activities as it was in her best interests! On one occasion, other pupils broke into the disabled toilet my daughter was using and threw her personal items around while sniggering and laughing.

Friends stopped asking our daughter on play dates and stopped babysitting which, as a family, we understood. What we didn't understand though were the hate messages I began receiving on social media from other parents. I began getting paranoid that all parents felt the same way about my daughter and I then distanced myself from everyone. It felt safer this way, but I also felt guilty that I had let my daughter down.

A question often asked of us was why we continued to let our child go through this experience. It is a question I often asked myself. It is a topic we often argued about as a family. Overall, we hoped that as the children grew older it would just stop. We also thought that the stigma and taboo of poo would be the same in any school, and believed the hate was due to ignorance about the condition. Before my daughter began school, I had discussed the condition with the school. My daughter began school in nappies, but this was frowned upon and we felt the staff did not really understand and needed to be educated about imperforate anus. But there was neither education to be accessed nor any information available on the subject.

We knew our daughter was going to live with this condition for the rest of her life and we did our best to teach her coping mechanisms, replacing her hurt with empowerment. The most important thing we did was to be on her side. We listened to her and hugged her. We didn't pity her but encouraged her to do her chores at home, to cook and to take part in after school activities as much as possible. These all had their limits as living with her condition often meant she was tired and would sleep for long hours. Ironically, we believed it was a good school. We had heard horror stories of children being sent home from school for soiling, or parents being called in every time the child soiled. We believe that it is a society problem, not just a school problem.

The best thing to happen was when her gastro nurse referred us to a group called Breakaway Foundation. As a family, we went along to a weekend with other families who had children with bowel or bladder problems. For the first time my daughter felt she wasn't alone with her struggles. Poo was no longer a taboo subject, and we cried and laughed over our shared stories. Of course, we didn't only talk about poo. We took part in activities and let our hair down and, as families that have been stressed for various reasons, we had fun!

Thankfully, now my daughter is accepted into her friendship group, she is becoming more confident again as her self-esteem builds. She is on a bowel management program that gives her freedom and control. She doesn't feel damaged or broken anymore. Our family life is calm and happy. We certainly hope that we have a lot more compassion for people living with incontinence than what people showed us. We know attitudes will not change until people are educated about it and it is discussed more.

If I were to do it all over again, I would most definitely home school my daughter away from the abuse she received on a daily basis at school. She had to receive counselling, and we were told that if this experience continues in high school her life will be ruined, as in their professional opinion she would most certainly develop mental illness. When I look back on that period of our life, I am not sure how we got through it. It is like a blur to be forgotten about.

My heart ached every day, seeing my daughter experience a loss of control with fear in her everyday life. It is time that the stigma of incontinence ends and that school staff and other professionals (as well as society in general) receive more education and training in awareness, understanding, compassion and support.

All children matter.

90. Resilient - Athan's story - Travis and Kendra (USA)

When Athan was born we had no idea that he would be born with any medical complications.

To our surprise we were told that he was born without an anal opening and he would be transferred to a nearby hospital to undergo emergency surgery.

The surgeon told us the operation would only take one hour, but it was the longest hour of our life. Little did we know this would become our new normal and it was just the beginning of Athan's journey. Over time, we found out that this was just the first of many surgeries and diagnoses he would receive.

He was diagnosed with Imperforate Anus, a tethered spinal cord, fused vertebrae and a genetic disorder called "Towns Brock".

It is so difficult to even begin to know where to start on how we have faced roadblock after roadblock as we have fought tirelessly since that day to make sure that Athan has access to the best medical care possible.

There were many times when we were faced with the thought of giving up trying to get answers. We weren't getting the right medical support as to why Athan was dealing with such difficult issues with his bowels and having no improvement at all.

We seemed to be forever visiting hospitals for emergency treatment and then returning within days, and spending so much time in the car. It has been a long road and it has never been easy.

When you looked at Athan you would never consider he had complex health issues as he was running around and smiling. But in the privacy of home, it was starting to take a toll on his emotional health. It was heartbreaking when he would be in the bathroom and saying, "my bottom burns" and "why does this happen to me, it's not fair".

As he couldn't have a bowel movement, he would always need an enema and, at one point, we would give him three a day and he would still get backed up. We were having to take him for weekly x-rays to make sure he wouldn't get backed up.

We decided to consider the Malone procedure so he could do his flush from the top through his belly button rather than his bottom. A surgeon told us that this surgery would change his life.

So, we decided to go ahead with it, but after he come home his belly button would ooze a lot and something just didn't seem right as the surgery site did not look right. When we would insert the tube into his "Mini-Ace button" in his belly he would scream from pain.

We eventually found out that the surgeon who performed the operation was not familiar with the surgery and the reason Athan was in such pain was because his appendix was on the outside and exposed and raw. It was incredibly distressing to be told this news.

This is where our story changed.

In sheer desperation and frustration, we decided that we would take another long drive and we drove to the Children's Hospital Los Angeles ER with five years of medical records in hand hoping there would be a doctor there who could help us. Thankfully, there was!

The doctors at CHLA corrected the surgery site and now Athan is pain free and is not backing up.

There have been countless times when we felt like giving up, but kids are so RESILIENT. They don't give up easily, so how could we have given up when our amazing son would never quit.

Chapter 7 - Parents/Family with Adolescent (13-17 Years Old)

91. Carter's Story - Erica Sousa (USA)

Our son Carter was born in November 2007, he was our first boy, as we already had two daughters. The next day as he still had not passed his meconium, we were advised by the doctor that Carter had been diagnosed with low Imperforate Anus. As we had never heard of the condition, I did a google search on the internet but could not find any information about Imperforate Anus.

We were told that he would be in the NICU for a few days, as we needed to learn how to perform dilations on him for the next few months.

At four weeks-old we found out he had stage two kidney reflux and that he would be on antibiotics for a year to prevent UTI's. He would also need to get ultrasounds every three to six months to see how the kidneys were growing and how well they were working. There was talk at one point that one of his kidneys was not growing that well, and it may need to be removed, which was concerning at the time. Thankfully over the years, as he grew so did his kidneys and he still has both his kidneys!

The dilations were awful, he would cry, I would cry, heck we all cried. We had to work up to a new size every six weeks, until he was up to a size fourteen. There was talk he might need a colostomy at one point.

At the same time, he was not gaining any weight. It was a struggle, as anytime he tried to eat he would throw up. Unfortunately, his paediatrician was not experienced in regard to Carter's complex issues. When he started to lose a lot of weight at six weeks old, we were advised to take him to the local hospital. He was admitted immediately.

Due to urgent concerns for his health, the next day we were transported to another Hospital for more specialised care. Over the next twelve days, he had many tests and we saw so many doctors. During his stay we learned he was a 'failure to thrive', as his weight was not at the normal level. He required a high calorie formula, might need a feeding tube later on and he had a skin tag on his anus. All his tests came back fine.

At eleven months old he had surgery to place a G-tube, muscle biopsy and remove the skin tag by his anus. We were told he would poop better, that he did not need a colostomy and he would start to gain weight.

We were very new to a feeding tube, and it was a struggle to adjust. For a long time, I thought I had failed him. Then I came to realize this was for the best, as he was not vomiting much, was slowly starting to gain weight and thrive.

We saw a geneticist and no serious issues were raised, other than he was going to be short, heck his dad is short, the whole family is not that tall! At one stage, we were advised by a doctor to stop with the feeding tube. He told us if we continued, he was going to be overweight. This shocked us, but after raising our concerns with specialists, we were advised that the G-tube was working well, so we continued.

We went through a period where we were seeing our Gastroenterologist (GI) every three months for weight checks and his poop issues which were going along well. But then slowly he began to struggle to poop and he was getting backed up, even though we were using MiraLAX and doing clean outs on him.

It was a struggle as we were wondering what else it could be, as we had been told his Imperforate Anus was taken care of! Unfortunately, the doctors we had relied on were slowly leaving and going to other hospitals and we were not getting the answers we needed. We ended up seeking a second opinion, but that was to no avail.

It was a struggle to potty train him, he would and could pee, but would not go to poop at all. Instead, he would always go and hide in his closet when he needed to poop, but as he was still in a pull up, we would take care of it when he was done.

He was around five years old when we ended up seeking a third opinion. The doctor we met was particularly good, had a plan to help our son and he also referred us to a new GI for his feeding tube. The doctor was having us do clean outs at home every weekend with magnesium citrate, and although it was working he was having lots of accidents and missing school a lot.

The GI was doing x-rays occasionally to see how backed up Carter was. This was very helpful, and he was the one who told us we needed to change his feeding tube every three to four months. We were not told this when he had his G-tube surgery. He hated getting his tube changed and he would hide all the time. It was a difficult adjustment for him, as previously we were only doing the change occasionally.

We continued to have pooping issues and at one stage we were recommended to try a special Botox treatment, but it did nothing to help him. He was maintaining his weight and height but was still not at the appropriate level, so the GI advised we add a nutritionist to our team to help him gain weight. They wanted to add a higher calorie formula. He also slowly started to eat some foods by mouth, which was a start after all those years and the feeding therapy finally started to pay off.

Then he started to get constipated and lose weight again. We were starting back with the clean outs again, which at this point were not helping with keeping him clean or with his weight. He was starting to throw up once again because he was full of poop. The nutritionist and GI at one point wanted us to add more formula to his diet. The nutritionist suggested we add even more formula to his diet, but as we had been through all this before I told her it was not a dietary issue.

The GI wanted us to see a specialist to do a 'stizmark test' which is a colon transit study that will allow your doctor to evaluate the function of your colon.

Out of sheer frustration and the desperate need for Carter to get the correct care and a better quality of life, I started to do my own research looking for a fourth option to help with his poop issues. He was getting older and was still wearing pull ups and missing school, so we needed help but had no idea who could help us.

I ended up taking my search to Facebook and found a support group that suggested I go see a colorectal doctor at who specialised in Carter's condition in Boston. I called them the next day and they were able to schedule an appointment for a few months later. Finally, I had a feeling that we were getting somewhere.

When we had our appointment, for the first time since Carter was born, I finally felt like his pooping issues were going to be addressed. The colorectal specialist we met was a breath of fresh air and she listened to us and could see how difficult things had been for us. She understood our son's struggle and presented us with a treatment plan.

This plan thankfully worked for us, and we also found out from the tests she conducted, that Carter's colon was super stretched out, and that parts of it would need to be surgically removed at a later stage.

But firstly, we needed to work on getting him totally cleaned out and then staying clean. I was thinking 'not again', as we had been down this route before. As per her instructions we did a huge clean out of him with MiraLAX and Gatorade. We were told to line the floor with puppy pads or something that you did not mind throwing away. When they mean a clean out, they mean it. I have never seen so much poop come out of such a tiny body. I was wondering how in the world he could hold that much poop. We did well, but it was not good enough according to the doctor, so he had to be admitted, as he needed to be totally cleaned out under medical supervision. He was not too happy because he could not eat, but they did get him totally cleaned out.

When we were sent home, he was going to start taking three to five Dulcolax a day. This new laxative was to help keep him clean. Even then he was still having accidents. He had a colon manometry done on him and we were told he would need a surgery. The doctor advised she was going to do a resection of his bowel and he would also get a Malone. After all, you have five feet of colon, so what is the point of keeping it all if it does not work. This was going to help him in more ways than we would have ever thought. He was thriving in so many ways. He started to gain weight, he is keeping clean and wearing underwear, which is something I thought would never happen. When the doctor initially said that to me, I laughed and said, 'yeah right'.

He was struggling with granulation tissue for a long time and I am glad to say he no longer has granulation tissue. Now if only we can figure out why his G-tube site is always itchy that would be great.

We are forever thankful for the Facebook group that helped us to get to the right place and doctor. We feel so comfortable with her and she listens to us and gets where we are coming from, understands his struggles and helps him. He thanks us every day for the surgery and finding his doctor!

I know our journey is far from over, but we feel so comforted that we are finally in good hands.

This plan thankfully worked for us, and we also found out from the tests she conducted, that Carter's colon was super stretched out, and that parts of it will need to be surgically removed at a later stage.

But firstly, we needed to work on getting him totally cleaned out and then staying clean. I was thinking "not again", as we had been down this route before. As per her instructions we did a huge clean out of him with MiraLAX and Gatorade. We were told to line the floor with puppy pads or something that you did not mind throwing away. When they mean a clean out they mean it. I have never seen so much poop come out of his tiny body. I was wondering how in the world could he hold that much poop. It was a good clean out but not good enough according to the doctor, so he had to be admitted as he needed to be totally cleaned out under medical supervision. He was not too happy because he couldn't eat, but they did get him totally cleaned out.

When we were sent home, he was going to start a new laxative to help keep him clean, he was going to start taking 3-5 Dulcolax a day. He was still having accidents. He had a colon manometry done on him and we were told he would need a surgery. The doctor advised she was going to do a resection of his bowel and he would also get a Malone. After all you have five feet of colon what is the point of keeping it all if it doesn't work. This was going to help him more ways than we would have ever thought. He was thriving in so many ways. He started to gain weight, he is keeping clean and wearing underwear, which is something I thought would never happen. When the doctor initially said that to me, I laughed and said, "yeah right".

He was struggling with granulation tissue for a long time, he needed to get a revision because of all the granulation tissue. I am glad to say he had no more granulation tissue. Now if only we can figure out why his G-tube site is always itchy that would be great.

We are forever thankful for the Facebook group that helped us to get to the right place and doctor, we feel so comfortable with her and she listens to us and gets where we are coming from and understands his struggles and helps him. He thanks us every day for the surgery and finding his doctor!

I know our journey is far from over, but we feel so comforted we are finally in good hands.

92. Our Story – The Penton Family (USA)

I woke up at two am to the feeling of my waters breaking. Up to that point my 32 week pregnancy had been uneventful, and I instantly knew something must be wrong. After arriving at the hospital, medical providers attempted to stop my labour but I delivered in just a few hours, despite their efforts. Owen was born weighing 3 lbs. 10 oz. and whisked away to the NICU. About thirty minutes later, a nurse came to deliver the news that he had imperforate anus and was scheduled for a colostomy placement in the morning. After visiting him for as long as we could, my husband and I returned to the room to try to rest and to pump (he could not eat with his impending surgery and was too young to nurse anyway). As a nurse, I had cared for a child with IA only once in my career, but I remembered that it accompanied a group of midline birth defects. I laid awake that night trying to recall what these were. The next day, I asked one of my nursing friends to bring up my textbook and I read all I could on VACTERL association and the birth defects that accompany IA.

Owen's first year is still a blur. I remember pumping breast milk every two to four hours, three surgeries, including a PSARP at six months and an ostomy reversal at eight months and countless specialist visits. Cardiology has discovered an ASD, VSD and multiple other cardiac anomalies and these required yearly echocardiograms for monitoring. Vesicoureteral reflux was found, requiring annual renal follow-up and two years of treatment with an antibiotic to prevent urinary tract infections. This resolved on its own after two years. He worked with PT/OT several times weekly for strengthening and began walking at about one and a half years.

They also provided great emotional support for the twice daily anal dilations that were required after his PSARP, to ensure his anus healed with the correct diameter of opening. I cried before and after each one and I am holding back tears as I write this now. The dilations were painful and required my husband and I to hold him down. I have never done anything that hurt my soul more, than watching his suffering and knowing I was causing it (even though it was for a sound medical reason). Later studies have found dilations might not be required in all cases, but it was the best knowledge we had at the time. Not all families may have to bear this burden in future cases. For those that do, I hope you can find some comfort in knowing that Owen has no recollection of this time and does not seem to have any long-term effects from it.

Following this came a few years that I remember being 'easy'. I call them easy because although the frequent medical provider visits continued, the major problems (that we knew of) had been surgically corrected. Bowel incontinence is expected of a one to three year old, so we spent the next two years in a period of quiet, with 'normal life' only interrupted by the management of his constipation. This began, almost immediately, after I weaned him at a year and has continued to this day.

Thankfully, his surgeons warned us of this, and he was placed on a bowel management regimen that combined laxatives, suppositories and enemas. I wish I could share what the 'magic' answer is, but it continues to change based on a variety of factors. The biggest challenges continue to be diet changes (especially those that occur with vacations, holidays and sleep overs), growth spurts and physical activity. As Owen got older, the correct regime depended on many factors, including his personal preferences. We used daily morning enemas when he was young, as this helped to keep him clean throughout the day at school. As he got older, he no longer wanted these, and we were able to transition to an oral laxative and diet. Including enough fibre in a kid's diet is difficult, but as they get older and are more aware of how eating certain foods affects their gut, it does get a little easier.

The next few years were the 'hard' years. It is not OK for a school aged child to be incontinent and thanks to his surgeon's advice and my own research, I knew achieving social continence was vital to ensure he could have a normal social life. As I mentioned before, we have never found a perfect answer. For a few years, enemas to clear his bowel and prevent (most) accidents during school were the solution. Later, at a specialist's recommendation we tried a polyethylene glycol laxative (which never worked, and most specialists now recommend against it for kids with IA).

For now, a senna laxative combined with fibre works well, 95% of the time. We try to anticipate things that will make his constipation worse and head things off. (Spending the weekend at a friend's house and eating junk food all weekend. We clean out with laxatives before [prevention] and after [treatment]. Having a growth spurt and the 'skid marks' start happening more. We go back to, every other day laxatives, instead of twice a week and adjust as needed. It helps that he is thirteen and can give feedback on how things are working.

When he was younger, I had to rely on supportive teachers and family friends. I wrote a letter to his teachers explaining in simple terms how his anatomy was different when he was born. That he could not prevent an accident if going to the bathroom was delayed (or sometimes at all). I emphasized how important it was to help him hide accidents and we developed a 'code word' to alert his teachers that he needed to visit the nurse, so that he could toilet and change. For his friends, I explained to their mothers and thankfully he found four close friends in kindergarten that he remains close to, to this day.

At first, his friends were unaware but gradually they noticed that he had occasional accidents. I will never forget a conversation my husband had with 'C' one day. He was spending the night and the boys had all gone on a bike ride. Owen had a major bowel accident during the ride and my husband texted me to help get things fixed when they got back home. While I was giving Owen an enema and he had a shower, 'C' helped my husband with work in the yard. He mentioned that he knew that Owen had problems with his stomach and that he would always help him hide it, because Owen always stood up for him when anyone picked on him at school too.

After getting through elementary and figuring out how to constantly adapt his bowel regimen to changes, I felt like we had gotten into a good routine. Owen was doing well in school, enjoyed Taekwondo in the afternoons, had close friends, went to sleepovers and had a life like all his friends (from my perspective). His renal problems had resolved, his cardiac issues were stable and did not restrict his activities in any way. Even his left ear hearing loss (which his school nurse found in kindergarten) wasn't affecting his grades or his ability to communicate. Anyone looking at our family from the outside would never know he had any medical problems.

That is when the back pain started. He had a major growth spurt at age eleven and shortly after started complaining that his back felt tight. Despite loving Taekwondo, he wanted to skip lessons and started having more bowel incontinence with physical activity. He had had an MRI of his spine several years earlier, to rule out tethered cord, and even though his conus was between L4-L5 (much lower than expected and suspicious for a tether), neurosurgery had elected a watchful, waiting approach, as he had no symptoms. In my research, I have found two schools of thought on this, and I would encourage other parents to research both to help determine the right choice for their child.

There are pros and cons to treating proactively (before symptoms occur) and retroactively (after symptoms occur) and it is not an easy decision either way. We knew back pain after a growth spurt was a problem and scheduled a follow-up with neurosurgery. If a tethered cord is present, growth spurts can stretch the spinal cord and this is often when the associated pain is noticed. After following the recommended six weeks of no physical activity (torture for an eleven-year-old), his back pain was not only just as bad, it was worse. Owen and my husband took a fifth-grade trip to Washington D.C.

and New York and found they had to cut sight-seeing walks short due to the back pain. We scheduled surgery shortly after and he had almost immediate relief. Post-operatively, after getting his bowel regime back on track (narcotic pain meds are horribly constipating), we again entered a period of 'normal'.

Owen finished his black belt recommended in Taekwondo and became interested in golf. He made the middle school golf team and all was well until we noticed he was restricting his swing. He said the old back pain was back. An MRI provided little answers (re-tethering is often difficult to detect and is related to scar tissue and other factors), but the symptoms were there. The back pain persisted and his constipation got harder to manage. One day, watching a movie, he suddenly had a bladder accident, something that had never happened before. We scheduled surgery (based on symptoms this time, as we had no imaging that could confirm a diagnosis).

For the second time, his neurosurgeon described how his spinal cord, 'sprang back up' when de-tethered. Prior to going into surgery, Owen calmly rated his pain as a seven on a scale of ten (ten being the worst pain you have ever experienced). Post-operatively he rated his pain as three, even accounting for the major operation he had. Pre-operatively, I never saw him grimace, moan, or cry. He never stopped his activity, he only slightly restricted it.

But during this time, I watched my happy child become restless and have difficulty sleeping. I share these symptoms as they are those I know all too well as the face of chronic pain; pain that is often discounted because it presents so differently than acute pain. As parents, I believe we need to be aware of these subtle symptoms in our children, so that we can quickly advocate for intervention if problems occur.

Today, we are ten months past his most recent surgery. We are back to 'normal' again, but I am acutely aware that this description may be temporary. Owen's next surgery is scheduled for Thanksgiving week, to fix a small rectal prolapse that makes him feel a constant pressure. For now, he is back at golf, doing well in pre-AP classes and has more friends than the kindergarten gang (although they remain close!). Many of his new friends are unaware of his medical issues and he shares, as he feels comfortable doing so. I no longer have to tell his teachers or other mothers about his medical problems.

He has a 504 (USA medical accommodations) plan that allows for toileting without restrictions at school. He advocates for his health as he feels the need, with the knowledge that his parents will support him if asked.

Owen is part of my inspiration. During these past thirteen years, I returned to school and became a nurse practitioner and completed my doctorate with the hopes I could assist others in finding the same path to health, I am helping Owen find.

In my experience, even among medical professionals, I have found that IA is poorly understood. VACTERL association is even more rare, requiring parents to become experts and advocates to ensure the best outcomes for our children.

What is next after this period of 'normal' for us? I do not know, but when we find out, we will adapt and overcome.

Rebecca, Mom

93. Aiden's Story – DeVries Family – Michelle, Mom (USA)

"Life isn't about waiting for the storm to pass, it's about learning to dance in the rain"

How do I even begin to describe what being a mom to a young man born with IA is like? When I look at my 13-year-old my heart explodes. There is not one day that I take for granted with him. The Good, The Bad and The Ugly. On most challenging days, I hold onto each one of these with dear life.

Aiden has pushed through so many surgeries and setbacks with an incredible will to never give up on himself. He's stronger than anyone I know and I love his fiery spirit. His name, Aiden, means "born of fire/the fiery one/little fiery one" in Gaelic and he definitely matches that description.

I can look back now at all that we've lived through with him and I can admit that it wasn't always so easy to talk about Aiden's medical issues without endless tears. To this day I still have not finished his baby book. Each time I've attempted to look through the photos I'm immediately bought back to the early days, and the anxiety rushes in like a tsunami. I'm not giving up and I know I'll finish that book one day, even if it takes me until his senior year in High School.

There are so many words that immediately come to mind when I think back to April 18, 2007. Immediately, when they put that tiny baby in my arms, I felt so much love that I thought my heart would burst. A beautiful boy with a healthy pair of lungs.

As the nurse whisked him away to complete the Apgar scoring, she gave me a reassuring smile that she'd return with him soon. Little did I know that my current state of bliss would change to feelings of panic & isolation in just under an hour.

Approximately thirty to forty-five minutes later, a team of Medical Personnel walked in without my baby but with concerned looks on their faces. I had an epidural plus they had given me some additional pain medication, so I wasn't the most coherent. I looked at my sister-in-law Laurie's face when she asked where the baby was, and she immediately left the room to get my husband. That was when I began to panic.

I will never forget the feelings of shock and helplessness as my husband and I heard these medical terms for the first time:

"Imperforate Anus, Anorectal Malformation, Fistula, Colostomy"

From that moment on, life would be changed forever. We had no idea how incredibly challenging Aiden's first year of life would be. We had just bought our first home together that December 2006. Our little boy would be born just a few months later. I had a pretty easy-going pregnancy, up until 20 weeks when I started to bleed. It was a Saturday night and the hospital thought I had lost him, only to find out ten hours later that I had Placenta Praevia and that the baby was ok.

Months later they would notice that my amniotic fluid was lower than typical. The doctors never seemed overly concerned. They would have me come in for ultrasounds to make sure everything was ok and kept tabs on my fluid level. At my 39-week check-up they discovered that my fluid was half of what it typically should be, and so they made the decision to induce me. At no point did they ever tell me the baby would have any issues.

Now that I look back at it, his kidneys weren't functioning well which most likely caused the amniotic fluid to remain low. He was also born with tethered cord which I had no idea is linked to Spina Bifida. I remember taking all kinds of tests during my pregnancy and I was never told if my scores were anything to be concerned about.

This happened during the years 2006-2007. It seems that now however, some people are finding out ahead of time if their child has any IA or similar issues.

Since we had just recently purchased our home, I was only able to afford three months of maternity leave. When I realised how involved his medical condition was, I asked my employer for an additional month off in order to make sure we found a medical team to help with his upcoming surgeries.

The entire four months went by in the blink of an eye, and it was filled with non-stop research and meetings with surgeons at three different hospitals. Aiden's first surgery, the colostomy, was performed after he was forty-eight hours old. He wasn't allowed to eat anything since birth. Visions of us watching that poor baby rooting for food are forever burned into our brains. They explained the risks of surgery on a forty-eight-hour old infant and then had us sign pages of documents giving permission to perform the colostomy. We watched helplessly as they wheeled Aiden away to surgery, praying that everything would go well.

Those days in the NICU are a blur and it would take a full year (2007-2008) to complete the necessary Pull-Thru and Colostomy Reversal Surgeries. During that same year he had a rectum prolapse repair and emergency surgery when his pull-thru stitches dehisced (ruptured).

As stressful as that year was, we were so happy to celebrate his first birthday with friends and family. We asked everyone to consider making a donation to Dr. Pena's foundation in place of toys or other gifts. We couldn't think of a better gift to thank this incredible surgeon and his team. He gave our son Aiden the best quality of life and we were forever in his debt.

During that first year, a (now late) dear friend of ours, Traci Wagner, researched and found an organisation called the Pull-thru Network on the internet. We joined it immediately. We attended our first PTN convention in New Orleans in July 2010.

We no longer felt so isolated and alone. We were finally in the presence of people that understood everything we were going through at the time. I finally exhaled and felt a little more like my old self again.

Since his birth in 2007, Aiden has had fourteen surgeries, the easiest surgery by far being the Malone and the most stressful being a tie between the Tethered Cord release & Kidney Repair.

When Aiden was very young, we were warned he may never be able to do certain things. We never once told Aiden any of this as we wanted him to challenge himself, and he continues to grow and become his own person. Aiden enjoys playing guitar, acting in plays, riding his scooter, skateboarding with his dad, going to Boy Scouts, snowboarding and, most recently, has started taking golf lessons with a friend.

Aiden with Dr Alberto Pena

The year 2018 was one of his most challenging since the first year of his life. Aiden had kidney failure and had to have a nephrostomy tube installed twice within a month of each other. I thought we may lose him and it was terrifying. While recovering in hospital he developed C-diff (an infection). After spending a gruelling month in the hospital, he then had to continue to quarantine at home for an additional week.

That April, a decision had to be made to either to remove the kidney or repair it. Aiden was eleven at the time, so we included him in the final decision. The surgeon explained the pros and cons of both and left it up to all of us. She gave us her cell number and asked that we text her our decision by 9pm. I will never forget looking at him as he said to us, I want the kidney repair. He said, "I understand that if the repair doesn't work, then I'll lose the kidney. I just want to give my kidney a chance". The rest is history and the kidney repair was a success. We have to continue to get ultrasounds and annual check-ups at Nationwide to make sure that his kidneys are OK. We are thankful that so far all is well.

What started as the worst year for him medically (Jan-April 2018) ended with an incredible week at Youth Rally in Boulder Colorado. This was the first time he was in a camp away from us for a week where he had to be responsible for his Malone flushes on his own. He grew up so much in that short week because he had to manage everything without mom or dad reminding him or being there to help him through. He knew he could ask any of the nurses for help, but he wanted to do it all on his own and he felt empowered.

The first two days of camp he was very homesick and I was ready to pick him up, but my husband kept telling me that he'll be ok and that this was normal. I had never been to a sleep away camp ever in my life, so I had no idea how scary it could be. By the third day I no longer received calls or texts and that made me even more nervous. As luck would have it, one of the counsellors was a young man that we met at a PTN conference in Georgia when Aiden was only five. He checked on Aiden and reassured me that he was having a great time. Knowing that Frank was there definitely helped me relax a bit more.

The main benefit of our son being born with IA is that we've been blessed with meeting so many incredible surgeons, nurses and parents all going through the same or very similar issues as children, teens and adults. We are especially blessed to have met so many adults living with IA. We continue to learn so much invaluable information from them.

One IA adult in particular, Mr. Greg Ryan, has become an incredible friend and mentor. Early on he shared with us his quote, that "**even though IA is a life condition, never treat it as a life sentence**". We absolutely love this and make sure that Aiden follows this mantra as well.

Greg celebrated 2017 Thanksgiving with us

No matter what life throws at our little family, we continue to learn how to "Dance in the Rain" of life.

94. Aiden's Story – DeVries Family – Dave, Dad (USA)

This is all I got, kid.

The woman was sweating and out of breath. Switching positions, she tossed the plastic baby around like a pair of nun chucks. Her job, a parting shot before we left the hospital, was to demonstrate the proper care of a newborn baby. It was laughable - totally useless and made even more so because our son had been born "different". Yeah, I know, that's vague.

But it was then, confronted with being a first-time dad, that I realised I had no idea how to be a good dad, especially to a kid with an uphill battle. How could I help him overcome the setbacks his body had left on his doorstep?

You want me to say stoma and imperforate anus and Malone, and that's about as much as I'm willing to reveal. Frankly, I've attended countless medical lectures throughout my son's life and I'm kind of done with describing things using the medical terminology. After a week in the NICU, my boy was coming home with a colostomy bag and I couldn't be prouder. While family members secretly gasped at his condition, I remember looking at him, his body a tentacled mess of cords and lines, and just smiling and being so happy to meet my son. He was just a concept last week – now here he was.

Upon arriving home, my wife and I realised that we were in way over our heads. Yeah, colostomy bag. They gave us like two or three bags and seals. The seals are the critical part; they fail and there's poop everywhere. All I knew was, it was our job to keep him clean. The objective was simple; cover the red bulbous openings that erupted throughout the day by gluing a bag to his stomach. The first weekend we ran out of supplies. I can't even remember what we did to mitigate that problem, but my wife can remember the details. Me, I just remember thinking, "I gotta get good at this".

I could always tell by my wife's tone when things had come unstuck - a terrified pitch, even whispered, that pierced the room, mall or party as she said, "It happened". We had a bag with scissors, powder, adhesive patches and prep wipes for the seals. There was more stuff too, but I forget what. At first we were a mess. We were nervous and made mistakes, but over time we got good at it. I think I was better at changing his colostomy bag, but that may be my ego speaking and my need to be "The Dad". All I knew was, when shit went down (or out), my blood pressure dropped, sound and movement decreased and the only thing that existed was my son.

Changing bags became meditative in a way, and when his colostomy was reversed at nine months I was never so happy to unlearn something and forget about a hard-won skill. Even so, I look back on that ability with pride, but have always felt like I didn't measure up to my wife's contributions to our family.

Over his 13 years, I've been in awe of my wife's abilities. Her command of scheduling and corresponding with doctors and hospitals, her bulldog like tenacity with insurance companies and the way she continually pushes my boy to develop social connections and new skills. She is the first person he runs to when he's sick. Her love seems endless, but mostly I am humbled by her "mom-ness". Moms like her are eternally mysterious creatures and I could never be one. I could never fill that void if she ever left this world.

So, since I could never possibly replace that "mom-ness", how can I be the best dad to him?

Despite the serious nature of his condition, I hope that when my son looks back on his life he sees some humour in all of it and how it helped us all cope as a family. My boy's strong spirit has carried him through more than 12 operations and procedures. While his friends complained of homework and screen time limitations, he complained about standing up after spinal surgery. While other kids made decisions about whether to go outside or play inside, my son made the decision of whether to remove one of his kidneys or not. These are really tough things for a kid to face, and if he focuses too much on his condition he may never be happy.

Right now, he's 13 and in the 8th grade. It's middle school hell, where kids judge you like it's a sport and he's not immune to his peers' scrutiny. He is shyer than his elementary school self but, at heart, I see the way he laughs at his situation and observes his contemporaries with a sharper focus than they can muster. He's intelligent, witty and ironic. He quotes stuff I have never heard of before and is able to make me laugh too.

I'll never really know or truly comprehend my contribution to his wellbeing from the countless others in his life. But I think that where one might otherwise worry, I have instead laughed at seemingly devastating social situations. As he grew up I tried to distract him, finding the poignant, funny moments and amplifying them so as to diffuse negativity and remind him that he is as perfect as the day I first met him.

I shall relate a few things I remember, written down before my aging brain makes them fuzzy and distant.

Before we proceed, you need to understand some terminology and how it's evolved over the years. Starting at age four, my son needed an enema every other night to clean out his system. (I know I should say colon or digestive tract but I won't. I digress...)

Anyway, he poops ever so slowly, almost glacially, and if left unchecked he'd go every hour. Hence the need for an enema to give him two days of peace.

So, at four he began doing his own enemas. No shame in that for him. He was little, but what did he know? As he got older, the enema term evolved into the more clandestine, suspiciously named "procedure" - like, "it's time for your procedure". And now, as 8th grade is in full gear, I just poke my head into the room, look past his friends and say, "You gotta do something for me so it's time for everyone to leave". I get it.! No one wants to be different in middle school!

So, that is what he has to do to survive this in world. Understand, I tried my best to turn this situation into a positive, or at least make it acceptable and (in the best of times) something to admire.

Before I proceed, I need to set something up. I have ulcerative colitis, which is nothing serious now, but in my 20's and 30's it was bad. It shaped my world view. I became less adventurous, preferred being at home, definitely avoided camping and developed an almost supernatural power in finding a bathroom in any store. It was like I had a radar!

So, when my son asked, "Dad, why do I have to do these enemas when Kevin doesn't have to do them?", I did my best to "draw" him a story where he was the hero. "Son" I replied, "if you were on a long hike, Kevin would have to poop every day or maybe even twice a day. He'd have to stop, find a quiet place and do his business. You, on the other hand, could go for two days without stopping. You'd get to the end of the trail first because that is your superpower". And because of my colitis I felt that. I really believed that and really conveyed it to him. I truly hope that it took.

Now I realise enema power is a gift he'd gladly exchange, but he doesn't have that option. We just make the best of it. But if a power isn't enough to help him on his journey, then perhaps he's learned to laugh. One particular instance highlights this well.

One day, in front of our house when my son was six, all the kids were surrounding my boy. I was eight feet away on our porch. I can't remember what they were playing but they were moving around a lot. As my son's foot dug in for a run, a turd fell out of his pants leg and all the kids saw it. In that split second, I looked at my son's face, and it wasn't like we'd practiced for this, but without hesitation we both started laughing out loud. Holy crap! A turd just popped into our lives! All the other kids saw the adult laughing and must have guessed it was OK, or at least a funny event not limited to the kid who bore my last name. It was a pure dad thing to do, like grading our farts like Olympic judges or complimenting each other's burps. It wasn't practiced but it was who we were.

Even so, as middle school bankrupts a kid's sense of humour at the best of times, I see his resilience take hold. Frankly, that's all him. I am, however, a willing conspirator in any ridiculousness at hand.

Lastly, one of the most important lessons I have learned, and one that everyone should take to heart, is to drop the schedule. Enemas, procedures, appointments, prepping, travel and tests all add up to feeling boxed in. Kids like my son...well...their whole world is scheduled. So, every year my boy and I travel somewhere (mostly Maine as we are a struggling family). We have family there that let us use their cabin. At the cabin, time shuts off. We schedule only things that demand it (like a start time to a movie, horseback riding or zip lining). Other than that, I give him a break. Smell the flowers kid. Forget where you have to be and just BE. Remember that. Remember your spirit is more powerful and more eternal than the body that limits you.

I won't be here for the end of his life, but hopefully he will have learned all of these things and taught them to others in need. Maybe to his own son or daughter. And don't hold back on the fart jokes! Girls should be able to laugh at that stuff too.

For now, his future is exactly as it should be - a mystery; one that will unfold, bringing challenges and joy. I hope he remembers that his mom and I love him with all our hearts, that we were amazed at his spirit and the way he overcame so much, that he mattered and that his hugs, especially as an 8th grader, are the reason we live.

We love you Aiden.

95. Drew's Story – Sherry (Canada)

Hello, my name is Sherry and I live in Newfoundland, Canada. I have a son that was born with IA on 3 July 2007. His name is Drew, and he is now 13 years old.

After he was born, Drew was looked over by the paediatricians and we were told there was a problem. It meant they had to transfer him immediately to another hospital. He was then medevacked to that hospital and, after seven days, went into surgery where they had to bring his bottom hole down.

After that surgery, we had to perform therapy on him every day with dilators in order to stretch his bottom hole. As he got older, we then had to use enemas to clean him out every day so he wouldn't get constipated.

As Drew continued to have problems, we then had to use enema's where we also had to use a tube with a balloon at the end. That balloon would blow up inside and trap a solution to enable him to clear his bowels. We had to continue this for a while.

When Drew was five years old, he had a tube placed inside of him with a trap door on the end. We were continuing to go back and forth to the hospital. That remained a part of our lives until he had stoma surgery, enabling him to use a colostomy bag. He had to have the bag for six months before his big surgery could be done.

It was so intense and stressful for us as the surgery took such a long time, and then we were told he had 50 percent of his large bowel removed and the colostomy was removed. The other part of the surgery was to join his small and large bowel to help with his bowel movements, but that took time to train again and again.

It's a little bit more complicated now, as he's going through a lot as he gets older. As far as we are aware, he is the only boy in the area where we live who has this problem, and it's really hard day after day for him. He has been taking Imodium to help him with his bowel movements, but he gets really stressed out with school, especially when it comes to doing stuff like tests and book reports.

I am trying to cope with it as best as I can, but I often get stressed seeing him go through this. He is trying very hard to keep up at school but it's difficult. One year he had to get help with schoolwork because he was so stressed out.

So, every day is a struggle for him and over the years he has developed anxiety. Sometimes he suffers from depression because of how he feels and what his body is going through with this condition.

Drew has been through so much with all his hospital visits, surgeries and procedures. He has had over forty-five X-rays done since he was born. I am fortunate that I have a lot of support from family and friends, and especially from my husband who is always here right by my side.

We know it's still a long road ahead for us and Drew with his condition, and it is a struggle for him each and every day. That is why I wanted to share our story with you and other parents with a child born with IA. I am tired of feeling alone and not having anybody to talk to about it, and its hard seeing my son like this. Some days are good, but some days are not.

96. Tav's Story – Kim and Luke (Australia)

Tavis was born by C-Section on 10 June 2005, and it seemed like he was a perfect, beautiful, "healthy" boy. Everyone was so happy. I fed him at around 8pm that night and, as much as he wanted to suck, he just didn't seem hungry. The same thing happened at around 1am. The next morning, I ran it by the nurse who took him for some checks and came back to tell me that Tavis was born with an Imperforate Anus. My first thought was "Oh OK, whatever that is", and later I learnt it meant he was born with no bottom hole.

I rang my husband and told him he needed to come to the hospital NOW. We were flown by air ambulance to a major hospital in Sydney. Tavis was taken to the Children's Hospital and I had to be admitted to an adult hospital due to my just having had a C-Section. My older sister, who lives in Sydney, went to sit with Tavis in intensive care until poor Luke could pack the other kids up and drive the four hours to Sydney to be with us. Luke finally came through the door with a wheelchair and took me to the Children's hospital to be with Tavis. I must say that my husband was an absolute hero in all of this. He was the one to be there for all the testing, the prodding and the probing and taking Tavis for his first surgery. Yet through all of this, Luke made sure I was back to my room for breakfast, lunch and dinner to keep me healthy so I would recover well from my operation.

We were absolutely blessed to have a wonderful paediatric surgeon assigned to Tavis. He informed us that Tavis's bowel was a high bowel. This is very unfortunate as it is hard to create an anus and pull the bowel down to meet the anus when you have a high bowel, so the prognosis was not as good as we had hoped. We took Tavis home a week later with his colostomy bag. Home life was crazy trying to balance a five-year-old and a three-year-old as well as give Tavis the time needed to keep him healthy. But we fell into a pattern and off we went juggling trips to Sydney and keeping life as normal as possible for Kiara and Declan. Living rurally, we had no-one nearby to support us.

Tavis had many appointments in Sydney for the next nine months, sometimes occurring fortnightly. When he was three months old, I worked three or four nights a week to gather enough money for petrol to get to Sydney, whilst Luke worked his normal full-time job. We were lucky enough however to have family in Sydney for accommodation.

At nine months of age, on 2 February 2003, we were back in Sydney for Tavis's big reconstructive surgery. This was to be a six-and-a-half-hour operation, the aim of which was to create an anus and bring the bowel down to meet the new opening. It was a very scary day and, looking back, we were so naïve. Halfway through the operation we were called to see the surgeon who advised us that his bowel was extremely high but he would do the best he could. It took a long time for Tavis to get over this operation and he was very unwell. Tavis had to have a couple more small surgeries due to problems which arose from the first operation. When his bowel was pulled down to meet the anus, the lining of the bowel frayed. We just had to hope and pray that the body would take over and mend the bowel.

On day nine of hospitalisation, a social worker came to see us as she was doing a survey about our stay. At this stage I feel I was coping (just) with the trauma that Tavis had been through, but I was fretting for my other two children. I had a bit of a meltdown and it was decided that Luke would drive back to Forster to pick up the kids and bring them back to Sydney. It was a big ask, but we felt we needed to be together. This is an area I'd like to see supported a little more. It is extremely hard to be separated from your children and sibling support is certainly important in this situation.

Three weeks later we were able to come home and be a family again. I had to travel to Sydney almost every fortnight for Tavis to have bowel explorations to keep an eye on how it was mending. Finally, the surgeon was happy with his progress.

On the 31 August 2006, Tavis had his colostomy closure operation, this being his tenth surgery! It was a piece of cake and all went well. There were big celebrations for his first poo! Then the expected nappy rash started. We knew that Tavis would have nappy rash, but nothing could prepare us for how severe it would be. It was like third degree burns. Tavis had no control over his poo and it would just leak out. He had to be changed immediately or the acid in the poo would burn his already painful skin. Sometimes we would change him every ten minutes. We did this for eighteen months, but Tavis had no quality of life and lived in pain twenty-four seven.

Amongst all this pain from the nappy rash, we also had to do the dreaded daily dilatations. Some days you could just do it and get on with your day and other days were just horrendous. I often dropped my other two children off to school and when I got back in the car I would burst into tears. The feeling that I had violated my own child was just too much to bear sometimes. I know this is not what I was doing, but it bloody well felt like it some days! Again, living rurally, I had NO support and I just hoped to God that I was doing it right.

After lengthy discussions with our surgeon, we were given some options to give him quality of life. The best option for Tavis was a thing called a Chait Button. No-one as young as Tavis had ever had this procedure.

In March 2008, at the ripe old age of two years and nine months, Tavis received his Chait Button! This allowed us to irrigate his bowel through a little button on his belly each night and keep him clean throughout the whole next day. At first it was a massive task to get Tavis irrigated plus get the other kids sorted, but it changed our lives dramatically. Thankfully, his everyday pain disappeared as his sore bottom cleared up, and we could lead normal lives during the day. We now have the bowel irrigations down pat and it has become part of our nightly routine. It is hard to go out for dinner or socialise much but hey, it's a million times better now he has his "special" button.

Tavis often complained of a sore tummy and we just related this to his bowel issues. At the beginning of 2011 it was time to find a local paediatrician. We had an appointment with him in Taree and, as the doctor was going through Tavis's history with me, he happened to ask how much red meat he ate. I told him that Tavis did not like red meat but I was very happy with his diet and didn't feel that it had affected him. The doctor sent Tavis for a blood test just to make sure his iron levels were OK. It was discovered however, that his iron levels were so low he would have to have iron injections. These injections were awful as they were extremely painful. By the third injection, which involved having to hold him down, I asked the doctor if there could possibly be something else causing the iron deficiency, as I was very happy with Tavis's diet and did not understand the low iron levels. He advised me that the only thing it might be was coeliac decease. I just laughed and said, "Well, it won't be that!". We then got Tavis tested for coeliac decease. The doctor called me a couple of days later and said that the blood test came back with a high reading for coeliac decease. Tavis was admitted to John Hunter Hospital in Newcastle for a bowel biopsy which confirmed that he did have coeliac disease.

Our paediatric surgeon had retired and our relationship with the hospital in Sydney sort of got lost because we had no doctor to refer to. Over the years it has been incredibly frustrating trying to find support in our local area. I have actually guided medical staff in what to do if Tavis's button came out as well as in any other related circumstances.

About three years ago I needed some advice and got onto the Stomal Therapist at the Sydney hospital, who was shocked at the amount of time that had passed with Tavis not having proper check-ups. So now we are under the care of a new paediatric surgeon.

This story is just a brief summary. I have skipped many traumas and tribulations but I feel we really need something in place to better support rural families. It is lucky that Luke and I are the sort of people who can cope and get through on our own. But I can see why families split in these situations.

I also strongly feel that we need something in place for siblings of children with IA, as their lives are thrown into absolute chaos. My son Declan, who is almost three years older than Tavis, has been fine but my daughter who is five years older than Tavis has had severe mental health problems stemming from the feeling of being left behind once Tavis was born. Luke and I put in so much time, effort and love into our other two children that we did not see this coming. Maybe if something were in place from early age it could prevent other families having to go through this dreaded spiral of depression.

Tavis's schooling has been up and down. He has a relationship with a psychologist, who he had not seen for about two or three years, but in 2018 he started high school and all the changes had obviously caused anxiety and stress. In turn, this affected his bowel and unfortunately he has had to come home a few days. So, he went back to see her and adjusted his thinking. His high school have been an amazing support, even inviting me to their whole staff meeting to explain Tavis's issues. He successfully attended the year seven camp and the school even invited his brother, who was in year ten, along as support.

Tavis is now in year nine and his mental attitude is so strong. He has amazing friends around him who are the funniest and most supportive and understanding crew. He is a talented Rugby League player and, with his dedication to training and maintaining his health, has had a remarkably successful year. He has just been selected to play for the North Coast Bulldogs squad. This is a next level up and will challenge us as a family to keep his health on track in order to cope with the travelling, training and anything else that gets thrown at us.

About a year ago Tavis started having problems with urinary tract infections and bladder leakage. The UTIs are painful and make him quite sick. But he has the most amazing mindset and still plays footy through the pain. Our GP is managing him at the moment until his appointment with a Urologist in November.

So that is Tavis's and our family's story! There are many things that happened in between the events that I have laid out here. At the end of the day, we have a beautiful boy who seemingly knows things we don't even know. He plays footy, surfs, spearfishes and leads a pretty normal life. Tavis has brought so much joy to our family and we are incredibly lucky to have him.

97. A Mother's Story – April (USA)

My name is April, and I am from a small town in North Carolina. I had my first and only child at the age of 30. I was assuming the birth would be normal, that all would be well and we would go home in a day or two with a healthy baby boy or girl. After my son, Nick was born, they placed him on a surface to take his temperature but were unable to insert the thermometer. I noticed a strange look on the nurses' faces but was unaware of what was to come. A nurse then placed him on my chest to start the feeding, when suddenly my son started gurgling. The nurse quickly took him from me and left the room. Soon after, the doctor came in, sat beside me and began to tell me what they had seen on my son's x-rays.

Honestly, it was all one big blur to me, and it still is. It was so overwhelming. The doctor was telling me that my son's oesophagus was not attached, which is why he was gurgling. He also spoke about his horseshoe kidney, that there was something abnormal with his heart and there was no anal opening. This, of course, was why the nurse could not get a temperature and why he would have to be transported immediately to a Children's Hospital for emergency surgery. The only thing I could comprehend at that time was that he needed to go to the nearest hospital, to save his life. When I was discharged the following morning, I went straight to Nick at the hospital. I was numb. I did not know what to think, what the outcome would be and I had no clue that this was going to be the start of a very difficult journey.

Fortunately, the procedures went well and he had his tracheoesophageal fistula repaired and a colostomy. After being in ICU for about a month we were finally given the OK to take Nick home. We started dilations, which were horrific, and soon took him back for another surgery to close up the colostomy and connect his colon. After his last surgery I remember the surgeon explaining what to expect for Nick's life, going forward. He said, in a nutshell, that potty training would be difficult and not to let him get constipated. He said that Nick would never be the biggest kid in the class, to give him MiraLAX in a cup of juice every evening, so that he would be cleaned out the next morning before school and good luck!

Seriously? Nothing more? This is not so bad after all. Right? Wrong. It was not that simple. Elementary school was tough, I was doing everything I thought I was supposed to do. I was mixing the MiraLAX daily, just as I was told, expecting him to use the potty the next morning to clean out and be good to go to school. Instead, Nick was having accidents almost daily. I would call the surgeon and all he would ever tell me was that I needed to figure out the right amount of MiraLAX to use. I tried many different amounts but could not figure out the 'perfect' amount. He had no control and would leak constantly. I called Nick's paediatrician for advice, but he did not have a clue how to help me either. I even called desperately wanting him to help me figure out a dosage for MiraLAX and they told me they could not give me that information. I would call his surgeon and all he could ever tell me was just keep trying the MiraLAX and sit him on the toilet for an hour. I was so desperate. I felt so alone and that no one else cared enough to help my son, but they also did not even know how to help him. The MiraLAX was not working, there had to be an answer, or a dosage that maybe someone I could reach would tell me. But that never happened. My son was having horrible accidents at school. But thankfully we had a plan in place with his teachers and the school staff. Nick could go to the office at any time, where his bag of extra clothes and underwear (with panty liners already in place) would be hanging in the principal's office, so that he could clean himself up. I was always on standby for a call to come, praying constantly that God would protect him from other kids seeing an accident on his pants.

One of the worst memories for my son was hearing kids ask, 'What's that smell?' He would know it was him and that he had had an accident. He would have to stand there and figure out a way to get to safety and to get changed. It still breaks my heart to think of what he went through. He could not play at recess without worrying, because a lot of his accidents happened while he was running and playing. If I saw him coming out of school with a sweatshirt or jacket wrapped around his waist, I knew he had had an accident, as that was his way of hiding it. Many times, he called and needed to be picked up from friends' houses because of having an accident. When I got those phone calls it was like I was on a mission. I would get to him as fast as I could, driving ninety mph, daring anyone to get in my way. I was always in a hurry to get to my child and rescue him from the situation. Those drives always felt like they took forever.

I am happy to say that by the grace of God, none of his friends or the other students at school have ever seen an accident to this day. Nick was able to do whatever he wanted, but there was always a chance of him having an accident, so we tried to always be prepared. From recess, to sleepovers, to playing baseball, to just everyday life, we could not get control,. It did not matter what I googled, or what we changed and tried. We were both getting so frustrated and discouraged. It was just plain hard.

I made the mistake, which I still regret to this day, of thinking he was just being lazy, that he could actually feel it and just did not want to stop playing with his friends and go to the bathroom. I even took toys away for punishment when he had an accident. Parents, please understand that **THEY CANNOT HELP IT**. Please do not make the same mistake I did. If I could give parents just one piece of advice, that is what I would want parents to know.

By the end of elementary school, I was determined to find help for my child. I searched the web and found a "Colorectal Center" in Ohio for children. I emailed a staff member and learned about the bowel management program. I knew this was where I needed to get my son and I was going to get him there, no matter what it took. We came up against several obstacles, including his paediatrician. We had to be approved by Nick's insurance, which meant his paediatrician had to put in some effort to get us approved.

So, I took all the information I had gathered over the years, along with information on the colorectal center's program and I will never forget what his paediatrician said, 'This is probably not going to happen, don't get your hopes up.' After many phone calls, trips to their office to get them to fill out the proper paperwork and many tears, they finally submitted what was needed and our insurance approved it. The hospital got Nick scheduled for July 2015. He was 12 years old and we were off to Ohio (an eight-hour drive) for a ten-day bowel management program.

It is so incredibly sad that we had to go that far away to get help and to no longer feel alone on this journey. I would have given anything to have a local doctor or nurse or anyone that was educated and familiar with IA to go to for help. One of the worst feelings was to feel completely alone, to feel that no healthcare professional knew how to help my son find a solution so that he could live a more normal life.

The bowel management program was a success. It turned out to be a simple switch to chocolate exlax chews, daily, and some fibre powder to bulk. Something so simple, that if we had known this years before we could have saved a lot of heartache. Do not get me wrong, it did not make everything perfect, but with the exlax, he was able to feel the sensation of having to go, unlike the MiraLAX which left him with no control. It was a game changer. We only had to figure out the amount that would work for him and we did that by trial and error. We also learned water, water, water. You must hydrate the colon. It is very important. We were able to get a lot of information on IA, as well as join a discussion group with Dr. Pena himself. We finally felt like we were not alone, there were actual doctors and nurses out there who understood and could help us.

Nick is now a seventeen-year-old and we have taken him off the exlax. He is trying to manage his bowels by drinking lots of water, keeping away from processed foods and staying active. If he has an accident, he knows that he has not hydrated himself enough. He will chug a water or two and usually that cleans him out quickly. As he has gotten older, it has become a lot easier for him (and me), because he knows his body well and can figure out what he needs when things are not moving through like they should. My son will be heading off to college in the fall of 2021 and he knows exactly what he wants to become. He will be studying psychology in the hope of getting his doctorate to become a clinical psychologist, focusing on paediatrics. He wants to be that 'someone to talk to' for those children born with birth defects and who need someone that can relate to them.

My son is a warrior, an overcomer and a survivor! Nick has a heart as big as the sky and I know God will use Nick to help young kids who struggle, just like he has. When Nick and I were going through such difficult times I would say to him 'I will fight for you until the day I die!' I meant it. I was determined to find help for Nick to improve his quality of life. I believe parents (especially us moms) will and should do anything it takes to help our kids.

I realized through all of this, that doctors do not know everything, so it is up to us to go above and beyond, through research, support groups and A LOT of prayer, to help our IA kids.
God Bless and know that you are NOT alone.

Chapter 8 - IA/ARM Adult with IA/ARM Child

98. Lightning Strikes Twice - Meghan Douglass (Australia)

Going in for my carefully planned caesarean I was feeling both nervous and excited. After nine months I was finally going to meet the little person growing inside me. Every scan had been perfect, so we weren't expecting any surprises. I'd known since I was a child that if I was ever to have children, I would have to have a caesarean. Because I was born with an Anorectal Malformation, a natural birth would be too dangerous.

Before we went in, the paediatrician went through a brief medical history with my husband and I to see if there was anything specific she should be looking for. I mentioned being born with an Anorectal Malformation. She said she'd never seen it in both a mother and child so she thought it was very unlikely our child would be born with one as well. Many doctors before her had said this to us, as well as a geneticist we had recently seen who said the chances of me having a child with it were no more likely than anyone else. We thought to ourselves, what are the chances lightning would strike twice in the same place? Turns out a lot more likely than we thought.

"It's a boy!" The obstetrician called out. I got a glimpse of this screaming purple looking baby covered in goo.

I'm a Mum... That's my baby, my little Archer.

My husband followed our screaming little man as the paediatrician took him to the side to check him over. They seemed to take forever and I desperately wanted to see him again but all I could do was lay there as they sewed me back up.

"Uh'oh..." I heard the paediatrician say.

That is not something you ever want to hear any doctor say, but I heard it and felt my heart stop. Even in that moment I never expected the news that was to come.

They handed me back my tiny little boy now fast asleep and wrapped up like the cutest little baby burrito, and then they told me it looked as though he had an Anorectal Malformation and which hospital would we prefer to be transferred to?

It happened faster than my brain could process. I was told I could hold him until I went to recovery and then he would be taken up to the nursery to wait until an Ambulance came to transfer him. They would do their best to transfer me too but that would depend on the availability of beds.

Too quickly he was ripped from my arms. Nothing was happening like we planned. I lay alone in recovery waiting for the feeling to come back into my legs so they could take me up to my baby. I couldn't get my head around anything we'd been told and I was alone, there was no one there to talk to and help me process anything, other than the nurse who occasionally checked on me. They finally took me up to him and I was able to hold him a few more minutes before he was strapped into a humidicrib to be taken to the local Children's hospital.

Shock was settling in as my brain finally came to terms with what was happening. It would still be hours before I knew the extent of what he needed but I had processed enough to know he was a lot more like me than we had hoped, and I had a fair idea of the journey ahead of us.

When I was transferred to the hospital and able to hold my beautiful boy again there was so much happiness in my heart but it was tinged with fear and sadness, knowing his life was not going to be the easy one I'd hoped and dreamed for him. The last thing I ever wanted was to inflict what I had been through on my children, but here we were with history repeating itself.

His first surgery was like torture watching him wheeled away from me again. He came out with a stoma and on a ventilator and that was the moment I felt my heart break.

I'd stayed strong until then and hadn't shed a tear but, in that moment, they came out in a flood. My baby boy wasn't even two days old and had already been through so much. I sat by him stroking his hair and crying for my little man, unable to hold him and comfort him the way any mother wants to comfort their newborn.

This was just the start of what has already been a long journey. Now, almost one year old, he has had four surgeries and many hospital visits. Every surgery was like a knife through my heart, as I had to let him go. I know this will shape my relationship with him just as it did for my Mum. I know how I deal with his journey will be shaped by my own. Growing up was not easy. No matter how hard I tried and wanted to be like everyone else I never was. I hope I can use everything I've learned to help my little man cope with and accept everything to come. We don't know the extent of what he will have to deal with yet but we know it won't be a normal childhood.

My differences have given me a strength that often comes across as a hardness. My need to protect and look after my son, no matter what, is strong.

One of the hardest things so far has been the feeling of the past repeating itself. I spent my life in doctors waiting rooms and now it's starting all over again.

I hope I have the strength to be what Archer needs and I hope I can always make sure he knows that, while he is incredibly special, he is not alone!

99. My Perfect Baby – Susan Setford (Australia)

Life has been hard over the last thirty years because our baby was born perfectly normal and healthy – or so we were told. I now believe it would have been easier to cope with her disability if we had known about it from day one. But since the professionals, whose job it was to know about these things, let us down, we started our journey as parents with a false sense of security.

Later, when her problem was discovered, if we had at least been given permission to call it what it was - a disability - I think we would have approached things much differently and would all now be mentally and emotionally less damaged. It happened at a time when the internet did not exist, so there was no easy way to research medical conditions and treatments, birth defects, doctors, support groups (which probably didn't even exist then anyway) etc. We had no choice but to put all our faith in the expertise, knowledge and advice of the doctors who just happened to be there as things unfolded.

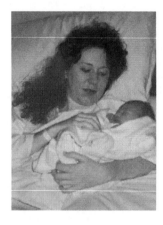

I was 27 years old in October 1990 when I gave birth to a beautiful little girl - Meghan. I'd had a dream pregnancy, my waters broke five days past the due date and, I'm not going to lie, the birth was an horrific experience that left me torn and bleeding like you wouldn't believe. But I had a perfect baby - the paediatrician told me so – ten fingers, ten toes and a healthy set of lungs. It was such a wonderful, happy occasion and worth every bit of the pain I had endured.

On her first night home, when I went to change her nappy, Meghan projectile-pooped horizontally across the change table all over my dressing gown. Hmmm, that's strange, but never mind, maybe it's just what all newborns do. Being my first child, how would I know any different? I'd heard that breast-fed babies had loose stools, so I put it down to just bad luck and bad timing. The next few months were happy and uneventful, but I look back now with sadness that I'd not even an inkling that something may be wrong.

Meghan was so very chubby, with a little bloated belly and arms and legs covered in "rubber band" creases. Much to everyone's great amusement, she would grunt, strain and go red in the face every time she tried to poop. So explosive were the poops that most of the time they blasted out the sides and top of her nappy. It was very frustrating, but still we didn't sense anything was wrong. I never missed the paediatrician or nurse appointments, and they never noticed a problem. So, despite things being a little different compared to our friends' baby experiences, she was just our beautiful, delightful little weirdo.

When Meghan was four months old, I started to feed her solid food. Very soon the poop stopped pooping and our GP sent us straight to the local Children's Hospital. There she was given a water enema and a consult from the paediatric surgeon. The poop had been cleared out of her, so everything should be OK now, right? But the surgeon was concerned and after a thorough examination we were told that she had an anorectal malformation. She would need surgery. Suddenly our world collapsed.

She was perfect. We had been told she was perfect. A congenital defect? What? How? Why hadn't anyone noticed before now?

The surgeon told us that he was able to perform a relatively new operation on our daughter called the Pena Procedure. I understand that he was pretty much a pioneer of it in Adelaide at the time, having recently been trained in the procedure overseas by Dr Alberto Pena himself. We felt lucky. There seemed to be a solution to her problem and we had just happened to come across the right person to do the surgery. But there is no nice way to describe what she was to endure. It entailed having her laid face down and literally cut open from butthole to breakfast time to surgically reposition her anus and rectum. We were terrified, but our impression was that putting it all back to where it should have been in the first place was the only way to give her a normal life.

As was usual back then however, doctors only told us what we needed to know in the moment. There was no warning of what was likely come later. We were to struggle alone on a wretched journey of trial and error trying to make things better for her and, when they were not, trying to make the appearance of normality. We would beat ourselves up for not being able to fix her constipation, wasting our time, money and emotional energy on bogus alternative treatments and therapies from people who did not, and could not ever, understand anything about her unique anatomy. Afterall, our child did not have a disability – she had a congenital defect that was fixed. Now she just had difficulties, which lots of people have for one reason or another. But there were plenty of people willing to offer useless and often unsolicited advice to a couple of desperate, extremely vulnerable parents who had not been (but should have been) told that things would likely never get much better and there was nothing we could do about it.

Meghan had the surgery at eight months of age. Ten days in hospital hooked up to monitors and morphine, our hearts were broken. She was such a strong little fighter and we loved her even more than we thought possible. There really is no greater pain to be felt than seeing your child suffering. That pain continues even to this day as we watch her still suffering.

From her first diagnosis until about the age of two, I had to perform daily dilatations to stretch scar tissue so (hopefully) bowel motions could easily pass. Then she had another operation to surgically dilate her anus and the daily dilatations continued. Thankfully, she does not remember any of this, but I do and it was traumatic for us both.

Our daughter spent the first eleven years of her life unable to poop on her own. Hours and hours were spent on the potty and then as she got older on the toilet, with her not even understanding what she was supposed to be feeling or doing. She never felt an urge to poop and didn't even really know how to push. I made all of her food myself, desperate to try and ensure that nothing would jam her up – no sugar, no cows' milk, no gluten, no bananas, no refined foods, no this that or something else, more fibre, more water, more going crazy trying anything! But it never helped. We gave her laxatives every day, trying just about every kind that was available but with little effect. At the end of each day, enemas were usually the last resort. Finally, by the age of about twelve she was able to manage toileting by herself, but it still took much time and effort.

I stand firm in my belief that if the language used by doctors had included the word "disability" then life would have been much easier for us. I don't mean easier on a day to day "trying to get her to poop" basis. I mean easier on a more general "getting other people to understand" basis. It would have given us permission to use the word too and help us to be more accepting of the fact that her problems were not going to go away. At school I could have said "my daughter has a disability and cannot stay overnight at camps" instead of "my daughter cannot poop and must not be out of my sight for more than 24 hours", or worse just simply say "no she cannot go" because I learned very quickly that no-one wanted to hear about her bottom, surgeries, laxatives, enemas etc because, quite simply, nobody likes talking about butts and poop.

To make matters worse, my daughter looked perfectly normal and so everyone treated her as normal. This can be good for a child who just wants to fit in. But in many ways it worked against us, because without any obvious context to explain why I appeared to be a neurotic helicopter mum, I think that I was mostly regarded as just a crazy person (even by doctors). A particularly insensitive relative once spoke very unkindly behind my back about how it was strange that I had not joined any mothers' groups when Meghan was a baby. The fact is they were simply of no use to me since no-one cared about the poop problems of a normal-looking child. Those groups provided no support for mothers struggling with anything way out of the ordinary, and I was far too busy anyway just struggling with caring for my daughter.

I remember specifically asking the surgeon, after Meghan's first surgery, if there was a chance that she could have other problems that had not yet surfaced. He told me quite categorically "no", there was no chance whatsoever. However, she did end up with many - a floating caecum which caused her large bowel to twist and required the surgical removal of one third of it, a rare tooth disorder called Dentin Dysplasia which will eventually cause her to lose all her teeth, an inflamed Meckel's Diverticulum which was removed by a resection of her small intestine, an autoimmune disease called Psoriatic Arthritis which causes daily inflammation and pain throughout her body, and fructose malabsorption disorder which I now believe may have been caused by years of antibiotic and laxative use destroying her gut microbiome. Not to mention the fact that she spent most of her childhood sick with colds, viruses, ear infections, croup and several surgeries for ear grommets. It is possible, I suppose, that none of these are related, but my instinct tells me otherwise.

Notwithstanding her outward appearance of being normal, as a child Meghan did not feel normal. Despite all the illnesses and surgeries, she has always been loving, kind, compassionate and highly intelligent. But she was also very shy, self-conscious and vulnerable. Bullied as a child, she was later as a teen and young adult susceptible to the manipulation and abuse of the worst imaginable predatory monsters. Although you cannot protect your child from everything, you can always be the safe place for them to land and we never lost our beautiful girl.

At least we had those first four months of "normal" after she was born, the memory of which I treasure, albeit tainted by my still smouldering resentment towards those who failed us when they did not diagnose her sooner. Meghan, however, never even had a single moment of "normal" with her first child, born only a year ago also with an anorectal malformation. His being much worse (he had no anus), he was ripped away from her the moment he was born and sent to another hospital to be operated on within the first 48 hours of his life. My disbelief and heartbreak cannot be explained. It feels like the universe is punishing us for I don't know what! But the advancements in medicine and technology, along with our own experiences, will hopefully make his journey with disability easier. And this time we will call it what it is – a disability.

Despite all the pain, fear, tears and trauma we have endured together, I would not change a thing. Our daughter is such a special person who we were privileged to have come into our lives and grow to become the beautiful, strong woman that she is today.

Meghan can now pass that strength on to her own special little boy, drawing on both our and her past experiences. I am devastated that she must go through the pain that I felt as a mother, but at least she can do it with a genuine understanding of what he is experiencing and feeling. She will nurture and protect him like no-one else can, and I look forward to giving both her and my beautiful grandson, Archer, the support and understanding that she and I never received.

Chapter 9 - Parents/Family with Adult Child (18+ Years)

100. Wilson's Story – Denise (USA)

You stink! You poop out your side. Don't play with him, he's a baby!

These words followed my son everywhere he went as he grew up in a landfill in the Dominican Republic. Kids yelled them out to him. Adults turned their heads away from him. Even his own mother expressed words of shame against him.

Having a "weakness" makes you vulnerable when you live in a world that is always on the brink of destruction. When your world is governed by the strong, having a hidden birth defect makes you a target.

In November 2011, a weak, sad, scared, vulnerable little boy stepped off a plane leaving an inner-city landfill in search of hope. A ministry and a hospital, a team of doctors and a host family all partnered together to offer hope to a little boy named Wilson.

At nine years old, Wilson had already experienced more trauma than most people would know in a lifetime. The third world is not the place you want to be if you need lifesaving and ongoing medical intervention, but that is where Wilson was born.

As with most kids with IA, Wilson's birth defect was discovered at birth. At three days old, he had his first operation. Unlike kids born in developed countries, Wilson's operation wouldn't be performed until it was paid for in advance. His family scraped together the necessary funds and his colostomy was placed. Pain medication and nursing care costs were not in the budget and so, only hours after his surgery, he went home.

Home was a house with a dirt floor and a tin roof. The roof was peppered with holes that allowed the tropical rains to enter at will. Home had a river of sewage running down the street, sweeping with it the excess garbage from the city. Home didn't have safe drinking water or surplus food. Home was a difficult place for a healthy child. It was a dangerous place for Wilson.

Two years passed while the family saved for the next operation. When the money was gathered, an anus was created. Again, with no pain meds, Wilson endured the operation and was sent home to recover. At the follow-up appointment, the doctor showed his mother how to do dilations. With no lubricant, the doctor shoved dilator after dilator into Wilson's newly created anus. He screamed and bled as he thrashed beneath the doctor's grip. Wilson's mother watched in horror as she was told to do this, and once again was sent home.

For three more years, Wilson's family saved money for his next operation - the PSARP or pull-through. Wilson was now five years old. His anus was constructed when he was two. The family travelled to the capital city for his next operation and Wilson and his mother overnighted in the hospital. When the doctor saw them there the next morning, he chastised them for still being there and told them to leave. They boarded a bus for a three-hour ride back to their barrio.

Again, Wilson did not have pain management. By this time, Wilson had learned that he could bite his hand and, at least for a moment, that would cause the other pain to go away. To this day he bears the scars on his hands from the constant biting that yielded open sores in an attempt to manage the pain.

Wilson's mother was concerned that her son was not stooling sufficiently and that the stool that did pass seemed to be in the form of a ribbon. The doctor dismissed her concerns. Within a few weeks, Wilson began to vomit stool. A week later, his intestines exploded. An emergency operation was performed to repair his intestines and Wilson was sent back home to recover. Within a month, his intestines exploded again. This time the doctor opened Wilson's side once again and placed a colostomy. The anus created at age two had constricted to the point of having only the slightest opening. It was not sufficient for passing the stool of a growing boy.

With no money to buy colostomy supplies, Wilson's mother went back to how she had cared for his colostomy originally. She placed a diaper over the stoma, wrapped his abdomen with an elastic bandage and a tight t-shirt and then pulled his clothes over it all. The binding was the only "colostomy bag" Wilson knew. They didn't have enough money to keep the diapers changed frequently so his skin broke down, the stoma bled and Wilson continued to suffer.

Wilson was now six and it was time for school. At the bottom of the hill, in the centre of the landfill that Wilson called home, was a school. It had two rooms and about 40 desks. It serviced the 600 families that called this space home.

Wearing his school uniform over the binding which covered his colostomy, Wilson headed to school. Wilson was shy and cautious; he had already learned that people can hurt you. He didn't trust easily and he kept his distance but the kids smelled him. They started taunting him. The taunting became physical.

The teacher tried to help Wilson by letting him leave a little before the other kids but the years of poor nutrition and limited activity had left Wilson physically weak. He couldn't outrun the kids. They threw things at him and laughed at him. Wilson withdrew into himself, protecting himself the only way he knew how, with isolation.

About this time, a ministry working in the landfill learned about Wilson's birth defect. They wanted to help but didn't know how. They tried to get him the help he needed in his home country but couldn't find doctors who knew how to help Wilson. They started looking for doctors in America who could help. It took three years before they found a hospital and doctors who would agree to take on Wilson's case pro bono.

In November 2011, Wilson arrived in America. This is where we entered his life, first as a host home and later as his family.

We learned about Wilson and his medical issues one week before he came. The ministry had made a video that told of Wilson's plight and asked for help so that he might receive the care he needed. Our family opened our hearts and home to Wilson and his mother. We drove them to appointments and prepared for the operation that would "fix everything". I look back now and realise how naive and ignorant we were. We had no understanding of IA and the lifelong implications that it holds. We had no idea what this little boy had endured and how it had scarred him, not only in his abdomen but also in his soul.

One operation turned into two. "Procedures" were needed to try to ascertain what had been done previously. We became "frequent fliers" at the local hospital. After 100 times under anaesthesia, I quit counting. Then their six-month visa expired and we applied for an extension. The extension expired with the end still nowhere in sight. Wilson's mother was done. Wilson was not the son she wanted. He had problems and she was done dealing with them and dealing with him. She had endured what she could and then six months after arriving in America she left. Wilson was nine and a half years old. He was in a foreign country, didn't speak the language and was living with people he had only known for a few months. Wilson's journey towards healing was taking another big turn.

We became Wilson's guardians and sought the medical care he needed. Even in a first-world context, with medical care readily available, dealing with IA is difficult for both the patient and the family. Doing this with a young man who had been highly traumatised was incredibly challenging. We had some amazing doctors who Wilson grew to love and trust. They poured all their energy and efforts into Wilson and he blossomed.

He had a new anus constructed. When the doctor said that dilations would be necessary, Wilson started crying, shaking and trying to crawl away. Even while under the effect of sedatives, Wilson remembered. I jokingly said, "You don't remember those. You were only two!" As tears rolled down his cheeks, Wilson shook his head to say he did remember, grabbed his leg and splayed it open to show what had been done to him. The mind does not forget.

Dilations were different this time. I would sit on the bathroom floor and let Wilson sit in my lap and cry, as he willed himself to trust me to do the dilation and not hurt him. The actual insertion of the dilator only takes a few seconds, but because of the trauma-induced panic it required an hour or more twice a day for months. Over time it got better. Wilson was learning to trust and that things could be different.

Eventually he had a successful PSARP. I had no idea how painful things would get. Wilson's bottom bled and the weeping tissue caused his clothes to stick to his skin. The tender tissue tore no matter how gentle I was. I remember vividly the day I looked at him walking with his legs bowed outward. I wasn't sure what was going on until he turned and I saw his blood-stained shorts. Wilson was so used to living in pain that he didn't realise there was another option! We soaked his bottom. He watched TV with his bottom open to the air and fan blowing in it. We offered pain medication but Wilson refused it. He didn't trust that we wouldn't hold him down and force it between his lips as had been done to him in the past.

Finally, the bottom healed and I thought we were done. But the constipation began. Soon we were doing enemas which were met with the same fear the dilators had elicited as we spent hours on the floor in the bathroom. In time, Wilson tolerated the enemas and things were going "well." But "well" wasn't really that good. Eventually Wilson had a Malone procedure (MACE) and was able to administer his own enema via his abdomen. This was the first time in his life that Wilson had control of his bowels. He was almost twelve years old!

At some point in Wilson's early childhood, a doctor had left a catheter in his urethra for two years! It destroyed the urethra and the valve that holds the bladder neck closed. Because of this, Wilson dripped urine continuously. By this point, even though he was socially continent for stools, he still needed diapers to be dry.

The local urologist did a bladder augmentation and a Mitranoff procedure to enable intermittent catheterisation. Unfortunately, he did a very poor job. Now Wilson leaked urine from his abdomen and his urethra! Wilson began to self-isolate and close himself off physically and emotionally just as he had as a little boy.

For three years, Wilson refused to allow another doctor to assess his situation until Dr Shumyle Alam accepted Wilson's case and offered him hope for the first time in his life. Words can never express what that means to a warrior child.

We lived with the constant stench of urine. Wilson always carries a backpack full of clothes with him at all times, and our lives revolve around wet clothes and the young man wearing them.

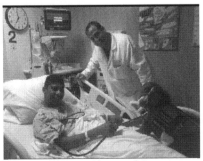
Wilson, Dr Alam and Amara

Wilson loves animals. Animals are safe because they don't say mean things. They don't look down on you and they stay with you regardless of your circumstances. Animals would provide the stabilising force that Wilson needed in his life.

The one thing Wilson always wanted from his home country was his dog. That wasn't something we could give him but we did get him a dog and immediately they became inseparable. They romped together on the farm and Amara became Wilson's best friend.

When Wilson took Amara to an agility class, the instructor recognised the signs of trauma and PTSD in Wilson. She helped Wilson train his dog to become his service dog. This revolutionised Wilson's world! With Amara at his side, Wilson's confidence increased. He was able to handle medical appointments with much greater ease. Amara accompanied him to all his procedures and operations, bringing with her the calming effect as only she could. Amara helped Wilson learn to talk about his birth defect for the first time in his life!

About this time, we found a trauma-educated therapist, Carol. Carol has been a steadying force in our lives for the past 4-5 years and is helping Wilson process all that he has endured. Some of it is medical, some emotional, some physical. Wilson has had to face the fact that his biological mother left him and, by her choice, has no contact with him. Carol is helping Wilson manage his trust issues and to get them more rightly aligned.

Our family

She is helping him understand that the past does not have to be repeated and that his new family will always be here for him. She is helping him see that the strategies he used for coping, when no one was there for him, are no longer necessary. The outward scars have mirrored inward scars.

When Wilson was sixteen years old, two huge things happened in his life. First, he met someone else with IA. After the meeting, he shared with us that until that day he really believed he was the only one with this birth defect. The second major turning point was that Wilson went to a camp where all the youth had some type of colorectal issue. There, he learned that he was truly not alone! He was able to spend a week with others like him and, for the first time in his life, there were others who understood what it was like to live with IA. These two occurrences helped Wilson choose to try "one last time" to let the doctors "fix" his bladder issues.

When Wilson came to us, we had no idea about IA, but over the ensuing years we have learned so much. We learned that there are Facebook groups and specialists to help with colorectal problems. Eighteen years ago, a baby was born into unexpected circumstances; nine years ago, he entered our world; three years ago; we were blessed to adopt this precious boy.

Today Wilson stands on the cusp of manhood.

The trauma he has endured will always be a part of his story, but it does not define him. God's hand has been on him from the beginning and I am certain He will guide him into a beautiful future.

101. D's Story, the Lewis Family – Mothers Perspective (UK)

D was our first child and first grandchild for the family. We attended all the classes and read lots of books, which just skimmed over any problems that might arise before or after birth. The pregnancy went smoothly. D (now in late teens) finally arrived six days late. The birth had no complications. At first glance everything looked well.... until the midwife went to check the temperature. She could not find a bottom opening. We will never forget the look on the midwife's face and her telling us a doctor was needed. Soon the room filled with medical staff looking at our son.

It was the longest few minutes of our lives waiting to be told our son had Imperforate Anus. We were in total shock. What did this mean? He looked so perfect, so how could it be? Maybe they were wrong. Doctors explained that D required an operation the next day, that his condition was very serious and without the operation he would die. He was allowed one small feed.

We were allowed to stay with him for a while before he went to the ICU. The hospital could not do the required surgery, so he had to be transferred to another hospital forty-five minutes away. On the day after he was born, D was transferred by ambulance for his first operation.

We still did not really know what was going to happen, or whether he would make it through, but there were no other options. Tests showed it was high IA, so the first operation was forming a colostomy. We learnt how to deal with bags rather than nappies for the next fourteen months. We were originally told D also had bladder problems and would be double incontinent for life. Those words still haunt me even now. He needed an in-dwelling catheter for the first six weeks.

After two weeks we came home to wait for his second operation (PSARP) pull-thru (which happened around nine months old). In the meantime, we had to cope not only with our first-born child but also two very complex medical issues with little medical support. In this time, we educated ourselves with research and medical jargon, as back then internet forums did not really exist. Knowledge and experience from a parent's perspective was not readily available. We felt very alone. No-one we knew had heard of the condition or had a child with it. It was very much learning as you go along. We felt very isolated and cut off from the world which had changed overnight. We became the carers and nurses for D, and it stayed the same for many years.

Financially we had to change our plans too. I became D's fulltime carer, while my husband worked a fulltime job. The days felt long and exhausting with many dilemmas along the way. I had to step up and deal with whatever was thrown at me. The self-doubt of being a new mum was exacerbated by the fact of having to make medical decisions based on sheer gut extinct sometimes. After many tests and procedures, the bladder problem resolved itself naturally, meaning we got rid of one tube and bag – hurray! But dealing with the colostomy was hard work.

Every stoma is unique, so every night my husband sat and cut stoma bag bases to shape, to lessen the chance of rubbing and the soreness when it stuck to the skin. In time the soreness got worse. Not only was our son growing and changing shape, but he was also getting more mobile. We had to be careful about him rolling on his front which caused lifting and then leakage from the bag, making crawling doubly awkward. Clothing choice was important with easy access a major priority. We bought a lot of cheap clothing as we had many blowouts! Soft dark clothing with buttons and poppers and trousers that did not rub the tummy scar- little things that helped.

After his third surgery which was the colostomy closure (around fourteen months) we hoped we would get the hang of things. But nothing prepared us for the sore skin when the bottom had to do what it was supposed to do. We endured months of trying every cream known to man (even one from Australia), most with little or no relief. D's bottom skin was so soft and delicate that it soon broke down with continuous soiling every day. Nothing would stop it. The skin got blisters and open wounds, and no-one could do anything to help take the pain away. He suffered, we suffered and at times we could not see a way forward.

I lived with guilt that I could not do anymore for him and that I had failed as a mother. The images of him howling with pain still haunts me, as well as the guilt that his condition was caused by something I did or did not do while pregnant, therefore my fault. Every day I still blame myself and wish life could have been so different for him and us as a family.

Many family memories are now based on hospital visits or operation dates (one of his operations was on Valentine's Day) which became more routine than proper family days out. Eventually D's bottom did heal up. Mainly due to the fact we trialled using a diary. What goes in, must come out right? We noted everything he ate or drank and when he weed or pooed, everything. It was a game changer which we still use to this day. It really helped us to move forward. After much deliberation we did go on to have another child, a daughter three years later who had no bowel issues and she too had to adjust to and accept our different version of family life. It has been hard sometimes, but we are a very strong family unit, who always have each other's back, no matter what.

Do not get me wrong, we still have bad days and ongoing struggles, but things are generally better. We use daily enemas with a set diet and routine for meals. Occasionally D still has episodes of soiling for no reason, but overall is able to live his life. Sticking to a diet has been a sacrifice to try and manage his soiling. He has suffered both physically and mentally with a lack of understanding from peers and others. Many shy away from wanting to educate themselves, as it is a hidden and private disability.

Many do not see the challenges that D deals with on a day-to-day basis. Not being able to socialise or join in with his friends or meet up, because he is eating tea or doing his enema stuff, can be very depressing for him and has led to difficult questions on occasions. We are a close family unit, but as he gets older it has been challenging as to how much support he requires from us. We want him to be as independent as possible, going forward. He has overcome more medical issues in his short lifetime than many will ever see. D will soon start Uni which will bring more uncertainty and worry, but he is a true IA warrior and with our help he will face the future head on.

102. D's Story, the Lewis Family – Fathers Perspective (UK)

Having your first child is scary enough, learning that they have serious medical issues is terrifying. I still remember being told in the delivery room that he did not have a bottom opening, a problem I had never even heard could exist. In one sentence from the midwife, my world changed. I tried to think logically, tried to ask sensible questions to understand the news, but inside all I could think was would my baby boy die? The doctors and nurses seemed so serious.

I remember going to phone my family, supposedly with good news....and having to tell them something was wrong, that we were waiting to find out which hospital would take him for emergency surgery. After that everything was a blur of doctors. It was information overload, so I bought a notebook and wrote down everything we were told. I am sure the doctors hated it, but if we were told differing opinions from appointment to appointment, we at least could question why the medical opinions had changed and quote the doctors' words without feeling we had misunderstood. It helped us get a handle on the different treatment options.

We gradually settled into a routine. How to make colostomy bags stick longer, how to cut enough spare bags every evening, how to ease bottom soreness after the colostomy closure, what to pack for hospital stays. We learned medical jargon, learned how to get our view across to doctors when we felt we were being pushed down a route which did not suit D.

An example of this was enemas. We started using micro-enemas, but they did not keep D clean all day. It was suggested we try larger Fleet enemas. D hated them but stuck with it for many months. Eventually one day he said that he hated them and did not want them ever again. He hated the volume of liquid and the subsequent cramps. Doctors wanted to try full wash outs with greater volumes of liquid. D was totally against this. In the end we asked to revert to micro enemas whilst re-evaluating options.

We started the food/poo diary to understand if there were certain trigger foods for soiling. Through trial and error with different foods and different meal and enema times we found a formula that worked. Evening meals needed to be at regular times with micro-enemas approximately one hour after. Timing and a fairly strict diet drastically reduced episodes of soiling.

As D has grown, we have discussed the options again. Does he want to try and eat everything (which kick starts the soiling) coupled with larger washouts, or does he want to watch his diet, but continue with micro enemas. To date he prefers to watch his diet as he still hates larger volume washouts.

We found that some consultants wanted to stick rigidly to set bowel management procedures and keep working through the different enemas, even if many involved larger volumes that D was vehemently against.

It took courage to say to doctors, that D's mental health was just as important as his physical wellbeing; that if large washouts were making him depressed, we needed another solution.
Now we have found a solution which works for us. We have had consultants ask us what we are doing, so that they can pass this on to other parents as alternatives for them to try.

The internet has enabled us to talk to other IA parents. We have learnt that whilst there are many bowel management routines to try, every IA child is different. Sometimes the system needs to be flexible enough to individually tailor treatments. Keeping a diary helped us isolate what was happening and find something that worked for us. It gave us information and examples when speaking to doctors, so that we could explain to them what was working for D and what was not.

It has been hugely stressful at times. We have made changes to our lifestyle to accommodate different mealtimes and evening enemas. But by advocating for a more nuanced approach to Ds bowel management, he is happier and more able to manage his condition into adulthood. It's up to him how he now deals with his meals and enemas but knowing that he can be clean of soiling for ninety-five percent of the time, gives him a benchmark as to what is possible and what works.

In addition to IA, D has also had to cope with three major operations in two years for scoliosis and kyphosis. Another huge learning curve with much stress to deal with, but in a way, the lessons we learnt as a family from IA have made us stronger and more confident when talking to doctors. D is a kind, caring and resourceful young man...or as he likes to joke, 'What doesn't kill you leaves you with a dark sense of humour and some unhealthy coping mechanisms!'

103. A Journey with Our Daughter – Parents, Tracy and Jeff (USA)

Our daughter was born with High IA along with a multitude of other VACTERL association conditions. As naive first-time parents, we could never have imagined the complex journey our little girl was to begin from the moment hospital staff whisked her away shortly after discovering she was born without a rectum.

It was a prolonged labour but nothing that caused any suspicion by the doctors and nurses she would arrive into this world with a complex medical condition. Shortly after her birth, once the umbilical cord was cut and she rested on my chest, the post-birth prenatal team began their examination.

Her father still vividly remembers the faces of the prenatal team as they discovered "something" during the exam. They noticed the cold stare of a father who sensed that "something" was not right, and immediately motioned him over from the side of my delivery bed to explain what they had discovered or rather, in this case, what they hadn't discovered. Our baby did not have a rectum.

Either intentionally or ignorantly, the team tried to minimise the issue and explained to Jeff that surgery would be required to create a rectum. A paediatric surgeon was to be called in to provide further examination and details of what was to follow. Still under the influence of medication and an epidural, I had no idea what was going on only a few feet away from my bed. I was later told that I had kept asking why I couldn't hold my baby after they took her out of the room.

Eventually, I was moved to a recovery room with another new mother who had her baby with her, along with a number of her other visiting family members. With each cry of the newborn behind the curtain, internal longings for my child intensified. Nurses checked on my "roommate" but rarely checked on me. Family members of the newborn were giddy with excitement as they held, coddled and adored their new arrival. They were completely oblivious to my anguish next to them, as I had yet to hold my newborn child since the initial placement on my bosom at birth. This was the beginning of a journey with parallel pathways; the path of the intense, complex and medically focused life of our daughter, alongside a long road of little to no understanding from an outside world.

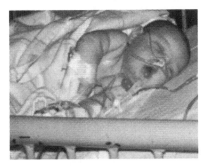

Jeff was torn as our daughter was life-flighted by helicopter to a hospital across town, where she was scheduled for a temporary colostomy the next morning. That day and evening, he travelled the forty-five minute journey back and forth to spend time with both me (his wife) at one hospital and our newborn daughter at another.

Prior to her surgery the next morning, the surgeon noticed some meconium at the base of her vagina and realized she had formed a fistula. He then made the decision to not continue with the colostomy and to weekly dilate the fistula. It was hoped she could successfully pass waste and then undergo a posterior sagittal anorectoplasty (pull-through surgery) at one year of age.

After a week in the PICU we left the hospital with the same emotions as any new parents, but also with the additional fears of unanswered questions about her medical condition. We left with scheduled doctor appointments and medical tests, sleepless nights, constant pain, incessant crying and no long-term prognosis.

This was certainly not what we signed up for as new parents and not at all what we had expected. It was all so overwhelming. Yet it wasn't about us, it was about our daughter and full attention on her care, needs and comfort became paramount, not just then but also in the years ahead.

With little guidance and limited information available on her condition, additional congenital defects revealed themselves with each medical exam. Her father and I did our own research and pushed hard for answers. We remained vigilant and quickly realised that we needed to be our daughter's advocate. This meant at times being bolder with our communication to our doctors than we otherwise would normally be. Yet in doing so, we grew to love her initial surgeons and developed a great relationship with them. What they lacked in knowledge about her overall condition was more than made up for with their care and compassion for our daughter.

They kept her alive, performing surgeries that years later were validated by other specialists as having been done properly, something we have learnt is not always the case for many kids having surgeries performed at their local hospitals.

As our daughter grew from a baby to a toddler to a little girl, we kept asking her doctors whether the things she experienced were normal. The answers were always "We have nothing to compare her to." In fact, one doctor even admitted that his initial observation categorised her in a group of only ten percent of kids with IA/VACTERL, then added "I actually believe she may be in less than one percent of that ten percent category or even one percent of that one percent." Such was the rare complexity of her many medical problems.

One of her doctors, who was chosen to be on a team that operated on the King of a foreign nation, sought answers from other colleagues around the world. Another doctor explained that she was learning more from her care of our daughter than she did during her paediatric residency.

We had so many questions and yet so few answers: Who do we trust? Who do we ask? What resources are out there? How will any specific procedure help in her future? What will be her future? How will she be accepted by her peers?

In addition to those questions, we longed to know how our daughter could be "fixed" and how to make life as normal as possible. We longed for people to understand her complexities, but IA/ARM isn't something easily spoken of even by the healthiest of people, since it involves areas of utmost privacy. We longed to be heard and as we tried to get the specialists to determine and understand how each of her specific issues were inter-related. There simply didn't seem to be any medical professionals that understood the whole picture as opposed to just the individual aspects.

As our daughter grew into her teenage years, puberty seemed to upend all elements of an established "normal" in her pre-teen years. Pain in all areas grew both in intensity and consistency. Infections began to become more frequent and more severe. Schooling became more difficult and friendships began to slowly fade.

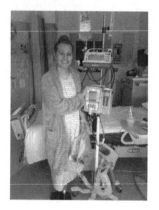

A search for psychological counsel for both our daughter and our family to help cope with the long-term medical needs, confusion, frustration and lack of direction proved as equally difficult as finding doctors that understood her medical condition. One psychologist actually reprimanded our daughter for complaining about the loss of friendships and asked her what her role was in those losses!

At the time of this writing, our daughter has just recently been released from another hospital stay. The number of times she has undergone procedures requiring anaesthesia is too numerous to count. The number of nights spent in a hospital bed is only outdone by the number of nights and days spent in her own bed being too ill to leave her bedroom.

Despite the difficult life and the challenges over the years, she continues to persevere. She encourages, motivates and inspires, not just younger kids with similar conditions, but also adults who have had routine medical procedures.

It is her desire to use her life experiences and her medical history to become an advocate for kids with long-term medical conditions. Although her college education started two years later than most her age and has been interrupted with the most recent hospital stay, the resilience ingrained from years of challenges will undoubtedly serve her well to accomplish and fulfill that desire.

Although our daughter has accepted that she cannot be "fixed", as her father and I had hoped over the years, her journey is far from over. She understands that there will undoubtedly be more medical potholes along the path. However, she refuses to allow the medical diagnosis to define her and be her identity. Instead, she allows the story of the parallel paths be told so others experiencing long-term medical challenges (of any type) and their families will possibly experience a far smoother journey than the one she and we have travelled.

When asked a few years ago to identify experiences that pointed at ancillary issues that came about as parents raising and caring for a child with IA/ARM, examples of trauma, education, insurance, medical support and medical care surfaced.

As it related to dealing with the trauma of having a child with long-term medical needs, it was easy as new parents to "stay busy" with all the demands of care in the beginning. As a result, it took away from the loving kind of parental bond needed for our daughter and created a "project" approach to parenting since there was so much to be done daily. Having to perform dilations three times daily for an entire year and one to two times daily for another half of year was extremely taxing on our emotions. It was hard to perform those procedures with our child looking up screaming and yelling "Don't hurt me!" As parents, having connected with other families through the Pull-Thru Network was vitally important in helping us to not feel so alone in addressing and performing these medical procedures as parents. For our daughter, as a teenager, connecting with other kids that shared some of the same medical conditions and procedures at an annual camp called Youth Rally created wonderful friendships

Determining the best route for education was difficult as parents and every stage of her schooling brought on new challenges. In High School, there was a decision on whether she should be put on a 504 Plan or an Individualized Education Program (IEP)? (Applies to USA only).

Each school district had their own interpretation and we needed to advocate for our daughter to navigate those interpretations; all in accordance with the mandates of the local school district and with state and federal laws. Questions arose...How do we stand strong for our child's education and learning? What programs are available at both local and state levels? Unfortunately, kids with IA/ARM don't fit in to the boxes or categories of what education systems have set in place for medical conditions and thus, she didn't qualify for certain accommodations. Her diagnosis being a chronic and invisible illness made it even more difficult. What about the protection of her privacy? Teams of teachers and administrators we did not know were set up to help guide her learning plan; but unfortunately required us to reveal privacy issues that shouldn't have been discussed. At times, it appeared that HIPAA (*Health Insurance Portability and Accountability Act)* laws regarding medical privacy did not apply to educational accommodations.

Insurance coverage for needed prescriptions and medical supplies was and is an on-going challenge. (Applies to USA only). Colorectal kids are not recognised easily in the supply field for insurance coverage. We had many costs denied because the best supplies were not the exact products that the insurance company wanted to cover, even though the products they would approve caused allergic reactions and worse, made infections more common. A big challenge is getting the insurance companies to understand and value the importance of each child born with IA/ARM as an individual; and that what works with one does not always work for everyone.

Our daughter's complexities have always affected each area of her well-being quite differently, with what could be described as a domino effect. As she got older and experienced hormonal, size and development changes, more issues and complications arose. Pain started around the age of eight and gradually led her to the point where she barely functioned from day to day. Her malformed spine began to grow a point at the end of her sacral mass and pushed directly out to her skin, slightly above her buttocks. Surgery was performed to grind the point to just before the spinal fluid, but this caused complications with other organs and the hospital staff didn't know what to do. They were not trained or educated in those other areas and thus, had nurses walk out of her hospital room never to return, leaving my husband and I to take care of her ourselves.

It is important to note that the purpose of sharing these details of our journey is to be of help to others, not a discouragement. The path might not be easy for those just beginning a journey, but information and knowledge of what may or may not lie ahead is intended to be useful in navigating that path. In addition, may the stories of our journey bring further awareness to the extended family members and friends of those affected by IA/ARM and allow it to motivate them to offer up additional love, support and advocacy along that path.

Footnote: Taylorann shares her story (No. 108)

104. Never Give Up – A Mum from Greece

Before 23 years, one boy with blue eyes came into our lives. He was the first baby in our family and we were all so happy for this special moment. At least so I thought.......

'Congratulations your boy is healthy and beautiful.... but without an anus.........' High Imperforate Anus.... I did not know what it was.... nobody knew. T'was here no internet, no Facebook, no other families to share it with. I was, we were, completely alone in this.....

The doctor who made him the colostomy for the first time, said that everything will be normal after a few months...so I took my baby home with this awful colostomy bag....my baby was sooo happy, in spite of all these problems,. Nobody could understand that he had a colostomy.

After one year ... the colostomy closed. Here our local surgeon told us to do dilatations every Tuesday. This was the first big mistake. I should have done these every day according to Dr. Alberto Pena's protocol.

As the years passed my son had continuing urine and bowel incontinence. Our doctor used to say that it will get better over the years.... but at the age of four, his urine incontinence still continued. Then after an x-ray we saw that he had no coccyx and two bones of his sacrum!!! What a surprise...we had done all the tests after his birth and yet no one had told us this......

What we have endured for thirteen years. Every hour and every day I changed him because of the mess.!!! Nobody told me what to do to keep him clean.... not even a simple enema was suggested......

It was just when the internet began to pour into our lives.... I was searching and searching when I finally found the IA Parents support group. I read that these kids will not have normal continence, that they should take either laxatives or use enemas.....and the parents talked of one name only, Dr. Alberto Pena. I was shocked because I did not know that the condition my son had was a real name!!!

I talked to the hospital where Dr. Pena was and after a year we managed to go there. It was such an unbelievable trip and I was so, relieved to find someone who knew what to do with my son's incontinence. Dr. Pena said to us that my son would be clean in a week...I could not believe it, after what we had been through for thirteen years.

My son, thank God, is a very social kid.... he has a lot of friends, but only one or two knew about his condition. So, after two types of medical treatment, the Malone, Mitrofanoff, bladder neck, bladder augmentation. My son was clean underwear ....so smile....I do not regret either of his operations.

The healing was the hardest thing after each surgery but the independence it has provided my son is PRICELESS!!! He told me after three months of being in Cincinnati .... 'I can't believe I get up from a chair and I do not have to look back to see if it's clean....' These words bring tears every time I tell them...

The truth is that every parent should speak about the problem. When I returned to Greece, I found more than 50 families like me!!!! Talk, Talk, Talk!!!!!! I am incredibly happy now and my son is happy too. The most important thing for kids is to have the quality of life they deserve.

His daily routine is doing the Malone once a day to keep him clean for twenty-four hours and doing catheterizations via Mitrofanoff every time he needs it....so simple if only our doctor known about it I would have been able to do all these before my son started school....

This is my experience of colorectal treatment in Greece......

105. From a Momma Who has been There – Michelle (USA)

On February 16, 1999, I was six weeks early with my son and the doctor said I believe nature is trying to tell us something and I think we need to listen. So, they took me in for an emergency c-section and our baby son Chad was born. He cried and his lungs sounded strong and we thought everything was great. They took me into recovery and my husband came in and was holding my hand and I knew something was wrong, but he wouldn't tell me anything.

The Paediatrician came in and said your baby has been born with imperforate anus and I just stared at her. it was like she was speaking another language because I had no clue what that was. She then said your baby has no butthole. Pretty simple words, yet what? How can that be? What does this mean? Will he die? I could not talk as I was literally in shock. I remember counting the ceiling tiles, I remember fifty-one. Over and over fifty-one.

Finally, they gave me medicine to help the shock. They informed us that Chad was being flown to a Children's Hospital, an hour from where we were. My husband met him there as I had to stay because

I had just had surgery. My heart was literally broken and on that helicopter. I prayed, not knowing a single thing about what this meant.

Fast forward to two days later. I signed myself out and met my husband at the hospital, to see my baby whom I did not get to hold. He was perfect in every way, except that he just literally did not have an anus. A birth defect I had never heard of. He had his first surgery at five days old and an opening and pull down was performed and a colostomy. He then came home four days later. I contacted the March of Dimes organisation to find out all I could about Imperforate Anus, but there was little to no information and the internet was not widely used at that time.

I felt so alone, so scared. I had no clue what we were doing or how to do it. When you hear that motherly instinct kicks in, that is all I had. There were no books, no internet, no families to lean on.

We did all the dilations and Chad grew over the next three months. When he had gained enough weight, he had his pull through surgery and he finally pooped normally for the first time. I cried. I had no idea that day, how many more tears I would shed over the years.

Chad struggled all through his childhood with incontinence and was bullied at school. He hated school. Somehow, we made it to his senior year, and he asked me if he could go to an alternative school which would allow him to attend only in the mornings. We talked with the school and decided to allow that, and Chad did a complete one hundred and eighty degree turn around. He came into himself and thrived. He learned how to take care of the situation and understood how his diet affected him.

He is now twenty-one with a full-time job and he has a girlfriend who he has shared this very private part of his life with. I am pretty sure she is 'the one'. Although physical activity makes his condition worse, he knows how to work around that. We are fortunate he is otherwise healthy. We are blessed and Chad is an amazing miracle that I am in awe of daily.

I finally found a wonderful group on Facebook, met Greg Ryan through this group and read his book. I am no longer in need of help each day but I love to help others when I am able.

If the young momma standing there crying when her baby first pooped at three months old had told me at twenty-one that my baby, my Chad, was going to be a happy, healthy, strong young man with the world in his hands, I am not sure she would have believed her. But my momma told me then,, 'Sis you never know what technology they will have in a year or five or ten, just hang on.'

So, to all the new parents that is what got us through... just hang on and give a lot of love. And I never treated Chad any differently from his older brother as I never wanted him to think this made him any less, or any different. We just were and are still hanging on.

106. Some Words of Advice for New ARM Moms

From a Mom Who Has Been There, Done That

Our daughter was born 27 years ago with VACteRL, including cloaca. She was our first child and was born full-term after an uneventful pregnancy. We were told when she was about three hours old that she had an imperforate anus (what do you mean, she doesn't have an anus?!) and heart murmur.

They told us they would be sending her to the Children's Hospital (in the middle of a snowstorm) about 40 miles away (and we couldn't go with her because the interstate was closed!) and that she may require surgery.

I think I spent the next nine days in shock, basically, as we learned about her other diagnoses during her NICU stay. She did not receive that emergency surgery since she had a fistula and passed her meconium. However, she should have...and did end up having emergency surgery to create a colostomy when she was 39 days old. In 1993, when there was no internet, we had to find other ways to find medical experts and get second opinions.

I learned quickly, though, that I had to trust myself and not to believe everything the doctors said.

Here are some things I've learned over the years, in no particular order:
- Ask questions, do your own research & educate yourself
- Take time for yourself
- Be prepared for the unexpected
- Find support for your family (parents, affected child & siblings) – Pull-thru Network (USA) has been a lifesaver for our family
- Get a second or third opinion
- Trust your gut instincts
- Remember bowel management is trial and error
- What works for one family, may not work for you, and vice versa
- No one knows your child better than you do
- For hospital stays, bring comfort items (blankets, pillows, slippers, favorite toys/games) for your child and yourself, along with plenty of snacks, phone chargers, and something to take notes on
- Teach someone else (family or friend) to take care of your child, so you can take a break
- Take a break – for a day, a weekend trip or week-long trip
- If you can, go back to work – it will help give you purpose and allow your child to depend on themselves and other adults, not just you
- Don't believe everything you read on the internet, including Facebook
- Remember no two ARM patients are alike, each one is unique
- Just because a doctor says something, doesn't necessarily mean it's true or pertains to your child

- Doctors and nurses are human, too. They make mistakes and have bad days like the rest of us.

- Experience is important, but not the only factor in choosing the right doctor for your child/family.

- Take notes at each clinic visit and during every in-patient stay.

- Keep a record of medications, procedures, surgeries, therapies, etc.

- Ask for copies of x-rays, CT's, MRI's and OP notes when they occur

- Always give yourself grace. Don't fret about decisions made in the past. You can only do the best you can with the information you have at the time.

107. Our Journey with Madeline - Thomas and Meredith Henwood (USA)

Looking back to that day in the middle of August 1996, when our journey with Madeline began, it would have been hard to imagine the twists, turns, ups and downs that we would experience in the years ahead. Those first few days were overwhelming, as we began to understand what a cloaca malformation was while visiting our daughter in the NICU at Thomas Jefferson University Hospital in Philadelphia.

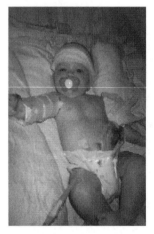

The youngest of four daughters, Madeline arrived as we were getting ready to move from the McGuire Air Force Base, New Jersey, to Northern Virginia and an assignment in the Pentagon. Trying to learn how to care for our baby girl's colostomy and suprapubic catheter, while simultaneously packing up our house and moving in with her grandparents, temporarily made for some long, stressful days.

One of the things that surprised us in the months after moving to Lake Ridge, VA, was how quickly we settled into a routine with Madeline and how something that had at first seemed so daunting—changing out a colostomy bag and taking care of a stoma—became second nature. We were also very fortunate that the surgeon, who operated on Madeline the day she was born, recommended we see Dr Alberto Pena at Schneider Children's Hospital outside New York City. After sending Madeline's records to him and talking with him once on the phone, we met Dr Pena for the first time on the evening before her PSARP procedure.

We have had many long days since that first trip to Schneider's and spent countless hours worrying about her while she has been in the OR. But that next day when we waited in the Ronald McDonald House for 13 hours to hear how the pull-through surgery (PSARP) had gone still stands out vividly in our minds. To this day we feel so blessed and grateful that we were referred to Dr Pena so quickly and were able to entrust our daughter's care to him for so many years.

In the years that followed Madeline's PSARP and colostomy closure, there were numerous procedures and surgeries that are familiar to the parents of a child born with a cloaca or anorectal malformation - prolapse repairs, dilatations, bilateral ureteral reimplantation, Malone procedure, dozens of VCUGs (imaging), etc.

Watching Madeline go through all of that was hard, but we always reassured ourselves that there would be a light at the end of the tunnel and Madeline would one day have a "normal" life. Yes, her "normal" would be a bit different than her sisters' daily routines, with the need for a nightly enema and intermittent catheterisation for the rest of her life.

But Madeline was able to do everything her peers did throughout elementary, middle and high school. We expected that once her anatomical malformations were addressed, or "fixed", the level of medical care would subside.

The period from Madeline's senior year of high school until the present day has shown us how naïve we were. Going into her final year of high school, Madeline began having difficulty swallowing. She was eventually diagnosed with oesophageal dysplasia and after multiple rounds of Botox injections in her oesophagus, she eventually had a Peroral Endoscopic Myotomy (POEM) at the Children's National Medical Center in Washington D.C. before her sophomore year at James Madison University.

Then, in the summer between her junior and senior years at JMU, she began having antibiotic-resistant bladder and kidney infections that continued into the academic year and resulted in multiple hospitalisations, including one in which she became septic. It was so scary to watch how sick she became that year and frustrating that the medical community struggled to diagnose the source of the infections.

Finally, an incredible Urology Fellow at CNMC took the time to listen intently to Madeline's symptoms and diagnosed a blockage in her right ureter. CNMC applied a series of "band-aids" - stents and eventually a nephrostomy - to get Madeline through her final year of college and to graduation. A week after she graduated, we drove her up to New York City to have her ureters repaired and her right ureter reimplanted by yet a another doctor.

As we had done so many times before, we breathed a deep sigh of relief when we brought Madeline home in mid-May of 2018. Unfortunately, within a week we had to rush her back to CNMC as she had developed an ileus. She ended up in the hospital for over a month and was also diagnosed with SMA syndrome. When Madeline returned home again in late June, she had a nasojejunal (NJ) tube.

The tube came out after we went to see the Dr. Belinda Dickie and the colorectal team at Boston Children's Hospital in August, but the pain and nausea Madeline experienced after eating never fully resolved. Over the course of the next two years, she had to go on total parenteral nutrition (TPN) twice and had NJ tubes placed several times. In January of 2020 she was diagnosed with postural orthostatic tachycardia syndrome (POTS) and this past August received an official diagnosis of gastroparesis.

As we write this in December of 2020, we are into our 7th week at Boston Children's Hospital. Madeline, who is now 24, was admitted on October 22 to have a gastrojejunal (GJ) tube placed along with a full hysterectomy. The initial surgery was followed by significant complications which, two weeks later, resulted in a laparotomy to remove a bowel obstruction. Thankfully, Madeline is being discharged on December 5 and we are heading home for the Christmas holidays.

While the early years were challenging, the last two and a half years have been the hardest and most heart-wrenching. Since she was a toddler, Madeline has been telling everyone who asked about her career aspirations that she planned to become a paediatric surgeon. During her senior year at JMU, when she was hospitalised a week out of every month on average, she still managed to graduate with honours on time while captaining her collegiate dance team to a national championship.

After graduation, she completed a post-baccalaureate program at George Washington University and received a Graduate Certificate in Anatomical and Translational Sciences. However, at a time when she should be halfway through her first year of medical school, she is still trying to cope with the debilitating effects of POTS and gastroparesis.

While her best friends from college are beginning their careers as teachers, nurses and accountants, Madeline struggles to get out of the bed in the morning and is wiped out by routine activities. While there has always been some trepidation about Madeline making the transition to independent adulthood, now the apprehension is more present and less easy to rationalise away.

This latest hospitalisation, with two trips to the OR in two weeks for major abdominal surgeries, will surely set her back even further. For us, the last six weeks have been the scariest experience of our journey with Madeline to date, watching her suffer, worrying around the clock after the first surgery when your intuition as a parent is screaming that your child is in trouble - that something is terribly wrong. And crying silently as your daughter Facetime's her older sisters just minutes before the second surgery to let them know what's going on and to tell them that she loves them, then sobbing uncontrollably later when you are alone.

This is the pain and heartache that so many parents of children with congenital defects know all too well. This is not what we expected as we looked ahead in those optimistic days and months following Madeline's PSARP and colostomy closure, when we naively envisioned our daughter becoming a woman. We will never forget the time a cocksure surgeon dismissively responded to our questions about Madeline's long-term prognosis by stating "don't worry, I don't see her consuming a significant amount of healthcare in her lifetime." If only...

Yet, the light at the end of the tunnel still shines for Madeline. While recovering in hospital she even managed to submit secondary applications to four medical schools. If there is anything we have learnt from her, it is the power of determination and perseverance. While we are working our worry beads, she is busy planning for her future as a physician.

While the journey has been arduous, it has also been incredibly rewarding and filled with as many smiles and laughs as tears. Madeline is blessed to have three supportive older sisters - they too sacrificed much over the years, as their parents were either away at hospitals with their baby sister or were maybe preoccupied and less attentive than they should have been. Now they are her biggest cheerleaders - her fan club for life.

There are also the relationships with the medical community Madeline has formed over the years that continue to be a source of comfort, support and camaraderie. Amazing surgeons like Dr Pena, Breech, Alam and Dickie stand out for their dedication to improving the lives of children born with cloacal and anorectal malformations. Countless nurses and clinical assistants (CAs), have been there day and night to care for Madeline and with whom she has built lasting relationships. When she marries, we expect more than just a handful of guests to attend who have given her an enema, placed her NJ tube or taken her temperature at some point in her life.

The last six weeks in hospital have been hard, perhaps the hardest six weeks of our lives. However, the one event during that time which best captures the absolute joy Madeline has brought into our lives was watching her create a Tik Tok dance video to the song "Boogie Wonderland" with nine members of the staff - four surgeons, three nurses, one social worker and a CA - in the hallway outside her room. She was grooving to the beat, GJ tube clearly visible below her pyjama top, a smile on her face as she interacts with everyone and, in that moment, not a care in the world.

Footnote: Madeline shares her story (No. 112)

Chapter 10 - Adults Living with IA/ARM (18+ Years)

108. Taylorann's Story (USA)

It is hard to sum up what my twenty years of life have been like in only a few words, let alone find the right words. Living with IA/ARM has been a journey. Due to that and other congenital defects, explained by my diagnosis of VACTERL association, my life has been overwhelmed by chronic pain, frequent sickness, a body that is prone to infection, daily medical care and approximately sixty surgeries.

At just a day old, I was life flighted to a hospital for surgery to get a colostomy. As they were preparing for the surgery and had started to sedate me, they discovered a fistula which had allowed the passing of meconium. They decided to hold off doing the colostomy since this opening at the end of my vagina was expected to allow stool to pass. After going home, my parents had to dilate me until further steps in my treatment could be planned. Even though I do not remember any of this I know that I spent each day in extreme pain, and that pain has continued for all the years since. Due to the many appointments, tests and procedures I had done in the early stages of life, many more anomalies were found and many more questions and issues arose. I was so different that my doctors told my parents "I was the one percent of the one percent." I was a complicated case and I still am. I was certainly not what you'd call a standard textbook case.

My childhood was challenging and traumatic. Bowel management over the years and the specific program I was a part of at six years of age was all horrific. I still shake when I think of it or if it is mentioned or I see an enema. Even medical supplies, which I use every single day, still cause me angst. Due to how complicated I was, the bowel management program took way longer than it was supposed to, and eventually no form of bowel management was even applied to my life because it was just too difficult. I went through weeks of tests, procedures, trauma to my body and tubes being shoved into me all for nothing. Since nothing made sense or worked for me, I just stayed the way I was, incontinent. Even though I was only six years old, my memories are still very clear.

I finally had the Malone procedure done when I was fourteen. Over the past six years with my Malone, doing a flush requires me to be in the bathroom for an hour and a half. It has been a blessing for sure, but it did happen much later in my life and it still comes with many complications and issues at certain times. If things are "off" or if I am dealing with other issues, I can be in the bathroom for hours and hours. I feel sad and annoyed, like I am "wasting" hours of my day sitting on the toilet for long periods of time. The aftermath of flushing can even make me feel quite sick, with pain in my stomach, extreme chills and no energy, which makes sense since I am emptying and depleting myself.

As a child, I was constantly out of school getting surgery after surgery done. I was constantly in hospitals and at appointments. I was constantly dealing with sickness, pain and infections. So, I didn't have much of a childhood. I couldn't get out like "normal" kids and enjoy childhood things. The surgeries and infections would land me in hospital for long periods of time. As I expressed before, since my medical problems were so complex and I didn't have anything to assist with my incontinence, I had to wear coverage on a daily basis up until the age of fourteen. I dealt with constant smells, trying to hide it from my peers and, even with the coverage, I still experienced leakage.

Growing up, my school did not understand, care or listen. I would get constant questions from my peers as to why I was gone for so long, why I was constantly in the nurse's office, why I would leave class whenever I needed, why I used a different bathroom than they did, and so on. As a result, kids started to find out because I would change in the girl's locker room stalls for gym class. I'd get questioned why I didn't just change in front of everyone like they all did. I wouldn't be able to participate in certain gym class activities due to my malformed spine. I'd have to leave class randomly to take care of my medical mess. I would be out of school for days on end due to sickness, pain or surgery. It was all these things that "normal kids" never had to deal with that I experienced.

I ended up getting bullied and no one wanted to be my friend because I was different. They only saw me as my illness. This continued as I was growing up and still goes on to this day. Not many see me for me, they only see me as a sick girl. I have personally been told by others that they think I am faking it. To this day, I still don't have many friends. I have a few special ones that see me as Taylorann, who are there for me and love me through it all. They try to understand the best they can. I am so thankful for them because with everything I have gone through, it has shown me that these friends are true gems in this world.

I am so thankful to have found different support groups, networks and camps that have blessed me with friends who "get it" and understand. These friends, the Pull-thru Network Conferences and Youth Rally have given me "a home" that I never had before. It has given me a certain love, care, understanding and support that is very hard to describe and it is so, so special.

My parents have also been my biggest supporters and advocates throughout my twenty years, which I am beyond grateful for.

As the years went on, so many things worsened. The bullying became extreme, I was getting sick more often and my pain was worse than ever. I had constant infections and a body that couldn't handle anything without becoming extremely weak. These issues would put me in bed or hospital for days.

That all continually happened growing up. Eventually, I ended up being home schooled for four years. That was a good decision for me health-wise as I was able to have my own schedule that worked with my body, but really it wasn't my preferred thing. I felt like I was trapped and in a prison. I felt like I was only at home because I was sick. After those four years I decided I wanted to be back in school, however I would say that I was only truly physically at the school one year in total out of my four years of high school. My body was so miserable from having complication after complication. During those four years, I was fighting with the school as well as fighting what was going on in my body. I didn't fit the school's normal box. It made me feel unworthy and like I was an object, not a person. It made me feel like no one in this world would ever listen, understand or care for me and what I was going through. Obviously throughout this, I had no friends and the friendships that I did have begun to fade. This was because, as I like to say, I was "out of sight, out of mind."

My body had an extremely hard time with everything that happens in teenage and adolescent years. That was when I had my Malone procedure done. It was a major surgery that included many other things during my freshman year of high school. This surgery amounted to a total of seven surgeries in one and lasted fifteen hours. My body did not know how to handle it. Adding all the medical craziness to a time of normal teenage issues was hard for me in every single aspect. My body did not accept this surgery at all. It was a long, painful and horrific couple of years after this surgery. Everything you could possibly think of went wrong. And beyond that, things happened that the doctors didn't even know were possible, and for which they had NO clue as to what to do.

This surgery was one that was supposed to change my life for the better, but that did not happen. It did change my life forever, but not in the way it was supposed to and I was so mad I wished I had never gotten it done.

I had a lot of recovering to do after this surgery. I spent months in bed and had new procedures to manage my body, which was all very hard to adjust to. While going through the process of recovering, learning and enduring the unimaginable in order to finish out my high school years, I ended up having an at home instructor.

My body eventually began to adjust to the surgeries that had been done, which I was so thankful for. However, in the middle of my senior year of high school a new complication arose. I almost went septic from it. It was a new issue that took a while to identify and was something new to add to the still growing list of the last twenty years. There was another major surgery done to try and "fix" that issue and again, because my body is so complicated, it was another long HARD recovery.

This time, as with every time my body is dealing with something, it messed up my bowel system very badly. My body now decides randomly if it wants to be constipated or have hypermotility. If I am constipated, my flushes will take HOURS. They will be excruciating as I have the worst cramps ever. My face gets flushed, as well as pale, and my lips become purple. I will get extremely nauseous as well. If it is hypermotility, I will not stop emptying stool with absolutely no control. It is then constant accidents for a full twenty-four hours, even when X-rays show that my colon is empty.
Having continual medical treatments and needing to use supplies each day is something that isn't "normal", but it has always been my "normal." Sometimes it will randomly hit me and I think "Oh that's right, this is not how other people pee and poop." Even though it's my normal, it is still hard at times knowing I have to pack an extra bag full of medical supplies just to stay at my grandparents' house, and then have to get all my supplies checked at the airport security. I must remember to order the supplies each month so I can stay alive. I need to have extra space to store all those supplies. And so, it goes on and on.

Going back to the end of my high school days, I was determined to graduate. It was a challenge, but I did it. However, I had NO life. I had no friends or social life. The things I loved were taken from me as I spent most of my time in bed, unable to get rid of excruciating pain and infections. I did nothing. The only time I got up or went anywhere was to go to the bathroom to sit for hours on the toilet. The trauma of my life is crazy. To this day, smells or what I see in a hospital or doctor's office can cause me anxiety. After approximately sixty surgeries, the operating room still gives me a small anxiety attack and I begin to shake. It's now just a part of the routine of each surgery. Even random smells can bring back memories of earlier years that I don't specifically remember but make me feel uneasy.

For many years I was scared of anyone wearing a white coat, even outside of the hospital. Bright lights anywhere reminded me too much about the operating room. I even have trauma from the people who were supposed to help me, whether they were doctors, nurses, psychologists, social workers, school staff or friends. Others wouldn't believe my complexity or thought I was just defiant. They didn't understand and told me things that made matters worse. Not being listened to was traumatic in itself. These days, it is still hard for me to trust anyone. Having had so many pokes, prods, experiments, procedures, surgeries, tests etc would explain why I feel the way I do.

Because of everything that happened up to the year 2018, I knew that after high school I was not going to be able to go to college like the rest of my peers. I knew I needed to focus on my health. There was no way, in the state I was in, I could go off to school. Since May 2019, after I recovered from my last major surgery, I have been able to have more of a "life" than I have ever had. BUT, while I have been the healthiest I have ever been, I still deal with crazy medical issues that doctors are still trying to understand. I still have extreme infections that land me in hospital for days and I still deal with a ton of pain and sickness.

It isn't always easy, but I look for what I can do and take out of the journey I have been on. I was determined to try school this year and am doing it online. I may be a bit behind on things and I may not know what is going to happen in the future (since I do not even know what is going to happen day to day), but I have a passion for patient and medical advocacy that has been inspired by all that I have been through. I am determined to use it somehow, even though I am unsure what will happen. But I refuse to live in fear.

I WILL keep going, even when it is extremely hard.

109. Acceptance - Lauren Stahly - 21 Years Old (Scotland)

When I was a child I hated talking about my Imperforate Anus/Anorectal Malformation (IA/ARM). I have a vivid memory of my bowel management nurse visiting my home to talk to my family about the options I had, I ran upstairs crying and hid until she left. I never spoke to my friends about my hospital visits, the enemas I received or the medicine I took. I have never spoken about how much hospital visits as a child have influenced my adulthood. Repetitive thoughts plague my mind reminding me of the many embarrassing examinations I received and the many students who were invited into my appointments to look at the "star pupil", staring at me and my body as if I were a zoo animal and not a real-life human being.

Regardless of the reminders my brain gives me about my time visiting the children's hospital I do not resent any of my experiences. I had excellent care and if it were not for those medical professionals, I would not be in the good position I am in now. They could not stop every accident or stop every stomach cramp, but I truly believe it is down to their knowledge, care and understanding (as well as that of my family), that I have managed to experience the quality of life I have today. For me, it is important to emphasize this is not a sad story. While I had hospital visits and accidents I also had (and still have) a loving family who have done everything they could for me and given me the best life I could have asked for. I was not shamed for my lack of bowel control. I was never made to feel like an annoyance when I spent nights awake crying due to constant UTI's and for this I am grateful, as I know this is not everybody's experience. My condition was treated as an everyday part of life, which it is.

Despite this, there will always be days I wish I had not been born with IA/ARM. There are days where I am in pain and when I cannot fathom leaving my house to go somewhere that may not have a toilet. There are days when I wish I did not need to use my RADAR key for the accessible toilets, especially when people question my need to use such facilities ("You don't look disabled"). To able-bodied people being young is the antithesis of being disabled and it is often the case that young people are not believed. I do not expect every single person to know exactly what it is like to have a congenital condition such as IA/ARM (for one because everybody's experiences vary even within the IA/ARM community), but I do expect understanding.

There have been countless times when strangers have made the assumption I should not be using an accessible toilet, despite having a RADAR key. One example being an elderly man belittling me when I asked if I could go ahead of the five people in line for the accessible toilet, none of whom had a RADAR key, each person held the door open for the next to avoid the 30p charge for the general toilets. I have heard people say to their friends as I leave an accessible toilet "what's wrong with her?" appalled a young person would dare to use such a facility. Toileting is a taboo subject and so, for myself, discussing my IA/ARM openly can at times be difficult. I have found it best not to reason with people who do not attempt to understand but instead to simply move on. It is not worth my time to be embarrassed about my body and its functions.

For me, I try to look past the negativity of being born with a disability and instead look to the positives. I try not to think of the accidents and instead look to what I have achieved in spite of my disability. I remember when I wanted to perform in the school talent show when I was a child, I had an accident shortly before I was due on stage but one of my older siblings picked me up and took me home. I got cleaned up put my outfit on went back to school and then performed in front of my entire group of peers, despite having an accident the previous hour. I have travelled to parts of the world I never imagined I would see. I have moved away from home to study something I am passionate about. IA/ARM has not made these things simple but life is not supposed to be simple, we are supposed to learn and grow, and being born with IA/ARM has awarded me the ability to look past difficulties. It has allowed me to see life from the perspective of someone who is typically seen to be at a disadvantage and it has allowed me to view my body as something incredible that allows me to live every day.

When I was at one of my regular appointments at the children's hospital, I made a paper daffodil with a play therapist while we waited for my appointment. I do not remember much about the actual event of crafting my daffodil, but I do remember the cheerful smile of the play therapist and her encouraging words. Once it was complete, I took my paper daffodil and gave it to my consultant as a gift. He was thrilled with it and he attached it to his notice board. The next time I had an appointment the daffodil was still there and the time after that. He kept my daffodil on the notice board until my last appointment and, to me, my paper daffodil has always been a reminder that I can get through anything. I managed all of the hospital appointments, I have (so far) managed to maintain my good health and I have managed to attend university despite my disability. Anytime that I am worried about my body I remember my daffodil and I know the troubling times will pass.

Meeting other adults born with IA/ARM online has been a hugely important step in my own personal acceptance of my condition. Previously, I knew of very few people who were born with IA/ARM and it seemed to me I was alone in my understanding and experience. While I have a hugely supportive circle of friends and family around me it has been incredible to talk to other people who live with this condition. Finding this incredibly supportive community has been one of the greatest things to come from being born with IA/ARM. Discussing my condition with other people in a similar situation has given me not the only the confidence but also the will to openly talk about my experience.

The change in perspective I have had over recent years has greatly improved not only my understanding of my condition, but my acceptance. I know I will always have stomach issues and there is a likelihood there will not always be a medical professional available who has an understanding of my needs. I have accepted there may come a time when I decide having a stoma again would improve my quality of life. I have accepted this will always be a part of my body and therefore a part of my identity. I cannot change this. Instead, I am thankful every day for the incredible life I have. I am thankful for the operations and medical care I received as a child. I am thankful for the understanding and acceptance from my family and friends.

110. My Story – Luca Garai (Hungary)

My name is Luca. I am 23 years old and currently attending medical school, pursuing my dream of becoming a doctor, specialising in paediatrics.

Actually, I don't know where I should begin my story because there are so many things on my mind. I think the best beginning would be my childhood. I have VACTERL, including an Imperforate Anus, and I suppose everybody knows what it is.

Honestly, I am one of the "lucky" ones when it comes to VACTERL because I got a "light" version of it. I can walk, I don't need dialysis or hormonal therapy etc. I had my first surgery as a newborn. I was a tiny baby and I weighed less than 1kg at birth. After my first operation I was put into an incubator and my parents weren't allowed to touch me until I was three months old.

After this time, little by little I started to grow, but I had to have other surgeries as a child and I had so many examinations and hospital visits. I was very fortunate I had a very warm-hearted and kind surgeon, he is the only part of my illness for which I am really grateful, because without my chronic illness we probably never would have had the opportunity meet to each other... I learned so much from him.

However, the day came when I had to go to school. I was so desperate and fearful because at that time I was suffering from incontinence and I had to wear a pad. Furthermore, I was put into normal school because I was not suffering from any learning disabilities.

I remember I always wore black clothes and I was so shy and reserved, I would read before school when I was alone, in the hope that no one would approach me. So, a book would become my companion every day at school to protect me.

Despite this, some girls eventually approached me and we started to play together and it was so nice to have friends. We have been friends now for 15 years.

We had great childhood and spent lot of time together, we would go on holidays together, have sleepovers etc. Of course, as we got older, I told them what the situation with me was. They were so understanding and they have never laughed at me.

We love each other still to this day and they have been a true blessing to me. They gave me so many good memories at school and in my teenage years.

I am full of good and kind memories despite the problems I had when suffering from my chronic illness. My friends helped to convince me that I could do everything with them and made me believe I could do anything in my life, that's why I know I'll be a doctor.

111. My Story – Sophie Oliva (USA)

My name is Sophie but my family and friends call me gopher. I am currently 25 years old and have my dream career. I am a paediatric nurse and love every second of it. I knew I wanted to be a nurse the day I met Mindy, a nurse who once cared for me at Cincinnati Children's Hospital. It was a dark and scary time, but she brought the light back into me! She inspired me! It was at that moment I knew my purpose in life was to be a nurse and change lives the way she changed mine. I was given the pain, birth defects and challenges so I could be the nurse who understands. In my mind A4 south will always be a special place.

A little back-story about me; I was born with an IA, a duplicated renal system and extra intestine but that is all... I promise. I came out full term at 5 pounds 3 ounces with big wide-open brown eyes. That is how I got the name gopher. I had my first surgery at one day old to fix the IA. Everything went seemingly well, we were told I had a good prognosis. On my first birthday my ureters were re-implanted, and all the kidney infections and pain were fixed! I potty trained perfectly, had a few cases of bladder, kidney and urethral stones, but I sailed through childhood. Except I always had the worst gas!!! I would be teased at school and bullied. My mom always made sure I lived life like a normal kid. I played sports (even though I was bad), I rode horses, played with friends and never let my belly pain impact my life.

When I was in about seventh grade, I started having a pain in my butt. I had what was called a rectal prolapse so basically my intestine was falling out of my butt. This was when my mom explained to me about the surgery I had when I was little to fix it and it may need to be repeated. We went to see a general surgeon and she ordered x-rays and tests. To our surprise, I was full of poop! My intestines were enlarged, and I had what was called a mega colon. That was when I got to experience my first colonoscopy and first experience with bowel prep. Anyone who has had a colonoscopy knows how vile that stuff is. It took multiple jugs to clean me out.

My mom was amazing and cheered me on the entire time. I was started on MiraLAX once I got cleaned out, but I kept having accident after accident after accident. What middle schooler wants to be having accidents? That is when the GI specialist offered me a colostomy bag. I felt this was something that was not right for me. Our GI specialist told us about Cincinnati Children's Hospital and the famous doctor, Alberto Pena.

My family worked extremely hard to raise the money for my mom and I to go to Cincinnati to see this specialist, as this was the only other option there was. I left in February of eighth grade in the middle of the school year.

We arrived in Cincinnati and it was my first time seeing real snow. My mom and I were in a crazy city, starting a new adventure to make my life the best it could be. After having many test and different procedures, Dr Pena looked at me for five seconds and said the first surgeon who did my surgery when I was one day old missed the sphincter muscle that was why I was having accidents. He then offered me the Malone, a procedure to create an opening so I could put a tube in my belly button and wash out my intestines from the top, if you catch my drift. There was just one catch. My mom and I had to stay in Cincinnati another four weeks. We faced the dilemma of "do we go home and try to come back again?" or "do we scrape by financially so I can have the best life possible?" That was when my mom made the decision I am forever grateful for. We stayed the extra four weeks and the doctors and nurses changed my life

Surgery went well. I was "NPO", nothing to eat or drink for 10 days. I got my nutrition from a PICC line, which stands for peripheral inserted central catheter. It was a big IV that went into the vein leading to my heart. My mom taught me then that no matter what I was faced with, the only way to get through it was to do it with a positive attitude. During that time, we adventured the streets of Cincinnati and came across many angels who changed our lives. We are still in touch to this day.

The decision my mom made to travel to Cincinnati is what made me the person I am today. If I hadn't gone to Cincinnati when I did, I don't think I would be the nurse I am now, traveling the world, in love with my best friend, or having the same passion and fire I do today.

One of my dreams was to go to Africa and provide medical care to people who otherwise do not get it. So, in 2019 you better believe I was on a plane to Africa with some nursing students to provide care to the people in remote villages. In that time frame we saw almost 5000 patients in six days, but more importantly, I was reminded that nursing is about more than medicine. It is about sitting down with someone and reading the bible with them or singing because you know no medicine can help them but sitting and singing provides more relief than any pill does.

During that trip, I was in a one-bathroom room with two other girls in a foreign country where almost every single one of us had stomach problems,

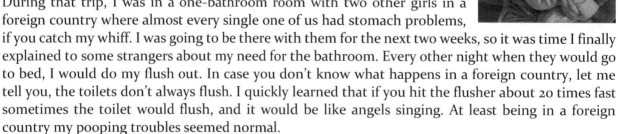

if you catch my whiff. I was going to be there with them for the next two weeks, so it was time I finally explained to some strangers about my need for the bathroom. Every other night when they would go to bed, I would do my flush out. In case you don't know what happens in a foreign country, let me tell you, the toilets don't always flush. I quickly learned that if you hit the flusher about 20 times fast sometimes the toilet would flush, and it would be like angels singing. At least being in a foreign country my pooping troubles seemed normal.

Also, in 2019 I graduated from nursing school with honours and I am now Sophie BSN, RN! It was one of the proudest moments of my life. Six surgeries and eight hospital admissions in four years of nursing school and I graduated with a Magna Cum Lade. I could not have done it without my mom teaching me to never let my health struggles be the reason I can't do something, and when I have a setback, to take a moment to cry and then keep going.

I remember going to hospital school, which I thought was fun. I remember nurses having me calculate my drip rate for my TPN and going up to the nurses station for paper and a pen so I could do my drug calculation exam.

I remember being in the hospital recovering from sepsis with nurses the day I got the call that I was accepted into nursing school. Nurses, doctors, and my mom are the people who shaped into the person I am today.

My newest accomplishment is mastering the transition from paediatric to adult care. I am lucky to have a Mayo Clinic in the same state, so I am able to have doctors that deal with complex medical problems just outside my backyard. I was so afraid of being lost in the healthcare system and not being listened to. There were gallons of tears and a lot of anxiety. However, with a binder full of medical records and a lot of education for the doctors, I finally have a care team that can manage me and I know I will be okay in the adult healthcare system. The next chapter in my life will include more international travel, more adventures, getting married finally and starting a family. I also hope to one day be able to go on another medical mission trip.

As I end my story, I leave you with some wisdom. So many of us have been given the gift to face and overcome our medical challenges. The way I see it is these medical challenges, these birth defects, these ailments or whatever you want to call them give us the chance to be extraordinary instead of ordinary.

The biggest thing I have learned throughout my life is that no matter the pain, the sadness, the challenges one goes through, it is important to remember you only have one life so you better live it and enjoy it before it is too late. And never limit yourself or live less because of your challenges!

I dedicate my accomplishments to my mother who taught me to never give up and to always see the light in every dark situation.

112. My Story - Maddie Henwood (USA)

About a year ago, my two-year-old niece snuck into the bathroom when I was starting my flush and decided she wanted to sit in the bathtub and hang out with me for a while. She knew that I had a special "belly button" but she didn't know what for. She curiously and intensely watched me as I inserted the catheter into my Malone and completely floored me when she gave me a round of applause after I taped the tube in place. I remember looking at her as she clapped and all I could do was cry. It was honestly one of the first moments in my life that the magnitude of how abnormal, and sometimes difficult, what I have to do on a daily basis as a result of my birth defect hit me. And yet, at two years old, my niece was able to recognize that I was doing something extraordinary. It's a moment I'll never forget.

PSARP at nine months

I was born on August 15th, 1996 with a high cloaca, inducting me into the One in 5000 community. After numerous reconstructive surgeries, I became what outwardly appeared to be a normal little girl, although behind closed doors my life was anything but normal.

While I am blessed in that my disability is hidden from view, that veil of privacy is also a curse because most people have no idea what it means to be me.

High School Graduation with my amazing parents

Sometimes I think being me is like running a marathon while carrying a 100lb weight on my shoulders—it can be done if I'm truly determined, but it takes a lot more effort to get to the finish line. Determination has never been something I've found myself lacking; however, I can honestly say that sometimes I struggle with why— why was I given so many obstacles, why did that higher power think that I was strong enough to handle all of this? Why was I given a life that always seems to be an uphill battle? The answer... the view from the top of that hill is completely worth the struggle.

This is even more clear as I write this from my hospital room at Boston Children's Hospital, my home for the last six weeks, after what I hope is the conclusion of the hardest three years of my life.

I'm very lucky in that until 2017, I didn't have any major health crises that impacted the other aspects of my life — at least it never felt like they did. In August 2017, I was diagnosed with a severe obstruction in my right ureter that was compromising the function of my right kidney. This resulted in numerous multi-drug resistant kidney infections that led to urosepsis and multiple hospitalizations. This happened to line up perfectly with the start of my senior year at James Madison University (JMU) where I was studying biology and pre-medicine. Early on in my diagnosis, I made the decision to continue my education at JMU despite my poor health and need for surgery.

I also had a great deal of responsibility on my shoulders with my collegiate dance team, the JMU Dukettes, as our coach quit very early in the season and, as team captain, the success of the program was in my hands. Through each hospitalization I juggled completing my college coursework with drawing out dance formations and choreographing for my team.

There were times when I would be on the phone delegating responsibilities to my teammates just minutes before heading into the operating room. In April 2018, I led the JMU Dukettes to the program's third national championship — I was septic and had surgery the week before our competition, and I am incredibly proud to say I made it onto the stage with my team one last time.

On May 7th, 2018, I graduated cum laude with distinction and two days later I was in the operating room in New York for my second bilateral ureteral reimplantation that I had successfully put off for nearly ten months. I wouldn't take any of these moments back and I don't regret a single decision that I made along the way. However, my body was significantly impacted by these health struggles and as a result, my life will never be the same.

While my kidney function is now stable, my GI tract was greatly affected in ways that we don't fully understand. As a result, I now rely entirely on enteral feeds and central line access to receive IV hydration.

In October, I underwent a nine-hour procedure at Boston Children's Hospital to place a gastro-jejunal (GJ) tube and a broviac central line so that I can maintain a healthy nutritional status while also having the quality of life I deserve. I also made the decision that during this surgery, I would have a hysterectomy and bilateral oophorectomy.

While this would typically be an incredibly hard choice to make, it didn't feel that difficult to me as I've spent the last ten years struggling with horrific pain with menstrual cycles, ovarian cysts, and endometriosis. Along with that comes medications that have their own side effects, like menopause or bone loss.

This surgery kick-started six weeks of unexpected complications and many important life lessons. The first complication, a fully collapsed lung, threw everyone for a loop. Why? Because my vitals were completely stable, and I was not showing any signs of respiratory distress. I then had to be rushed right into interventional radiology to have a chest tube placed while completely awake with no medication to keep me calm — an experience I hope no one else has to go through. However, it taught me how much my body has learned to compensate for the pain it fights every single day of my life. On the same day, my newly placed GJ tube flipped so the part that was meant to be in my jejunum was in my stomach. This meant that at the same time my chest tube was placed, the IR team was also digging around in a brand new incision to try to get my GJ tube back into place.

My first time outside after surgery

Fast forward one week, seven days of vomiting and retching, I was being rushed into a seven-hour emergency laparotomy at 6pm. The recovery after this surgery was harder than I could have ever imagined. I was so defeated after the first time I tried walking and only made it about ten steps before nearly passing out. I spent hours beating myself up over being so weak.

I expected myself to be stronger and I felt like I had let myself down. I quickly realized that I needed to give myself more credit. In the three weeks before that moment, my body had fought through trauma after trauma and while my mind and spirit were strong, my body needed some time to catch up and heal.

I have spent my whole life being complimented for how strong I am, and I think at some point that made me think that I couldn't be weak, both physically and mentally or emotionally. As a result, I failed to recognize the negative emotions that come along with living with a chronic illness.

Until the last few years, I genuinely felt like my birth defect hadn't affected me emotionally and mentally. However, the traumas I experienced in the last three years have forced me to face the emotions that I had previously ignored — helplessness, defeat, fear, sadness, and sometimes even anger.

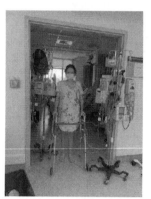

Back on my feet again

I learned that in those moments of weakness, I tend to shut off my emotions and put on a brave face, or I express those emotions instead in anger towards the people who are just trying to help make things easier for me — because I'd rather them think that I'm angry or frustrated with them than have them see how much pain I'm truly in. I also learned that in keeping those emotions bottled up, I made it a lot harder for myself to heal once the storm passed.

I don't think that I'm alone in this. I think that a lot of kids that grow up with chronic illness learn how to be strong at a very young age. And then in order to protect our loved ones, we keep on a brave face to hide any weakness. We also adapt to our lives so quickly that catheterizing, living with a stoma, or doing enemas becomes normal. When in reality it's not normal, it's a lot to deal with and it's also painful and emotionally taxing at times. It's not the easiest life to live, but it's what makes us unique. I think we all deserve to give ourselves a little more credit for that. It took that moment with my niece a year ago to help me start to recognize these things and I know I still have a lot to learn.

The experiences I have had as a result of my anatomical uniqueness have played an integral part in shaping the person I am today, providing me with an enduring sense of empathy and a deep passion to pursue a career in medicine. I dream that one day I will improve the quality of life of my patients like my doctors did for me. I will one day become a dedicated and compassionate physician who fiercely advocates for her patients, instils them with hope, and provides them with unparalleled support on their path to recovery.

113. Melissa's Story (USA)

My name is Melissa, I am a 25-year-old female and I was born with an Imperforate Anus along with a rectovaginal fistula. I have lived most of my life with minor incontinence but with chronic constipation and stomach pain. Colace, MiraLAX, and enemas really helped me throughout my childhood. I have also suffered from anxiety and depression.

Going into adulthood without a specialist by my side was quite scary. I had no idea what to expect so I transitioned blindly. Thankfully, I started menstruation normally and got pregnant with my first child at 18. I was nervous about delivery but was told by my normal OBGYN that I could deliver vaginally without problems. My first vaginal delivery went great with zero complications.

After my pregnancy I developed sacral joint issues, I spent a lot of time getting injections that ultimately did not help in the long run. I got pregnant again at 21. During this pregnancy I was practically bedridden due to sacral joint problems, which I later found out is common within the IA Community. I delivered again vaginally with no complications.

It was not until after this pregnancy I developed stage 3 vaginal and rectal prolapses. The prolapses caused pain, pressure and more issues for my already chronic constipation. I revisited my paediatric gastroenterologist who recommended I go to an adult urogynecologist to see what the next steps in treatment should be.

The new doctor recommended I either wait it out and try multiple pessaries to hold in my prolapses or have surgery that could potentially fail after five, ten, or twenty years. I weighed the odds for my personal situation and decided to choose surgery. At 24 years old I had a hysterectomy leaving my ovaries, Sacro colpopexy with mesh, and rectopexy. Although the surgery went well, I ended up having damage done to my femoral nerve during my procedure. I felt like I lost ten pounds of pressure off my pelvic area after the surgery!

Finally, I could have a bowel movement without struggling. I was so happy that my surgery had been a success.

Two months later, I started having constipation issues again. Stool was not moving as smooth as it had right after surgery. The intense abdominal pain and pressure returned. Little did I know that my recently repaired rectal prolapse would soon reappear. The depression hit all at once. I felt so let down that the surgery I just recovered from had failed.

My surgeon said there was nothing left she could do to help me that would not put me at risk of the formation of another rectovaginal fistula. I felt abandoned, alone, and scared. How would I be able to live without going to the restroom? How would I deal with the day-to-day aches and pains of prolapse?

Thankfully, with the wonderful support of an adult based IA Facebook group and another fellow IA patient, I was recommended to a doctor that specializes in transition care from child to adult IA patients. I was very scared to see a new doctor, so I waited to see how far my condition would deteriorate. After a trip to the emergency room for constipation I felt it would be dangerous if I waited any longer. I finally reached out to the doctor states away and scheduled for a virtual visit.

Portrait by Michelle Collins

After visiting with the doctor online, I felt at peace about being in the hands of a doctor trained in anorectal malformation care. She recommended I try a Peristeen enema to keep clean and remove stool. Once I was having frequent bowel movements, we would see what the next steps in treatment should be.

So here I am, 25 years old and still learning new things about how to live with my condition. From my personal experience, the best advice I can give someone is to take it day by day, trust in the Lord, find a support system and do not ever take your life for granted.

The grass is not always greener on the other side. Life is what you make it and a little positivity and humour can go a long, long way.

114. Blair's Story (USA)

My name is Blair. I am a 29-year-old female born with IA with a recto-vaginal fistula. I'm sure like many families, my mom was told the doctors were unsure if I would have a monthly cycle, let alone have children of my own, only time could tell. I did in fact have a normal cycle.

I was 17 when I went for a regular female exam for the first time. The doctor seemed puzzled and asked questions about sexual activity and tampon usage. She said there was a mass and couldn't reach my cervix. I then followed up with a different doctor for a second opinion (the doctor that delivered me). His nurse practitioner did the examination with success and it was concluded at the time of the first exam I was constipated.

I was still unsure if I would be able to carry children or even get pregnant. When I married my husband at 20 we had decided that we would just go about life and if we got pregnant, that was wonderful and if not we would look into adoption and fostering.

Within the first two months of marriage, we found out we were expecting our first child (a girl)! Everything went fairly smoothly except for some urination difficulties and constipation. I was able to deliver vaginally with the help of forceps. I did tear considerably and had to be stitched up. The first two weeks were hard and I was afraid to have a bowel movement because I didn't want to tear the stitches.

When our oldest was just shy of two we found out we were pregnant with our second (a boy). This pregnancy was very smooth and I didn't have any issues with constipation. He was delivered vaginally with no help.

Another two years down the road we found out we were expecting for a third time (a girl).

This is where things started to change for me as about halfway through this pregnancy I developed a bladder prolapse. I was told it might return to normal after the baby was delivered. I had a long labour, just shy of 24 hours. Which was unexpected because I had been in labour twice before. Again, I was able to deliver vaginally.

Just five months after baby number three was born, we were surprised to find out we were expecting again (a girl). This pregnancy was the hardest on my body, I think because it was so close to the third pregnancy. The bladder prolapse returned but fairly early in the pregnancy.

Again, I was told that it might return to normal after the baby was delivered. This pregnancy didn't have complications either. She was delivered vaginally too!

My bladder prolapse sadly didn't return completely back to normal but doesn't give me any major problems, just frequent bathroom visits.

A year after my fourth child was born, I decided to acquire my medical records from when I was an infant. That was when I realized I had had a fistula repair. I had known about it but had very little idea of what it all entailed or what it meant. That's when I realized the fact I had delivered four babies vaginally without any major complications was a miracle and a blessing!

I want to share my story to give hope to the young women and girls who wish to one day have a family. Always talk to your doctor (I have discovered there are test that can help determine which birth method is right for you) and keep an open mind.

Sister - Belinda, Mom - Leah, Nana - Johanna and me

Families can be made up of all kinds of people from all over the world, not just blood.

I hope my story inspires someone to reach for their dreams of having a family one day, no matter what that looks like.

115. Jordane's Story - 30 Years Old (France)

My parents already had two children together when they had me, and two others from a previous union. A big family of three sisters and one brother, we had a strong family bond. My mother received an abundance of love from her children, making her want another, she dreamed of a son for her husband. She wanted me more than anything and no one could quench her thirst for motherhood. Determined to force her destiny, she waited impatiently to become pregnant. After two years, the universe was still not granting her wish. She declared forfeit, with death in her soul.

But Mother Nature saw fit to grant this gift from heaven to my parents. At the end of the summer of 1989, one month after giving up, my mother was pregnant. Excited, she prepared for my arrival for months struggling to find a name that pleased her. She didn't suspect how simple this would be. In spite of everything, she and my father chose one worthy of my atypical story. Six months went by smoothly, until the day my mother suffered a placental abruption. She was infused for the next three months until she gave birth. The ultrasound revealed one of my kidneys was hypertrophied which could resolve itself, in which case, intervention would not be necessary.

There was a one in two chance of this happening but today I have only one kidney. The most unbelievable anecdote remains my mother's foreboding the day before my arrival. She had a premonition in a dream that would haunt her for years, the birth of her baby born without a mouth. That nightmare was like a warning to prepare her psychologically for what lay ahead. This unbreakable bond between us had created a heightened sixth sense in her. No one at the clinic believed her when she told them I would be born the next day. But at midnight the team at the Clinique du Parc had to rush to stop the bleeding. An hour and a half later, I was there, thanks to the intervention of a male midwife who performed a caesarean section.

My dear mother was stitched up and exhausted. She had to rest so I was transferred to an incubator in another clinic. This was what she was told, but the truth was quite different. The surgeons were waiting for my father's arrival the next day to announce the terrible news; I was born without an anus.

Shocked, they decided to fight for my survival, the battle began. I stayed ten days in an incubator, a protective unit reserved for sick children. In spite of this I caught staphylococcus aureus a few days after birth. Already weakened by my congenital condition, antibiotics were administered until the deadly bacteria disappeared.

My mother and I, when I was 18 months old

We stayed at the Clinic for a month to ensure no new danger could further damage my already fragile health. Night and day, huddled in my mother's arms, regained my strength. After receiving detailed explanations from the staff, my courageous mother set about the task of taking care of my ostomy as I continued to recover.

The reconstruction of an organ is a big operation, especially on a baby for whom a long general anaesthesia (nine hours) can have repercussions.

Unfortunately, the surgery was delayed due to the condition of my lungs, which were not as strong as they should have been, and the surgeons recommended postponing the operation to avoid any major risks that could compromise my health. This meant that I would have to have a colostomy while waiting for the surgery to be performed.

One month after my birth we were able to go home, happy to start a real family life (or almost). Fate was hanging over us with my daily vomiting. I couldn't lie down because I was crying so much, vomiting until I choked. With no solution to ease my pain, my mother was forced to stand me up against her so I could sleep. Convinced I was in pain, she sought help from a doctor who accused her of developing a parental attachment that was dependent on me.

Depressed and helpless, she used the last thing she had left, her maternal instincts. She went to a pulmonologist who confirmed her doubts, telling her I was suffering from gastric reflux. This was the result of a lack of closure between my oesophagus and stomach. Food I ingested was going back up my digestive tract and into my lungs, causing me to choke. Not to mention the suffering caused by the inflammation of the mucous membrane, which explained my incessant crying. But I was born under a lucky star, walking allowed my small body to build up muscles, repairing this anomaly that had insidiously added itself to my clinical picture.

This was already more than enough for such a small being to have come through. At least that's what my parents thought until the first case of bronchitis appeared. Then a second, a third, and so on... This continued for almost 15 years. The trips to and from the C.H.U. of Purpan never stopped, the bronchiolitis stuck with me like a magnet.

A battery of tests revealed another abnormality; absence of bone plaque in the spinal cord, a mild form of spina bifida and the upper part of my left lung was not formed, as well as the bronchus, which was atrophied.

I still suffer from respiratory insufficiency living with only 43% of my respiratory capacity. This is in part because I rejected any treatment when I reached pre-adolescence. I could no longer tolerate the shadow of a drug in any form having spent years on oxygen, corticosteroids, antibiotics and other inhalation treatments. I am paying the price today, but I am lucky enough to be able to breathe on my own.

My father and I at Valras Beach. I was shouting for joy every time he came from work.

When I was in elementary school, despite the harassment I'd been subjected to for several years, I'd gotten through the hardest part. Once again, hope was the quality that best defined me. But one winter night, my life changed again. I woke up my mother in panic. A flood of blood had descended on our home like a tsunami. I stood there, prostrate before a pool of blood while my mother panicked, barely awake. It was a traumatic several weeks of blurred memories and amnesia before I received my diagnosis. Back in the operating theatre, a six-hour operation was performed, during which the medical team poured blood, sweat and tears to keep me alive.

Thanks to the remarkable work of the surgeons and many bags of blood, I survived. My parents waited for hours, wondering what had happened to me and why I deserved to suffer so much. The diagnosis, the vein in my liver had exploded. It was like a time bomb for me at eleven years old. Varicose veins lined the walls of my already traumatised oesophagus. Blood clots kept dilating the affected vessels day after day leading to portal hypertension caused by atrophy of the portal vein. This was too much to add up to an already complicated past. All my parents wanted, was for me to be able to live again.

I was half immersed in unconsciousness for almost two weeks, unaware of what had happened to me. I heard everything but could do nothing except listen: the ringing of monitoring devices, E.T. on the TV on my right, my sister who came to visit on her birthday, my mother always at my side, her hand on my stapled belly the only thing relieving my post-operative pain, the high-pitched sound of laughing gas being administered daily and so on. So many things today are still so precise and blurred at the same time.

I especially remember the day I was told I could leave, the day I could walk normally again. The crazy horse, my childhood nickname, had returned to gallop. No matter what the obstacles, this was all I could think about. I hadn't eaten anything, drunk anything, or put my foot on the ground for more than a month. I had to relearn everything like a newborn baby. But when I have an idea in my head, nothing and no one can stop me. So much so, I almost opened my belly going too fast with my rehabilitation. I was a conqueror, but I wouldn't have thought the same ordeal would happen to me again two and a half years later...

In spite of life's trials, I am still standing. So, I was going to face this second round at all costs. I had a second bypass, an appendectomy, a Meckel's diverticulum, a digestive infection, a dozen general anaesthetics, another infection (this time pulmonary), and a third operation on my anus. All in the 17 years that followed. I would be lying if I said I didn't still suffer from the after-effects, but I'm lucky to be able to walk, eat and just live, thanks to the unfailing love of my mother who protected me for many years without me knowing.

My Mom, sublime as always

Thank you mom and thank you dad for staying by her side. I love you all. I don't intend to leave it at that, as the road ahead is full of pitfalls and my health problems are far from being solved. Most of all, I am happy and satisfied to have been able to gather so many memories.

The body is an extraordinary machine capable of adapting to so many things that can upset our emotions in so many ways, to the point of causing a black hole in our minds when the limit of what we can bear is reached. This happened to me, and I am so proud when I look at the effort I made to remember.

For a long time, I had come to think the story I was told was not my own, so many pieces were missing, so many anecdotes necessary to retrace the thread of my life. Today I am relieved to have been able to reappropriate it and others can now use it.

I am thirty years old, it has been many years of medical examinations, each more invasive than the last, to find the truth about my health condition. I made the choice to have surgery to regain a comfortable life.

I had to go back to the drawing board to reconcile the daily difficulties I faced for many years: incontinence and organ descent. It sounds frightening but it is not inevitable, not since the intervention of Dr Portier, Colorectal Surgeon at Rangueil. Thanks to him, I am a new woman who has regained a large part of her freedom and femininity. I can't say that I have total control of my rectum, but there is a clear improvement.

This operation revealed many long-buried secrets; I was born with two cervixes, a spinal deformity and a low attached marrow. This is known as V.A.C.T.E.R.L. syndrome. However, I have not given up on wanting to turn this story into an opportunity.

I wish to put my passion for writing at the service of those who live apart from society because of their digestive suffering. This is a refusal to put up with social pressure at the risk of humiliation and being pushed out of the social sphere. Hundreds, what am I saying, thousands suffer in silence? No one sees them in the shadows, silencing the evils carrying them to the abyssal darkness of their morbid diathesis. And yet I see them because they come to me when they hear me talk. That is why I have decided to take up this injustice by delivering my testimony, hoping to give courage to all.

I have walked the streets and the depths of the web to find people like me. I have found no one except abroad. So, I decided to become a voice other Francophones could find and see a bright future for their family, friends or child. One out of 5000 are born with this condition and millions suffer from problems with their intestines and associated organs. This is a large percentage of people put aside in society in psychological distress. Even if disability is more accepted in the professional world, discrimination persists and can damage self-esteem. Changing this is important to me because I have experienced it many times.

I would like to refer families to health channels specific to their condition, because there are too many associations dedicated to unrelated causes. This is problematic when raising awareness of a rare disease or medical condition. These teams are there to create one contact for consistent medical follow-up to avoid errors and erroneous diagnoses in the face of a rare disease.

One month after my operation - February 2020

Having made progress in the first part of my project, I wanted to write this as a reminder of my priorities, but also to thank everyone who contributed to my success.

The task was a difficult one given recent events that have taken place, but far from impossible.

116. HOPE - Carolina's Story (Brazil)

On the afternoon of 26 October 1990, after a painful and complicated delivery, little "Hope" showed up in the world. A Brazilian girl whose surname "Esperança" means hope. Well, you can see that I was born with "hope" in my name, and that's why I never lost my faith.

As soon as I came into the world, the doctors informed my mother I would be a child who would undergo many surgeries during my life (in total, there were six procedures in 30 years). That's enough for a lifetime, right?

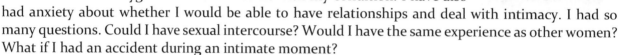

My diagnosis was VACTERL syndrome, I have only one kidney, I had obstruction of the oesophagus, scoliosis, my left leg is shorter than the right one and I have an imperforate anus. It was not imperforate but attached to the vagina.

I have had difficulties throughout my life concerning going to the bathroom, as well as with the hygiene issues that come with my condition. I have also had anxiety about whether I would be able to have relationships and deal with intimacy. I had so many questions. Could I have sexual intercourse? Would I have the same experience as other women? What if I had an accident during an intimate moment?

Several other things have made me sad, thoughtful, furious, all at the same time. It was tough to go through all this, my family and friends have always been there for me, helping me and believing I could go beyond a mere diagnosis.

Today, I have a degree in Literature and I'm also a translator and proofreader. I love watching movies, TV series, listening to music and singing, even though I can't sing that well. I also love spending time with my family and friends, travelling and doing sports.

Sometimes I feel a bit of the sadness that accompanied me years ago, but now I can cope with it better. I once heard that telling our story and not crying while doing it means we have overcome this sad situation. But I disagree because I think sadness will always be there to remind us what we have been and who we are now.

The scars are not just the physical ones on our bodies, and I do have those because of the surgeries mentioned above, the scars also go much deeper and are as invisible as they are painful.

117. Lyn's Story - 34 Years Old (Philippines)

Hi everyone, actually, I don't know how I am going start this story about my life as one of the IA adults from across the world. Well maybe a short intro will do. I'm 34 years old, was born and raised in the Philippines and I am the second of five children.

My father was a fisherman and my mother was a full-time housewife. They were just like any normal family when their first daughter was born. Everything was perfect, everyone was happy. After two years, mom gets pregnant again, there are no signs anything is wrong with the baby. With excitement, they look forward to the new bundle of joy.

After 3:00am on 17 March 1986 my Mom delivered another baby girl and another new, cute little angel comes into the family. In the morning, the midwife came back to bathe their newborn, but to her dismay she noticed that I didn't have an anus, it was totally closed. She immediately told my parents and rushed me to the main Children's Hospital in Manila. It was gross because they said poo came out of my mouth, I could have died.

Just after my birth I had a major operation, poor little baby. When I came out of the operating room I had a colostomy. My parents, especially my mother, were crying all the time. She asked herself what went wrong and why this had happened to her baby. They left everything to the doctors who were looking after me, because they didn't understand what had happened.

None of our relatives, friends or even acquaintances have the same condition so they had no one to reassure them that everything would be fine, only the doctors knew what to say to comfort my parents. They kept coming back to the hospital for more than two years to check my condition. Then, they noticed another problem, this meant another operation when I was two years old.

That surgery was to get a vesicostomy for urination. I now had a colostomy and vesicostomy and the way people looked at me was awful. I felt like an "alien" because of my body. The doctors told my parents that my condition would be much better if I was to keep the colostomy rather than operating to create an anus. They told them that if I had this surgery, I would never leave the toilet because I wouldn't have any control. So, without any understanding but fearful for their daughter, my parents chose to keep the colostomy.

I had no memories of my early childhood, relatives have narrated some moments to me like; I'm always crying and they are the ones who took care of me. One thing I remember, when I had my colostomy bag as a child, is the skin surrounding my colostomy would get a rash and it felt like I was burnt. My parents were worried, so they used pieces of cotton cloth to cover and make a bandage over the area, and that's what I have been doing until now. I have not used a colostomy bag since.

I don't have many memories of my time in day care. All I know is I almost didn't get into elementary school because my mother was worried the teachers might reject me. But I insisted because I wanted to have bags, pencils and paper. In short, I felt envious of my brother. It seems so childish now. So, against other people's advice, my parents enrolled me in school. It was so hard for me, having a vesicostomy that was nonstop excreting urine and I always felt wet. I was also having accidents through my colostomy with no parents and no one else around to help me.

There were times that no one wanted to sit beside me, but no matter what, I never wanted to stop going to school. I would only tell my mother when she saw me crying. After that I never showed my mom that I was upset because I didn't want her to stop me from going to school, which I attended until I graduated elementary. All the bullying, ridicule, rejections and teasing I chose to keep to myself.

When I entered high school, we didn't inform the school about my condition because by that time my vesicostomy was closed and I could pee normally. But accidents still happened. Sometimes I wished it was always raining so I had an excuse or they might not notice and I wished that I could blame it on cat poo at school.

I had schoolgirl crushes but I kept them a secret. I found some close friends and told them about my condition but it was not a big deal to them and that's what I loved most about being in high school. During my college days I still had accidents. I remember once, a classmate staying away from me because she thought I had pooed myself. I almost broke down and cried because no one could help me. Sometimes I would wish the soil would eat me and I could just disappear.

But I'm very proud to say I still managed to graduate, after all the hardship in classes, I made it.

Graduation 2010

I was confident that I could find a good job even though I have a rare condition because I am now a graduate. But starting to apply for jobs was just another reason for me to get depressed. I would have an accident even when I was just on the bus, so how could I go to the interview when I smelled messy. If I went home I would be late and lose the opportunity.

When I finally got a job, I only lasted five months. I never told the management because I was afraid that if they knew about my condition, they would never hire me as I would have accidents, but the use of the toilet was limited. I just dealt with it until I finished the contract.

At a work outing in 2013

At my second attempt to find work I let the management know about my condition so they could give me extra time if I needed to change, but things didn't work and I felt so rejected. I cried but no one knew.

Since then, I never let anyone in my family know I am crying because of my condition. I don't want anybody to look at me with pity. I can manage all the pain and hurt but never the way they would look at me.

My family don't know that I have this depression, these worries and fears about myself. When I'm in pain I don't let them know.

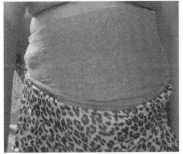

What I wear to protect my Colostomy

When my colostomy bleeds without me knowing why, they don't know. When I feel something strange in me, I never tell anyone. Why? Because they can't help me, they will only feel sorry for me and I don't want to see that.

Sometimes I wish my life would end because all I have are hardships, problems and pains. I just wanted to shut myself off from everybody. I wanted to be alone because I always fart.

I don't want to go out because an accident might happen. I just wanted to be all by myself.

I always asked myself, how could I explain my condition to people if I am the only person on earth that has this? Thinking that I was the only one in the world made me feel so alone and I wanted to kill myself because no one would understand what I am going through. Imagine, even the doctors told my parents it's better to stay this way. I would sometimes hear of a child born without an anus, but I still felt alone because I know that doctors can make their lives better compared to my day. Technology and medicine get more innovative and high tech all the time. They are lucky compared to me. I still feel like an "alien".

One time I felt so down, all I could do was cry and I couldn't go outside of my room because my eyes were swollen from crying. I then did a Google search trying to find people with the same condition and people older than me who live with what I have. I found some parents, which was a relief, but I really wanted to find other adults. Then I received a message from a man named Greg Ryan saying there was group of adults with the same condition and asked me if I would like to join. I didn't hesitate and said YES immediately. I wanted to meet people like me. I wanted to know how they live their life and I wanted to know if they also feel embarrassed most of the time.

I became one of them and I felt I found a real family after reading some of their stories. I couldn't help but say "thanks God", I found out I am not really alone and that I am not an "alien". But sometimes reading their stories I don't understand what they are talking about when they use words like dilations, enemas, high IA, low IA, PSARP, reversal, etc. When they talk about toilets, I feel sad, as I can't relate to them.

I'm afraid to ask any questions just in case they advise me to go and see a doctor. I can't do that because my childhood doctors are not here and my parents don't know where they are. When I do see a doctor now, all they do is advise me to go to where I was operated on because only that hospital has my records. If only I had money but being unemployed I can't make these inquiries.

Sometimes feel weak so I stay at home and rest. Lucky, because after a day I feel better, but something happens that bothers me. There are times my colostomy bleeds hard and it feels like it's being crumpled but only for a day.

When it reaches two days, I start to feel afraid and all I do is cry silently in my room. I thought of the group, but I was hesitant to do anything.

Because Greg Ryan had contacted me initially and made me feel very welcome and comfortable, I don't know why, but I sent him a message asking if he knew why my colostomy was bleeding. I told him I don't know a doctor who can help me and Greg said he would make some inquiries through his medical contacts to see if he could find me a doctor.

Within 24 hours I received great news that I never expected, Greg had the name of a doctor and incredibly he was near me in Cavite. The doctor was Dr Jason Castro and Sir Greg became my path to meet this specialist. Immediately I made an appointment to see him and he was able to see me in two days!

I felt nervous, worried and afraid, so much emotion, but after I met Dr Castro, I felt relief, thanks God. It's really when everything seems so unfair that there is someone God sends to us to be our unexpected strength when we are feeling so down.

It was Sir Greg Ryan that God used as my way to meet Dr Castro. Thankful isn't enough to express how grateful I am that God never forgets I am alive.

Dr Castro and me

Dr Castro has recommended I get some tests performed to see if it is possible to have my anus created, but I have to wait to save enough money to do this as it is at another hospital. But at least I know Dr Castro is there for me now and that the adult group is as well.

I know I'm not alone anymore.

118. TRIUMPH - Against All Odds – Tino (Zimbabwe)

I am Tinotenda Mudarikwa, a 35-year-old Zimbabwean national born with an Imperforate Anus.

Since birth, I have had difficulties going to the toilet, which is something that has affected my academic, social and economic life. Dealing with my condition day to day has been a psychological battle and because of this, it has always been hard for me to socialise with different people.

Growing up in sub-Saharan Africa, Zimbabwe, my family and society had convinced me that ancestral gods had cursed me while I was in my mother's womb. I learnt to accept I was the black sheep, an ugly smelling duckling who would die an outcast.

When I was a child, going to school was very difficult. Due to the faecal incontinence caused by my IA, I did not know, and could not control, when stool would come out, so I had frequent accidents (messing and soiling myself). As a result, I was always smelly which caused me to be anti-social.

Often, I would have to change my undergarments, I had no one to confide in or understand what I was going through. I had no friends and other pupils used to call me all sorts of names. I remember they nicknamed me "stinking guy". I was the last person people wanted to sit with in class.

The more I grew up, the more pain I endured, and the harder it got to go to the loo. On average, I could be in the toilet for about 30-45 minutes battling, struggling and at times failing to defecate.

As for my adult life, I was forced to endure another surgery in 1997 to enlarge my anal opening. I have had three surgeries so far, the last being in 1997. My health is still compromised, and I do not enjoy the basic right of access to good health care as a citizen of Africa.

The toilet continues to play such a pivotal role in my life. The word toilet is used more often in my part of the world than the word bathroom. The word anus is used more often than anal opening in our school system. The phrase toilet seat is a phrase I have recently embraced and adopted as we grew up having learned the word "chamber" instead of toilet seat. Growing up I dreaded the "chamber", especially the public one in boarding school, as it was dirty 200 times out of 100. I would prefer to use it the week where my group was on cleaning duty.

The type and kind of language I use today is more universal for everyone around the world to understand. What hurts is, a big number of my own people seem not to understand still, as I have not managed to provide material in our own mother language.

Just yesterday, 29 October 2020, an official publication explained stoma in this way, "... a child born with no anus had a hole drilled on her stomach for excretion..." This is an isolated example of incorrect terminology being used to address anorectal malformation awareness.

Generally, people in our society and those who suffer from such ailments believe that it is as a result of witchcraft or evil spirits. I have also discovered that people who suffer from rare diseases and disabilities lack the communication and education to open up about their medical problems. Many do not have access to information because these rare ailments lack exposure and so, those affected tend to remain silent and die quietly.

For me, my life changed in 2017 when I searched the term "Imperforate Anus" on the Internet and came across an Australian, Greg Ryan, on Facebook and he was the first person in my life who I had ever spoken to about my condition. He then introduced me to the "Adults living with IA/ARM" support group.

Joining this group liberated me from the psychological prison I was in, all my life. It was consoling and comforting to learn there are other folks out there who were born with my exact same condition, some were even worse than me.

As 2020 comes to a close, it is saddening, disheartening and discouraging to see the state of anorectal malformation/imperforate anus awareness in my country and Africa as a whole. Even before COVID19, IA/ARM and rare disease awareness was still NOT addressed at all.

Yet the numbers of sufferers in my hometown and the whole country are so overwhelming for an infant organisation run by an individual who boasts of no resources, no finances, just full of passion.

It is a waste of energy to blame the general public or policy makers. I ask myself what I did in my private space to create awareness about IA/ARM in Africa. The few individuals who decided to follow my cause have since stepped back. The problem is I am begging for assistance on a daily basis.

Rare diseases only affect a small amount of people, unlike HIV/AIDS, Cancer, Cholera and Malaria. More resources and media exposure are given to the diseases that affect the masses, but this phenomenon HAS to change. There is need for dissemination of information to people who are in the marginalized and rural communities.

I would be doing a disservice towards my advocacy efforts if I were to present a picture that Africa, and Zimbabwe in particular, were on the rise in ARM awareness let alone rare disease awareness. NO. I put pen to paper, sharing my story in all honesty without sugar coating anything.

I am aware this piece of literature might not be as relevant to the main purpose of this book. Seeking relevance to fellow IA patients, caregivers and prospective partners is an element I find very difficult to adhere to, as the needs in the rare disease space in my country are much different from the rest of the world.

What does a young man with nothing but passion do to fill this gap?

To fill this gap, in 2018 I successfully registered a non-profit organisation called Rare Diseases & Disabilities Africa Foundation (RaDDA Foundation). The logic was to address my condition as an invisible "unseen" disability.

· RaDDA Mandate

Championing for the fundamental human rights concerning all persons with rare diseases & disabilities found in Africa

In addition, the Government of Zimbabwe through its Ministry of Health & Child Care recently approved a 5-year Memorandum of Understanding between themselves and the RaDDA Foundation to support this cause and recognize Rare Disease Day OFFICIALLY in my country.

RaDDA
FOUNDATION

Tinotenda's mother

The following is an extract of an article written on Tinotenda which was featured on the front page written by Thandeka Moyo-Ndlovu, Health Reporter for the "The Chronicle", Bulawayo's daily newspaper on 14 November 2020, where his mother was also interviewed.[1]

"Tinotenda's mother, Ms Winnie Moyo, says raising her first born son was emotionally draining although, she has always been convinced he was a special boy.

Wistfully, she recalls her anguish when Tinotenda underwent an unsuccessful operation when he was two days old to correct his condition.

"I had to undergo a Caesarean section operation to deliver Tino, my first-born child, only to be told he needed an emergency surgery two days after his birth. His life had always been marred with pain and tears and I recall how twice he wanted to drop out of school because he was always being ridiculed for his condition," says Ms Moyo.

"I remember vividly how every day I had to wipe his tears after school after being labelled and laughed at because he was stinking. I had to do my best to ensure he was clean, but he had tough school days, especially when he went to Thekwane High School."

According to Ms Moyo, Tinotenda could have passed his O-levels with flying colours had he been a normal child though she is still grateful he completed his studies.

"Tino was offered a place at Mpopoma High School for A-level but due to his condition he decided to quit and never finished his studies. However, I am happy because despite all this, God has been faithful. My son is doing well in life.

I actually didn't think he would live to this day because children with his condition would die in infancy."

Tinotenda's mother adds that she was made to believe he was suffering as a result of witchcraft but she has since discovered it's a rare condition.

"I know we have women who may have children living with disabilities and we know our society is not kind enough to accept that such can happen. I encourage them to embrace these God given gifts because He has great plans for each and every one of them despite condition and disabilities."

Reference:

1. "35-year-old battles rare condition everyday" - Saturday Chronicle, Bulawayo, Zimbabwe. 14th November 2020. Page 1, Written by Thandeka Moyo-Ndlovu, Health Reporter

119. Living with Cloaca – Chelsea Mullins (USA)

It was Sunday, September 8, 1985. My parents were in Wichita, Kansas with my grandfather (dad's dad) who had just had a heart attack. All of my family were over there at the time praying my grandfather would make it through the day. My mom was 32 weeks pregnant and doing pretty well up to that point. ---- A little back story, they had told my parents around 20 weeks that there were abnormalities on the sonogram. They told my parents I had downs syndrome, I would never talk, never walk and I would be fully dependent on them for my entire life. They even gave them the option of aborting the pregnancy. At the time, my parents had been married for ten years. They had tried to have a child for so long and there was nothing a doctor nor a sonogram could say or show that would make them consider abortion.

She started having some back aches and some mild contractions, then her water broke. She had everything planned in my hometown of Hutchinson, Kansas. She was not delivering me anywhere else! So, my dad, the good man that he is, along with my aunt who is a nurse, raced her back home (45 miles or so) so I could be brought into this world. Delivery didn't go as planned and they ended up doing an emergency C-section. Back then you weren't even awake, so my mom didn't get to hold me until two days later. Knowing my mom was in good hands, he went on to find out if he had a daughter or a son!

After delivery, they told my dad he had a healthy baby boy. That of course was far from the truth after more investigation. They then said, you have a daughter, and she is in critical condition. We need to life watch her to WICHITA! Mind you, this is where they had just come from. They told my dad I had no openings on the outside and it was vital that I had surgery as soon as possible.

At this point, my poor dad had his wife recovering from surgery, his daughter in a helicopter flying to another city and his dad in ICU healing from a heart attack. Somehow through all of that, he and his twin brother beat the helicopter to Wichita. He still to this day says he wasn't going to let me be there without him.

I was admitted to the NICU and was assigned to the only paediatric surgeon in the state of Kansas at that time. My father was watching the hours go by and still no surgery. At 15 hours old, my father approached the nurse's station and pleaded for them to help me. He knew that if I didn't have surgery very soon, I would never make it. The nurse assured him I was on the list. Just as my father returned to my incubator, the doctor walked up. He said very few words and walked away. My father was livid.

Thankfully, I made it through my first surgery without many complications.

In 2014, I was asked by Cincinnati Children's Colorectal Center if I would like to write about my life living with cloaca, this is the piece I wrote which was featured on their website.

"5 years ago, my future mother-in-law said something to me that has stuck with me all of these years. It was a question that made me evaluate where I had been and how to have a better outlook on the condition I was born with: anorectal malformation (ARM) and cloaca.

She asked me a simple question:

Do you want to be known as someone who is defined by her diagnosis, or someone who has overcome it?

I chose to overcome it. I'm not saying that it was easy, because it most certainly was not. But I realized that the years of tormenting myself had done nothing to help me. The years of questions like, why me? What am I? Who am I? What do they think of me? 10 years of fighting with who I am and being angry that it happened to me didn't help me move forward and consider who I wanted to be.

After some time had passed and a lot of self-reflection, I came to the realization that I wanted to help people by becoming a nurse. I wanted to eventually be a wife and mother.

So Dr. Bruce Tjaden, my reproductive endocrinologist at the Center for Reproductive Medicine in Wichita, Kansas, walked me through my gynaecologic and obstetric options. I had been seen by Dr. Peña, the founding director of the Colorectal Center at Cincinnati Children's, since I was four years old, where he performed multiple reconstructive surgeries to help correct the anorectal malformation and cloaca, which included multiple posterior sagittal anorectoplasty's (PSARP).

Dr. Tjaden answered all of my questions from the medical perspective, like what sex will be like for me, what my chances are for conception and can I give birth to a baby?

In order to potentially fulfil those goals, he explained that my vaginal stenotic ring would need to be removed, due to the shortening of my vaginal canal. Because this procedure is not his area of expertise, he encouraged me to explore my options. I found Dr. Lesley Breech's name on the Cincinnati Children's website, and I set up a consultation with both Dr's. Breech and Peña. We reviewed multiple options and completed testing.

When I was 25 years old, my husband (boyfriend at the time) and I decided that having a redo PSARP and vaginoplasty was the best option for me. This was a very extensive surgery where they took a piece of colon and elongated the vaginal canal to allow for sexual intercourse. Eventually when I was married and ready to have children, Dr. Breech walked me through my options for becoming a mother.

Because of multiple abdominal surgeries, pregnancy was not an option for me. But using a surrogate might be. We tried in vitro fertilization (IVF) with a gestational carrier in April of 2012. My husband and I knew this was the only way we would have a biological child. One of my co-workers was extremely gracious and offered to carry. This started the process. We only did IVF once. Unfortunately, I did not respond well to the ovarian stimulation and was only successful in retrieving and fertilizing one embryo. We transferred that embryo back and found out a few weeks later that we did not become pregnant.

This was very difficult time. We questioned why? But then the picture became clearer. Adoption may be the answer in expanding our family.

We adopted a baby girl seven months later. The birth mom was absolutely amazing. She gave me as close to the childbirth experience as I could have. She allowed me to be in the labour and delivery room and I even held her leg while she was pushing. I got to cut the umbilical cord. And we left the hospital with a beautiful baby girl who has been the light of our lives.

I was also able to find a suitable, rewarding career path. I am an infertility nurse practicing with a Reproductive Endocrinology and Infertility Clinic. It has been incredibly therapeutic to help patients who are in similar situations as I was. There is comfort in camaraderie, and it feels amazing helping someone's dreams come true.

I'm sharing my story because I want other females out there to know that there is a light at the end of the tunnel. Regardless of your age, having an ARM and cloaca is challenging and can be isolating. But you don't have to let it define you as a person. You can overcome this.

Seek professional counsel if you are feeling isolated, angry, or depressed. I wish I had done it sooner. I found journaling helpful to relieve some of the weight on my shoulders when I couldn't speak with someone.

I wrote a blog during our infertility process and made it public after. This allowed outpouring of support and other people bearing their difficult situations in creating their families. It created more friendships and confidants to help during those tough times.

Choose supportive friends and partners. I picked them carefully and was always cautious to whom I revealed my condition. My closest friends growing up threw parties for me each time I had a major surgery. I waited for a very long time – even a year – before I told my partners the full scope of my gynaecologic situation. I'm not saying the length of time is right or wrong, what I am urging you to do is to consider what is important to you and stick with it. Privacy and finding an understanding partner were paramount to me.

Don't be afraid to explore your gynaecologic and obstetric options. Sit down with your OB/Gyn and outline what you hope to achieve and what is possible, based on your specific condition. While pregnancy wasn't an option for me, it can be for many other females with cloaca. In fact, Dr. Breech told me that many young women with cloaca should be able to carry a baby. Reconstructive procedures may be necessary to make this happen, but it is possible.

Above all, please know that it can and will get better. Believe in yourself. You have overcome more than a lot of people will in a lifetime, already! Enjoy life. Sometimes, just letting go, will allow you to find a different part of who you are."

After that article was published, I decided to search Imperforate Anus on Google. I hadn't had many opportunities to meet others born with the same condition, other than a few chance meetings up to that point in my life. I never felt the sense of community, people that could understand my day-to-day struggles.

That "Google" search changed everything!

The Pull-Thru Network popped up and my world was forever changed. This led me to not only meet others in our community personally, but also discover a network that created support and friendships that I will cherish forever.

Not only did this provide me with the support I needed, it showed that my journey could help other families. It opened up the opportunity for me to be elected as a Pull-Thru Network board of director, as well as being involved in the creation of the "Adults living with IA/ARM" Facebook support group with Greg, who now is one of my closest friends even though we live on opposite sides of the world.

Most importantly this has given me an ability to speak to adults and families from all across the world, allowing them to know that we are all in this together.

120. My Story – Michelle Collins (USA)

I was born on 2nd of September 1986 in Montgomery, Alabama. My father told me I was immediately rushed to another hospital in a larger city right after I was born. He told me he followed along in his own car to be there with me. I was diagnosed with an Imperforate Anus and had several surgeries, but I don't know much else about my condition or what I went through as a child.

I didn't fully understand my condition until I was in my late 20s and started doing my own research. I had a relatively normal childhood I thought, until I was older and realized how different things were for me. In my 20s I began to get UTIs frequently and began seeing the on-campus nurse practitioner regularly.

My mother passed away when I was 22. I got very sick a week after her funeral and had a fever, so I went to the emergency room thinking I had a kidney infection. Once there they tested my kidney function, they told me I had stage 3 kidney disease.

In a matter of weeks, I went from a normal college student to losing my mother and becoming chronically ill. This was one of the hardest years of my life. I continued school even though I wanted nothing more than to stay home in bed. I had decided I'd finish for my mom. I wanted to show her I could do it.

Unfortunately, the hardest years were yet to come. In college I met my future husband and even tried to scare him away by explaining my bleak future on our first date. However, he is a great person and decided to go through life with me.

By 2014, I became increasingly sick. My kidney numbers continued to decline, and I was put on dialysis on 9th of October of that year. It was a devastating time in my life. I have always been fiercely independent and worked since I was 16, but because of the dialysis I could no longer work.

My husband and I decided to move to Houston, Texas because of the transplant hospitals in the city. I also had family nearby, which helped with the decision to move. We were living in a small town in Alabama at the time and I wanted to have access to better healthcare. I started dialysis in Texas shortly after the move. I became very depressed and anxious just with the general idea of dialysis. I went to dialysis Monday, Wednesday and Friday for three hours.

I couldn't work and I had lost my sense of purpose because I was exhausted all the time. A few months into dialysis I found that I needed a reason to make myself go to dialysis. I had picked up crafting projects at home when I had the energy to fill my time since I wasn't working.

One of my first times I painted at dialysis and shared on my Instagram page

So, I decided to take my love of calligraphy to dialysis. Practicing hand lettering and calligraphy at dialysis gave me what I needed. It was exciting to have a scheduled time to practice. Soon I was interested in painting with watercolour.

Painting is my passion

This became my regular activity at dialysis. It helped me keep my mind off what I was going through. The pain, fatigue and general feeling of being unwell all disappeared when I started painting at dialysis. I started looking forward to it. Which was monumental for me, my mental health, as well as my physical health.

From there I worked on my business and even wrote a calligraphy course at dialysis. It truly changed my perspective on this hard time.

I was able to explore, find something I'm passionate about and I was pretty good at. Growing up I only took the required art classes and was convinced I was terrible at it. My mother, father and brother are all artistic and I just assumed it skipped me. Turns out I just hadn't taken the time to develop that muscle. In a lot of ways, I think of my time being sick as time I needed to grow, find myself, and find something that I'm passionate about.

I received a kidney transplant after almost five years on dialysis. I had a living donor and I was inspired by her gift to give something back to my community. A year after my transplant I painted a series of organ transplant

My Self-portrait

recipients and donors. Painting portraits of these people is something that gives me purpose. I think it's incredibly important to honour donors and share stories of others who have gone through transplant surgery. It's helpful for the families of loved ones lost to know their loved one is a hero.

I continue to advocate for organ donation as well as the use of art as therapy for people like me.

I hope that my art brings awareness, understanding and healing for those who have Imperforate Anus as well.

121. Isabella's Story (USA)

Hello, my name is Isabella. I have been trying to recall my earliest conscious thought of being. It should have been something beautiful or heart-warming, but it is of looking down and seeing a reddish blue bump sticking out of the left side of my tummy, which I would later find out was a Stoma/Colostomy.

I struggled throughout my childhood and have experienced quite a few corrective surgeries since the creation of the stoma and the pull-through rectal surgeries, but I don't recall any of that. I have been told that I also had a fistula between my intestines and bladder. I've also experienced other related issues with my bladder having my ureters re-implanted in my bladder at least twice.

As well as some other surgeries in my genital area, my genitalia were never quite normal. I've experienced quite a lot of poking and prodding and very invasive surgeries "down there" both as a child and adult. I have always felt like my privacy was invaded and was used as a sideshow due to my unique conditions and I still feel it is not normalized to this day.

I was also born with cross-fused kidneys, which as a child caused regular reflux back into my kidneys, this has been happening again for at least the last three years. So, I suppose I really have one kidney with two ureters.

I grew up in a very broken family. I'm not sure how much my parents were involved in being there during these surgeries and don't believe I had proper dilations. Unfortunately, I have not been able to locate all of my earlier medical records, so there is so much of what procedures and treatment I had which are still a mystery to me.

Throughout my childhood I had to keep what I was going through a secret. I had to wear diapers up to and through the third grade and to deal with quite a bit of picking on and teasing during those years at school. As I was brought up in an environment where "children are seen but not to be heard" in a highly Christian family setting, it just added to the burden of what I was dealing with, both physically and emotionally.

The doctors were considered "Gods" by my family, so there was no questioning them about my care, so I had no one to turn to and no real direction was given to me personally. I had no knowledge that there were others like me going through similar situations. I definitely felt like an alien, an outcast of sorts.

So, through all of this, most of the time I was never told what exactly was wrong with me or what my condition really was. I was made to feel like it was all my fault. I was spanked and demeaned whenever I soiled myself. I was then made to wash out my under garments in bleach water to scrub the poo out. I was on a strict schedule of enemas every night, which was done by a parental figure well into my late teens, but never given a reason why I was having all these problems.

I aged out of the medical system I had relied on most of my life around the end of my late teens. I then left the area and was shunned from the family because I had left the fold. So, I have never had true knowledge about my body and what I have to live with. I haven't been able to afford or find proper medical care for most of my adult life.

I have tried to explain to doctors what I did know, or remember, but as that was so limited, the medical care provided has been substandard since my early teens.

I have mostly kept these things a secret and I remember trying to find someone like myself several times over the years but to no avail. I recently had some X-Rays done in a local chiropractor's office. I then found out that I have no Coccyx or tailbone, two cervical ribs in my neck, two extra ribs on the bottom of my rib cage and an extra vertebra. To find that out at the age of 46 just reinforced my lifelong passion to find my medical records. What else could I have and not know!

I have lived 47 years, had multiple X-Rays and other tests, however I have never been privy to my condition or capable of meeting anyone else who has lived with it. I recently made the decision to try and find more information and started a new search for answers on the Internet. I found a website mentioning IA/ARM, which was the ONE in 5000 Foundation website and that led me to the ONE in 5000 support groups and FINALLY I found others who were living and dealing with IA/ARM.

It's only been two months since this happened and to be honest, I'm still trying to get my head around it. As I read other adults experiences, I can relate because of what I have endured and still live with to this day and how my IA/ARM has such an effect on my daily life.

For the first time in my entire life, I now actually feel like I have some hope that I may be able to find the right specialists who can give me the answers to my problems. As well as get the right care and treatment that I believe I deserve, which will improve my quality of life.

I am so thankful for Greg Ryan who took the time to write his book about his life living with IA and shared it with the world and has spent so many hours of his life trying to help so many of whom have this condition. Writing books, spending endless hours setting up group forums where we can discuss these situations in detail. Where we don't have to live in secret.

Thank you for reading part of my story.

122. Until Recently – John Aherne (USA)

I've often wondered what the moments after my birth were like for my mother: how terrifying to hear that "something was wrong", how scary to see a chaplain come in and baptize me because I was in "danger of death", how helpless to have me taken from her by doctors, how lonely to lie there alone, her arms empty, her heart aching, her little boy being poked, prodded and opened up by strangers in a room far away from her.

Until recently, I never reflected on what the experience was like for me. How terrifying, scary, helpless, and lonely I must have felt to be born into this new and violent world.

I have several scars from my childhood surgeries to address my IA, including a long, jagged one on the right side of my torso that's impossible to miss. I've had fun over the years telling tall tales of how I got the scar: that it was the result of a cut-throat preschool program I attended in the Bronx, a tiger attack in Kenya, being jumped in prison, or medical experiments that occurred during an alien abduction. I've thought about reconstructive surgery to correct my scar, imagined what kind of tattoo I would design to cover it, and regretted not marrying the two people who found my scar very, very sexy.

Until recently, I never knew the truth about how that scar came to be on my body. As often as I told outlandish stories to other people, I never knew the truth of which specific surgery left its permanent mark on me.

I'm fine. I've said these words so often, you may as well engrave them on my tombstone. "John, you've had an accident, do you want me to call your mommy to have her pick you up?"

I'm fine. "Did the kids make fun of you at school again today? Do you want to talk about it?"

I'm fine. "My name is Dr Klein, and I specialize in helping special boys like you understand your feelings. Would you like to talk to me?"

I'm fine. "We've been dating for two years, and you won't open up. Unless you start telling me what's going on in that heart of yours, I'm not going to stick around."

I'm fine.

Until recently, I didn't realize that I am, in fact, not always fine. In many ways, I've had a full and wonderful life, such a life is possible with IA! I've travelled the world, run marathons, gotten a graduate degree, changed careers and done things the little ten-year-old boy who felt so smelly, friendless and broken never even dared to dream he could do. I watch what I eat (no yellow peppers, please!), do my daily enema, get off the toilet, and get on with my life. And I truly enjoy life today.

But until recently, I've never taken the time to see how IA has impacted my heart and my mind as well as my body. I've truly lived "a secret life," as Greg Ryan, the editor of this anthology, uses to describe life with IA. I've spent an unfathomable amount of mental and emotional energy keeping the secret of my IA from other people, but also myself.

Until recently, I've never had the courage to talk to my mother or get a hold of my medical records to find out what surgeries were done and get a full understanding of my diagnosis.

Until recently, I've never learned to acknowledge, identify, or name the shame, embarrassment, loneliness, brokenness and fear I felt as a child and still feel today.

Until recently, I've never let anyone become close to me, or allowed myself to become close to anyone, for fear they would find out about my IA.

Until recently, I never realized that some of the problematic ways I've tried to cope with life, especially the way I used alcohol, are linked to my unwillingness and inability to look at how IA has shaped me.

Until recently, I thought the only scar I had was the visible one.

Until recently, I thought I was alone.

Until recently, I didn't think I needed any help. But I am grateful to have found a good counsellor who is helping me talk about my experience and my feelings and encouraged me to find and connect with the ONE in 5000 Foundation, and the Facebook support group for "Adults living with IA/ARM".

Today, I am filled with hope and optimism for my future. I feel in the marrow of my bones that learning more about my medical history, reflecting on my experience with IA, and learning how to talk about it and share my story, will heal some of the scars I might have picked up along the way.

Until recently, I thought life was as good as it was going to get. But today, I think the best is yet to come.

123. My Story – Carlo Anselmo Jr. (USA)

I am One in 5000. It's sort of like being part of a secret society that only a few people get to be a part of. However, being born with this rare congenital birth defect has taken me on an interesting journey throughout my life. It's been a journey that only a few people out there could relate to, but I would like to share what my personal dealings with this defect are and what it has been like for me.

I was born premature in April of 1984 at St. Joseph's Hospital in Queens, New York. I was immediately transferred to New York Hospital (NY Presbyterian Hospital) where I went under the knife less than 24 hours after being born to have a colostomy placed. I would have this colostomy for a few years before I underwent reversal surgery and had the PSARP performed on me by a general paediatric surgeon, Dr Frank Redo at New York Hospital.

It was quite a journey for my parents to raise a child where there was extraordinarily little known about imperforate anus and how to properly care for a child born with this defect. They knew of no other parents who had a child born with this defect, which they could have relied on for support and reassurance. It would not be until 35 years later, my mother would finally meet other parents whose children were born with IA at a picnic organized by members of a local Facebook IA group. It was also my first-time meeting others born with the same birth defect as myself.

As a young child, I knew I had been born without an anal opening and I had surgery to correct it. My parents made sure to let me know about my medical history at a young age. I was also diagnosed with hearing loss by the age of five and I had to wear a hearing aid. With a hearing aid I could not hide my disability. My peers were able to see the hearing aid sitting on my ear and I would always be asked about it. I knew I was different from all my peers early on, dealing with this double whammy. I was not able to hide from both and my occasional accidents were embarrassing to admit.

The one incident that always stuck out in my memory, where I could distinctly remember I was truly different from my peers was when I was in Pre-K. I remember it was during our playtime and I was running around having fun with my classmates when all of a sudden, I had an accident. I remember feeling too embarrassed to let my teacher know I had pooped myself, so I did not say anything. I just continued playing with my peers while I was completely soiled.

I remember being woken up during nap time by one of the aides in the classroom and having to go with her to the bathroom so she could help me clean up and change into a clean set of clothes. I remember she had left the bathroom door open and seeing other classes walk by while I had no pants on, I felt completely ashamed others had seen me like that. It was at that exact moment I realized I was completely different from others, and I knew I had to protect myself from others by keeping my condition a secret as a way of coping with my defect.

One of the major ways of coping with my IA early on was through music. My father always had the New York oldies station, CBS-FM, playing in the car whenever he was driving anywhere. I was always entrenched to the sounds of Elvis Presley, Dion & the Belmonts, Carl Perkins and so many other greats from the 1950's, whose music came blaring out of those car speakers. It was in that car I realized how powerful music was in helping me feel better about myself. I realized that through music I was able to escape the reality of dealing with my disabilities and escape from myself.

As I came into my teenage years, I discovered my own music, Punk Rock. It was music created by other young teenage kids who also felt like they were different and did not necessarily fit in with their peers. These outcasts sang with a purposeful message about being different from everyone else and that it was ok to not fit in with others, just simply be proud of yourself and embrace your uniqueness. This kind of message truly spoke right to my core as a kid coming of age. I finally felt I belonged somewhere and it was ok to be different.

This loud, fast music spoke to me like nothing else had ever done. This was my drug of choice. I knew I could always rely on it to help me feel better about myself. There were bands whose messages were anti-drugs and anti-alcohol, and their message helped me steer clear away from those two things at a young age. I never needed to rely on substances to deal with my embarrassing birth defect. Simply dropping the needle on a record was all the high I needed to make myself feel good. As a result, I became a fanatical record collector and still am to this day.

Going into my late 20's, my IA became more of a challenge to deal with. All of a sudden, I started having more issues with bowel control. Up to that point in my life, I was very fortunate to have been able to have incredible control of my bowels, with a few occasional accidents. I was never put on any bowel management programs. My doctors never presented this option to my parents. We had no clue such a thing existed that could help me stay clean and empty.

However, as I reached my late 20's I found myself having to go to the bathroom way more frequently than I did when I was a child. This problem got progressively worse as I came into my 30's. I was just simply too embarrassed to approach any of my doctors with this problem, I felt they would not understand what the problems were.

Dealing with my continence issues would take a turn for the better when I discovered various IA groups on Facebook. In one of the groups, I met a few local mothers who had created their own private local group where they would all interact with other local families who had a child born with IA. These mothers accepted me as an adult with IA in their little group with open arms. It was through some of these amazing human beings I found a local paediatric colorectal physician who agreed to treat me as an adult patient.

After going through a few tests, we tried bowel management by taking Ex-Lax chocolate squares. This turned out be a nightmare, as I was going to the bathroom 2-3 times an hour for six hours straight the day after taking it. I was unable to get anything done at work, and I became even more stressed out dealing with my continence issues.

We figured out I had hypermotility and the senna squares exacerbated the situation. The next thing we decided to try was taking Benefiber every night before going to bed, and this made all the difference for me. It helps me to get a much better bowel movement every morning. It's not perfect, but I am able to empty out better and I am feeling more cleaned out than I have before.

These days in my mid-30s, I no longer feel embarrassed about my birth defect. I tell others about my condition in hopes of spreading awareness about this rare congenital condition. Educating others about this malformation can help take away the taboo of talking about it.

I feel that there should be no shame in the fact I had no control over how I was born. After all I am One in 5000 and there is nothing wrong with that.

124. When Life Gives You Lemons... Elizabeth Wilson (USA)

Behind the couch in the corner of our living room was my hiding spot. I would go there when I heard my mom say, "The visiting nurse is on her way, Beth!" Instantly I knew what that meant. Time for her to fix my "impacted rectum." What five-year old understands the meaning of an impacted rectum? If that child was born with an imperforate anus, like I was, then that meant the warning bells had been sounded. God, I hated how it hurt and how different it made me feel. The suppositories were the absolute worst, and I still remember the embarrassment and awful feeling of having them put inside me.

But my mom kept it positive, saying that I had surgery in 1967 at Boston's Floating Hospital, which only about one hundred other children had had before me to prevent the need for a colostomy bag. I was one of the lucky ones. She would tell me how my father followed the ambulance to Boston on the day I was born so that I could receive proper care. She also told me about the daily dilations during my first year of life to help keep me open so that I could eliminate properly.

Living with an imperforate anus was a big secret for me. It wasn't something that I would tell people. When I was little I was prone to constant bowel accidents and mom would tell the school nurse about my situation. Back then there was no need for a 504 plan so it was just kept between the nurse, the teacher and my parents.

As I reached puberty, I remember having horrible periods. I mean I was down for the count vomiting, having diarrhoea and practically fainting. I now believe the painful periods were related to my birth defect. This also included a bicornuate uterus and vaginal septum, which were not discovered until I was in my twenties. One summer morning I walked to the local tennis court for my tennis lesson. "Aunt Flo" struck around 10.00am, and instantly I started feeling sick. There were no cell phones at the time, so the instructor asked a mother to take me home in her car. We were almost home when I defecated in her car. It was the absolute worst moment of my life, and it still brings tears to my eyes to think about how incredibly gross I felt and how sorry I was for messing up her car.

Since that event, I have been reluctant to drive in cars with people other than my own family. I watch what I eat during the workweek and I have to be so careful about eating fatty foods at restaurants, which might cause an episode. I never eat breakfast before work and carry Imodium and a change of clothes wherever I go.

I remember losing ten pounds about two weeks before my wedding because I was so scared I would have an accident walking down the aisle. I lived on a diet of bananas and baked potatoes for days up to the wedding. Luckily everything worked out fine on the big day, but this is just one example of how my life is controlled by fear of having an accident.

The toilet is my best friend. I can figure out where a restroom is within ten seconds of walking into a new store or establishment. One time I visited a friend in upstate New York and she had cooked Tiramisu. I didn't want to hurt her feelings by not eating any, so I obliged. Afterward, she took me to the grocery store where of course I needed to use the restroom. She remarked at how I was able to find the restroom so quickly. Friends may remark about how they would never use a bathroom at a gas station or at the train station, but for me, any restroom is a kindred spirit.

I am now in my mid-fifties and, as one ages, gravity kicks in. I have to be more careful of my diet and yes, I admit that I wear Depends. At first I was embarrassed about it, but at this point in my life I'm no longer ashamed. It's sort of like a security blanket for me and I know it's weird, but it provides me with a little security that helps me get through the day.

I am happily married to a wonderful husband who has been nothing but patient, loving and accepting of me. He loves me for who I am and is always there for me when I have had a bad day or if my stomach acts up. I am also so lucky to share that we have two beautiful daughters. Before we were married the doctors said that I would be prone to miscarriage because of my birth defect, and I did need to have two scheduled caesareans to avoid ripping my rectum during childbirth.

There is so much to be grateful for in my life and I am so lucky to have been brought up in a loving family. My mother truly saved my life when I was little. She was there for me every step of the way and I will always be so grateful for that.

If I were to give advice to kids with IA, I would tell them that they are special and unique in their own way. They have a beautiful life ahead of them and they should be proud of how strong and brave they are.

125. My Life with Imperforate Anus – Suman Roy (England)

I was born April 1970 in London and straight away the nurses knew there was something wrong. I had no hole in my back passage – known as Imperforate Anus. As this was a life-threatening condition, I was rushed across town to London's largest children's hospital where I had an emergency colostomy performed.

My imperforate anus was part of a larger condition called VACTERL association, in the USA it's often known as VATER syndrome. I also had scoliosis of the ribs including a cervical rib, an absent kidney and conjoined fingers on my right hand.

I have vague memories of life with a colostomy bag, the main one being how sore my skin would get on my belly and how much I hated it. When I was about two years old my colostomy was reversed and I had a pull-through operation, which cut a hole for my anus and pulled the intestines through to join them up.

Unfortunately, this caused complete bowel incontinence, as I had no functioning sphincter. People with stomas have a bag to collect the waste since there is no way to control how and when it comes out. Well, I effectively had a stoma without a bag. I would mess myself unpredictably up to 20 times a day, although sometimes I would have a few days respite due to blockages in my bowel.

During follow-up appointments when I was maybe 5 or 6 years old, the doctors tried to get me to practice squeezing more. I tried, but without actually checking the sphincter function, they were worse than useless and my parents followed their lead. They blamed me for my accidents, not realising that these weren't accidents, just something that was always going to happen. My mother used to say I should sit on the toilet longer, not realising that as my bowel was always open it made no difference how long I sat there. The stool would come out when it was ready, not when I decided.

Because of this culture of denial from my parents and doctors, I was left feeling like a freak and had to just find a way to deal with it myself. I believed that nothing could be done about my problem medically, otherwise those doctors would have done it by now.

From a young age, I taught myself to make my own pads by taking large wads of toilet paper, folding them up, and placing them in my underwear to catch the accidents and then changing them every time. If it got messy, I would use the water from the toilet bowl to wet toilet paper and make wet-wipes to clean up with.

I did everything I could to hide my shameful condition and on the whole, I think I succeeded. This taught me resilience and the need to be better than I otherwise would have been, which allowed me to achieve more. I got through school with good grades, went to college and university and eventually got a good job as a software engineer.

Incontinence is a recognised disability but I was not told this and never knew about the help that could be offered. If I had been recognised as having a disability, I might have had a less traumatic childhood especially at school. But ironically, I might not have achieved as much as I did if I had been placed in a 'special school'.

I was married in 1998 and had two beautiful daughters. Unfortunately, my ill-health was one of a number of factors that led to my divorce in 2009 and my borderline personality disorder and depression led to my being admitted to a psychiatric hospital for three months. It was during this time that a nurse noticed my incontinence episodes and, with the help of a mental health advocate from the charity "Mind", I was given the confidence to approach my GP (doctor) about getting the incontinence looked at again.

In the UK we have 'continence clinics' which can prescribe incontinence wear and pads, but my GP claimed to have never heard of them when I enquired. I was annoyed, but a subsequent appointment with a better GP led to my referral to a specialist colorectal hospital, St. Marks in Harrow. After anal manometry, a number of ultrasounds and other tests, I finally learned the truth. I never had any chance of controlling my bowels, but there was a way to manage them.

I was prescribed Peristeen, which is a colonic irrigation system that you perform yourself or with the help of carers, whilst sitting on the toilet. I do this every night and it's made a huge difference to my life. I still need to wear pads 24 hours a day, but the number of times I have accidents has been reduced from many times a day to a few times a week.

I've been using Peristeen since 2010 and though it can be uncomfortable and it has risks of its own, including bowel perforation and electrolyte imbalances, I'd recommend it to anyone struggling with this condition.

I'd also like to say that even when things look bleak, you can succeed

126. D. N's Story (Africa)

Well, my story begins 51 years ago. Looking back, much of childhood seems a blur, but one thing I know was that I had a happy, healthy childhood with a few hurdles along the way. I was fiercely independent and strong willed. Growing up with four older boys, and being the only girl, I was protected, loved and spoilt.

Thinking back to my early years, having IA didn't really bother me. I just learnt to get on with it. I had to, there was no other choice. My mother never treated me any different, so learning to deal with my IA problems was left up to me. I learnt in school how to get undressed in the change rooms (locker rooms) by changing in the toilet cubicles or taking my time, so I was the last girl out. Learning to wear school jerseys around my waist and of course lots of toilet paper. Teachers were made aware of my IA, so I had more freedom if I needed to get to the loo.

Wearing skirts was a big plus. I could always turn them around if there was a stain on my skirt, and then sanitary pads become my best friend and so did my period. I think girls have it a lot easier than boys. We can get away with more excuses. Whenever someone saw my scars, I made up such incredible stories about how I got them, it should have had me winning an Emmy. I think one story I told was that I jumped out of a helicopter without a parachute.

As a child growing up with a disability, you learn to lie, you learn to become defensive, and you learn to think on your feet. You are quick to retaliate and lash out at your environment and everyone in it. It's so easy to self-destruct.

Meanwhile, without knowing it, you sink into despair, self-hatred and loneliness. But you also learn to grow. My teenage years were filled with apprehension. Boys, the opposite sex! I never went to a co-ed school. Having grown up with four older boys, I knew about boys and men, but being intimate or having one as a boyfriend was another story altogether.

Then one day a TV commercial came on, it was on laxative tea. I was 16 years old at the time. It changed my life! For the first time, my tummy worked properly, and I trained it as a parent would train their toddler in potty training. I trained my mind. My acne disappeared and no more accidents in my panties. I could wear what I wanted to, go out with boys, go dancing, party with my girlfriends, travel to Europe and have a long-term relationship with a guy.

No one was EVER any the wiser as to why I had scars or that I had IA. I became a master of deceit, all to hide the fact that I was born "abnormal".

If ever asked about my scars on my tummy, I would say a half-truth, that my bowel twisted when I was six months old and I had to have emergency surgery (that is true). I kept it short and simple. You'd be surprised how people accept things and move on.

I was one lucky baby because I was born with a very low IA. Also, because I had found a laxative tea, which has helped me with bowel function and control, and I had a very supportive family.

I'm very blessed to be married to a man who knows all my secrets and loves me for who I am. Though I've never been able to have children because of the scar tissue created by the bowel twist surgery. I am very blessed to be here and to share my story.

The advice I can offer to those who are going through so many challenges or are parents who have children born with IA, is to be kind, be patient, understanding and supportive to yourselves and to those around you.

Blessed Be,
D.N.

127. Adawehi's Story (USA)

I was born in Falfurrias, Texas, but we actually lived in Laredo, which is a twin city half in Texas (USA) and half in Mexico. My mom would always talk about why they decided to have the birth in Falfurrias. Around that time in the 1970's, Laredo was having issues with babies being stolen on the border. My mom also said when I was born all the nurses wanted to hold me one last time before I went home from hospital.

I wasn't diagnosed with an Imperforate Anus until two months of age and had my surgery in South Texas in the city of Corpus Christi. I have no memory of my early years, but I can only imagine how difficult it was for my parents. 50 years ago, there wasn't very much help or understanding about special medical conditions.

My memory starts when everything was great in school in south Texas. I never felt different. I love how wonderful all the people still are in South Texas. Then my dad had to look for work so we had to move. We moved to East Texas, and what a different world that was.

I have to explain, my dad played a lifesaving role in our local area catching rattlesnakes and milking them for antivenin as a way to make extra money. I guess I should tell you about my ancestry so you can fully understand. I am Native American, Scandinavian and European from the Colonial days here in America, and my Native American Culture saved my life.

Unfortunately, my mom became ill in East Texas. She was diagnosed with Paranoid Schizophrenia. We aren't sure exactly when she became sick, just when she was diagnosed. My parents stopped taking care of my special needs when I was around six years old. My mom needed all of us to help her out. I missed a lot of things growing up, that's why a lot of my milestones were missed.

I had to have further surgery in 1974, for which I was left sterilized, no longer able to have children of my own. I also suffered a brain Injury from a car accident 1977. I wish I knew more about all my medical issues from that time, but I haven't been able to access my records.

My mom's health deteriorated and when I was around nine she was admitted to a mental hospital for six months. During that time, I had limited parental support as my dad was working three jobs to support us kids and my mom was in hospital. This was a very difficult time for me and living in a camping facility was frightening at times. We then moved to another part of East Texas.

When I started at the new school, I was bullied a lot but overcame my problems by playing sports. I played Little Dribblers Basketball in Elementary school, my basketball team was the best and those bullies I played basketball with were only good to me on the court because I was pretty good at basketball. That was the first healing place for me. Sports taught me how to work for a goal, how to be a team player and to never give up on that goal. My determination is something I still carry with me.

I finally got transferred to another school for high school but couldn't play sports there. I wasn't related to the right people. But at this new school, in my adolescence, I fell in with the wrong crowd and started making very poor decisions. This was when my childhood experiences started to take its toll on me. I went to the edge of depression and the implications of my early surgeries really started to show. I was viewed as not dating material, and I ended up getting into trouble with the law due to drug and alcohol related issues.

I was subsequently arrested, but by that time I knew I really needed some help and was sent to a program run by the Texas Prisons. That's where I received my GED (General Educational Development). I went in at age 17 and was out before my 19th birthday.

When I was released I had a really tough time making ends meet. This whole time I never complained outwardly about my medical issues, I chose this at an early age. But I was still very much depressed and in a dark place in my mind and that's why I reached out to my ancestry and felt very connected to those ancestors. I started going to public Powwows just to be there.

I did stay out of trouble and quit that life by the time I met my current husband, and then I started having some difficulties with my conditions. My husband is very compassionate and loving and is helping me to rediscover my disabilities so I am able to get the care I have needed all this time.
I still don't have my disability paperwork because, here in America, I have to prove that I have been getting treatment for my conditions. I have no medical records except for the surgery I had at two months old. I can no longer work due to my health, but I realize now that I am on a new road and look forward to exploring how far medical advancements have come and seek the right treatment.

I am so grateful that children born with IA nowadays can get the right medical treatment and support from the start, which wasn't available to me and my parents.

There's a lot more to my life story, I am just grateful to share this part.

In the Indigenous world sharing our story is what helps us all move forward, walk in beauty, help others heal by healing ourselves and becoming strong people.

My native name Adawehi means "Angel" in English.

128. Kelly's Story (USA)

I was born in 1968 and diagnosed with an Imperforate Anus at our local hospital. They transferred me to a Children's Hospital Emergency Department and once they realized the situation, I immediately had pull-through surgery. My mom had to stay at the local hospital while my dad was able to come visit me every day I stayed in Boston. It's really weird to read my hospital records from 50 years ago and read about my surgery, how I did, what I ate and the times I stooled.

I can't begin to comprehend what my parents had to endure. My mom told me that after my surgery, I stayed in the hospital for about two weeks and the nurses would give me dilatations to ensure my anal opening didn't close and taught my mom how to do them. When I was discharged my mom was instructed to continue with the dilatations, but as they didn't have any dilatation rods back then as they do now, she had to use her pinky finger with some Vaseline.

She told me about how I screamed and how hard it was for her. She was alone a lot while my dad worked or slept from the night shift. My mother remembers all of the stress and the guilt she felt from having to hurt me and make me cry. I remember none of it. But to say I consider my mom to be a "Rock Star" is an understatement!

At that time there were no support groups or social media to learn about special conditions and there seemed to be no one who had gone through it before. The doctors made it seem like it was a fluke sort of thing that just happened, that she didn't do anything wrong and that I should be just "fine". I soon realized that the word "fine" had a completely different meaning to me than it had to others.

"Fine"

I guess "fine' is pooping in the chair in kindergarten in front of all your classmates and then having to stay in the bathroom forever until your mom showed up to bring clean underwear. I remember raising my hand that day and getting yelled at by a Nun because I said, "can I go to the bathroom and not may I go to the bathroom". I ended up leaving a present on the chair for that Nun!

"Fine" is always having to remember to pack extra underwear in your school bag just in case you have an accident so you could change. By second grade I was already being bullied by a certain boy. I was always anxious that he would find out about my problem and announce it to the classroom or make fun of me even more.

"Fine" is having your younger sister give you the underwear she was wearing because you had soiled yours and she would always go without. Wherever we were she'd hand it over. She never got angry about it or refused my mother's request to give it to me. It was always given quietly and she never made a big thing about it, I will always love her for that.

"Fine" is having accidents or having to run off course into the woods to poop during every cross-country race in high school. The exercise always seemed to bring on accidents. One day my coach drove me home after one particular race and I knew I smelled in the car. I just wanted to die of embarrassment. He never said anything about it, but I remember everything.

"Fine" is accidentally pooping during an intimate moment with your college boyfriend. All of a sudden he tells you, you've had an accident and you didn't know something had come out. I've never spoken of that to anyone before. We didn't stay together.

"Fine" is going for a romantic walk with your husband, realizing that you're going to have an accident and not being able to make it home in time. Instead of holding hands I made him walk in front of me so he couldn't see the stain in my pants. I just didn't want him to think of me that way. IA impacts every aspect of your life no matter how small.

"Fine" is finally summoning up the courage to seek adult colorectal medical assistance for your IA at the age of 49. I went to the colorectal surgeon to talk about my problems and to see if he could help me. He asked me to lay on my stomach on this special table that rises up, but your head is lower than your butt which is exposed and up in the air to do the examination. He looked and spoke to me and asked if he could have some other doctors see my surgical area. I then saw all these feet standing behind me and I knew they were looking at my butt like an animal in a zoo. That's how I felt anyway... they didn't talk to me... only my doctor asked me questions. That was my first attempt to get medical help since I had left paediatric care as a child!

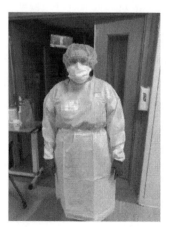

I've had my children bring me a change of clothes when I have had an accident in the woods and been unable to walk home. I would have been seen with poop stains. I couldn't hide the accident. To them this was normal. "That's just mom" they would say. Wish I was known for my fantastic pancakes or how I decorated for Christmas but it's more about my bathroom issues.

I currently work as an Intensive Care Nurse and, thankfully, the bathroom is very close in my department. I've never had a job where the bathroom wasn't near me but sometimes it could never be near enough. I always know where the bathrooms are, you have to have this awareness and it is just an instinctive habit now.

I am 52 years old and I think about my IA every day. Is my pad straight? I frequently feel for its position and I hope no one sees me or I wonder if they can see it through my pants.

I take medication to help with diarrhoea. I have Irritable Bowel Syndrome (IBS) as well, so not only do I have diarrhoea frequently but, because of the IA, I can't control it. I've had a sacral nerve stimulator placed years ago but I really don't feel it's made any difference.

There are many more stories in my head other than the ones I've written but I just wanted to describe a small piece of what my life has been like with IA. Despite my lot in life, I've tried to make the best of it. Some days I go from laughing at myself or crying about it all.

I've found a man who loves me regardless and, even though we have been married for 26 years, I still don't want to share a lot of poop stories with him... trying to keep the romance and all. I have two beautiful boys, well men now, who know one day they will be wiping my butt. It's an ongoing joke! Seriously, they've stepped up when I needed their help at my most embarrassing moments.

A doctor's perception of "fine" is not really "fine" for the person who has to live it. I know some kids and adults have had things much tougher than me. Many people have had the latest procedures and medical equipment to help them live their best life. Everyone's journey is different. We all make the best of it.

Make your "fine" the best you can.

129. The Show Must Go On – Dan (England)

My name is Dan. I was born with IA in 1965 at St. James Hospital in Leeds. Within hours I was rushed to Leeds General Infirmary where I had, what was considered at that time, a ground-breaking operation performed by Professor John Goligher. He was considered in the sixties to be one of the leading surgeons in IA /ARM surgery, in short Professor Goligher saved my life and here I am 55 years later still drawing breath.

When I was asked by Greg to submit an article for the book I was delighted, however this left me with the challenge of what to write as I was sure many contributors would write similar articles and ideas as me. So, I decided to write about my approach to IA throughout my life so far and my relationship with my bowels.

It's never been an easy relationship. Sometimes it's been like dealing with a rebellious teenager and at other times a 90-year-old pensioner. Generally, I think I can safely say there have not been many occasions where I have had a normal day.

I could go on for pages and pages, but I will just settle on a couple of examples:

Out and About

I am always amazed when someone says they have to go to the toilet and are back out in 5-15 minutes, this still surprises me even now. Like most with IA, if I am able to go in and come out within 30 minutes that is a bonanza day to me. From an early age this has led me to fear getting caught out when I am in public.

The trepidation of facing the porcelain portal of public punishment all the while feeling the grumbling teenager inside you shout incessantly, "I'm coming out, get in there, I'm coming", makes you break out in a cold sweat and tremble all over. There are a number of things going through your mind at this crucial time and it comes in the following order:

Do I have the time to make it?

Is my body going to be able to hold the tsunami of poop currently blasting its way towards my open orifice or will an old sea captain jump out in front of me shouting "Thar she blows!!!"

Will there be an empty cubicle?

Or will I be faced with a row of closed doors? Meaning I have to desperately do the "squeeze my butt cheeks together" dance to hold the aforementioned tsunami. Hoping once a cubicle does become available, I will be able to walk in normally without soiling myself.

Will there be a working cubicle lock?

If there was an Olympic event that specified you had to sit on the toilet, defecate, wipe and pull yourself together. All this while having one foot pressed against the toilet door looking like a one-legged madman trying to unfold wet spaghetti in the dark with your hands behind your back, then all members of the IA community would win a Gold medal every time.

The, what smell will I make prayer!

You think desperately "what have I eaten recently and what smell will I generate?" Then you begin the smell prayer, "Oh lord please make the gaseous emission I am about to create be very low on the smell generation scale, in your name, thank you lord, Amen". This will hopefully stop the usual walk-in comment of "Bloody hell, has something died in here!" This means you have to stay in there at least until the shouter has gone because you don't want anyone to know it's you who created something that will rot the tiles off the wall.

Will there be any toilet paper in there?
This is the crucial one. You make it in time, you sit for half an hour or more, the lock works, no mention of the smell prayer, everything is going great, you think you've finished, you look up... and whisper "Bugger..." Your gaze settles on the empty toilet roll/paper dispenser.

Anyone with a sphincter will say, "Oh I know, I've had Diarrhoea"... no dear this is a regular day for me...

Taboo Subject

I have been a musician since I was very young, and I enjoy that part of my life. The performing, the entertaining people, bringing happiness and joy, at least, I hope. Over the years this has brought many challenges and yes, I have to admit there have been some accidents. When you are performing you cannot stop and go to the toilet, it's just not possible.

This has meant that yes, I have performed with soiled underwear in a most uncomfortable position but as the old adage goes "The Show Must Go On".

You never know by looking at someone what they are going through and within the IA community I think this is very applicable to all who have the condition. We need to champion this, the need to get the message across of who we are and how different we are.

A friend of mine once said, "Can you not be registered as disabled?" and to be honest I don't know. I am sure there are IA/ARM people who are in a worse off position than me and yes, they probably do need to be registered disabled to assist in their general living state so they, and their families, have the support they need.

There is a current problem in the world. No one likes to discuss poo. It's as simple as that. The by-product of the human body we create is not acceptable to discuss in polite society. It's seen as a taboo subject, not to be talked about, something of disgust and revulsion. Yet any parent of an IA/ARM child will discuss it and will be quite open in their approach and handling of faecal matter. This brings me to my last tale about how we have become immune to our approach to the taboo subject.

My current partner Dawn and I had only been together for a matter of months when late one night her toilet had become blocked and had proceeded to overflow all over the bathroom floor. Yes, we were awash with "Brown stuff". Well, we set to the task and I dove straight in (excuse the pun) and proceeded to assist in cleaning up, plus I got the toilet unblocked and the bathroom was spick and span again.

After we had finished, Dawn was terribly embarrassed about what had happened and asked me how I had been able to do what I had? I explained that the last 55 years had given me a unique perspective on the said item and that it will always be there for me and always has been. Over the years I have cleared up many accidents and messes of varying degrees, so I had become desensitised to it and just dealt with it.

So, what am I getting at? Basically, "The Show Must Go On". Whatever incidents or accidents I have had over the years it must go on. We need to talk in wider circles about IA/ARM, we need to talk about poo, we need to talk about everything. Only by bringing it all into the light will we be able to make sure the younger generation will have a better life and treatment, so they may not suffer the ridicule, mental anguish and instability some of us have.

We need to talk.

130. My Story – Katrina Marie Tyler, 63 Years Old (Shropshire UK)

Diagnosis

1959 - My Mum and me

Tracheoesophageal Fistula with Oesophageal Atresia
Cloaca with Anorectal Malformation
Volvulus – Bowel resection and colostomy (reversed at 18 months)
Bicornuate Uterus
Abnormal Fallopian Tubes
Hemi vertebrae
Extra thumb

A childhood lost

Always anxious, frightened, fight or flight mode, always alert, expecting the worst. Alone and sometimes terrified of what was happening and what was going to happen.

Loss of control

Adults asking questions I had no answers to; "why did I poo in my pants?" Projecting their anxieties about my future onto me, a lost child, struggling to understand their grownup language and medical jargon which accompanied it. Told I must work hard at school, must get a good job or no one would want to marry me... That I would never be able to have children.

I hated the physical loss of control, when my body would not behave as it should. Many times, I would be unaware of faecal leakage until it was too late and my only warning was a horrible smell oozing out of my underwear. I hated being unable to correct or at least improve the situation. Quite by chance when I was about 10 years old, I discovered that folded toilet tissue in my knickers absorbed some of the faeces and the tissue could easily be flushed in the loo. I was still left with that nauseating smell and bits of faeces which had somehow managed to avoid the wad of tissue and soak into my pants but at least it was all a bit more tolerable, until periods started then it was a desperate mess.

Isolation

Hospital 50 miles from home, no facilities for parents to stay, so far away they could not visit every day.

I remember planning my escape from the ward and walking down several flights of stairs before a nurse found me and returned me to my bed. I would stare out of the windows thinking I could see my home over the top of the high-rise buildings.

Watching the "ward round" from a distance, feeling so scared, knowing they would eventually come to me, invade my space with their strange unrecognisable language, their probing hands. Biting the arm of a nurse, she hurt me pushing that stiff rectal tube in my already damaged, abnormal rectum.

After this they started giving me sedation prior to the soap and water enemas. I think that was worse as this just made me hate them more, they could do what they wanted and I couldn't fight back, falling into an abyss, hearing their voices but not being able to respond, to protest, or to protect myself from their prying eyes and fingers. I would wake up and have no idea what the doctors had done, I would be cross with myself that I hadn't been able to stop them, that I was not strong enough to put up a fight, to escape.

Painful invasive examinations and procedures, lights above my head when wheeled into theatre for yet another manual evacuation, the overwhelming smell of anaesthetic gases, the hateful, horrid anaesthetic mask. Doctors peering at me over masks, so desperately scary...

I was always bloated, uncomfortable, gaseous, hideously constipated (17 days was my longest without a bowel action) or uncontrollable diarrhoea. There was no in between, no normal. So many medications, laxatives and enemas, making me feel sick. The toilet was my enemy, I was made to sit for what seemed like forever, and there was always a man's face in the water, staring at my bottom. He made it much harder to relax, to push, not that that would have done much good. I never told anyone he was in the toilet, my mind was playing tricks... I guess.

Smell

Foul faecal smell pervading everything, on my hands, under my nails, up my nose, in my underwear. Parents being told by Paediatricians I'm "naughty", no one, including medics, understanding the implications of absent muscles, absent nerves, scarred from surgeries occurring at birth, failing to function correctly.

I couldn't help being constipated or soiling, yet I was made to feel it was somehow my fault and eventually I believed it was. My parents were told I had "behavioural issues", I read that in my notes many years later. How wrong they all were. My physical body couldn't comply and somehow, I was labelled "naughty".

Striving for independence, washing soiled pants, putting them to dry on the radiator, not really clean, the smell of faeces filling the room, my Mum getting cross. Never enough toilet paper in the house to meet my needs, always needing loads, sometimes using newspaper, inevitably blocking the toilet drainage system.

Socially isolated at school, always "smelly", embarrassed, bullied, felt different, ugly, hideous scars remarked on frequently in the shower block after physical education sessions. Children can be so very cruel. Learning to swim, bits of faeces leaking out into the swimming pool, trying to scoop them up and shove them in the filter system, strangely no adult seemed to notice... or maybe they did.

Sports: running around made faeces sneak out into my pants, what to do with the stinky mess at school.... only babies soil their pants, it is so often viewed as dirty and anti-social.

I shared a bed with my younger sister, which meant my sleep was superficial because I worried that I would soil our bed. I remember waking and realising my faeces was on her leg, dried on hard and difficult to budge. I remember trying to clean it without disturbing her... the smell lingering on my hands.

Adulthood –A Life Rebalanced – The power of positive touch, of understanding and of love

1983 - Our Wedding Day

Adulthood provided me with the opportunity to learn about, to understand and to accept my conditions, living alongside it and managing it as opposed to always being at odds with it.

I developed strategies to manage my unpredictable bowels. Spare underwear and tissues are my constant companions.

I was told I would never marry - when I was about nine years old, but in 1983, Mike and I were married.

In 1988 Mike and I adopted 2 sisters - Stephanie and Roberta, we became the parents to two beautiful little girls. In the autumn of our lives, we are now blessed with boisterous grandchildren to keep us on our toes and we are very lucky to spend wonderful days with our precious family.

Our daughters, Stephanie and Roberta

2020 - Mike and me

My husband thinks I am hyper aware of smell and I can get quite paranoid about bowel odours. He is probably right, but I know I can't change that sensitivity now.

I trained to be a nurse, caring for very sick and life limited children helped me to appreciate the gift of good health. So many children are faced with much higher, harsher mountains to climb and sadly many never reach the top.

I see myself as lucky, I have a wonderful life with my truly incredible husband by my side. He has helped me enormously on this journey and continues to blow me away with his unconditional love. I have amazing family and friends and with their love and support I have reached the top of my personal mountain. In my opinion acceptance is essential, gaining emotional strength from sharing my experiences with family, friends and others born with similar abnormalities. Being proud of who I am rather than ashamed.

I am determined that ARM does not define me. Sometimes it is hard to be positive and I honestly do allow myself periods of reflection and wonder what life would have been like if my embryonic self had taken a different pathway, but it didn't, and this is me 63 years on and still dancing. I was given a life and it is my responsibility to grasp it with both hands and live that life to the fullest.

Parents

I share my ARM journey to recognise and honour my amazing parents, Neville and Patricia, who were just 17 years old when I was born, many would say just children themselves. They rose to the many challenges I and the medical professionals presented them with, this was the United Kingdom in the 1950's, there were only General Practitioners for support, no Community Nurses, Stoma Specialists, no one for 50 miles who understood my health needs.

1957 - My parents Wedding Day

My parents advocated for me and they gave me the tools to face my future with courage and confidence, they believed in me, they loved me.

Family contributions

My sister Cheryl:

"I have memories of Katrina's 21st birthday celebrations. Our father gave a moving speech about how "she didn't want to come into the world"...well I am glad she did and I am very proud of all her achievements."

My brother Steve:

"Her tenacity is remarkable, her attitude inspiring, where others may have given up Katrina has been a role model and has provided a platform for others to gain knowledge about her condition."

My husband Mike:

"I am honoured she chose to share her life with me."

I would like to take this opportunity to thank Greg Ryan. He has helped me remove the overcoat of embarrassment and shame that has weighed heavily on my shoulders for many years, I now walk tall and free.

131. Imperforate Anus Congenital Birth Defect Poem and Story by Verona Endrizzi (USA)

IA/ARM Poem

Most babies like myself born in 1953 had little chance of survival

Parents and family of mine had no knowledge, experience or support

Embarrassment, shame, humiliation, self-loathing for 6+ decades

Remnants of terrible memories relating to my IA

Facebook community of Adults with IA/ARM became my life support

Overcoming psychological, social and emotional turmoil since birth

Respecting and loving myself just the way I am without fear of rejection

Accepting that my IA doesn't define me or acknowledge I'm not normal

Too many unexpected "accidents" looking for nearest bathrooms and exits

Exposing myself to family, friends and others openly about my condition

Adapting to a new life with my "Rosie" stoma and colostomy forever

Never knowing or meeting any other IAs created a deep sense of loneliness

Understanding future challenges exist but have more control over my life

Success and confidence now mine

Thank you from the bottom of my heart to the IA/ARM community. You're now my family of choice and not birth.

My Story - Verona

Who is an IA? What is IA? Why does IA happen? When does IA happen? These are questions and answers I've been grappling with for 67 years, since my birth in 1953.

I'm an IA adult and have always known that I had an imperforate anus. Why I have IA was never fully known or explained to me in medical or biological terms by my parents or doctors. What is IA? I found out decades later, when I started researching my congenital birth defect in order to understand and accept myself. Years of traditional therapy never helped or gave me the answers I needed so I kept investigating.

My epic journey, similar to others' stories like myself, was fraught with physical, emotional, social and psychological struggles. It's been an epic chronicling of my turbulent life thus far, but not anymore. I am now empowered to love myself and try to help others with IA, of any age, understand and accept their own life's paths.

Way back when I was born in 1953, my parents excitedly awaited the birth of their twin daughters without any experience with babies, twins, or caring for a newborn with life threatening issues. I was a 3lbs 15oz preemie rushed off to be operated on at 12 hours old for an imperforate anus. My parents were told to summon a priest to give me my Last Rites (I'm Jewish btw), to which my father said, "Absolutely not. If that baby doesn't go to Heaven, then nobody goes to Heaven".

That story still wells tears in my eyes. Truth is most babies like me at that time never survived because of lack medical knowledge, technology and everything else it took to save an IA infant. Fortunately, I had an OB/GYN who remarkably never gave up on me and saved my life. There weren't even neo-natal units or Children's Hospitals in those days.

Growing up I never knew today's terminology: pull-through, high IA, low IA, birth defect, obstruction, constipation, irrigation, dilations, colostomy supplies, or any other terms used. My parents just told me I was "fixed" and that was that. Ostomy supplies were bandages wrapped around my stomach to catch my bowel movements and to prevent my intestines from falling outside, which meant immediate trips to the emergency room.

We had many of those over three years before my colostomy was reversed. Can you imagine what it was like when other parents were overjoyed their child was potty trained at three and my parents were elated, I could even have a bowel movement into a diaper? Luckily those memories escape me but weren't evaded completely, they were buried deep into my subconscious for so many years to come.

My first IA memory was my father dragging me off to the doctor kicking and screaming, because the doctor would probe my anus, which hurt like hell. I couldn't scream loud enough to make it all stop. Little did I know that it was to "fix" me with anal dilations. No one told me.

As I grew older, I have horrible memories of being terrified that someone would eventually find out I had had a colostomy for something I couldn't prevent but which would cause me a lifetime of loneliness, embarrassment, shame, confusion, and self-loathing. I couldn't share any of my fears or anxieties with anyone, not even my parents.

My own children never knew how I felt, they only knew the visible complications. No one knew how I suffered, which led to a future of many unsuccessful counseling sessions, fear of rejection, (why not I was born as damaged goods, supposed to have died, rejected) real or not. If I could look back at myself, I would hold that little girl, named Verona after her maternal grandmother who would help care for her, tightly making sure she knew she was lovable, worthwhile and valuable in spite of her birth defect.

My parents never labeled me as having a birth defect, so I didn't refer to myself having one until I was 52. For that I'm glad, but even so, I believed I wasn't normal when I so much wanted to be like everyone else.

Life went on. Several gynecological surgery repairs related to my IA/colostomy surgeries, two C-sections to avoid fistulas, hysterectomy and a constant roller coaster of constipation, diarrhea, and incontinence. Public shame and embarrassment haunted me. Fear of being exposed kept me hostage and silent. Having to make excuses and explanations for myself to people made me crazy with expectations of rejection. Where could I hide after public accidents? Where were the nearest bathrooms and exits?

Everyone I was with always felt safe and secure, knowing I had the answers to those questions, but not me. I was always on guard. Who else awakes everyday wondering if they'll have a bowel movement, when and where it'll happen, how it will happen, or how they'll feel after whatever happens? My lifetime of fears gave birth to my new direction.

In my 50's I discovered a temporary solution to my dilemma. I found out about artificial bowel sphincter implants (aka ABS implants) performed by a well-known colorectal surgeon in L.A. In fact, I had three of them over a 15-year period of time. In reality, they were only Band-Aids, temporary "fixes" for my IA issues.

What happened next? I sought spiritual counseling and energy healing which were far superior to my traditional therapy sessions. I discovered that my IA congenital birth defect was the root of all my dysfunctional relationships because I feared rejection, I was unworthy, I wasn't valuable, I didn't deserve respect, honor, or love. After all, I wasn't supposed to live, right? I was defective from birth but miraculously survived, because I had other things to accomplish in this life. It's been my spiritual journey to where I am now which is: I love, respect and honour myself, I am worthy, valuable and worthwhile. I am lovable!

Today, I'm healing. I've forgiven myself for all my mistakes and failures. I understand what happened and now have resources and information.

I discovered my Facebook family and community of support from Adults with Imperforate Anus and One in 5000, filled with other IA's I will meet in person someday. **I AM NOT ALONE**.

I am unafraid. I am empowered. I am in control of my life.
I will continue asking questions and seeking answers but never alone and never lonely.

I have "come out" to many friends, family, acquaintances and even strangers. And it feels so, so good to be me! To be continued...

132. My Poems - Greg Ryan (Australia)

So much has happened to me since publishing my book "A Secret Life - Surviving a Rare Congenital Condition" in 2017 and establishing the ONE in 5000 Foundation at the same time. But the one thing that hasn't changed at all is my ongoing health battles, both with my IA as well as my mental health.

I have found that writing poems has really helped me to express how I'm feeling. This first occurred back in 2001 when I suffered my first mental breakdown and was diagnosed with Major Depression and Severe Anxiety. At the time, I had no idea what was happening to me and I found it very difficult to express what I was going through.

Because of my IA, there was always a reason why I would have physical problems. As a child, I had accepted that it was my lot in life and that it would be a lifelong issue. But dealing with mental health issues was a whole new ballgame for me and I struggled greatly. Then, for some reason (and I still have no idea how it occurred) I started to write poems as a way of expressing my thoughts, as I just couldn't talk about it let alone even understand it myself. There is no doubt I needed some sort of release, but I had never contemplated writing a poem in my 37 years up to that point.

Maybe I was in denial, but somehow I felt if I had started talking about it openly then I may divulge my IA "secret" inadvertently as a way of justifying why I had my breakdown. I felt like I was in a no-win situation, as the acceptance and understanding of having a mental illness twenty years ago was nowhere near what it is like in 2020.

I felt like I'd been dealt a double whammy of living with the shame and stigma of an invisible bowel condition plus an invisible mental health condition.

My only outlets were talking to my doctor and psychiatrist and taking my medication. So, writing poems became very important to me.

Over the years I have shared my poems only with very close friends, and even when I wrote my book, I only included one poem. It has taken me up until mid-2020 to actually share just a few of the poems on my Facebook page.

With everyone being so incredibly open and sharing with their stories I now feel this book is the right platform to share some of my poems, to express both my physical and emotional journey of living with IA.

The one thing I have learnt is that mental health is as important a concern as the physical challenges faced by the IA/ARM community.

I hope you find my poems written over the last 20 years interesting.

Greg Ryan

Portrait by Michelle Collins

PARENTS

When I was born with no bottom,
My parents where in total shock

But from that day forward,
They became my absolute rock

Their unconditional love,
Has got me through each day

The one thing that has helped me,
Deal with what has come my way

The journey that ensured,
Many times, laced with tears

But with my parents by my side,
They would always allay my fears

Even when I was hurting,
In pain and wanting to hide

They would never leave me,
And be always right by my side

So, for anyone with a child,
With a bottom like mine

With the love of their parents,
I know they will be just fine

TOILET AND ME

Living with an Imperforate Anus
Is such a rare condition,
Where I can't trust my body
To have a regular bowel motion

It causes anxiety and angst
As I live a life in doubt,
Because I have no idea
When I may get caught out

Ones toilet habits are a subject
Unfortunately, of stigma and taboo,
But when living with IA
It just becomes a part of you

To go to the toilet for me
Is an adventure each and every day,
But throughout my life
I have not known any other way

It's a war that I wage
Between the toilet and me,
But the battle scars I carry
No one else can see

Even though it's become
A normal part of my life,
It's still hard to face the toilet
As it's always a fight

It can be a friend or enemy
Depending on the day,
But the toilet and me
We just don't know any other way

SCARRED

The scars on my body,
Are visible for all to see

The scars in my mind though,
Are visible only to me

I can justify to myself,
The scars that people can see

I can't however justify,
The scars only seen by me

The scars on my body,
Maybe have cut so deep

That's why my mind,
Is so fragile and weak

Even though my life,
At the moment is hard

I will come through in the end,
No matter how scarred

NORMAL

If I could be granted one wish it would be
"To feel normal"

To live through this illness
"Nothing seems normal"

I look in the mirror and say
"Well, I look normal"

I talk to my family and friends, they'd say
"I sound normal"

I walk down the streets, do people think
"He's not normal"

The thoughts in my head, I know
"Are not normal"

The question I ask myself is,
"Who is normal?"

To do this makes me wonder,
"What is normal?"

But to me to get thru the day,
"I must feel normal"

So, in my own mind I have to believe
"I AM NORMAL"

DEPRESSION

This is such a confronting illness
Which is so hard to control,
And the more you deny it
The more it takes hold

I've learnt to live with it,
By taking things day by day,
Because if I don't accept this,
I know it will never go away

For so long I pretended,
That everything was fine,
But now I'm accepting
That this problem is mine

I'm holding on to the belief,
That my life can get back on track,
By acknowledging my old self
May never come back

I now accept this illness,
Which has changed my life forever,
And looking forward to a life,
That I know will only get better

ANXIETY

I live with constant anxiety
And am always on the edge

But the fear of the unknown
Is what fills me with pure dread

I try to control my environment
With everything I do

I know it's totally unrealistic
But for me it's so very true

I live my life in a bubble
In a way to protect myself

Because the ramifications I know
Adversely affect my health

If I look really nervous
As well as subdued and meek

That's my way of showing
I'm still feeling anxious and weak

So, when I go and face the world
It's with a very personal hope

Is that no matter what situations occur
I'm able to show the ability to cope

PANIC ATTACK

I get overwhelmed with fear,
When a panic attack occurs

It's a feeling that consumes me,
Which I find hard to express in words

When my body goes into meltdown
And I don't know what to do

As all you do is wonder,
What is happening to you

The thought of absolute terror,
Hits like a giant wave

And the effect it has on me,
Can last for days and days

I then try to comprehend,
Why I suffer attacks of these kind

But I hope they will stop,
As I get stronger in my mind

SELFISH

When you suffer a mental illness,
The world must revolve around you

I realise this come across,
As a very selfish view

It's the only reason,
I can give to explain

How hard this is to control,
The thoughts from the brain

You live your life,
Feeling self-conscious and meek

It's easier to be alone
Being selfish and weak

To confront the world,
Is so hard to do

Because it makes you realise,
The world doesn't revolve around you

THE REAL ME

I have to live in a world,
Where my life is a lie

And I put on a charade,
Just to get by

But I have to deal with the fact,
That I live a different way

To everyone else around me,
Each and every day

So I don't let anyone see,
How my moods ebb and flow

Because the last thing I want,
Is to let my vulnerability show

I have never let them,
See the real me

Because I've been too scared,
What they will really see

But I live for the day,
That I can let them all see

The special person I am,
And that's the REAL ME

SOMEONE AGAIN

I want to believe I'll be someone again

But I can't, I'm too scared

But I can't, I don't know how

But I can't, I am forever tired

But I can't, I don't trust my body

But I can't, I have no confidence

But I can't, I'm a burden

But I can't, I'm selfish and lazy

But I can't, my mind and body are broken

But I can't, I live by words, not actions

But I can't, I feel unsafe away from my room

But I can't, I look for answers I can't get

But I have to believe, I'll be someone again

TEMPT FATE

Should I unveil my secret,
Is something I wonder

But how people will react,
Is what makes me ponder

Will it help me or hinder,
My mental health struggles

Or is it easier and safer,
To continue to live in my bubble

Should I just do what,
I've done all of my life

And keep it a secret,
And totally out of sight

Or I should I show courage,
And be bold and true

But it's such a difficult topic,
And is considered so taboo

To be hard on myself,
is now a familiar trait

Which makes me question
Is it the right time to tempt fate?

A SECRET LIFE

I was born with a condition
That no-one else could see,
So I kept it as a secret
And hid the real me

To deal with its stigma
Or to try and explain,
I knew would be too hard
And just cause me more pain

So I learnt to live with it
By taking each day by day,
Even with the knowledge
That it would never go away

So I got on with my life
With the hand I got dealt,
And adapted and adjusted
No matter how I felt

I'd be lying if I said
It's been an easy ride,
But I'm proud to say
I've been able to survive

Then after 50 years
The time came to be,
So I unveiled "my secret"
To all close to me

It was emotional to those
Who had no idea at all,
And it made me feel proud
As I opened up and stood tall

Then it made me realise that with
All my struggles and fight,
Is that I'm proud of what I have achieved
Living "A Secret Life"

Chapter 11 - In Memoriam

133. Our Romeo, Growing His Angel Wings - Amie Goodwin (Australia)

Dave & I found out we were expecting a baby on Tuesday the second of October 2018. Once we told the kids, Ava, Tahj & Indigo that they were getting a little brother our family conversations changed to only talking about 'Baby G'. I had a relatively easy pregnancy and was so excited to watch Daddy Dave become a father for the very first time. We had our ultrasounds at 12, 20, 26, 29 and 31 weeks and everything seemed perfect. But at thirty-two weeks we were told our baby had an abnormal heart. Right then and there I went into labour and was taken by ambulance to the Royal Women's Hospital.

At 34 weeks, on the 7th May 2019, after two red buzzers, a dropped heart rate, and almost a general anaesthetic, Romeo Miller Goodwin joined our family. The first words I said once holding him on my chest were 'He's so perfect.' Shortly after he was taken to the Royal Children's Hospital with his proud Daddy. This is when we found out the extent of Romeo's congenital abnormalities. Dave rang me and said, 'Babe, Romeo doesn't have a bum hole'. They were words I did not even know could possibly come out of anyone's mouth. I was so confused. How was that even possible?

A few hours later when I arrived, Dave took me to see our perfectly imperfect baby boy. We found out that our Romeo was born with multiple internal plumbing issues involving his heart, oesophagus, trachea and bowel.

At eight hours old Romeo went in for eight hours' worth of life saving surgery for his TOFF-OA and imperforate anus, where he was given a gastrostomy and colostomy.

This is where our journey truly begun. We were assigned our Neonatologist, and of course Romeo got the top dog, Professor Rod Hunt who is also the Director of the NICU. We met with Rod the day after Romeo was born and he told us our Romeo would only have a ten to twenty percent chance of survival. But Rod did not know us, and he did not know that our son had his Mumma's country blood. We were told that out of all of Romeo's conditions, his ARM would have the most negative impact on his life and were left with the possibility of saying goodbye to our Romeo.

But we let Romeo dictate his own life and path from there. The next five and half months was the Romeo show. There was not any rule book or journal article that would predict what he would do next. Romeo managed to pull through and overcome every obstacle that was thrown at him, including open heart surgery at two weeks old.

The next few months were a constant rollercoaster where the lows, unfortunately, came more often than the highs. I became a professional colostomy bag changer, and what was meant to be our biggest burden, became the most 'normal' part of our day.

I started joining Facebook groups to connect with other parents and then contacted Greg Ryan. Greg came and met me at RCH for coffee and instantly I felt OKAY about Romeo's ARM and began getting excited about the life that was ahead of him. Greg was a walking example that these little babies will one day still be able to live normal lives and take any opportunities that are presented to them.

Dave and I changed our mindset and decided that it was up to us to make sure Romeo lived a normal life, despite the medically complex challenges that continued to come his way.

We fought hard to get Romeo home. We never knew how much time at home we would have, but we wanted to show him what life was about. The journey home was one of the most emotional parts of this whole experience. The mental load that shifted from us the moment we walked out of the NICU doors was enormous. Finally, after 140 days, we did not have to leave our baby boy any longer and we could all be together as a family. Being able to sleep with Romeo and not have to ask permission to leave the room, was something I had always taken for granted.

Arriving home was a surreal moment that we had only ever dreamed of. We let Romeo live life to the fullest and did not treat him like a sick baby. We let the dogs lick his face, we dragged him to school pick up and drop off, kids sports, brunch, wineries, the dentist and Bunnings. You name it, we did it. Our baby room that we had originally set up for him now resembled something similar to a pharmacy, or the NICU stock room, with shelves full of medical supplies for this stoma and tracheostomy. But somehow, it was all so normal.

We were fortunate enough to spend 23 nights at home with him. The kids made our life easy and were always insisting that they hold Romeo and snuggle on the couch, or in their beds with him. As always, he had us all wrapped around his little finger.

On Thursday 17th November, Dave woke me up as he was leaving for work and handed me Romeo. All dressed up, fed and ready for the day. As he left, he mentioned that he thought Romeo was a little blue, but we were not too concerned, after all, it is Romeo.

However, by 12.30pm Romeo had started to change colour more often, I called for the ambulance and as I had been trained at the hospital I knew what to do when this happened. I started doing manual breaths for Romeo. By 7.30pm that night we landed back at the Royal Children's Hospital via helicopter. We never thought that our time with Romeo would be coming to an end. Romeo spent the last few days of his life surrounded by all of his family and friends.

We had always promised Romeo we would take him to the zoo to see the lions, so we honoured our promise. The day before Romeo grew his wings, Dave, myself and our nurse walked him over to the zoo where all of our family were waiting. We laughed, cried, and enjoyed what would be our last family outing with our son.

The staff at the RCH had heard all about our wedding plans and I had given them the date which was less than two weeks away. Our plan was to have Romeo home for the wedding.

However, due to his declining health to, the staff and our friends rallied together, to have our wedding at the hospital the next day. instead. But Romeo, being Romeo had other ideas. That day was about him...like every day. He did not want us to have our wedding at the hospital, so three hours before our ceremony was due to start, he began to rapidly deteriorate.

We knew this time would come, but nothing could have prepared us.

Our brave boy passed away in my arms, with his Daddy cuddling us both at 4.45pm on Monday 21st October. Finally, his battle was over and he was at peace.   He did not need to fight, and he was with the angels. You see, Romeo was too beautiful for this world of ours. His time with us was short, but he has left a mark on our hearts to last a lifetime. He has taught us all to never give up, to live in the moment and to always keep looking forward.

Two weeks later, Dave and I still got married amongst the whimsical trees of the Redwood forest. We did not have guests and instead had just ourselves and our children alongside our Celebrant, Photographer and Cinematographer. It rained the entire day and the kids told me it was Romeo's tears falling from heaven. They say that it rains when heaven meets the earth, and that is why we could feel Romeo all around us that day. Our boy was watching his Mummy & Daddy unite forever from the heavens above.

It was not the Wedding we had planned, but the difficult circumstances have given us the tools to create a marriage that will last the test of time. After all, would we ever be ready to have our Wedding without our son? Romeo taught us that life is far too precious to live with fear, and the importance of grasping any opportunity to create memories with the ones we love.

"To our Darling Romeo,

Thank you for blessing us by being your parents. Thank you for the short, but beautiful time we had with you. And most of all, thank you for teaching us gratitude and the real meaning of what it means to live!

Love Mamma, Daddy,
Ava, Tahj, Indigo and baby brother (due May 2021) xx"

Chapter 12 - ONE in 5000 Foundation

The ONE in 5000 Foundation was established in August 2017 as a not-for-profit organisation to aid and support anyone affected by the congenital condition called Imperforate Anus (IA), also known as Anorectal Malformation (ARM).

As the condition is rarely acknowledged outside this extremely small sector of the community, it therefore does not attract the resources needed. Those affected require ongoing physical and emotional medical care, families need information and support, and doctors and nurses need professional development.

To achieve this objective, we are committed to the following four outcomes: **Awareness** of ARM; **Information** regarding mental health and economic issues; **Medical** advice and best practice; **Support** emotionally and if feasible, financially. These ambitions form the basis of the acronym that we call our A.I.M.S.

To align with these objectives, the ONE in 5000 Foundation has been represented at International Paediatric Colorectal conferences in the USA, London, Paris, Vienna, Zurich and Melbourne. This has enabled us to build important personal relationships with leading paediatric colorectal surgeons and patient organisations from around the world. It has resulted in a collaboration of projects including research studies, global webinars and co-authorship of a chapter in an internationally released paediatric colorectal textbook.

Our website **www.onein5000foundation.org** provides a global online resource for the ARM and wider community.

We provide regular updates in out "latest news" section, share medical educational IA/ARM videos, provide a FAQ section and offer the opportunity for patients and parents to describe their own experiences. We also have a Medical section which details a global list of paediatric colorectal and mental health medical professionals and their hospitals.

Samuel & Ursula (Rare Disease Ghana Initiative)

We have been able to assist in funding and organising much needed surgeries for two young IA/ARM children from Ghana, Africa.

Subsequently, we have set up a program called "Help for Ghana Project", in collaboration with Samuel Agyei Waife (Rare Disease Ghana Initiative), where we forward unused stoma supplies obtained from our worldwide network to Ghana for distribution.

Supplies delivered to Korle-Bu Teaching Hospital, Accra Ghana

Our first shipment of four boxes of 750+ unused stoma supplies, graciously donated by Australian families, were sent to Ghana in August 2020. These have already been distributed to children's hospitals for IA/ARM families. We have also received donated supplies from families in the USA and UK which will be shipped to Ghana in early 2021.

On 28th March 2018, I was honoured to be invited by Senator Anne Urquhart of Tasmania, to attend the Australian Parliament House in Canberra as her guest.

Senator Urquhart gave a parliamentary speech in the Senate Chamber in which she detailed my journey of living with IA/ARM and shared her thoughts on my memoir and the detailed the work of the ONE in 5000 Foundation.

Most importantly, this was the first time that Imperforate Anus/ Anorectal Malformation had been mentioned and discussed in any Parliament in the world.

Senator Anne Urquhart and me 28th March 2018 Australian Parliament House

Our organisation has a very active and influential online presence on social media platforms such as Facebook, Instagram, Twitter and LinkedIn. Under the ONE in 5000 banner, we have reached thousands of people globally. This includes members from the IA/ARM community, our medical network and many from the general public.

We have a Facebook public page where we provide regular information and a closed "Research group" where the global IA/ARM community have a safe, private and monitored environment to discuss IA/ARM issues and provide support:

- ONE in 5000 Foundation - Imperforate Anus/Anorectal Malformation (public page)
- ONE in 5000 IA/ARM Research Group (closed group)

We have also been able to establish the following closed Facebook Support Groups and public pages where families can connect with others in their own respective countries in privacy and for personal support:

- ONE in 5000 Australia Support Group
- ONE in 5000 UK Support Group (United Kingdom)
- ONE in 5000 France (Malformation Ano-Rectale, Imperforation Anale/Anus)
- ONE in 5000 Canada Support Group
- ONE in 5000 NZ Support Group (New Zealand)
- ONE in 5000 Philippines Support Group (IA/ARM)
- ONE in 5000 Hong Kong Support Group
- ONE in 5000 ARM Awareness Group in Bangladesh

- Udruženje za pomoć i podršku roditeljima i deci sa anorektalnim anomalijama "JEDAN u 5000 Balkan" (ONE in 5000 Balkan's Page)

If you would like to create a ONE in 5000 support group in your country or region and be a part of the ONE in 5000 family, please contact us on the email address at the end of this chapter.

We are affiliated with the following local and international organisations:
- Colorectal and Pelvic Reconstruction Service (CPRS), The Royal Children's Hospital Melbourne, Australia
- Rare Voices Australia (RVA)
- Continence Foundation of Australia (BINS4Blokes Campaign)
- Pull-Thru Network (PTN), USA
- Pediatric Colorectal and Pelvic Learning Consortium (PCPLC), USA
- eUROGEN - European Reference Network (ERN), International
- Global PaedSurg, International

We also have ONE in 5000 Foundation Brochures, which we are able to distribute globally for families and hospitals, and which contain all the information provided in this chapter.

The brochure has become a very important resource for our community as we strive to increase awareness and understanding of IA/ARM.

Our email address for any enquiries is:

info@onein5000.org

Chapter 13 - Patient Care

Due to the severity of the condition, the majority of children will require urgent surgical intervention. The following information relates to the surgeries and ongoing care required for children with an ARM.

This important information has been provided by Associate Professor Sebastian King, Director of Colorectal and Pelvic Reconstruction Service (CPRS) at The Royal Children's Hospital Melbourne, Australia, and his team.

The RCH has had a well-established and internationally recognised role in the management of children with colorectal and pelvic conditions. Initiated by Professor F. Douglas Stephens in the 1950's, there has been an ongoing clinical and academic focus upon children born with congenital colorectal conditions, particularly Anorectal Malformation and Hirschsprung Disease.

With the added interest, expertise and international reputations of Mr E. Durham Smith, Mr Justin Kelly and Professor John Hutson, the Department of Paediatric Surgery and Urology have provided world-class care for children, adolescents and families affected by colorectal conditions.

'I was incredibly fortunate that when I was born with Imperforate Anus in 1964, we lived in Melbourne and my family and I received the most wonderful care and support for the next twenty years. Initially by Prof. Stephens and then Mr. Kelly. I owe my life to these wonderful surgeons and the nursing staff at Royal Children's Hospital Melbourne, Australia.'

Greg Ryan

Greg, Mr. Justin Kelly, Wendy and Max Ryan
(Greg's parents) in 2017

The following list details the most common surgeries, treatments and issues associated with ARM.

Formation of stoma

Colostomies and ileostomies are two different types of stomas. A stoma is an artificial opening which allows a child to pass stool to the outside of their body. During an operation under general anaesthesia, the surgeon will bring the healthy end of the bowel to an artificial opening in the child's abdominal wall.

This means that stool will be pushed through the bowel into the stoma, where it is collected into a bag and disposed of. This gives the body a safe way of managing stool prior to the PSARP/LAARP surgery. The stoma is nearly always a temporary measure.

Posterior Sagittal Anorectoplasty (PSARP)/Laparoscopically Assisted Anorectoplasty (LAARP)

The PSARP is performed under general anaesthesia. During the surgery, the child will be placed face down on the operating table. The surgeon will make an incision down the midline of the child's bottom, between the cheeks.

The surgeon will then separate the layers of muscle, fat and connection tissue in the area until they locate the rectum. The surgeon will lift the rectum up and away from the urinary tract (in boys) or vagina (in girls), and then surgically position it within the anal sphincter muscles to create an opening.

During this operation, the surgeon will also ensure there are no vaginal anomalies (in girls) or urological anatomical issues (in girls and boys).

The LAARP is performed under general anaesthesia. During this surgery, the child will be placed on the operating table and will undergo laparoscopic (keyhole) surgery. The rectum will be separated from the surrounding strictures and will then be surgically positioned within the anal sphincter muscles to create an opening. During the operation, the surgeon will ensure that there are no vaginal anomalies (in girls) or urological anatomical issues (in girls and boys).

After the PSARP/LAARP the child will be admitted to hospital for seven to ten days. This is to ensure that they have recovered from the surgery, have their pain managed and are able to drink, prior to going home.

Anal dilatation/dilation

After surgery, the body has a natural tendency to close the surgical wound as part of the healing process. The care of the child after their PSARP/LAARP includes a treatment to prevent the anal wound closing. This is known as anal dilatation and may be required to keep the newly formed join in the bowel open to the right size. Dilatation includes placing a metal dilator into the child's anus once or twice per day. The dilator will slowly stretch the anus to the correct size for the child's age.

Closure of stoma

The stoma is usually closed three to four months after the PSARP/LAARP. For the procedure, the surgeon will reconnect the two sections of bowel and close. Typically, your child will not be able to eat for 48 hours. This allows the new connection between the two parts of the bowel to heal. Children usually start passing stool within two to three days, and most children may be home shortly after they begin passing stool. The child will be in hospital for five to seven days after the closure of their stoma.

Once the above three surgeries have been completed, children with ARM may continue to have issues and require ongoing care, which could involve the following:

Buttock care

Buttock care to prevent nappy/diaper rash is important. Nappy rash is a dermatitis confined to the areas covered by the nappy/diaper. Nappy/diaper rash is not caused by one thing but may be due to a range of problems. The most common cause of nappy/diaper rash (sometimes called diaper dermatitis) in children is irritation.

Toilet training

A common question asked by families is when will be the right time to toilet train their child? Children with an ARM are often delayed in their toilet training by six to 12 months. It is important to get the bowel in the best shape possible prior to commencing toilet training, and your medical team will work with you and your child to do that. It is important to remember that there is no rush to toilet train.

Bowel management

Children with ARM may suffer from different levels of constipation, diarrhoea and/or incontinence. Bowel management is a planned way to clean the large bowel of stool regularly. It helps a child stay clean, avoid accidents and wear regular underwear. Bowel management may include the use of diet, medicines, laxatives and/or enemas to slow down or speed up the bowel with the goal for the child to have a daily bowel movement and remain clean in-between.

Psychological wellbeing/Mental Health Support

The impact of a diagnosis of an ARM on a patient and the family cannot be under-estimated. There may be issues with parental anxiety related to the care for their child, particularly with regards to the need for operations and the role of anal dilatations. In addition, parents may be concerned about the long-term outcomes for their child, especially for bowel and bladder continence.

There is also increasing recognition of the need to provide psychological support for the children with an ARM throughout their childhood, and into adulthood in some situations. This support may take the form of dedicated psychologists and social workers, as well as the entire surgical team caring for your child.

Reference:
1. Colorectal and Pelvic Reconstruction Service "Information for families booklets" (2020) - The Royal Children's Hospital, Melbourne Australia (www.rch.org.au/cprs)

Glossary

You may find that there are many words/terms that you are not familiar with when reading the stories in this book. I include the following which will assist in an explanation of each of their true meanings.

Anal Dilatation/Dilation – Refer to Chapter 13 - Patient Care

Anorectal Malformations - Male

- **Perineal fistula** – in this type of ARM, the anal opening is slightly closer to the scrotum than it should be. This may be obvious at birth, or it may be diagnosed when the child is older and develops constipation.

- **Retrobulbar fistula** – this is the most common type of ARM in males. The rectum ends in a fistula that joins the urethra (urinary tube). There is no anal opening in the normal position on the skin. It is usually obvious at birth that the anus is not present.

- **Rectoprostatic fistula** – in this form of ARM, the rectum ends in a fistula that joins the urethra (urinary tube) as it passes through the prostate. There is no anal opening in the normal position on the skin. It is usually obvious at birth that the anus is not present.

- **Rectobladderneck fistula** – this is a rare and more complex form of ARM. The rectum ends in a fistula that joins the bladder (organ where urine is stored). There is no anal opening in the normal position on the skin. It is usually obvious at birth that the anus is not present.

- **Anorectal Malformation with no fistula** – the rectum ends in a blind pouch and does not connect to anything. There is no anal opening in the normal position on the skin. It is usually obvious at birth that the anus is not present.

Anorectal Malformations - Female

- **Perineal fistula** – in this type of ARM, the anal opening is slightly closer to the vagina than it should be. This may be obvious at birth, or it may be diagnosed when the child is older and develops constipation.

- **Rectovestibular fistula** – this is the most common type of ARM in girls. In this type of ARM, the anal opening is just behind the vagina, within the vestibule. The vestibule is the space in the vulva into which both the urethra and vagina open. A rectovestibular fistula is usually diagnosed when the anus is not in the normal position or when stool (poo) is seen coming out of an area next to the vagina. This is normally diagnosed at birth but sometimes may not be diagnosed until the child is several months old. There may be associated anomalies in the genital tract.

- **Anorectal Malformation with no fistula** – the rectum ends in a blind pouch and does not connect to anything. There is no anal opening in the normal position on the skin. It is usually obvious at birth that the anus is not present.

- **Cloaca** – this is the most complex type of ARM in girls, and occurs when the three tubes (urethra, vagina and rectum) are all joined together in a common channel. The length of the common channel may be short or long, and treatment is different for each child.

- **Cloacal exstrophy** – a rare and complicated defect that occurs during the prenatal development of the lower abdominal wall structures. (The cloaca is the part of an embryo that develops into these structures) A child with cloacal exstrophy is born with many inner-abdominal structures exposed. A portion of the large intestines lies outside of the body, and on either side of it are the two halves of the bladder. In males, the penis is usually flat and short, sometimes split in half. In females the clitoris is split. Oftentimes in cloacal exstrophy there may be two vaginal openings.

ACE procedures – antegrade colonic enema (ACE) procedure allows fluid to be put into the colon through the abdominal wall. This washes out the colon (like an enema) but is easier to perform and more efficient than a conventional enema. Several types of ACE procedures have been developed including a cecostomy, in which a hole is placed into the abdominal wall directly into the colon, and the Malone procedure, in which the appendix is used as a conduit.

Anorectal manometry – a rectal motility test that measures the nerve and muscle functions of the rectum and anal sphincter. During this test, a catheter (flexible plastic tube) is inserted into the anus and then into the rectum. A small balloon on the end of the catheter is then inflated gradually and this causes the nerves and muscles in the rectum and anus to start to squeeze. These signals are picked up by sensors contained in the catheter and recorded by a machine. The test takes about 40 minutes.

Anus – the external opening of the rectum. Closure is controlled by sphincter muscles. Faeces are expelled from the body through the anus during the act of defecation, which is the primary function of the anus.

Barium enema – test given in order to perform an x-ray examination of the large intestines. Pictures are taken after rectal instillation of barium sulphate (a radiopaque contrast medium).

Clostridioides difficile (C. diff) - is a bacterium that can cause symptoms ranging from diarrhea to life-threatening inflammation of the colon

Catheter – a flexible tube used to drain fluid from or inject fluid into the body. The most common catheters are the Foley catheter, used to drain urine from the bladder, and intravenous (IV) catheters inserted into veins to administer fluids.

Cecostomy –
1. Opening between cecum and exterior: a surgically formed connection between the interior first part of the large intestine and the outside that is made through an opening in the front of the abdominal wall.

2. Surgery to join cecum to exterior: an operation to form a surgical connection between the interior of the start of the large intestine and the outside, through an opening in the front of the abdominal wall.

Chait cecostomy appliance – one type of appliance (button) available for use in a cecostomy.

Colostomy – surgical approach in which a section of the colon is brought out through an opening (stoma) created in the abdominal wall. Stool then passes into a small bag securely fastened over the opening.

Contrast enema – a test which uses X-rays and a special kind of enema solution and/or air to take pictures of the colon or large bowel, which is the lower part of the intestines. The test shows the doctor if there are abnormalities of the colon or distal small intestine.

Diarrhea – frequent passage of loose, watery stool.

Double diapering - is an alternative to a stoma/colostomy bag by placing a diaper over an ostomy and still use a diaper for bladder

Enema – technique for emptying the bowel by introducing liquid into the rectum to loosen the faeces and provoke a bowel movement.

Failure to thrive – a medical term which denotes poor weight gain and physical growth failure over an extended period of time in infancy. Often abbreviated to FTT, the term has been in medical use for over a century. As used by paediatricians, it covers poor physical growth of any cause and does not imply abnormal intellectual, social, or emotional development.

Faecal incontinence – the inability to control bowel movements or gas.

Fistula – an abnormal passage, opening or connection between two internal organs or from an internal organ to the surface of the body.

Hypospadias – a congenital anomaly in boys resulting in the abnormal location of the urethral opening. This is often associated with penile curvature (chordee). The hypospadiac opening may be within the scrotum or just below where the urethra is normally found. Hypospadias repair places the urethra in a normal location and removes the abnormal foreskin. Chordee repair is performed simultaneously. Complications are uncommon but may occur more often with more severe forms of the disorder.

Ileostomy – an operation in which the end of the small intestine, the ileum, is brought out through an opening in the abdomen. The contents of the intestine, unformed stool, are expelled through this opening into a bag called an appliance.

Ileus - A post-operative complication that is characterized by the loss of forward flow of intestinal contents. It is often accompanied by abdominal cramps, increasing abdominal distension, constipation or vomiting, electrolyte disturbances and dehydration.

Laxative – a substance (food or medicine) taken to cause a bowel movement.

Malone procedure – the procedure connects the appendix to the umbilicus, creating an orifice with a one-way valve mechanism through which the patient can administer the enemas. The procedure allows the patient to irrigate the colon from above (antegrade enema) instead of from the rectum (rectal enema). Variations on this technique may include connecting the appendix to the lower abdomen and/or using other native tissue in cases where the appendix is not available or is being used for another procedure.

Meconium - is a newborn's first passing of stool. This sticky, thick, dark green poop is made up of cells, protein, fats, and intestinal secretions, like bile. Babies typically pass meconium in the first few hours and days after birth. But some babies pass meconium while still in the womb during late pregnancy.

Mic-Key/Mini Button – a skin level tube type appliance used for a gastrostomy (in the stomach) or for a cecostomy (in the cecum/colon).

Mitrofanoff appendicovesicostomy (Mitrofanoff procedure) – attaches the appendix between the skin and the bladder in order to provide an outlet for urine. In the procedure, a surgeon removes the appendix from its place at the end of the cecum. The appendix is then washed and an opening made at its blind end. One end is connected by sutures to the bladder and the other is connected to the skin. Urine is typically drained several times a day by use of a catheter inserted into the Mitrofanoff canal. If the appendix is not available for use, a different part of the intestines may be used.

Nasal Gastric Tube (NG) – a tube that is placed through the nose into the stomach that is used when a child cannot eat by mouth or requires more calories to grow. An NG tube can also be used when a bowel clean-out is needed (for instance, prior to surgery) to avoid having to drink a large quantity of bowel prep medications.

Neurogenic bladder – condition in which the control of urinary bladder control is disturbed. Symptoms include frequent or urgent urination, loss of the urge sensation, inability to empty the bladder even though the urge may be present or loss of bladder control, which then empties itself irregularly and spontaneously.

Neonatal Intensive Care Unit (NICU) – is a hospital service that provide care for sick and preterm babies in the first few weeks and months of life. These babies may be premature, of low birth weight, or have congenital or other conditions that impact upon their health or survival.

Ostomy – operation to create an opening (a stoma) from an area inside the body to the outside.

Percutaneous Endoscopic Gastrostomy Tube – a surgical procedure for placing a feeding tube without having to perform an open operation on the abdomen (laparotomy). A gastrostomy (a surgical opening into the stomach) is made percutaneously (through the skin) using an endoscope (a flexible, lighted instrument) to determine where to place the feeding tube in the stomach and secure it in place.

Peristeen - is a Transanal Irrigation System for people who suffer from faecal incontinence and constipation by using a rectal catheter.

PSARP/LAARP – Refer to Chapter 13 - Patient Care

Prolapse – the bulging out of any mucosa lined structure, usually used to refer to as a rectal prolapse, when the rectal wall bulges out past the anal opening. This can occur following surgery for anorectal malformations, and also rarely occurs in a patient who has never had surgery.

Rectum – the final portion of the large intestine. It empties stool from the body through the anus.

Reflux (of urine) – the backing up of urine into the ureters and/or kidneys. This happens when the bladder is full and is not regularly emptied.

Saline – a solution of salt and water. In medicine, saline is a salt solution that is adjusted to the normal salinity of the human body. Home-made saline used in bowel management is made by adding one teaspoon of plain or kosher salt to 500cc of warm water.

Sepsis - is a life-threatening condition that arises when the body's response to an infection damages its own tissues and organs.

Sphincter – a circular muscle at base of bladder neck and also around the anus, which controls opening of the bladder and bowel respectively.

Stoma – a surgically created opening from an area inside the body to the outside.

Tethered Spinal Cord (TC) – a neurological disorder caused by tissue attachments that limit the movement of the spinal cord within the spinal column. These attachments cause an abnormal stretching of the spinal cord.

Urethra – the tube which conveys urine from the bladder to the outside. The female urethra is very short, extending from the bladder to the urinary opening at the vulva. The male urethra is longer, extending along the length of the penis. It also conveys the seminal fluid.

Urinary incontinence – the involuntary loss of urine.

Urinary Tract – passageway from the pelvis of the kidney to the urinary orifice through the ureters, bladder, and urethra. There is an upper urinary tract (2 kidneys and 2 ureters) and a lower urinary tract (bladder, sphincters and urethra).

Urinary Tract Infection (UTI) – infection in one or more parts of the urinary system that occurs as a result of bacteria growing in the urinary tract; not everyone with a UTI develops symptoms, but when they do occur, symptoms develop suddenly and include a burning sensation while urinating

Vesicostomy – an incision made in the bladder allowing urine to pass through an opening in the abdominal wall.

Voiding Cystourethrogram (VCUG) – a specific x-ray that examines the urinary tract. A catheter (hollow tube) is placed in the urethra (tube that drains urine from the bladder to the outside of the body) and the bladder is filled with a liquid dye. X-ray images will be taken as the bladder fills and empties. The images will show if there is any reverse flow of urine into the ureters and kidneys.

VACTERL – Refer to iii - What is Imperforate Anus (IA)/Anorectal Malformation (ARM)?

References:
1. Pull-Thru Network (USA) Resources section (Glossary) – www.pullthrunetwork.org
2. Colorectal and Pelvic Reconstruction Service "Information for families booklets" (2020) - The Royal Children's Hospital, Melbourne Australia (www.rch.org.au/cprs)

Acknowledgements

I would like to take this opportunity to acknowledge and thank the following people who have supported me in my life and assisted in making this book possible.

Firstly, without my parents, Max and Wendy, I am nothing. The unconditional love and support they give me is impossible to express in words. My brother Brad, sister-in-law Peta and my wonderful nephews, Archer and Jack all play such an important part of my life.

I have been incredibly fortunate to have been cared for and treated by such wonderful doctors ever since the day I was born. Recognising their contribution to my life is essential, so thank you, Mr. Nate Myers, Prof. Douglas Stephens, Mr Justin Kelly, Dr David Dammery, Prof. Fred Hocking, Prof. Adrian Polglase Dr. Angelo Pacella, Dr Con Mitropoulos and Prof. Mark Walterfang.

I greatly appreciate Assoc. Prof. Sebastian King for accepting my invitation to write the foreword for the book and assisting in the medical sections. His wonderful support and encouragement to me personally and the ONE in 5000 Foundation has been pivotal.

To Anne Holland, thank you for being of such great assistance as a sounding board for me as well as assisting with the editing of the book, and for penning such a lovely piece on the back cover.

One of the great aspects of this book for me has been the friendship I have developed with a fellow IA/ARM Adult, Meghan Douglass and her mother, Susan Setford. They have assisted greatly in the editing process and assisting me throughout the project. Also, at the end of the process, Meghan's father, Lyndon who assisted greatly in formatting and setting up the book.

I'm sure you will all agree, the cover design of the book is very powerful. This was created by Tahlia West, a wonderful IA/ARM mother who volunteers her time to do all the ONE in 5000 Foundation graphic design work.

A special thanks to Michelle Collins, IA/ARM Adult who graciously offered to paint portraits of some IA/ARM children and Adults to accompany their stories.

I have been incredibly fortunate over the last few years to attend International Paediatric Colorectal Conferences and meeting the world's leading IA/ARM medical professionals. I would also like to recognise them individually for their support and encouragement to me personally, but more importantly, the incredible care and treatment they provide IA/ARM patients.

Thank you; Dr. Alessandra Gasior, Dr. Marc Levitt, Dr. Carlos Reck, Dr Jason Frischer, Dr Richard Wood, Dr Alberto Pena, Dr. Andrea Bischoff, Dr Laura Judd-Glossy, Prof. Wout Feitz, Dr. Ivo de Blaauw, Miss Naomi Wright, Mr. Jonathan Sutcliffe, Dr Jeff Avansino, Dr Belinda Dickie, Dr Rebecca Rentea, Dr Alejandra Vilanova-Sanchez, Dr Aaron Garrison, Dr. Jacob Langer, Dr Shumyle Alam and Dr. Jason Castro.

Also, this wouldn't be possible without the ONE in 5000 Foundation team. Thank you to our executive of Les Cameron, Greg Male and Jo Ewen. Also, our online global team of Chelsea, Ange and Trent, Kendra and Travis, Blair, Bec and Katie who are such great supports to me.

Finally, this wouldn't have happened without our IA/ARM global community and ONE in 5000 Foundation family for sharing their incredible stories.....THANK YOU!!!!

Greg Ryan

Made in the USA
Columbia, SC
19 July 2021